The Structure of the Lexicon

Natural Language Processing

5

Mouton de Gruyter
Berlin · New York

The Structure of the Lexicon

Human versus Machine

by

Jürgen Handke

Mouton de Gruyter
Berlin · New York 1995

Mouton de Gruyter (formerly Mouton, The Hague)
is a Division of Walter de Gruyter & Co., Berlin.

∞ Printed on acid-free paper which falls within the guidelines
of the ANSI to ensure permanence and durability.

Library of Congress Cataloging-in-Publication Data

Handke, Jürgen.
The structure of the lexicon ; human versus machine / Jürgen Handke.
p. cm. – (Natural language processing ; 5)
Includes bibliographical references and index.
ISBN 3-11-014732-7 clothbound (alk. paper)
ISBN 3-11-014786-6 paperback (alk. paper)
1. Lexicology – Data processing. I. Title. II. Series.
P326.5.D38H36 1995
413′.0285′635–dc20 95-35380
CIP

Die Deutsche Bibliothek – Cataloging-in-Publication Data

Handke, Jürgen:
The structure of the lexicon : human versus machine / Jürgen Handke. – Berlin ; New York : Mouton de Gruyter, 1995
(Natural language processing ; 5)
ISBN 3-11-014786-6 brosch.
ISBN 3-11-014732-7 Gb.
NE: GT

Disk conversion with $\TeX$: Lewis & Leins, Berlin. – Printing: Gerike GmbH, Berlin. – Binding: Lüderitz & Bauer GmbH, Berlin.
Printed in Germany

Preface

The motivation for this book grew out of a dissatisfaction with textbooks about cognitive science, a relatively new discipline that tries to integrate psychological, philosophical, linguistic, computational, and to some extent neurological insights to explore cognitive processes. There are numerous books and articles that discuss specific topics from their particular points of view, but an interdisciplinary approach that combines the research results of psychological and computational studies is not available.

In this book an attempt is made to investigate the central component of natural language processing, the lexicon, trying to unite the results of linguistic, psycholinguistic and computational research. The lexicon is in the centre of interest in many ways: linguistic theories increasingly rely on the lexicon as a central component of grammar. Modern generative theories of grammar, for example, incorporate a lexicon that not only contains the basic grammatical properties of the words that are required for the generation of sentences but also numerous aspects that were previously generated via syntactic rules. Thus, a major issue in theoretical linguistics is to specify the nature and the content of lexical entries. Theories of natural language processing, on the other hand, have acknowledged that the lexicon is central to natural language processing. The internal structure, the content and the strategies of accessing lexical information have been the focus of psycholinguistic research for a long time. Even though many aspects of human lexical processing have been revealed, there are still a number of issues that are beyond our judgement. Finally, computer programs that are equipped with linguistic knowledge have to incorporate a lexical database. Whether such a machine-readable lexicon can be organised according to psycholinguistic principles depends not only on the results of psycholinguistic research but on computational issues such as program design, database management and processing efficiency.

This book integrates linguistic, psycholinguistic and computational approaches towards the lexicon, hoping to provide a mental model which may serve as the basis of an efficient lexicon implementation. The addressees of this book are thus linguists, psychologists and computer scientists, or all those who are interested in dealing with natural language phenomena.

The book is divided into three sections, a theoretical linguistic section, a psycholinguistic section, and a computational section.

The theoretical linguistic section is introductory in character and not essential for the reader well-versed in the field. In chapter one the reader is first introduced to the most important issues in natural language processing and to the relevant terminology. At the end of this section, a working model of natural language processing is presented, which outlines the central role of the lexicon and serves as the basis for the remaining sections. Chapter two deals with the organisation of lexical entries. It discusses the enormous complexity of information associated with each item in the lexicon and familiarises the reader with the relevant theories and formalisms of presenting this information.

The second section deals with human lexical processing. Chapter three outlines the phases prior to lexical processing, that is the phases in which contact with the lexicon is made. In order to access the entries in the lexicon and the information associated with them, the sensory input has to be analysed and identified. In chapter four the central stages of lexical processing are discussed. On the basis of spoken or written input, the principles of word recognition and lexical retrieval are outlined. This chapter tries to convert the insights into word recognition into some general principles about the overall architecture of the lexicon. Since a uniform theory about the structure of the lexicon does not exist, we will have to discuss the arguments and experimental findings leading to the existing theories about possible lexicon architectures.

The final section discusses the structure of machine-readable lexicons and the computational strategies for retrieving information from them. In chapter five we examine the general principles of database management and file structure in order to find out about economical and efficient ways of implementing a machine-readable lexicon. As a result we will discuss a lexicon architecture that realises a number of principles of the mental counterpart but also makes use of strategies which are confined to presently available machines. Chapter six illustrates how such a lexicon can be employed in a commercial natural language processing system.

Annotations

In order to distinguish different linguistic units, the following notational conventions are used throughout the book. Words that are used as examples are presented in italics (e.g. *word*). If a word does not exist but is in line with the orthographical conventions of a language, it is marked with one, if it is tactically impossible, with two asterisks (e.g. English **worce*, ***wroce*). Phrases are presented in inverted commas (e.g. "a phrase"), lexical access units are written in capital letters (e.g. UNIT).

The phonemic transcription used in this book is based on Gimson (1962) and can also be found in Longman's Dictionary of Contemporary English (LDOCE).

All benchmark tests have been run on a 80386 IBM-compatible machine, with 4 MB RAM, 33 MHZ speed and 21 msec harddisk access time.

Acknowledgements

Many people have directly or indirectly contributed to this book. Special thanks go to those who read through preliminary drafts and pointed out errors and suggested improvements: in particular, my colleagues Christopher Moss, Ingo Plag, David Smith and Michael Völtz, who went through the contents very carefully, making suggestions where possible. I am especially grateful to Monika Schwarz, who provided me with invaluable comments about the theoretical linguistic and the psycholinguistic section. Furthermore, I am indebted to my students who attended my seminar of the same title and contributed with many fruitful ideas and proposals. Some of them even took the trouble to read the entire manuscript, pointing out misunderstandings and bad explanations. Concerning the computational section, my co- author of various articles, Klaus Deiß, deserves special thanks, since his ideas about the implementation of machine-readable dictionaries stimulated my programming ambitions to a large extent.

Special thanks are due to Bill Stevens, one-time fellow-student and old friend, who made a major contribution by not only examining my use of English but also by making numerous suggestions about the structure and the contents of the book.

For any remaining errors, I must take full responsibility.

Marburg, October 1994

Contents

1. Natural Language Processing 1

2. Entries in the Lexicon 49

3. Pre-lexical Processing 113

4. Lexical Processing 162

5. Machine-Readable Lexicons 223

6. LexEcon; an On-Line Machine Readable Lexicon 296

7. Summary 311

Appendix A. Writing Systems 315

Appendix B. Lexicon Production 322

Appendix C. Tools 330

Notes 347

References 359

Index 381

1. Natural Language Processing

"Speaking and understanding the speech of others are things we do every day. Under normal circumstances we do these things effortlessly and, it seems, almost instantaneously. It takes almost no effort and very little, if any, conscious thought to turn our thoughts into words and sentences in order to communicate them to others; and, likewise, we ordinarily have no trouble in getting at the thoughts that others express in their words and sentences."
(Matthei/Roeper 1983: 13)

The use of natural language is one of the most complicated human cognitive activities.[1] Despite its great complexity humans use language like breathing or walking with great ease, applying little or no conscious effort. In contrast to other mental tasks like calculating or playing games, where we are aware of sequentially going through a number of thought processes, the stages of natural language processing are much more difficult to inspect. Various disciplines combine their efforts to investigate natural language and the cognitive abilities underlying language processing. This enormously difficult enterprise can be approached in three different ways.

The *linguistic* approach tries to investigate the rules and principles according to which natural language operates. The study of natural language has a long tradition. Modern linguistics emerged from comparative philological studies in the 19th century, which have their roots more than two thousand years ago. Even though the philological approach was by and large responsible for the birth of modern linguistics, it was only in the second half of the 20th century that a move away from philologically-oriented language studies to a more structural approach could be observed. With the advent of Noam Chomsky's generative model of a theory of grammar in the 1960s, a new direction in linguistics was manifested. Central to this direction is no longer the investigation of actual linguistic behaviour, but the study of the underlying linguistic knowledge which a native speaker has mastered. This distinction between *competence* (the internalised knowledge) and *performance* (the use of language) led to new goals of linguistic research. Today linguists seek to describe and explain the mental rules and principles underlying human linguistic ability. They want to postulate general principles which apply to all languages in order to set up a structural framework for natural language in general. Since no other natural languages than the ones spoken on earth are known, linguists refer to such principles as *linguistic universals* and to the resulting framework as *universal grammar.*

The theoretical linguistic framework can be put to the test in various ways. First, we can look at performance data and investigate the cognitive ability of human subjects in experimental situations, confronting them with linguistic data in the laboratory, or observe their spontaneous use of language in real-life situations. Secondly, we can perform long-term observations, especially during the first years of childhood, to explore the principles of language acquisition. This *psycholinguistic* approach, which combines the insights and research strategies of psychology and linguistics, seeks to develop a model of language processing, taking into account theoretical linguistic data, experimental results, and the strategies according to which children acquire their mother tongue.

A third approach has become available with the arrival of the digital computer. With its help we can simulate language processing, or at least some stages of it. Especially in the area of representation formalisms, the *computational* approach, which integrates information science, psychology, logic and linguistics, has been very helpful. In almost all areas of linguistic research, but most importantly in the areas of meaning representation and grammatical analysis, the contribution of computational linguistics to the study of language in recent years is enormous.

Both linguistics and psycholinguistics have been stimulated by the results of the studies in computer science, especially in artificial intelligence, since the mid-1970s. This mutual influence between linguistics and psycholinguistics, on the one hand, and artificial intelligence, on the other, led to a new interdisciplinary approach, which is referred to as *cognitive science.* Studies in cognitive science seek to answer the following central questions (Schwarz 1992: 14):

- What sources of knowledge do humans utilise in order to perform such complex cognitive tasks as speaking, hearing and thinking?
- How is this knowledge organised and represented in the mind?
- How is this knowledge put to use and what cognitive processes underlie the application of this knowledge?

The following sections will illustrate these aspects. On the basis of some selected linguistic examples, the reader will be introduced to the fundamental research topics and the relevant terminology in these areas. The remaining part of this chapter will deal with the central aspects of natural language processing. We will outline the components and levels of human natural language processing to arrive at a working model which will serve as a framework for the following chapters. Parallel with this discussion, a number of hypotheses and theories and the relevant terminology will be introduced.

1.1. Ambiguity and the Study of Language

One of the most important differences between natural and artificial languages is the phenomenon of ambiguity. While natural language constructions may allow more than one interpretation, artificial languages, for example computer programming languages, do not exhibit ambiguous structures. Actually, it would be disastrous for a computer if an ambiguous structure in a computer program permitted several alternative interpretations leading to completely different results.

Here are some examples of natural language ambiguity which serve as the basis for our subsequent discussion. They exhibit ambiguity at wordlevel as well as more complex types of ambiguity depending on the integration of the respective sentence into a more general context. Note that example (1a) is meant to refer to ambiguity in speech, while the remaining examples illustrate the phenomenon of ambiguity in their written form.

(1)
a. /ˈaɪskriːm/
b. They can fish.
c. Have the boys take their exams!
d. The chickens are ready to eat.
e. The Smiths saw some eagles when they were flying to Italy.
f. John kissed his wife and so did Bill.
g. I'll come to your party on Saturday!

In order to integrate the three approaches the following steps have to be performed: first, a sound theoretical basis of ambiguity which defines the linguistic problems underlying ambiguous constructions has to be provided. Using these insights, we should then be able to perform experiments contrasting ambiguous with unambiguous data, hoping to explore the mental activities involved in the processing of such structures. Finally, the computer will be applied to language material, to serve as a kind of testing device. Based on a precise formal description of ambiguity and a sound processing hypothesis, an attempt can be made to develop an ambiguity processing algorithm which tries to simulate human processing strategies.

1.1.1. The Linguistic Approach

Obviously, the types of ambiguity displayed in the examples above can be attributed to completely different theoretical-linguistic aspects. An overview of the branches of theoretical linguistics (figure 1) might be helpful in this respect.

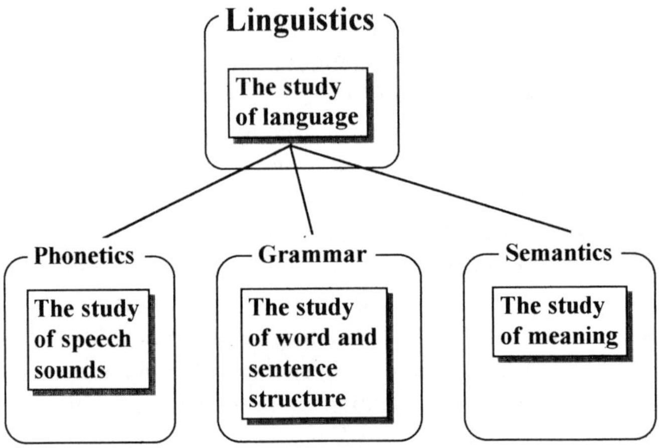

Figure 1. The branches of theoretical linguistics

The examples in (1) can be used to illustrate the fundamental aims of the major linguistic branches.

(1a) is a phonetically-based example of ambiguity. The construction is deliberately displayed in a code which makes use of *phonemes*, the fundamental units in phonology. As shown in figure 1, *Phonetics* (spelt with a capital "P") deals with the study of speech sounds. This study can be undertaken in two ways. On the one hand, we can look at the sounds without reference to a specific language, studying the articulation of speech sounds, their acoustic properties, and the auditory impression they evoke. This area is referred to as *phonetics* (spelt with a small "p"). The fundamental units of phonetics are referred to as *speech sounds* or *phones*. They are represented in square brackets, where as many as possible phonetic details are presented, for example [t^h].

Over and above the phonetic study of speech sounds, we can look at their function in one particular language. For example, we might want to explore the function of the sound [ð] (the voiced dental fricative, in English more commonly known as "th") in English or German. While its function in English is to distinguish pairs such as *thick/sick* (/θɪk/ /sɪk/), it has no specific function in German. This different functional status can be shown if one replaces the alveolar fricatives /s/ and /z/ by their dental counterparts. While this would have severe semantic consequences in English, where pairs such as *sick* and *thick* would no longer be distinguishable, in German the meaning of the respective words would not be affected. As soon as we begin to study the function of speech sounds we enter the area of *phonology*.[2] To differentiate speech sounds or phones from phonemes, the functional sound units in a particular language, phonemes are presented in slant brackets, for example /t/. With this background we can now return to our example (1a), which can be interpreted in connected speech as "I scream" or as "ice-cream". Phonologically, that is in terms of the phonemes involved, the difference between the two interpretations cannot be highlighted. Phonetically, however, the interpretation of (1a) depends on the ways in which phonetic cues mark word boundaries. While the interpretation of (1a) as "I scream" involves a long diphthong /aɪ/, a fairly strong fricative /s/, and relatively little devoicing of the liquid /r/, the second interpretation as "ice-cream" exhibits different cues, such as a reduced /aɪ/, a weaker /s/, and a devoiced /r/ (Gimson 1962: 300).

The examples (1b) to (1d) are all cases of *structural ambiguity*, where the respective sentences can be grammatically analysed into different structures. The analysis of the structural properties of language is the central task of *grammar*. This branch of linguistics can be subdivided into *morphology*, the study of the structure of words, and *syntax*, the study of sentence structure. Some scholars use the term grammar in a much wider sense, to include to some extent both phonology and semantics, with syntax used for the central portion (Palmer 1971: 13). In other words, they equate the term grammar with "theory of language". To avoid any confusion we will suppress the term grammar where possible and refer to morphology and syntax respectively.

The structural ambiguity of (1b) depends on the analysis of *can* as a modal auxiliary ("They are able to fish") or as a full verb ("They put fish into cans"). Since this type of ambiguity solely depends on the syntactic category of a lexical item, it can also be referred to as *categorial lexical ambiguity* (Small et al. 1988: 4).[3] This case of ambiguity, then, can be attributed to the area of morphology. Note that the addition of a morphological formative such as *-ed* can disambiguate the sentence ("They canned fish" is not ambiguous any more). The processes of morphological alternation are discussed in detail in section 1.3.3.

A similar case of structural ambiguity is presented in (1c). Again, the interpretation depends on the syntactic category of one word. *Have* can be analysed as an auxiliary verb or as a full verb, resulting in completely different expectations about the continuation of the sentence. If the admittedly strongly favoured analysis of *have* as an auxiliary verb is chosen, we expect the sentence to follow the general pattern of a yes-no question with a past participle, in this case *taken,* occurring somewhat later in the sentence. However, this is the wrong analysis in (1c) and we feel stranded when the word *take* is reached. This phenomenon has become known as *garden-path effect*, where the listener is strongly biased towards one interpretation and can hardly or not at all recognise the alternative. In our example (1c) the correct alternative is to analyse *have* as a full verb in the sense of "Let the boys take their exam!".

In (1d) we are also confronted with a case of structural ambiguity, yet of a different kind. On the one hand, we can interpret (1d) as "The chickens are boiled and we are ready to eat *them*", on the other hand, it can be understood as "The chickens are hungry and *they* are ready to eat something". The analysis of the words into their syntactic categories does not reveal any difference between the two interpretations. Here, the cause of the ambiguity is the interpretation of the subject of the reduced infinitival clause "to eat". (1d) is a case of structural ambiguity, since the clause "to eat" has two possible syntactic structures. It can be analysed as "The chickens eat something" or as "Someone eats the chickens", where the phrase "the chickens" can either function as the subject or as the object of the embedded infinitival clause.

A completely different type of ambiguity can be found in (1e). Here, the interpretation does not depend on the phonetic or grammatical properties of the items in the sentence but on the meaning of the words involved. The sentence is ambiguous because it is not clear who is flying, or, more precisely, to whom the pronoun *they* refers. Both eagles and the average family (on board a plane) can fly or be flown and are thus possible referential candidates for *they,* using different flying devices though. If we replace *eagles* by *mountains,* the interpretation is clear. In this case, *they* must refer to the Smiths. Our general knowledge about flying and possible flyers leaves us with only one interpretation. Hence, we have a case of semantic ambiguity, with the specific problem of pronominal reference. For this reason, this ambiguity type can be referred to as *(semantic) referential ambiguity.* Example (1f) also exhibits a case of *referential ambiguity*, where the reduced construction "and so did Bill" may relate to Bill's own wife or to John's. In (1e), the ambiguity has to be resolved on the basis of the context, which will have to determine the exact relationship between John, Bill, and their wives.

Another case of ambiguity is featured in (1g). Here, the interpretation of the utterance as a promise or as a warning depends on the relationship between speaker and hearer. It is thus a case of ambiguity which arises when language is put to use. The investigation of the function and use of language is referred to as *pragmatics*. This branch of linguistics can either be subsumed under the heading of semantics or it can be assigned an independent status.[4] In any case, we can refer to this type of ambiguity as *pragmatically-based ambiguity*.

Having linguistically described different types of ambiguity, we can now ask how the human mind copes with these constructions. Is language processing complicated by ambiguous constructions, do we have less time for additional cognitive activities, or are ambiguous structures processed with the same ease as unambiguous ones? To answer these and other questions is a central task of psycholinguistics.

1.1.2. The Psycholinguistic Approach

The relationship between theoretical linguistics and psycholinguistics can be characterised by a comparison. The linguist provides a framework of natural language, but does not explain how this model is applied. The psycholinguist, by contrast, studies how people use language. A linguistic model, then, is a blueprint of natural language; a psycholinguistic model is a description of how it is used. Have a look at the following examples which illustrate this relationship.

(2) a. The boy the cat bit yelped.
 b. ??The boy the cat the mouse feared bit yelped.
 c. ??The question the boy the lion bit answered was complex.
 d. The boy whom the cat bit that the mouse feared yelped.

These sentences exhibit the possibility of relative pronoun deletion in those cases where the relative pronoun is the object of the relative clause ("The boy [whom the cat bit] yelped"; *whom* = object, see Quirk et al. 1985: 1250ff). While this rule works perfectly well in example (2a), it causes severe problems in (2b) and (2c). However, the awkwardness of these examples is not due to any violation of a linguistic rule. Rather, it is a consequence of a memory problem where the relationship between noun phrases and their corresponding verbs, i.e. between "the boy" and "yelped", is discontinuous. In (2a) this relationship is disrupted by two elements: "the cat" and "bit". In (2b), however, too much material disrupts the relationship between "the boy" and "yelped" and thus causes a memory problem. Figure 2 illustrates this problem in terms of a 'stack-principle'. If we think of our mind as a stack which collects linguistic material as it comes in and tries to establish relationships between the incoming elements, we immediately see that the intervention of "the cat the mouse feared bit" between "the boy" and "yelped" causes a memory overload and thus a processing problem. This problem can only be overcome if the relationship between the noun phrases and their verbs is made more explicit, as in (2c), or if they are adjacent, as in (2d).

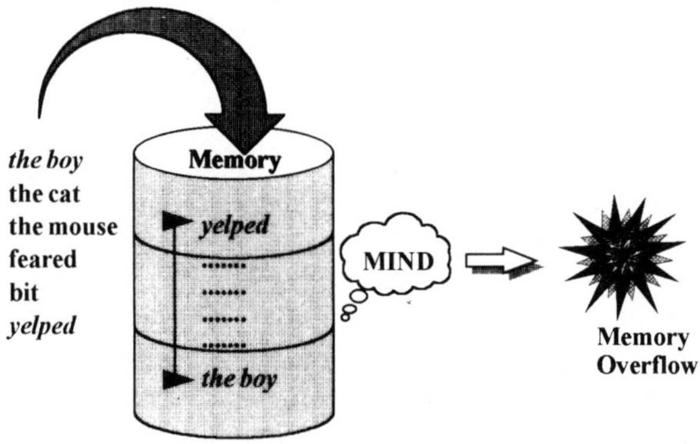

Figure 2. Relative clauses and human memory

Thus, the rule of relative pronoun deletion, which is linguistically unconstrained and can theoretically be applied infinitely often, has to be restricted psycholinguistically. Memory limitations do not allow more than one application of this rule. Figure 3 illustrates the central branches of psycholinguistic research.

In this book we will primarily deal with language processing, the branch of psycholinguistics that studies the processes from thought to linguistic output (language production) and from linguistic input to thought (language comprehension) and investigates how linguistic knowledge might be represented in the mind. The other branches of psycholinguistics deal with the acquisition of language and the implications of this process for human language (language acquisition), and with the study of the neural basis of

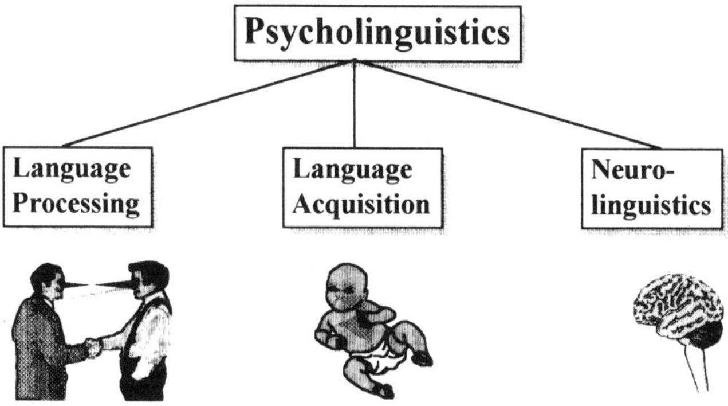

Figure 3. The branches of psycholinguistics

language, i.e. the relation between language and the brain (neurolinguistics). These branches of psycholinguistics will not be the centre of interest in this book, but research into language acquisition will be dealt with from time to time. It may provide support for some of the central ideas of adult language processing.

Let us now return to the processing of the ambiguous structures in (1). A central psycholinguistic question in this case is: do ambiguous structures slow down processing or not? The numerous experiments that have been carried out in this area (see, for example, Foss/Hakes 1978: 120ff) indicate that ambiguity increases the difficulty of comprehension, but it is a short-lived effect. This, in turn, suggests that two possible processing strategies can be applied. On the one hand, one could postulate a *parallel processing,* in which case all possible interpretations of an ambiguous construction are processed until an ambiguity resolution point is reached. This resolution point can be the general context, for example the knowledge about flying in (1e)[5], or the immediate context such as the past participle *gone* in "They have gone", which disambiguates *have* to an auxiliary verb and not to a full verb as in "They have time". On the other hand, one can assume a *serial processing*, where one interpretation is chosen. If it is the correct one, fine; if not, a strategy of *backtracking* has to be applied. This is a method of returning to a previous choice-point and trying again with an alternative (Barr/Feigenbaum 1981: 258). Backtracking requires a significant amount of bookkeeping, since it plunges ahead with a single alternative and keeps track of the other possibilities, i.e. of all the alternatives not yet tried (Winograd 1983: 63). For example, in (1c) we seem to be strongly biased towards an interpretation of *have* as an auxiliary verb and consequently assume a yes-no question to be processed. The occurrence of *take*, however, suggests a reinterpretation of the sentence as a command. Hence, we go back to the initial choice-point *have* and try the alternative. It seems likely that both serial and parallel strategies are employed. In the case of ambiguous constructions with a high bias towards a specific interpretation, a serial strategy seems likely; in cases with no or low biases, parallel processing might be used. For example, the sentence-initial occurrence of *have* and its bias towards an auxiliary verb seem to support the serial strategy, while the sentence-internal occurrence of *have* favours a parallel strategy until a resolution point is reached. We will return to this issue in section 1.5.

To sum up, psycholinguists are not primarily interested in the description of linguistic phenomena but in human performance when confronted with it, for example, in the processing strategies applied in the case of ambiguity.

1.1.3. The Computational Approach

Although theoretical linguists, psycholinguists, and computational linguists have rather different approaches and outlooks, they are all ultimately concerned with understanding linguistic processes. Instead of setting up a theory, however, computational linguists develop procedures and architectures for handling natural language input and for generating natural language output. To do this, they employ the insights from a number of more or less related disciplines which are exhibited in figure 4.

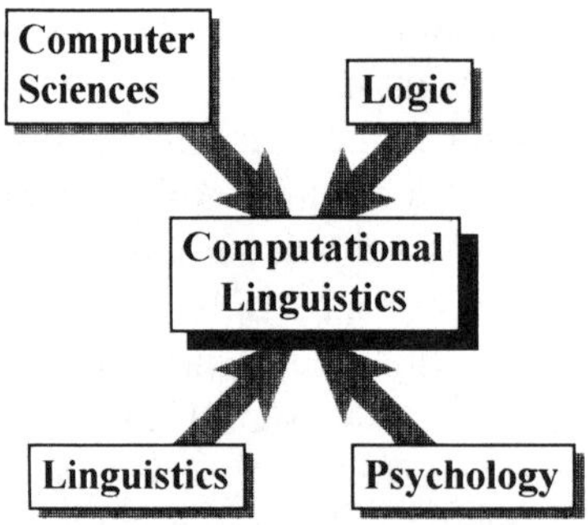

Figure 4. Computational linguistics and its main neighbouring disciplines

The contribution of computer sciences is obvious. Aspects such as program design, programming techniques, and general implementation issues pursue the general goal of achieving the highest possible efficiency of programs that can handle natural language data. Logic, by contrast, delivers rules and principles with which complex structures can be broken down into smaller units and thus transferred to a machine. Psychology deals with human strategies of cognition, and linguists seek to unveil the structure of language.

Interest in computational linguistics has two motivations. One motivation has always been the development of practical systems which involve natural language. Figure 5 displays the main application areas of such systems.

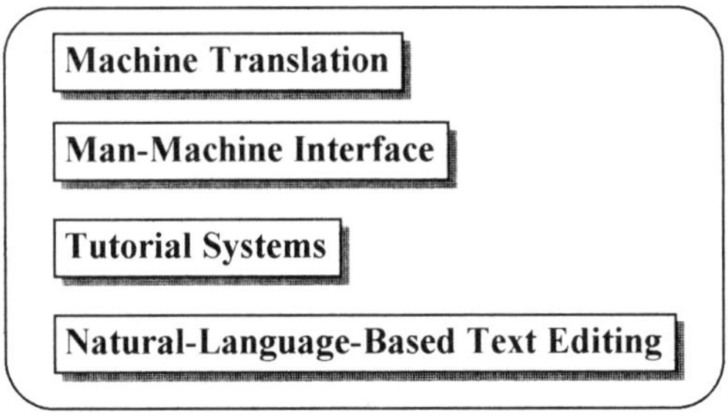

Figure 5. Computational linguistic applications

(a) machine translation

The necessity of machine translation becomes obvious when one considers the enormous range of translation services required in multi-national organisations such as the United Nations, NATO, or the European Union. The EU, for example, with nine official languages[6], could drastically reduce its annual expenditure if machines instead of human translators were employed (Blatt et al. 1985: 3ff). However, despite extensive research in this area, which started in the 1950s, little progress has been made. The reasons for the lack of success are linguistic and computational. On the one hand, linguistic theory does not provide answers to all problems of machine translation; on the other hand, software and hardware problems restrict the implementation and the design of machine translation systems to a certain degree.[7]

(b) man-machine interfaces

Man-machine interfaces, that is the possibility of communicating with the computer in one's mother tongue instead of a specific command language, can be applied to a wide range of purposes. Some of them have already been realised, others will be soon available.

(b1) natural language operating and help systems

The computer's internal processes are directed by the operating system, which is a computer program consisting of a number of specific commands. These have to be learned and applied by the human user. One way of by-passing this command language is the use of a menu-driven surface, where each command is replaced by a specific symbol. Alternatively, one could use a natural-language-based operating and help system which handles the central commands on the basis of natural language input. Both menu-driven and natural-language-based systems increase the degree of user-friendliness of the computer and make it accessible to a much larger group of people.[8]

(b2) natural-language-based data base access

One of the great advantages of computers is their almost unlimited capacity for storing data on external storage devices (for example, harddisks, magnetic tapes, CD-ROM, etc.). Using such devices databases can be made available which supply the user with knowledge within a very short interval. Library databases, for example, contain information about several thousands of books, including information about their contents and general information such as author, publisher, etc. To access this information, however, specific commands have to be learned by the human user. Again, the use of natural language can simplify database access, allowing even the inexperienced human user to work with machine-based database systems.

(b3) natural-language-based information retrieval

Much of the information we use appears in written natural language form – books, journals, reports. To make available this information, computational linguists are interested in developing automatic information retrieval systems that extract the relevant information from a text. This reduced text could then be employed in question-answering systems, or it could be directly displayed on a screen. Despite the massive interest in this application, little progress has been made. This is due to theoretical-linguistic reasons and to the complexity of the primarily scientific texts (Grishman 1986: 4).

In summary, computer systems that use natural language as a mode of interaction with humans seem to be much more convenient than systems that employ complicated command interfaces or command languages.

(c) tutorial systems

Educational applications of computer technology have been under development for a long time. Today, research in this area predominantly concentrates on the use of the computer as an assistant to the human teacher. Computer systems that are used for tutoring purposes are called *CAI* (Computer-Assisted Instruction) systems. In the early 1970s they were equipped with specific knowledge (e.g. in geography) and with rudimentary natural language processing ability (e.g. Carbonell's SCHOLAR system, 1970), turning them into *ICAI*-systems, where the first character stands for "intelligent". Today, such systems are alternatively referred to as *ITS* (Intelligent Tutorial Systems), and a special class, which can be applied to the area of foreign language teaching, has been termed *ILTS* (Intelligent Language Teaching Systems, see Schwind 1986) or *ICALL* (Intelligent Computer Assisted Language Learning, see Zähner 1991). The primary application areas of modern ITS are the natural sciences, mathematics and computer programming. An ITS consists of the following fundamental modules (Kunz/Schott 1987):

- a knowledge base
- a user-model
- a tutorial component
- a dialogue component

The knowledge base contains the knowledge about the material to be presented to the learner. The learner's progress is recorded in the user-modelling component. Together with the knowledge base, this component is responsible for a proper arrangement of the tutorial material, according to the progress level attained. In the tutorial component the actual presentation of the material is administered, and the dialogue component controls the interaction between the human learner and the machine. Ideally, this dialogue will be in natural language. Today's systems, however, are not capable of using natural language freely. The reasons are similar to the ones mentioned above: theoretical-linguistic limitations and implementation restrictions.[9]

(d) natural-language-based text editing

The most widespread application of the modern computer is its use as a word processor. Using a word processor, one can easily create and manipulate text material and can – over and above the standard techniques – make use of utilities such as style sheets, footnote organisation or a thesaurus. Further tools include hyphenation programs and spell-checkers. However, these often lead to undesired results. The English language, for example, makes use of a morphologically-oriented hyphenation system. Applying the hyphenation program of a standard word processor, words such as *greenish*, *yellowish*, etc. will be correctly split into their roots *green* and *yellow* and the suffix *-ish*. However, words such as *English* or *longish* will either be separated wrongly (**Engl-ish*, **lon-gish*) or - for the program to be on the safe side - no hyphenation offer will be made. A similar phenomenon occurs with words that are a case of hyphen vs. zero-hyphen. Examples are *re-count/recount*, *re-cover/recover*, etc. The hyphenation problem is even worse in languages with a phonology-based hyphenation strategy. In German, for example, words such as *Staubecken* or *Spieleröffnung*, can be split into two completely different but meaningful parts: in *Stau-becken* and *Staub-ecken* the first possibility means "water reservoir" and the second "dust corners"; *Spiel-eröffnung* means "game opening" and *Spieler-öffnung* means "player's orifice" or "player's opening". [10] In all these cases the correct hyphenation alternative can only be chosen if the word processor is enriched by natural language principles and rules, in this case by principles that allow the machine to achieve a certain level of text understanding.

The need to develop computer programs capable of 'understanding' natural language input has led to a second, less practical, branch of computational linguistics. This branch focuses on the processes underlying natural language processing, trying to model human processing strategies and thus imitate at least some aspects of human performance. This far more cognitive approach to computer science is today subsumed under the heading of *cognitive science*. One branch of this relatively young field is concerned with the representation of knowledge, that is the formalisation of human experience and general aspects of meaning in order to facilitate search and inference operations. (We will return to this branch of computational linguistics and the problems of knowledge representation in section 2.3.3.).

Both approaches, the more practically-oriented and the cognitive one, normally interact. The requirements of practical systems often lead to research in better understanding of the underlying linguistic processes, which in turn results in an improvement of the actual implementations.

Returning to our ambiguity problem in (1), we now know that computer programs with natural language ability have to cope with ambiguous structures, just like the human mind. Whether the same disambiguation strategies can be made available to machines is not only a question of the results of theoretical-linguistic and psycholinguistic findings but also a matter of implementation efficiency. While structural, semantic, and pragmatic ambiguity can only be disambiguated using enormously large knowledge bases, some types of lexical ambiguity may be resolved using strategies which are computationally efficient but cognitively inadequate. For example, ambiguity resolution strategies relying on the immediate local context can easily be implemented and made very efficient (Hindle 1983; Handke 1991b), yet they are completely different from human disambiguation strategies. In section 6.2. we will show how such a local strategy for ambiguity resolution can be implemented.

1.2. Natural Language Processing and Cognition

As already mentioned, linguistics, psycholinguistics and computational linguistics (as a sub-branch of artificial intelligence) can be subsumed under cognitive science. A central question of cognitive science concerns the relationship between natural language processing and general cognition. The main question here is whether it is possible to isolate a natural language faculty from other cognitive activities or not. Two opposing positions have been formulated to answer this question. The *modular* approach treats the language faculty as an autonomous component of the mind. It is closely related to the Chomskyan tradition of generative grammar (Fodor 1983; Chomsky 1988). The *holistic* approach, by contrast, does not regard language as an autonomous subsystem but as an ability which can be explained by general cognitive principles. This view can be associated with cognitive-oriented approaches to language theories (Anderson 1983; Langacker 1987).

(a) the modular approach

The main arguments in favour of a modular approach are presented in Fodor (1983), where a general description of modularity is presented. Fodor lists the following basic properties of a module:

- modules are domain-specific
- modules are mandatory
- modules are fast, they operate automatically
- modules are informationally encapsulated

If the language faculty is considered to be an autonomous subsystem (module) in the mind, it has to satisfy these criteria. It can be shown that, by and large, this is the case.

The domain-specific character of a module, that is, the fact that a module is highly specialised and has access only to specific information, can be attributed to the language faculty. For example, the aspiration part and the absence of voicing in the context of ['tʰeɪm], symbolised by the diacritic [ʰ], is essential to mark the difference between *tame* and *dame* in English. Speech perception experiments have shown that a voicing/aspiration portion of approximately 30 msec is sufficient for the perceptual difference between [tʰ] and [d]. However, if the aspiration part is isolated and presented to listeners without its natural language context, it is perceived as whistling (Fodor 1983: 49). In other words, there is a clear-cut difference between speech and non-speech perception, or, in terms of the modular approach, the language faculty is specialised for the processing of input embedded in natural language context.

Considering a module to operate in a mandatory fashion means that a module operates irrespective of one's wishes. One cannot simply switch off a module and make it non-operational. Transferred to the language faculty, human listeners are incapable of blocking comprehension when listening to an interlocutor. Whenever a speech signal reaches the hearing, humans start processing it, whether they want to or not.

That the speed of natural language processing is amazingly high has long been known. Depending on the actual speech rate, several dozens of phones can be produced and perceived per second, receiving little or no conscious attention, and it seems that language processing is, by and large, an automatic reflex-like process (Levelt 1989: 28).[11]

Informational encapsulation, finally, means that modules are autonomous and that their interaction is basically a unidirectional process. In restoration experiments, where the listener has to complete constructions of all kinds with missing information (for example, missing phones, missing words or even sentence fragments), higher levels are addressed to solve the task. The missing phone in /ledʒɪ__'leɪtʃə/ (*legislature*) is restored if information from the lexical level is incorporated; the missing segment in /ðə '__i:l ɪz ɒn ðɪ 'æksl/ (The __eel is on the axle) can be filled in if the context is integrated. (/'wi:l/ is certainly a much better candidate than /'hi:l/ or /'si:l/).

In summary, it seems that the modular character of the language faculty has been well established in the light of these and other arguments.

(b) the holistic approach

The holistic approach claims that there are only few language-specific adaptations, and that the language faculty is governed by general cognitive principles. In contrast to the modular approach, the proponents of holism reject the autonomous character of the language faculty and define natural languages as open systems which are influenced by general cognitive activities. The basic grammatical properties of a language result from general processes of conceptualisation which relate to various areas of human experience. Linguistic phenomena, then, can be described by general semantic or conceptual principles. For example, the degree of well-formedness decreases the higher the conceptual distance between the focal elements involved (Langacker 1983: 25):

(3) a. A body has two arms
b. An arm has an elbow and a hand.
c. ?A body has two elbows.
d. ??A body has two hands.

Note that (3d) is less acceptable than (3b) since the conceptual distance between BODY and HAND is much higher in (3d) than between ELBOW and HAND in (3b). In other words, well-formedness is not solely a matter of grammatical principles but it is a reflex of general semantic-conceptual and functional information. Language is entwined with general cognition.

Even though it is not clear whether language is a specialised mental module or not, it is attractive – at least from a research point of view – to assume an autonomous natural language expert in the mind capable of dealing with specific inputs (speech, written language) and generating a specific output. The modular approach can serve as a framework for experimental research. Applying Fodor's criteria, one can inspect the nature of the input, make predictions about the nature of the output, and define the degree of interaction with language processing and other cognitive activities.

1.3. Subprocesses of Language Processing

The main purpose of natural language is communication. Various modes of communication are employed to convey thoughts and messages. The most commonly used modes are the oral-auditory mode, speech and listening, and the visual mode, writing and reading. The remaining communication possibilities (tactile, gustatory and olfactory) play only a subordinate role in standard communication processes.

The situation is slightly different if we consider computational linguistic applications such as man-machine interfaces. Despite some considerable progress in speech synthesis and speech analysis, it is by and large the visual mode of communication which serves as the basis for an interaction between humans and machines.

Both the oral-auditory and the visual mode can be employed in two directions, as output channels and as input channels. That there is a link between the input and output mode is obvious. In producing speech we are constantly monitoring ourselves, i.e. we invoke our comprehension system (see Levelt 1983, for a discussion). If this were not the case we could not detect and correct speech errors. On the other hand, it can be assumed that in the initial stages of the comprehension process, especially at the level of speech perception, a number of production levels are active (see section 3.2.1. on active theories of speech perception).

Similarly, when we write down something, we constantly look at the result and activate the comprehension system of written language. In other words, we check our written output by reading it. That the reading process involves a number of language production activities has been experimentally supported (see section 3.5.) and thus research has led to a range of reading models. As a summary, the picture of figure 6, which outlines the central communication modes and their actual realisations, emerges.

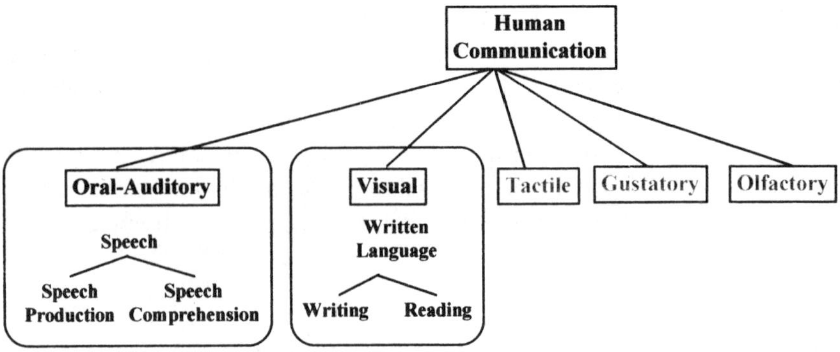

Figure 6. Modes of communication

Assuming a specialised language faculty, one can speculate about its internal structure. As in any scientific discipline, it is useful to divide the overall problem into a number of subproblems (Garnham 1985: 4), in the case of the language faculty into a number of subsystems and processing levels. Although this book focuses on high-level or cognitive processes, we will include low-level processes such as auditory and visual analysis. The treatment of these stages of language processing is necessary to get an idea

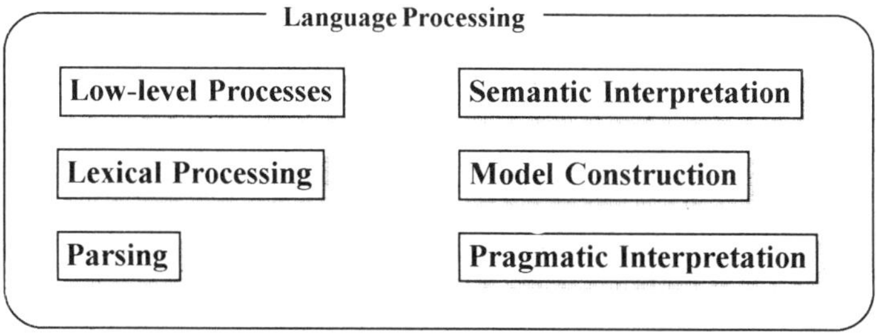

Figure 7. Subprocesses of natural language processing

of the early steps of language processing. Fig 7 provides an overview of the subprocesses involved in language processing.

A central question in cognitive science concerns the relationship between language comprehension and language production. Psycholinguists have for a long time concentrated on studies in language comprehension, primarily for experimental reasons: language production is much more difficult to control in the laboratory than comprehension. However, three main observational techniques, the study of disfluencies, the study of speech errors, and the study of aphasia, have shed some light on the process of language production. Meanwhile, enough results have been obtained to outline the differences and similarities between the two modes, one of the most important tasks being to establish to what extent language production and language comprehension share processing mechanisms and rules.

From an efficiency point of view it seems plausible to postulate each processing mechanism and each rule system only once. For example, it would be a wasteful duplication of information if the language processor made use of two mental lexicons, one for production and one for comprehension. However, there is strong experimental evidence that this is not the case (Garnham 1985: 221). Likewise, we can assume one general knowledge base, which is made use of in production as well as in comprehension. Despite these similarities, there are differences between production and comprehension. One difference concerns the sequence of the activation of the various mechanisms. Assuming a sequential model of language processing, language production starts with a thought or an idea, to eventually produce a spoken or written output; language comprehension, by contrast, first performs an acoustic analysis of the incoming signal, before a message is generated.

In this book we will be primarily concerned with language comprehension processes, that is with speech comprehension and with reading, for the following reasons. First, a good deal of literature, containing numerous experimental results, is available on language comprehension. Secondly, we are not interested in the physiological activities required in the production of language. The innervation of the active articulators in speech, and the control of hand movement by the central nervous system in writing, are of minor interest in this book. And, last but not least, we only deal with one component of natural language processing in this book, the lexicon. The main tasks and functional properties of this knowledge system can be explained on the basis of language comprehension.

1.3.1. Low-level Processes

Not all processes involved in language processing are cognitive (Garnham 1985: 4). In speech production the articulators have to be set into motion and in the production of written language the motion of the hand has to be precisely controlled. Both processes are physiological rather than linguistic. They involve subconscious movements of bodily organs controlled by the central nervous system. The comprehension of language also involves low-level processes. Prior to cognition an analysis of the sensory signal has to take place and make the results available to the understanding system. We will see in chapter three that there are two central input channels to the human language processing system, one for speech and one for written input. Both input signals are enormously complex and require highly specialised analysis mechanisms.

In the case of written input, the recognition device has to cope with lines and curves of characters, with shapes of words, and with more or less complex non-alphabetic symbols. The complexity of the analysis of print becomes clear when we realise the multitude of variants of one single character. The characters of the word *cat*, for example, can be written in various ways:

cat, CAT, *cat*, cat, cat, **cat**, cAT, Cat, etc.

However, irrespective of their realisation we have little or no trouble identifying each character and thus each word. By analogy with the concept of the phoneme (section 1.1.1.), characters which are identified as the same can be grouped into graphemes. A *grapheme* is thus an abstract concept corresponding to a character, or, to draw the parallel with the phoneme, it is the head term of a family of related characters. Like phonemes, any grapheme may have different realisations. On the basis of the examples above, the grapheme "A" has the following members: A, A, *A*, A, 𝔄, A.[12] Further realisations of "A" can be found in figure 37 (chapter III). Despite the enormous degree of graphological variation and the numerous sources of variability, the human visual recognition system is capable of correctly identifying written language with great precision. The process of identifying written alphabetic characters has become known as *optical character recognition* (OCR). In section 3.1.2. we will discuss the central implications of perceiving the written signal in general, and of OCR in particular.

Another, even more complicated, low-level analysis process is the perception of speech. From the acoustic input, which normally occurs against background noise, specific cues and characteristics have to be abstracted. However, not all acoustic information is required to decode the spoken message. In fact, to handle the entirety of acoustic information contained in the speech signal would possibly overload the speech recognition system. The enormously complex speech signal contains frequencies between 10 and 10.000 Hz and it embodies intensity variations over a range of 30 dB (Fry 1979: 129). To cope with all these aspects, which take place many times a second, would certainly be a waste of processing effort. In order to process the acoustic signal we discard quite a portion of information and concentrate on a few extremely important acoustic features. These features are referred to as *acoustic cues* In section 3.1.1. we will have a detailed look at such acoustic cues and discuss the central mechanisms involved in the perception of speech in order to model the low-level analysis of speech.

In summary, low-level processes extract various properties from an input signal, which conveys an enormously large amount of information in an extremely short time interval and is normally intermingled with a good deal of background information. To cope with these aspects, the processor applies complicated strategies to work out those properties of the sensory signal that are necessary for higher levels of language processing.

1.3.2. Lexical Processing

The goal of lexical processing is to retrieve the stored knowledge associated with a word in order to generate a meaningful interpretation of an utterance. There are various aspects that make the task of lexical processing particularly difficult, among which are the following:

(a) segmentation

The problem here is that the input signal is not neatly segmented into words. While in written language - at least in phonographic alphabetic writing systems - individual words can be identified by spaces, punctuation marks, or upper and lower case, the segmentation of spoken language into words is a complicated process.[13] Here are some examples to illustrate the segmentation problem in spoken English (stress marks have been deliberately omitted):

(4) a. /pi:stɔ:ks/
b. /ðəweɪtəkʌtɪt/
c. /ðəsædpəʊɪtrɪmembəzəlɒŋəgəʊtaɪm/

Here are the theoretically possible interpretations of these examples:

(4) a'. peace talks / pea stalks
b'. The way to cut it. / The waiter cut it.
c'. The sad poet remembers a long ago time. /
?? Thus add poetry members along a goat I'm.

In (4a), we are faced with a problem of word-internal segmentation, or *juncture* (Gimson 1962: 299). Phonologically, the two interpretations cannot be differentiated. Only phonetically can a distinction be drawn. In this case, a slight aspiration of [t^h] and a resulting boundary between /s/ and /t/ evokes the interpretation of the input as "peace talks". However, it is doubtful whether such minute phonetic differences can be utilised in rapid connected speech such as (4b). Again, it could be argued that low-level perceptual impressions, such as the perceived length of the diphthong /eɪ/, decide which interpretation has to be favoured. An alternative could be to incorporate high-level information, such as the linguistic context, which determines the segmentation of the acoustic signal into words and thus the interpretation of an utterance. On the basis of low-level processes alone, we might arrive at extremely odd interpretations such as "??Thus add poetry..." in (4c'), which is phonetically plausible but semantically out of the question. (We will return to this issue in section 3.6).

(b) the nature of the contact representation

Lexical processing begins when the fundamental perceptual properties have been extracted from the input signal to contact the central human word-store, the *mental lexicon*. An important issue in this respect concerns the nature of representation, with which the mental lexicon is activated. We will see in subsequent chapters that all sorts of contact representations have been proposed to mediate between the initial phase and higher levels of lexical processing (Frauenfelder/Tyler 1987: 3). Figure 8 provides a first overview of the main aspects utilised to extract information from the spoken and the written input signal.

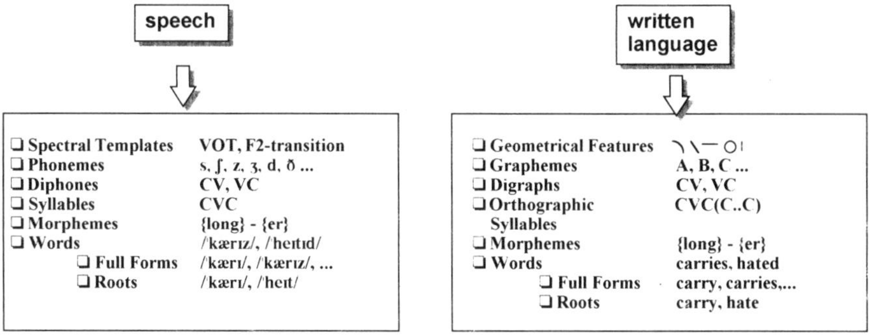

Figure 8. The nature of the contact representations
Annotations: VOT = Voice Onset Time, F2 = Formant 2, C = Consonant, V = Vowel

As figure 8 suggests, a whole range of representations is employed to contact the lexicon. Spectral templates, for example, are fundamental acoustic properties encoded in the speech signal, just as geometrical features are the basic properties of written information. Both constitute low-level aspects of processing. It will be shown in subsequent chapters that these as well as higher-level aspects such as syllables, morphemes, or words, are also employed as mediators between the input signal and lexical processing.

The type and the internal organisation of the elements in the lexicon, it may be argued, are influenced by the nature of the contact representation. For example, if the lexicon is contacted on the basis of syllables, then it is likely that the mental lexicon organises its access units in terms of syllables rather than phonemes.

Two fundamental concepts of lexical processing deserve our specific attention: *lexical access* and *word recognition*. According to Tyler/Frauenfelder (1987: 6ff) *lexical access* refers to the point at which the various facets of the lexical entry contacted become available, whereas *word recognition* defines the end-point of the selection phase, that is the point at which a listener is able to decide what lexical entry he identified.

While the process of 'word recognition' is relatively unproblematic, the term 'lexical access' is confusing in many ways. First, it is used fairly inconsistently throughout the relevant literature. In contrast to Tyler/Frauenfelder, Garnham (1985: 43) defines 'lexical access' as the retrieval of a word form from the lexicon on the basis of perceptual and contextual information, and 'word recognition' as the identification of one remaining word candidate. Aitchison (1992: 53, 95) views 'word recognition' as a two-stage process: at the first stage, the stage of 'lexical access', the input is matched against possible words, and at the second, the multiple possibilities are narrowed down to one candidate. This view is paralleled by Zwitserlood's (1989) approach, where stage one of the word recognition process is defined as 'lexical access' and stage two as 'lexical selection'.

Thus, we are confronted with various different interpretations of the term 'lexical access'. On the one hand, it is viewed as the initial stage of the more general process of word recognition (Aitchison, Garnham, Zwitserlood), on the other hand, it is defined as the retrieval of lexical information (Tyler/Frauenfelder). In both cases, the term 'access' seems to be interpreted too narrowly. To 'access something' means to 'reach' or 'make use of something'. Thus, the process of 'lexical access' should rather be interpreted as 'making use of the lexicon' or 'preparing the lexicon for use' just as we open a dictionary before we actually start reading in it.

Such a generalised interpretation is much more plausible if we consider the computational interpretation of 'access' in the sense of 'file access', which is normally read as 'making use of a file' or 'preparing a file for read/write operations'. Thus, it seems reasonable to extend the term 'lexical access' and consider it synonymous with lexical processing henceforth. The process of making available lexical information, i.e. 'lexical access' in Tyler/Frauenfelder's sense, will be referred to as *lexical retrieval* instead.[14]

The relationship between word recognition and lexical retrieval is assumed to be sequential. Most theories of lexical processing claim that word recognition precedes lexical retrieval. This in turn raises the question whether either of the two stages can be by-passed. Put differently, is it possible to retrieve information from the mental lexicon without recognising what was heard, or, vice versa, is it possible to perceive a sensory input, i.e. hear or read a word, without understanding it? The answer to these issues places some very important constraints on models of lexical processing recognition. Since the third and the fourth chapter are dedicated to the stages of lexical and pre-lexical processing, we will not pursue these questions here.

1.3.3. Parsing

The parsing process can be subdivided into two subprocesses: the identification of the internal structure of words (morphological analysis) and the analysis of sentence structure (syntactic analysis). Both processes are often subsumed under the head term *grammar* (Palmer 1971: 13). Since the term grammar has, in the Chomskyan tradition, also been used to refer to a general theory of language, it will by and large be avoided in this book (see also section 1.1.1.).

(a) morphological analysis

Morphological analysis is concerned with the internal make-up of words. But what can be considered to be a word? Morphologically, a word is the actual realisation of a *lexeme*, the fundamental unit of the lexicon of a language (Matthews 1972: 22).[15] For example, *dies*, *died*, *dying*, and *die* are forms or 'words' of the lexeme DIE. According to Quirk et al. (1985: 67ff), words can be subdivided into two general classes:

- open-class words
- closed-class words

While open-class items (nouns, full verbs, adjectives, adverbs) allow the creation of new members and thus constitute classes which are unlimited in number, closed-class items (prepositions, pronouns, determiners, conjunctions, auxiliary verbs, interjections) are closed in the sense that they are highly resistant to the addition of new members and can only exceptionally be extended by processes of alternation. In other words, closed-class words are limited in number (Huddleston 1984: 120ff). Consequently, the number of words in a language depends on the productivity of the processes capable of extending the open-class items. These *morphological processes* can be subdivided as shown in figure 9.

The task of morphological analysis, then, is to find out the basic building blocks of which open-class words are constructed. These building blocks, or *morphemes*, constitute the smallest units of grammatical analysis (Matthews 1974: 13). By convention, morphemes are presented in curly brackets. They can be *free*, for example *table*, or *bound*, e.g. *-s*. Free morphemes serve as the basis for further morphological processes. They are generally referred to as *roots*. The terminology in this area is very fluid. Some linguists draw a distinction between *root,* the fundamental morphological unit, and *stem,* the

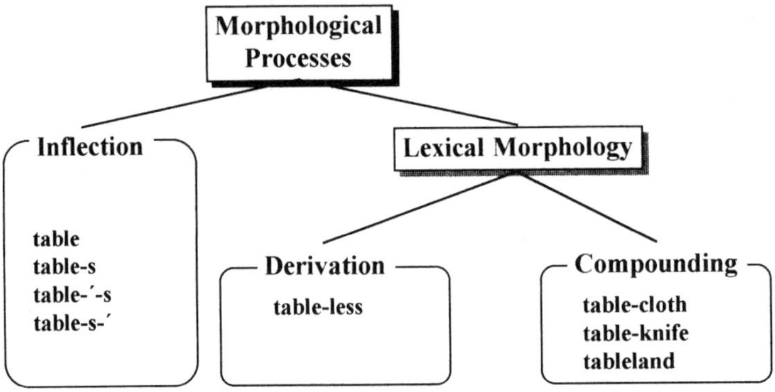

Figure 9. Morphological processes[16]

basis for inflectional processes. According to this distinction, the following root and stem relationships can be postulated:

farm	→	root, also a stem
farms	→	root/stem + inflectional affix
farmer	→	root/stem + derivational affix = new stem
farmers	→	stem + inflectional affix

In English this distinction seems quite trivial. In languages, however, where reduced forms can be generated, it makes sense to postulate such a specification. For example, in German derivatives such as *Röschen* /'rœsçən/ ("little rose"), the diminutive *-chen* does not attach to the nominative singular form *Rose* /'ro:zə/ but to a lesser form, in this case *Ros-*. This lesser form would then be the root and the resulting derivative, *Röschen*, which serves as the basis for further inflectional processes, the stem. For reasons of generalisation across languages, we have good reason to make use of this differentiation henceforth.

The actual realisation of a morpheme is referred to as *morph*. The examples in (5) illustrate the different phonological realisations of the plural morpheme in English.

(5) a. {cat} + {s} → /'kæts/
b. {dog} + {s} → /'dɒgz/
c. {rose} + {s} → /'rəʊzɪz/

Bound morphemes can also be referred to as *affixes*. Affixes in turn can be classified into *prefixes* (affixes that precede the root), *infixes* (affixes that are inserted into the root), and *suffixes* (affixes that follow the root).

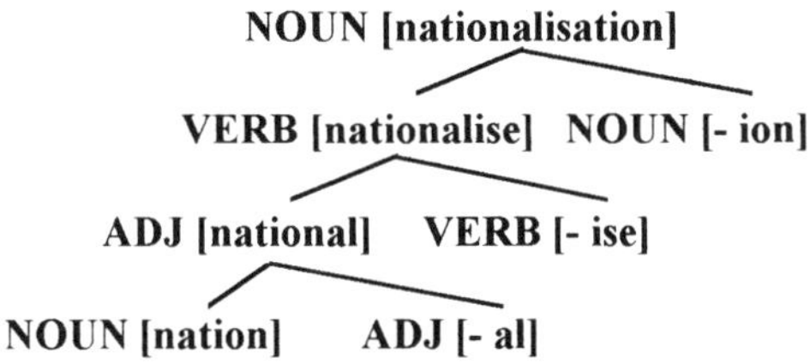

Figure 10. An illustration of affixation [17]

Somewhat natural antitheses to infixes are *circumfixes*, which attach discontinuously around a stem (Sproat 1992: 50). Examples of this type can be found in Indonesian, where the function of an affix cannot be derived from the prefix and the suffix of which the circumfix is composed.

The process of combining an affix with a root is called *affixation*. Figure 10 illustrates the process of affixation on the basis of the derivative *nationalisation*, which consists of the root *nation* and the resulting stems *national*, *nationalise* and *nationalisation* respectively.

(b) syntactic analysis

The syntactic structure of a sentence determines the relationship between the words in a sentence. It indicates how words can be grouped together to form phrases, to what extent words modify other words, and what words are syntactically most important.

The parsing process extracts the structural properties of a sentence and eventually produces a representation which contains the general syntactic aspects of the sentence, such as tense, voice, etc., and represents the basic syntactic functions and their internal syntactic make-up.[18] Let us illustrate this on the basis of:

(6) The man gave a book to John.

A possible functional syntactic representation of (6) could look like this:

[(Sentence-Features:
(S-Type: Declarative)
(Tense: Past)
(Voice: Active)
(Aspect: Perfective, Simple)[19]
(Mood: Indicative))

(Syntactic Functions:
 (Subject: (MAN, Definite)
 (Direct Object: (BOOK, Indefinite)
 (Indirect Object: (JOHN, Proper))]

Over and above the generation of a functional representation, several grammatical properties are constantly being checked during the process of syntactic analysis. The following ungrammatical examples illustrate some of these features:

(7) a. *John are at home.
 b. *John gave.
 c. *John put the book in London.

Sentence (7a) is ungrammatical because the subject *John* and the main verb *are* do not agree in features, in English primarily in number. While *John* is a third person singular noun, *are* is a plural verb or a verb denoting the second person singular. In other words, the morphological information associated with the lexical entries *John* and *are* is incompatible and the parsing process would reject such a construction.

(7b) is ungrammatical, since the syntactic context for *gave* is illegitimate. *Give*, traditionally known as a ditransitive verb, requires two objects as its arguments. Again, the parser would show such a construction to be ungrammatical.

A similar case is exhibited in (7c). Once more, the syntactic context for the verb is ungrammatical. *Put*, at least in this interpretation, typically requires an object and an adverbial of place in its immediate context. Given example (7c), this requirement seems to be fulfilled: "the book" is the object and "in London" is the adverbial of place. However, "in London" lacks the quality of "containment" such as "in the car", "in the garage", "in the bucket", etc. Likewise the object of *put* is illegitimate if it lacks any physical structure as in "*He puts *democracy* in the bucket." In contrast to (7b), we are confronted with a case where the syntax parser incorporates general knowledge about nouns and verbs to decide whether a sentence is ungrammatical or not. Such knowledge is associated with each lexical entry of a language. For the verb *put*, this can be specified as follows:[20]

PUT: (SUBJECT [+ANIMATE])
 (OBJECT [+PHYSICAL OBJECT])
 (ADVERBIAL [+PHYSICAL OBJECT, + CONTAINER])

To sum up, on the basis of lexical and morphological information associated with each element in a sentence, the parser generates a functional structure and constantly examines the morpho-syntactic properties of the respective elements in the sentence.

1.3.4. Semantic Interpretation

Generating the functional structure of a sentence is just one step towards building an understanding of a sentence. Over and above the structural properties of a sentence we need to determine its meaning. The process of generating and representing a sentence's meaning is called *semantic interpretation*. Recently, a distinction has been drawn between aspects that primarily have intra-linguistic relevance and aspects that relate to external domains (Schwarz 1992: 49). Such a two-level model suggests that the process of semantic interpretation can be subdivided into two stages: the generation of a linguistic-semantic form which has no contact with external domains, and the generation of a structure which has access to the outside world and incorporates general knowledge. In computational linguistics these two levels are referred to as *logical form* and *conceptual representation* (Allen 1987: 193ff).

(a) logical form

The first stage is concerned with the rules and principles of the language in question and is thus essentially linguistic in character. It is an intermediate representation between the syntactic functional structure, on the one hand, and the logical or conceptual representation of a sentence, on the other. One problem which has to be solved at the level of logical form is the disambiguation of word meaning. Just as words can have several syntactic categories, they can have different meanings, or *senses*. For example, the word *fly* has for each of its syntactic categories (noun, verb or adjective) several senses. In the Oxford English Dictionary (OED) the interpretation of *fly* which denotes the winged insect alone exhibits eleven different senses. Another noun interpretation which derives from the verb *fly* has eight senses. The first stage of interpreting a sentence semantically has to narrow down the multitude of word senses on the basis of the lexical knowledge of the word. Various techniques of representing word meaning are available in this respect. They range from more or less syntactic techniques, such as selectional restrictions, to semantic representation techniques, such as semantic networks or frames. These and other techniques are discussed in section 2.3.3.3. They help to disambiguate expressions such as:

(8)	a.	a swarm of flies	(two-winged insect)
	b.	a two-mile pigeon fly	(the action of flying, obsolete)
	c.	to travel in a fly	(a quick-travelling carriage)

(b) conceptual representation

Very often, it is impossible on the basis of linguistic considerations alone to determine the correct sense of a word. Here are two examples:

(8) d. a one-centimetre fly
e. a one-mile fly

Only the integration of general knowledge and human experience, in this case the relationship between length, insects, and the action of flying, helps to establish the correct sense. This second level of semantic interpretation, then, builds a conceptual structure which allows the drawing of inferences and conclusions. That human experience is often a key factor in the semantic interpretation of a sentence can be illustrated using the following examples:

(9) a. He read a book about music in the last two hours.
b. He read a book about music in the last century.

The central problem of these two sentences concerns the relationship between the act of reading and the adverbial of time "in the last ...". While in sentence (9a) the temporal adverbial is external to "a book about music" and describes the length of the reading process, (9b) exhibits a relationship of the opposite kind. Here, the adverbial "in the last century" relates to "a book about music". How do we arrive at such a conclusion? Clearly, our knowledge about the relationship between a human action such as reading, human lifetime, and time in general, guides our interpretation process.

Whatever the internal stages of semantic interpretation, the main task of semantic analysis is to give a precise account of the meaning of a sentence. In the sentences below, for example, we would like to generate a conceptual representation that expresses the fact that, despite their syntactic differences, they have essentially the same meaning:

(10) a. The man gave a book to John.
b. John received a book from the man.

Syntactically, both sentences behave similarly concerning their direct objects (in both cases "a book") but conversely concerning their subjects and their indirect objects. The latter are realised by prepositional phrases. Semantically, however, both sentences are almost identical in meaning. This can be expressed by the following variant of a conceptual representation:

```
[ACTION: TRANSFER
         (ACTOR  MAN, definite)
         (OBJECT BOOK, indefinite)
         (DIRECTION   (SOURCE  MAN, definite)
                      (GOAL    JOHN, proper))]
```

Expressed less formally, this representation means that an actor of the type MAN transferred an object of the type BOOK from himself to an individual called JOHN. The primary difference between (10a) and (10b) is thus not a difference of meaning but one of focus. In both cases, *John* is the recipient, but only in (10b) *John* is also the focus. Such a conceptual representation not only expresses the meaning of the sentence but it also helps in the drawing of inferences from it. Consider the following two sentences:

(11) a. The man went to the station.
b. The man arrived at the station.

The conceptual representation for both sentences is basically identical:

```
[ACTION: TRANSFER
         (ACTOR  MAN,definite)
         (OBJECT MAN,definite)
         (DIRECTION   (SOURCE  unknown)
                      (GOAL    STATION, proper))]
```

However, there is a difference. While we cannot be sure whether the actor has reached the goal in (11a), *arrive* clearly implies that the actor MAN is at the station. Hence, the conceptual interpretation of ARRIVE necessitates that the GOAL of the TRANSFER-action is reached. In other words, (11b) conceptually implies that "the man got there". That this inference is legitimate can be shown by a co-ordination test:

(11) a'. The man went to the station and he didn't get there.
b'. ??The man arrived at the station and he didn't get there.

The co-ordination of the sentence with the negated presumed inference leads to a contradiction in (11b') but not in (11a'). This demonstrates that the inference is correct for (11b) but not for (11a).

In summary, the process of semantic interpretation has to fulfil the following tasks: it has to specify the meaning of the words in a sentence, it has to define the meaning relations between the words and phrases in a sentence, and it has to couple linguistic interpretation techniques with general knowledge in order to generate a conceptual structure.

1.3.5. Higher Levels

Beyond the syntactic analysis of sentences and their semantic interpretation, two further levels are involved in natural language processing. One such level is concerned with the building of a model of the discourse and the situation which the actual sentence describes. The second of these higher levels determines what to do with that model; expressed differently, it defines what message is conveyed.

(a) model construction

Speakers and listeners keep track of what is being talked about. They introduce and reintroduce referents (persons, objects) and make assumptions about them, they change topics; in short, they build mental models. Levelt (1989: 114ff) distinguishes four types of knowledge structure on the basis of a two-person interaction. The first kind of knowledge is the knowledge which the speaker believes he shares with his addressee. It is called *common ground*. The second kind of knowledge is a collection of knowledge structures which the speaker believes he has successfully transmitted to his interlocutor. These *own contributions* are mixed with the *interlocutor's contributions*, the third knowledge structure. The remaining knowledge structure is the *information yet to be conveyed* or the *communicative goal*. All four knowledge structures constitute the speaker's discourse model, which is defined by the speaker's plus the interlocutor's contributions.

In addition to the discourse model, humans build general performance models of the interlocutor which contain information about the interlocutor's preferred interaction modes, a rough characterisation of his linguistic competence, an assessment of the interlocutor's memory ability, and an indication of what his goals seem to be for the remaining dialogue. In other words, we build a model of what the interlocutor knows, how he thinks, what he memorises, and how he learns. The process of inferring a person's cognitive state from his performance can be called *cognitive diagnosis* (Ohlsson 1987: 204). Research into the modelling of these aspects has primarily been carried out in the area of ICAI (see section 1.1.3., above), where computer systems used for teaching are equipped with a user-modelling component that represents the student's understanding of the material to be taught (Bumbaca 1988: 228).

(b) pragmatic interpretation

The level of pragmatic interpretation determines the communicative intention of a sentence, or its *illocutionary force*. In section 1.1.1., we illustrated on the basis of example (1g) that the illocutionary force of a sentence hinges on factors which are well beyond linguistic considerations, for example, the relationship between two interlocutors. The most direct way of expressing the illocutionary force of a sentence is by using verbs which belong to the class of *performative verbs*: *warn*, *promise*, *believe*, *pledge*, etc. For example, a promise can be expressed using the verb *promise* in the context of "I promise you ...", an assertion can be made using "I believe that ...", and so on. However, the pragmatic interpretation of utterances is often complicated by the fact that the message a speaker is trying to convey is different from what he actually says. In an extreme case, a speaker wants to convey the opposite of what he actually says in order to create an ironical effect. A performative verb such as *promise*, then, can be used as a warning, provided that the general circumstances permit such an interpretation. The pragmatic theory of speech acts, which goes back to Austin (1962), approaches phenomena of this kind, but constructing an adequate theory in this area is very difficult since many contextual influences play a role in the interpretation of natural language.

Another aspect of pragmatic interpretation deals with the fact that speakers adhere to a general principle of co-operativeness. This principle, which was first formulated by Grice (1975), defines a general framework of conversation where speakers mutually assume that their contributions are purposeful, well-conducted, or, more generally, co-operative. The *co-operative principle* is supplemented by four maxims that Grice considers to follow from it:[21]

- the principle of quality
- the principle of quantity
- the principle of relation
- the principle of manner

These maxims are not scientific laws that determine the operation of natural language processing; rather they serve as defaults or norms that can be violated, or, to use Grice's terminology, 'flouted'.

(12) a. Speaker A: "Can you pass me the salt?"
Speaker B: "It's a nice day."
b. Speaker A: "What time is it?"
Speaker B: "My watch is broken."

In (12) we are confronted with two examples of a violation of the maxim of relation, which essentially says: be relevant. In both cases, speaker B's contribution is superficially irrelevant as an answer to the question asked by speaker A. However, such a violation does not necessarily lead to a failure of the conversation. Assuming that any contribution is purposeful or co-operative, the language processor tries to establish a relationship between question and answer, to work out what was meant. Such a relationship is called *conversational implicature*. In example (12b), this relationship is obvious: "on broken watches one can't read the time; speaker B has such a watch and can thus not answer speaker A's question". Speaker B's answer in (12a), by contrast, is really irrelevant, unless we construct something like "under normal circumstances speaker B never passes the salt to A; however, since it is a nice day he will make an exception".

Both levels, model construction and pragmatic interpretation, are processes which are well beyond the scope of the central linguistic levels: phonetics, grammar and semantics. They are enormously difficult to define, and, despite more or less precise theoretical underpinnings, these extremely complex high-level processes are very hard to capture. Computer programs which incorporate the entirety of high-level knowledge have not been implemented yet; however, there have been attempts to integrate at least fragments of such knowledge (see Allen 1983, for example).

1.4. The Architecture of a Natural Language Processing System

Having outlined the subprocesses involved in natural language processing, we can now convert the insights into a working model of language processing which will serve as the basis of our discussion henceforth. Figure 11 proposes such a framework.

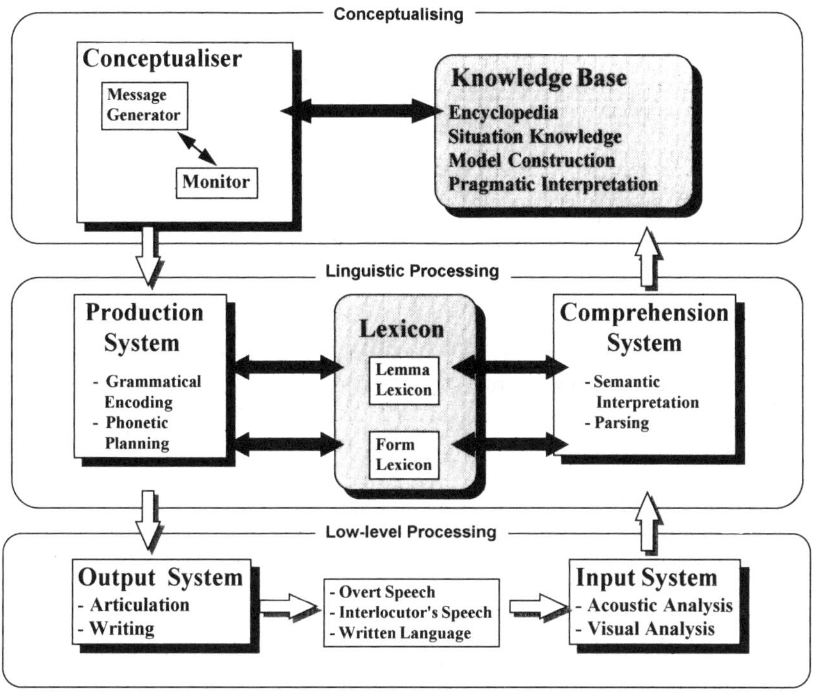

Figure 11. A framework of language processing

The model in figure 11 is based on the language production model of Bock (1982) and Levelt (1989). It suggests that a natural language processing system has the following ingredients:

- three processing levels:
  - conceptualising
  - linguistic processing
  - low-level processing

- two general stores:
  - the knowledge base
  - the lexicon

The conceptualiser is responsible for the high-level processes which were outlined in section 1.3.5. It interacts with a powerful knowledge base which supplies the general knowledge necessary for the generation and interpretation of a message and keeps track of the discourse. The counterpart of the knowledge base at the linguistic level is the lexicon. It supplies the information about the words of a language. It incorporates a morphological component (here the form lexicon) whose complexity depends on the language type, especially on the degree of synthesis of a language. A language is *synthetic* if its words can be split into component parts. By contrast, a language is *analytic* where there is a ono-to-one correspondence between words and morphemes (Comrie 1981: 39ff). English and German can be located somewhere between these two extremes. However, German morphology is much richer than English, since German words allow a much wider range of morphological variation. Hence, German is more synthetic than English and requires more complex morphological processes.

The remaining modules are concerned with the central linguistic processes (parsing and semantic interpretation) and with low-level processes as described in section 1.3.1.

Let us have a closer look at the processing levels of our working model.

(a) the level of conceptualising

The main task of the conceptualiser is to generate a conceptual structure in the process of planning speech, and to interpret incoming messages in speech comprehension. It interacts with the knowledge base, where general factual knowledge and experience as well as discourse-specific knowledge (for example, knowledge about the interlocutor) is stored. The conceptual structure defines the basic conceptual properties of a sentence to be generated or analysed (see section 1.3.4. (b)).

Several techniques for representing conceptual structures are available. Their main aim, however, is the same: to describe the fundamental conceptual dependencies of a sentence. Example (13) exhibits two examples of a conceptual representation, Jackendoff's theory of conceptual structure (1983 and 1990) and Schank's conceptual dependency theory (1975).

(13) a. John put the car in the garage.

b. Jackendoff's conceptual structure:

```
[EVENT          PUT
     (PERSON    JOHN)
     (THING     CAR)
     (PLACE     IN
     (THING     GARAGE))]
```

c. Schank's conceptual dependency representation:

```
[ACTION             ATRANS
     (ACTOR              JOHN)
     (OBJECT             CAR)
     (DIRECTION          (FROM  NIL)
                         (TO    GARAGE))]
```

The representations are fairly similar. They relate a number of categories (person/actor, thing/object, etc.) to a predicate. Also the individual concepts such as JOHN, CAR, etc. are in both cases spelt with capital letters to indicate that they are lexemes and consist of a set of meaning components, such as JOHN (human, male, adult) or CAR (vehicle, 4-wheels). The primary difference concerns the definition of the event/action. While Jackendoff proposes a representation which is close to a syntactic predicate-argument structure (see section 1.3.3.), Schank's representation is much more general in character. The action type ATRANS (*A*bstract *TRANS*fer), for example, is just one of eleven primitive actions in the conceptual dependency theory. Also, the representation frame and its structuring into ACTOR, OBJECT and DIRECTION is independent of the type of action and remains unchanged (see section 2.3.3.3.). Example (14) compares both representations on the basis of a further example, where PTRANS stands for *P*hysical *TRANS*fer:

(14) a. John is coming.
b. Jackendoff's conceptual structure:

```
[EVENT          COME
     (PERSON    JOHN)]
```

c. Schank's conceptual dependency representation:

```
[ACTION             PTRANS
     (ACTOR              JOHN)
     (OBJECT             JOHN)
     (DIRECTION          (FROM  NIL)
                         (TO    NIL))]
```

In summary, the two theories differ in their presentation of semantic categories and their relationships within a message. In any case, a conceptual representation of whatever type is generated by the processor, either to be converted into a grammatical structure in language production, or as a result of the process of language comprehension.

(b) the level of "linguistic" processing

At the linguistic level, we have to differentiate between language production and language comprehension.

In language production, the conceptual structure is translated into a linguistic structure. This process is carried out in two stages. One stage is responsible for syntactic and semantic aspects. It converts the conceptual structure into a syntactic structure which describes the main structural properties of a sentence (i.e. subject-verb-relations). At a second stage the syntactic structure is mapped to a phonetic string which can be forwarded to the lower levels of language production. This conversion process is mainly concerned with phonetic and morphological information.

In language comprehension this process is reversed. The incoming signal is first transformed into a morpho-phonemic string and then augmented with syntactic and semantic information. It is eventually converted into a conceptual representation.

The subdivision of the level of linguistic processing is reflected by the partitioning of the lexicon into two parts, a lemma lexicon and a form lexicon. The lemma lexicon handles those aspects of the lexical entries that define a word's syntactic and semantic properties; the form lexicon specifies an entry's morphological and phonological aspects. We will elaborate the internal structure of lexical entries in great detail in chapter two.

(c) the low-level processing system

In speech production, the linguistic level generates a phonetic plan which serves as the basis for the articulation of the sentence. Before the articulators come into action, however, the phonetic plan is to be transformed into a physiological program which serves as an instruction to the central nervous system and eventually results in audible speech or in physiological actions to produce written output.

On the comprehension side, the incoming speech signal from the interlocutor (in case of a conversation) or the speaker himself (via bone conduction) is acoustically analysed in the perception component. Through various intermediate stages this component transforms the sound wave into a linguistically interpretable structure consisting of phonetic and phonological properties (phonemes, syllables, intonation contour, etc.). The result is a phonetic string which can be analysed by higher level components. Alternatively, the comprehension system can be confronted with written input. In this case, the written symbols have to be recognised before higher levels come into action. Whether the analysis of written information proceeds along the lines of general vision, or whether it is a highly specialised technique which may even involve additional phonetic techniques is not entirely clear. We will look at the relevant experiments in section 3.5.

Central to the entire system is the lexicon, the knowledge system which is the central concern of this book. It contains the words of the language and a large amount of information associated with each word. The centrality of the lexicon has today been acknowledged by linguists, psycholinguists, and computational linguists.

In linguistic theory, for example, numerous grammar models have been developed which assign a central role to the lexicon.[22] Take the class of Unification Grammars as an example. In GPSG/Generalised Phrase Structure Grammar, HPSG/Head-Driven Phrase Structure Grammar, and CUG/Categorical Unification Grammar, the lexicon not only contains the information about the words, but it is used as a control unit to examine the well-formedness of the sentences generated by the model. Hence, it is not surprising that many linguists see their primary task as developing grammar models with a large lexicon that satisfies the needs of the grammatical rules.

The centrality of the lexicon can also be attributed to technological aspects. In order to use the computer as a means of communication, large databases which contain information about the items to be communicated have to developed. However, such databases are built in accordance with the principles of engineering rather than linguistic theory or psycholinguistic insights, i.e. they satisfy practical needs and only rudimentarily theoretical linguistic considerations.

As already mentioned, the lexicon can be subdivided into two parts, a form lexicon and a lemma lexicon. The reasons for this split, and an exact description of the information contained in each subcomponent, are given in great detail in section 2.3.1.

Before we turn our attention to the lexicon, we have to address an issue which has been a central research topic in cognitive science for some time. It concerns the possibility of interaction between the components of a language processing system.

1.5. The Interaction between the Components

Any framework of natural language processing must do more than just list and describe each component of the system. It must also specify how the components act together to generate overt speech or a conceptual structure. Figure 11 lists all the components in a neatly ordered form, from high-level to low-level processes in language production, and, vice versa, in language comprehension. At the same time this implies that any output of one component is simply passed on as input to the next, suggesting little or no interaction between the components. An alternative would be a model where the components constantly interact with each other and all operate simultaneously or parallelly.

In fact both models have been suggested in the literature. A model in which the components act serially and independently of each other is called a non-interactive, or *autonomy model* (Garnham 1985: 186). Figure 12 presents such a model from the point of view of language comprehension.

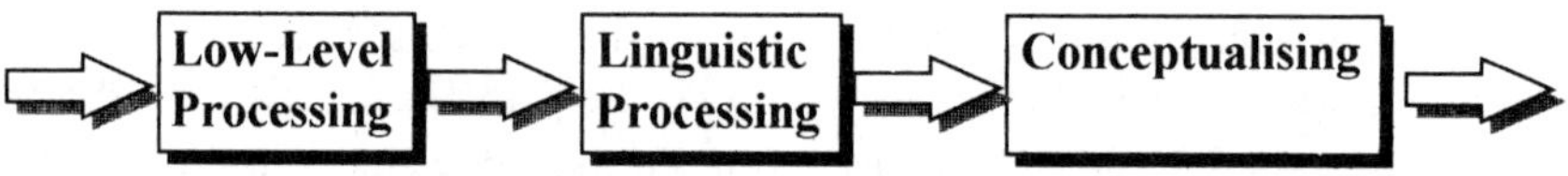

Figure 12. A non-interactive or autonomy model of language processing

Essentially, the autonomy model says that all low-level processing takes place before all linguistic processing, and all linguistic processing before all conceptualising. In other words, the flow of information is *serial* and *bottom-up*.[23] The term 'serial' means that there is a unidirectional flow of information through the entire system, and that the components receive their instructions in a strict order. Autonomous models were suggested to account for the analysis of speech errors, such as Garrett's layered model of language production (Garrett 1980). An advantage of autonomy models concerns their testability in psycholinguistic experiments, since the experimenter has precise conceptions about the task of each module as well as its input and output (Rickheit/Strohner 1993: 52).

In a series of word-monitoring experiments in the 1970s Marslen-Wilson showed that strict seriality cannot be maintained as a parameter of language processing.[24] It was demonstrated that there is not only a multidirectional flow of information between the components of language processing but also a constant interaction between them. For example, the identification of a clause boundary, essentially a syntactic problem, is influenced by the intonation contour of the incoming signal, the identification of word sense is by and large influenced by the context, and so on. Thus, we are confronted with *top-down* effects, where high-level information influences lower levels.[25]

Figure 13 shows an *interactive* model of language processing, where all three components of language processing operate in parallel, and at least two of them constantly interact.

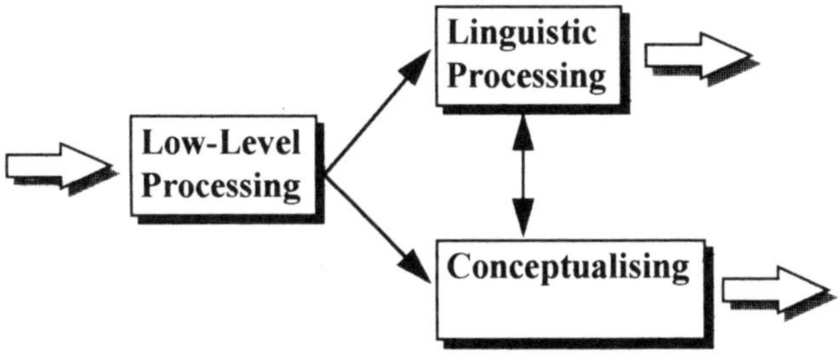

Figure 13. An interactive model of language processing

Whether low-level processes can be included in the interactive process will be discussed in section 3.6., when we reconsider the segmentation problem in spoken word recognition.

The interactive model has been proposed in several variants. A weak interactive theory of language processing claims that the level of conceptualising can influence linguistic processing. It says, for example, that in the case of ambiguity, one interpretation of the incoming sentence is to be preferred. In a stronger version of interactivity, the level of conceptualising not only influences but constrains the level of linguistic processing (Garnham 1985: 188ff).

A third variant suggests a compromise between the relative autonomy of the levels of processing and their parallel activation (Rickheit/Strohner 1993: 55). It says that all components of the language processor can operate in parallel, however on different parts of the construction. Such an *incremental* model makes sense especially in language production, where some sort of *lookahead* must be possible to generate a sentence. Levelt (1989: 25) gives the following example: the phrase "sixteen dollars" can alternatively be pronounced /sɪks 'ti:n dɒləz/ or /'sɪksti:n dɒləz/, with the word stress either on sixTEEN or on SIXteen. Depending on the choice, the intonation contour of *dollars* is heavily influenced. Hence, for the right stress pattern to be generated for the first word, the non-segmental phonological aspects of the second word must be available. In fact, most speech production models suggest that by means of a 'subconscious' lookahead technique the anticipation of segments is fundamental to the production of language

(Borden/Harris 1980: 138ff). In an incremental model, as suggested in figure 14, then, we are confronted with a different kind of parallelism, where all components are active but work on different parts of the construction. This technique can also be referred to as *pseudo-parallelism*.

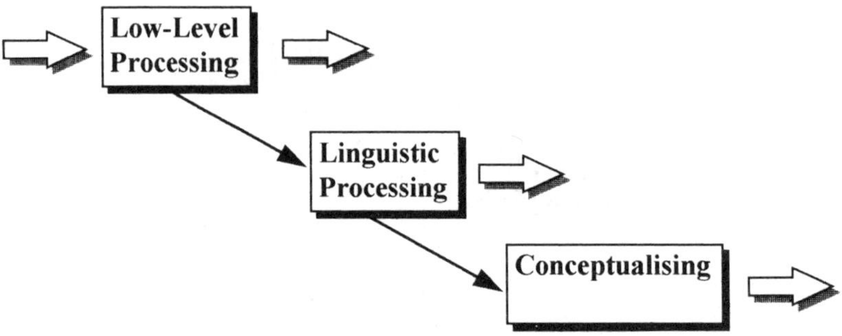

Figure 14. An incremental model of language processing

Processing models which incrementally employ their modules are not only relevant for the process of language production but are also very attractive for computer implementations. Present computer architectures do not permit strict parallelism, due to their processor design. Even though recent developments, such as the Connection Machine[26], allow parallel processing, standard applications in computational linguistics use processing strategies of an incremental kind with a limited lookahead. One of the most influential implementations in this respect is Marcus's PARSIFAL (1980).

1.6. Connectionism

Since the mid 1980s cognitive scientists have begun to explore a new framework for thinking about cognitive processes. Prior to that, it was common to think that information processing proceeds along the lines of the von-Neumann computer.[27] According to this *conventional* or *symbolic view of computation*, processing was considered as a sequence of discrete operations, and memory consisted of a set of separate stores. For example, the relationship between vision and language processing can be described as a relationship where the visual system sends an abstract message to a general receiver in the language processing system, which decodes the message and retrieves the appropriate linguistic reaction.

An alternative approach still accepts the computer and thus the use of concrete information processing models as a useful approximation of the macrostructure of human thought, but believes that an alternative framework seems more appropriate for the description of the microstructure of cognition. This new approach is called the *connectionist framework* (McClelland 1988: 107). On the theoretical side, it is based on an abstraction of our current understanding of the information properties of neurons; on the technological side, it relies on the feasibility of building parallel computers (Feldman/Ballard 1982: 205/206). Returning to the relationship between vision and language processing, this view suggests that there are numerous indirect links between the visual system and the language processing system. These links, or connections, hold between a large number of individual processing units at different processing levels.

Figure 15 illustrates the differences between conventional computing and connectionism on the basis of the visual input "brown fly". While the conventional model establishes a symbolic link between the visual system and the language processing system (shown as a double-lined arrow), the connectionist model establishes the connection between the two levels via a number of specialised processing units and their appropriate connections. The units have been drawn as boxes and the connections by simple lines.

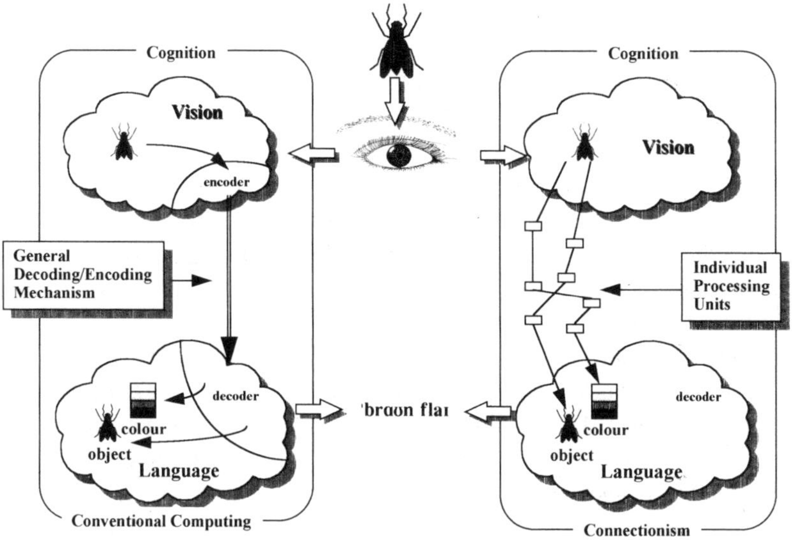

Figure 15. Conventional (symbolic) computing vs. Connectionism

Actually, the connectionist framework is not that new. As early as in the 1950s, computer pioneers, such as Marvin Minsky and Seymour Papert, began to think about modelling cognitive processes in terms of neural models or *neural networks*. Unfortunately for the subject, they concluded that, due to the number of connections established in neural models, they are combinatorially too complex and should be dismissed as models of cognition. It was not until the 1970s that neural networks were reconsidered as suitable models of human information processing in general, and of natural language processing in particular. Since a number of models that evolved from research into neural networks, especially those models that result in actual computer implementations, deviate from the anatomy of the human ideal to a considerable extent, the term *connectionism* was introduced. Today, we have two terms that essentially mean the same thing: *neural network*s and *connectionism*. However, according to the terminology used in the United States, the present stronghold of this young and growing discipline, 'neural networks' is used as the more general term, while 'connectionism', or its modern variant 'new connectionism', refers to those models that are also computer implementations and serve a specific purpose, for example, the processing of natural language (Kemke 1988: 145).

In its modern interpretation, the term 'connectionism' describes the importance of the interaction between neurons in modelling artificially intelligent systems (Ladd 1986: 110). Essentially, the connectionist approach tries to model the basic functions of the human brain by means of networks of connections among simple processing units (in the case of the brain, neurons). However, there are differences between the connectionist approach and the physiology of the brain. They concern, among others, the number and the function of the connections between the processing units.

Sometimes connectionist models have also been referred to as *parallel distributed processing* or PDP-models. Basically, these models are specific classes of connectionist models that emphasise the fact that processing activity is a result of interaction between a large number of processing units (McClelland 1988: 108).

A connectionist model consists of two primitives, *units* and *connections*. Units, also referred to as nodes, are simple processing devices with associated activation values. These values result from a weighted sum of the inputs to a unit and from other units. The interaction between the units is based on connections. Connections, also called links, may have positive weights, so that an input may excite or inhibit the processing unit that receives the input. The total set of processing units and connections is normally referred to as *network*. A fundamental premise of connectionism is that the individual units do not transmit large amounts of information. Instead, they compute information on the basis of a set of appropriate connections to a large number of similar units (Feldman/Ballard 1982: 208).

Not all connectionist models follow the same architecture. In fact, a wide range of architectures is possible. At one extreme, a network may be structured in such a way that it contains a set of totally interconnected units, where each unit receives its input from the environment and passes its results back. Figure 16 illustrates such a network.

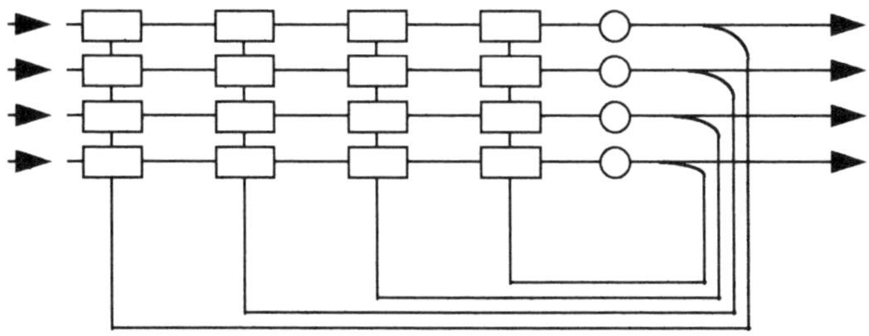

Figure 16. A fully connected network (after McClelland 1988)

More restricted versions define processing units that under certain circumstances may receive no input from the environment. Further restrictions concern the connections between the units and the values associated with them. Figure 17 illustrates this architecture on the basis of a simplified model of visual word recognition.

Central to the architecture of a network as presented in figure 17 is that the connections may be excitatory between mutually consistent units (black lines) and inhibitory between processing units whose processing results are incompatible (grey lines).[28] Thus, the feature processing unit responsible for the identification of a curved line excites and is excited by R, as well as by all words beginning with R, but at the same time it inhibits units for other letters in the same position, for example H, and all words beginning with H.

An important aspect in connectionist models is the notion of *activation*. Each processing unit is associated with an activation value that is altered by the incoming information. In accordance with representations in a computer, activation values may be binary (ultimately zero or one), or they may be graded. As shown in figure 17, activation may spread through the network; for example, the activation of R may spread to all processing units at the word level which have R as their initial letter. Another related notion is called *activation threshold*. The activation of a processing unit may depend

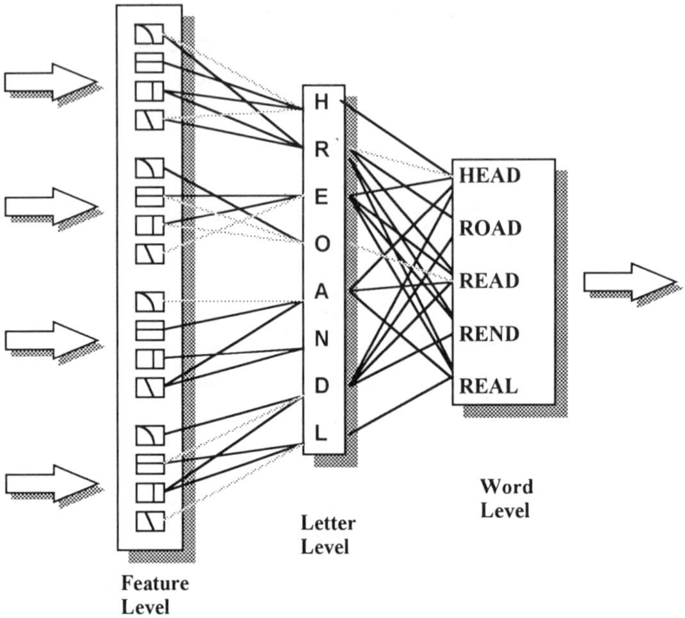

Figure 17. A network with excitatory and inhibitory

on a certain value which has to be reached. By contrast, a unit may be deactivated if its activation value falls short of a certain threshold.

Connectionist frameworks are often evaluated by means of computer simulation; however, implementations of connectionist models have to be taken with care. First, present computer architectures are not capable of simulating the type of parallelism that activates several processing units of a network at a time, and, secondly, computers only allow a discrete sequence of actions (Schade 1992: 18). Nevertheless, the connectionist framework is a promising alternative to traditional models and it provides a valuable set of tools for constructing models for a wide range of aspects (McClelland 1988: 121).

We will see in subsequent chapters that networks, such as the one in figure 17, are enormously powerful models for the description of natural language processing phenomena in general, and aspects of low-level and lexical processing in particular.

1.7. Summary and Outlook

In the previous sections, an attempt has been made to introduce the reader to the central research areas and to the relevant terminology of linguistics, psycholinguistics and computational linguistics. All three disciplines are concerned with the processing of natural language. While the theoretical linguist seeks to define the rules and principles underlying natural language processing, the psycholinguist deals with the mental processes involved in the production, comprehension and acquisition of natural language. Whether linguistic knowledge stored in the mind corresponds to linguistic formalisms is a further question for psycholinguistics. The cognitively-oriented computational linguist, by contrast, simulates the mental processes underlying language processing, seeking support for the theoretical findings or the development of alternative algorithms. The more practically-oriented computational linguist tries to augment computer programs with linguistic knowledge, to apply the machine to natural language processing tasks such as machine translation, tutoring, etc. Ideally, such programs use processing strategies identical with or similar to human processing strategies. Present hardware design and demands on computational efficiency, however, often force the programmer to implement ad hoc algorithms which are functionally adequate but operate very differently from human processing strategies.

Natural language processing - whether performed by humans or by machines - is an amazingly complex activity. Several levels and subprocesses are more or less simultaneously engaged in the analysis and the generation of natural language. Low-level processes such as the analysis of the sound wave, the identification of symbolic shapes, or the stimulation of certain muscles, as well as high-level processes which analyse and generate linguistic and conceptual properties, contribute to natural language processing. Central to a natural language processing system is a word-store, the lexicon. It provides information on the words of a language, ranging from phonological to semantic aspects. Essentially, the lexicon is a gigantic database containing several thousand entries, allowing extremely fast access, very efficient storage principles, and highly flexible techniques of data manipulation.

The remainder of this book is about the lexicon and tries to integrate linguistic, psycholinguistic, and computational linguistic insights. The following chapter is primarily interested in representational issues, addressing, among others, the following questions:

> What does the lexicon contain?
> How is the information associated with the items in the lexicon organised?
> What formalisms are employed to represent this information?
> According to what principles is the lexicon organised?

Chapters three and four concentrate on the processing of lexical information by humans. The following questions are of major interest in these chapters:

> What kind of input channels does the lexicon employ?
> How are the various low-level processes related to one another?
> On the basis of what type of information do we know whether an input is a word or not?
> How do humans retrieve the items and the information associated with them from the lexicon?

The remaining part of the book will discuss the possible ways of implementing a large lexicon on a computer, trying to make use of as many human strategies of processing lexical information as possible. It will be shown that machine-readable lexicons can exploit some of the strategies of human lexical processing and lexicon organisation, but we will also see that there are numerous areas where the simulation of human strategies leads to a wasteful complication of the administration of machine-readable lexicons and to a reduction of the processing efficiency of the respective access algorithms.

In other words, we will speculate about the contents of the lexicon (chapter two), the principles of pre-lexical (chapter three) and lexical processing (chapter four), and the architecture of a machine-readable lexicon (chapter five) and its actual implementation (chapter six). We will not speculate about the acquisition of the lexicon; however, the integration of specific aspects of lexical processing in infancy will shed some light on strategies for accessing the mental lexicon.

2. Entries in the Lexicon

"A speaker's mental lexicon is a repository of declarative knowledge about the words of his language".
(Levelt 1989: 182).

Language is a communication system employing arbitrary symbols. These symbols, normally words, have to be stored. Three techniques of storage are available: words can be listed in a reference book, they can be saved on storage devices connected to computers, or they can be kept in the mind. Depending on their application area and their task, one can draw a further distinction. Word-stores that are primarily consulted for the reason of information retrieval are referred to as *dictionaries.* By contrast, word-stores that constitute a component within a natural language processing system are called *lexicon.* Figure 18 illustrates this typology of word-stores.

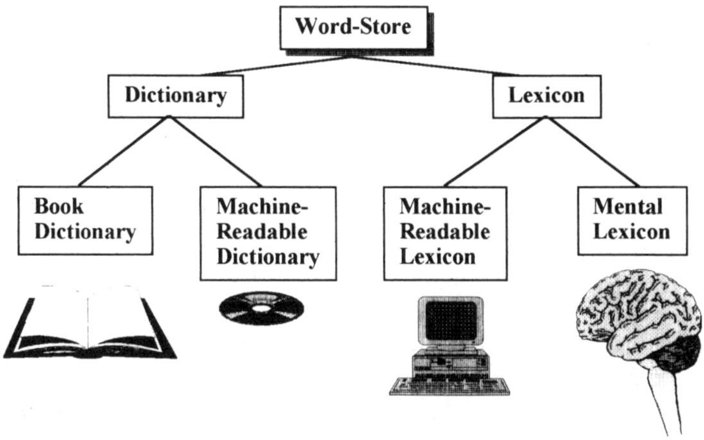

Figure 18. A typology of word-stores

Book dictionaries have been around for a long time. The most common types of book dictionary are encyclopaedic monolingual dictionaries, bilingual dictionaries, or dictionaries for special purposes, such as synonym dictionaries, foreign word dictionaries, etc. Machine-readable dictionaries were only made available in the late 1980s, when book dictionaries such as the Oxford English Dictionary were transferred to a machine-readable format.[1] Normally, machine-readable dictionaries are delivered on special storage devices such as CD-ROM or large removable harddisks. Additionally, the use of such dictionaries requires the use of specific software.

A lexicon, by contrast, is the central module of a natural language processing system (see figure 11), whether human or machine. It closely interacts with the other components of the language processor and provides detailed information about the words to be produced or comprehended. There are no machine-readable lexicons available that represent the entirety of the words of a language. At present, machine-readable lexicons concentrate on the words required in specific application areas, such as weather reports, geological terminology, etc. The mental lexicon, by contrast, is at every speaker's disposal. Yet, despite extensive psycholinguistic research over more than twenty years, its exact structure has not been revealed (see Aitchison 1992: 59).

To sum up, the following terminology will be used henceforth:

(book) dictionary	↔	reference word-book
machine-readable dictionary	↔	electronic book dictionary
machine-readable lexicon	↔	natural language word-store on machines
mental lexicon	↔	natural language word-store in the mind

All types of word-store feature a number of parallels. They contain a large number of items which are defined linguistically. The collection of information associated with an item, that is the item itself and its linguistic specification, is referred to as *lexical entry.* Each lexical entry is specified for its meaning, its phonological and morphological properties, and for some basic aspects that determine its syntactic behaviour. However, if we look at the representation techniques involved and the content of the representation, numerous dissimilarities emerge. Moreover, the internal organisation of dictionaries and lexicons differs enormously. While dictionaries list their entries in alphabetical order, the mental lexicon must be organised along different lines, for the following reasons. First, there are languages without alphabet-based writing systems or with no writing systems at all. It would be very difficult to explain why speakers of a language with an alphabetic writing system store the entries in the mental lexicon alphabetically and speakers whose language lacks an alphabetic writing system use different organisational principles for their mental lexicon. More importantly, an alphabetic way of storing lexical entries would imply that, presuming a linear search strategy, the search time required for items occurring early in the alphabet would be much shorter than that for items starting with *z-*. This is certainly not the case. Moreover, an alphabetic organisation would imply that speech production errors occur where accidentally an alphabetic neighbour is accessed, for example *bane* instead of *band.* Such exchange errors have not been found. Hence, the mental lexicon must be organised according to completely different principles. Whether machine-readable lexicons use the alphabet is a matter of implementation and computational efficiency. We will return to this question in chapter five.

Another quite important difference between the various types of lexicon concerns the possibility of manipulating their structure. While dictionaries contain a fixed number of items with fixed content, lexicons permit the addition and the extraction of items, as well as the alteration of the information associated with them.

The following major issues will be addressed in this chapter:

- Which words should be listed in a lexicon and which ones should be excluded? In other words, what items are separate lexical entries and what items are not?
- What kind of information is associated with a lexical entry?
- What formalisms are employed to represent the specification of lexical entries?

In answering these questions we will see that there are fundamental differences between the word-stores, not only in terms of their internal structure, but also concerning their content.

2.1. Lexical Entries

While the size of a dictionary depends on its application area and its purpose, the exact number of entries in the mental lexicon of an average adult speaker is controversial. Aitchison (1987: 6ff) reports that the number of words a native speaker of English *knows* can be estimated as between 50.000 and 250.000. This immediately raises two questions: first, what does it mean to *know* a word, and, secondly, what do we understand by the notion *word*?

Looking at the different estimates of the size of the lexicon and the respective experimental observations (for example, word definition tasks), it is quite obvious that *knowing* is always equated with *understanding,* i.e. with the passive vocabulary. The active vocabulary of a native speaker, that is the words a speaker is actually capable of using in speech, can hardly be judged, since this would involve the observation of one speaker during a long, perhaps a lifelong, period. For this reason, estimates about the size of the mental lexicon are always equated with the passive vocabulary.

The number of words in the lexicon depends on what we understand by *word.* In section 1.3.3. the following terms were introduced:

Lexeme	–	the fundamental unit of the lexicon
Word	–	the actual realisation of a lexeme
Morpheme	–	the basic building block of a word
Root	–	the free morpheme that serves as the basis of morphological alternation
Stem	–	a free morpheme that serves as the basis of inflectional processes
Affix	–	a bound morpheme

Let us illustrate these terms on the basis of the word *farmers.*

Lexeme	FARM
Word	farmers; other words: farm, farms, farming, farmed, farmer, farm's, etc.
Morphemes	{farm,} {-er,} {-s}
Root	farm
Stem	farmer
Affixes	-er, -s

Theoretically, there are two extreme positions about the content of a word-store. At one extreme, it is fairly clear that homonyms such as *swallow* (the bird vs. the act of swallowing) count as two different lexical items.[2] At the other extreme, words that differ only in their inflectional suffix, such as *walk* and *walked,* count as alternate forms of the same lexical item. Between these two extremes are numerous cases whose status is not so clear. Take the following examples (Jackendoff 1990: 76):

(15) a. Joe climbed for hours.
b. Joe climbed down the mountain.
c. Joe climbed down the rope.
d. Joe climbed through the tunnel.

Here we are confronted with four different senses of *climb.* We will see below (section 2.3.3.1.) whether such cases be treated as four separate lexical items, or as variants of a common item. In principle, we can define the senses of a lexical entry as variants of one lexeme if we can establish a systematic relationship between them. For the four senses of *climb* in (15) this would mean that they can be subsumed under one entry, since in all cases the subject (Joe) is travelling some path. The different status of the complements does not affect this basic property of *climb.* Before we return to issues of this kind, let us examine the matter of consulting word-stores. The main question in this respect is, what counts as a separate lexical entry?

Basically, there are two conceptions about the items listed in a lexicon. On the one hand, we could confine ourselves to listing only those forms in the lexicon which serve as a basis for the generation of further forms, i.e. roots or stems. Such a strategy can be referred to as *minimal listing hypothesis* (Butterworth 1983). The resulting lexicon architecture is called *root lexicon.* On the other hand, we could opt for a lexicon containing all possible words of a language. According to this *full listing hypothesis,* all words have a lexical representation. The resulting lexicon is referred to as *full-form lexicon.*

There is even a third, somewhat hybrid position. It concerns the implementation of machine-readable lexicons. Most machine-readable lexicons and their corresponding access algorithms are designed to process written input. This in turn means that they have to cope with orthographical variants, such as *carry, carries, carried,* etc. In a full-form lexicon such variants would simply be listed; in a root lexicon they have to be analysed by an additional algorithm. For languages with little orthographical variation, there is a third possibility, the storing of morpho-graphemes.[3] In such a *morpho-graphemic lexicon* we would list morpho-graphemic roots, such as *carrI* and *carrY,* where the final elements "I" and "Y" are placeholders that serve two purposes. On the one hand, they stand for their own orthographical realisation in actual contexts, i.e. "Y" is realised as *y* and "I" as *i*; on the other hand, they are symbols that determine the affixational possibilities of an item. For example, the "I" in the morpho-graphemic root *carrI* can be combined with {-s} and -ed, the "Y" in *carrY* with -0 and -ing. To illustrate the fact that "I" and "Y" are not actual letters but variables they have been capitalised.

Table 1 specifies some selected lexical entries on the basis of their orthographical access forms.

Table 1. Items in the lexicon

Root	WALK	CARRY	JOG	HATE
Full-Forms	WALK	CARRY	JOG	HATE
	WALKS	CARRIES	JOGS	HATES
	WALKED	CARRIED	JOGGED	HATED
	WALKING	CARRYING	JOGGING	HATING
Morpho-Graphemes	WALK	CARRY	JOG	HATE
		CARRI	JOGG	HAT

2.1.1. Roots

A root lexicon excludes all those items that are morphologically and semantically fully compositional. In this case, the word-store does not contain words, but items that serve as a basis for morphological processes. Such items are called roots; hence we could call the word-store root lexicon. But what exactly are roots?

The exact content of a root lexicon depends on the definition of morphological and semantic productivity. Obviously, inflectional variants, i.e. words which are generated by adding an inflectional affix to a root, should not be listed in the lexicon. They are morphologically and semantically fully compositional, since the syntactic category (word-class) and the basic features associated with the lexeme do not change. Hence, the words in an inflectional paradigm can be excluded from the lexicon, only the root being included:[4]

(16) a. Words: walk, walks, walked, walking
Lexeme: WALK Root: walk-
b. Words: table, tables, table's, tables'
Lexeme: TABLE Root: table-
c. Words: quick, quicker, quickest, quickly
Lexeme: QUICK Root: quick-

Bearing in mind that most open-class words in English can generate four inflectional variants and we only want to include the respective roots in the lexicon, the number of lexical entries in a root lexicon can be reduced considerably.

The definition of roots becomes far more complicated when we turn our attention to lexical morphological processes. Superficially, derivatives and compounds can be analysed into one or several roots. Hence, we might be tempted to exclude these items from a root lexicon and generate them by a rule. Items such as *movement* and *peace-movement* would then be excluded from a root lexicon and be generated on the basis of their respective roots, *move* and *peace*. However, it is not as simple as that. The definition of derivatives and compounds as separate or as decomposable lexical items depends on the degree of stability of the lexical processes involved. While in inflectional processes most aspects associated with the lexeme are kept stable, lexical morphological processes can involve, among others,

– a change of syntactic category	Noun: *table*	→	Adjective: *tableless*
– a change of stress pattern	/'prɒdʌkt/	→	/prɒdək'tɪvətɪ/

or, more generally, lexical morphological processes lack the stability of inflection. Hence, derivatives and compounds should be contained in the lexicon. This would certainly be the simplest solution, but it would increase the size of the lexicon. If we can find words generated by lexical morphological processes whose properties are regular and can be inferred using general principles, we can considerably reduce the number of items in a root lexicon.

Let us look at derivation first. It may be argued that this process is not fully productive since it generates words which are semantically unstable in many cases:

(17)	a.	destroy	→	destruction
		qualify	→	qualification
		elect	→	election
		divert	→	diversion
	b.	generate	→	degenerate
		nominate	→	denominate

This is certainly true for derivational processes such as *-ion* suffixation (17a) or *de-* prefixation (17b). For example, while *destruction* can regularly be defined as "the process of destroying", *qualification* is not neccessarily "the process" but "the result of qualifying". Likewise, the interpretation of the prefix *de-* in *degenerate* is systematic in describing "the process of action reversal". In *denominate,* however, *de-* emphasises the "process of nominating" rather than reversing it. Thus, the meaning of some of these words is not always a result of their component parts. Also, the processes of *-ion* suffixation or *de-* prefixation are confined to a relatively small group of items. Thus, all those derivatives which involve the slightest degree of instability should be defined as separate entries and listed in the lexicon. Yet, there are derivational processes which are highly productive and generate words whose meaning can be recovered using stable principles:

(17) c. walker (Verb-Noun Derivation)
d. tableless (Noun-Adjective Derivation)
e. quicken (Adjective-Verb Derivation)

Derivatives of the type verb + *er* typically allow an interpretation of the type "someone who *verbs*" or "an instrument with which one can *verb*", adjectives derived from nouns by the addition of -less are usually interpreted as "something without *noun*", and verbs derived from adjectives via the -*en* affixation generally mean "to make *adjective*". Thus, derivatives of the type *walker* (*walk* + *er* → "someone who walks"), *tableless* (*table* + *less* → "something without tables") and *quicken* (*quick* + *en* → "to make quick") can in most cases be generated on the basis of their roots and may be excluded from the lexicon.

While in derivational processes roots are combined with affixes, compounding involves the combination of two or more lexemes. Compounds may or may not have lexicalised. That is, if the meaning of a compound is the result of the combination of its components, a compound may be excluded from the lexicon; if not, it has lexicalised and should be listed in the lexicon. In other words, the criterion of semantic stability is the key factor for assessing the status of compounds.

For example, the compounds in (18) are semantically regular.

(18) a. walking-stick= a stick for walking
b. table-cloth= cloth for tables
c. quick action= an action which 'is' quick

Their meaning can be interpreted using the following strategy: an X for Y (18a) and (18b), an X is Y (18c). In other words, the compound head (the rightmost element, here X) is modified by one or more elements on the left-hand side (Y). This strategy of compound interpretation becomes even more obvious in very complex compounds:

bathroom → room of the type bath
bathroom towel → towel for bathroom
bathroom towel designer → designer of bathroom towels
bathroom towel designer congress → congress of bathroom towel designers

Such 'regular' compounds should not be listed in a root lexicon; they can be analysed in terms of their component parts. However, this strategy of interpreting compounds fails in (19). The meaning of these compounds cannot be recovered by interpreting their components. Hence they should not be excluded from the lexicon.

(19) a. walkman * a man who walks
b. table-turning * the turning of tables
c. quicksand * sand which has the property to be quick

So what should be listed in a root lexicon?

Proponents of whatever lexicon format agree that all free forms are roots, that is non-compositional words that can occur in isolation. Thus, open-class words such as *table, quick, walk,* whose roots serve as the basis for morphological processes, should be represented in a root lexicon. Closed-class words should also be represented in a root lexicon, even though they rarely occur alone. Also, their meaning cannot be defined formally but has to be related to their function in specific environments. The conjunction *and,* for example, may not only express a relationship of coordination, but also one of contrast (Allwood et al. 1977: 27). Despite these difficulties, closed-class words must be contained in the lexicon, only their meaning must be represented using different techniques.

The inclusion of compositional items, whether generated by processes of inflection, derivation or compounding, depends on aspects such as semantic decomposability and generative productivity. It has been shown that inflectional and a number of derivational variants are fully decompositional and highly productive. Hence, they do not require a listing in the lexicon, only their roots should be represented. This in turn means that the lexicon must be closely connected to an additional store containing affixes and morpho-phonological affixation rules (see section 2.4.).

2.1.2. Full-Forms

A lexicon which lists all possible words of a lexeme is referred to as full-form lexicon. At first sight, such a format seems out of the question. Too many redundancies would unnecessarily enlarge the lexicon. In English, for example, most nouns permit the generation of four variants (basic form, genitive singular, plural, genitive plural). Since the number of nouns is theoretically unlimited (due to the possibility of generating compound nouns), the inclusion of all four forms in the lexicon would increase the size of the lexicon enormously. However, for languages with little morphological variability, such a lexicon structure is not that ludicrous.

Further arguments for a full-form lexicon come from the computational realisation of a lexical database. They concern the processing efficiency and the manageability of the program. For example, a lexicon for a specific domain, such as weather reports or geology, requires only a limited number of entries. In such a case, a computational system with a full-form machine-readable lexicon may be more efficient than a system that incorporates a smaller lexicon that has to be supported by a complex component processing morphological variants. Furthermore, a full-form lexicon is computationally much easier to handle and more user-friendly. Aspects such as lexicon extension, editing, etc. can be dealt with more easily in a full-form lexicon. (We will return to issues of this kind in chapter five).

Over and above issues of implementation efficiency, there are psycholinguistic arguments for as well as against such a lexicon structure. Wolff (1984: 9) reports on psycholinguistic experiments indicating that there are no processing differences between simple words and compounds. By contrast, she also mentions experimental results where morphologically complex forms are more difficult to process than simple forms.

2.1.3. Morpho-Graphemic Forms

The design of a machine-readable lexicon depends on a number of issues which are, by and large, independent of psycholinguistic considerations. One demand concerns general computational aspects. Any computer program has to be implemented in such a way that it economically exploits the systems sources, i.e. the internal and external storage capacity available and the processor. Secondly, the architecture of a machine-readable lexicon is highly dependent on its application. A domain-specific lexicon which contains only a few hundred items is probably much easier to handle as a full-form lexicon than as a root lexicon with complex morphological and orthographical alternation processes. For a domain-independent machine-readable lexicon with several thousand items, however, a full-form lexicon would be less economic. Since it wastefully duplicates a certain amount of information, it might exceed the storage space available. Especially in synthetic languages with a rich morphology, for example the Balto-Slavonic and the Romance languages, full-form machine-readable lexicons are problematic.

Machine-readable root lexicons, by contrast, are fairly economical; however, they require the implementation of an additional component that handles morphological and orthographical alternation. In such a component, items such as *making* or *running* are internally transformed to *make-ing* or *run-ing*. These are enormously complex processes. For example, the analysis of *running* into *run-ing*, not only requires the careful inspection of the orthographical structure of the input (r u n n i n g), but it also needs access to the phonological code /'rʌn/ of the stem (since /ʌ/ is a short vowel and the syllable is stressed, the rule of consonant doubling can apply, (Handke 1989: 145)). The complexity of this component can be reduced considerably, if the lexicon does not list roots but morpho-graphemic forms. Now, we would have two entries, RUN and RUNN. Both would be linked with a list of morphemes with which they could co-occur. Admittedly, morpho-graphemic forms enlarge the size of the lexicon. However, in languages with relatively little orthographical alternation, the number of additional elements is limited. In English, for example, the lexicon size would increase by a factor smaller than two.

In summary, then, morpho-graphemic forms are suitable alternatives for machine-readable lexicons, especially for languages with little morphological and orthographic variation.

2.1.4. Items in the Lexicon

From a linguistic point of view, a root lexicon architecture seems highly economic and efficient. Moreover, there are various theoretical linguistic models that fully rely on a root lexicon and an additional rule system by means of which compositional word-forms are generated. Kiparsky's (1982) lexical phonological theory, for example, is dependent on a subdivision of the lexicon into roots and affixes. Unfortunately, experimental data suggests that the story is not as simple as that.

Various researchers evaluated the possibilities of organising the basic forms and their morphological variants in the lexicon. In discussing experimental data from speech perception, speech production, reading, and aphasia, Emmorey/Fromkin (1988: 134) concluded that affixes and base forms (roots) are processed differently. Despite the high degree of economy in such a minimal listing hypothesis, which only lists base forms and generates the variants by a system of morpho-phonological rules, disappointingly little experimental evidence was found to support this position.

Butterworth (1983) outlined the possibility of an alternative view, the full listing hypothesis, where all words have a lexical representation. A somewhat weaker hypothesis says that the morphological variants of a root are related within a lexical entry, that is, that forms such as *flies, flying, flew, flown,* and *fly* can be found under the same lexical entry or address. The phonological or graphological structure in language comprehension, and morphological features such as tense, number, etc. in language production, would then take care of triggering the relevant item within a lexical entry. Such a hypothesis was not rejected; however, no evidence could be collected that such a group of related words has a common base form or some sort of abstract heading. Thus, a full listing hypothesis seems much more likely than previously thought.

Henderson (1985) rejected the full listing hypothesis and concluded, on the basis of production experiments and speech errors, that morphological regularities are conceived of as rules which permit a reduction in the amount of information to be stored. Further arguments against the full listing hypothesis come from Hankamer (1989). On the basis of agglutinative languages, such as Turkish, he argued that the lexical entry includes representations of morphological structure, so that affixes are processed via the root.[5]

Evidence from studies into the mental lexicon of bilinguals lends further support to this position. Myers-Scotton (1993a:12) reports on intrasentential codeswitching data involving an agglutinative language such as Bantu, which suggests that noun and verb roots have separate entries from their affixes which accompany the realisation of a noun or verb in monolingual speech. At the same time, codeswitching data in non-agglutinative languages, such as English, suggest that morphemes may be entered in the same entry as their heads.

Sproat (1992: 110ff) also argues for a minimal listing hypothesis. The fact that speakers are able to coin as well as to comprehend new words, such as *giraffishness,* indicates that they have some knowledge about roots and affixes and are thus aware of the morphological structure of their language. Further arguments involve evidence from specific cases of aphasia, where the generation and comprehension of prefixes is impaired (Sproat 1992: 111).

Despite many arguments in favour of a minimal listing hypothesis, we are still confronted with two opposing views, a full listing hypothesis, which stores all morphological variants in a full-form lexicon and a weaker position, which excludes morphological variants from the lexicon and generates them using morphological rules. As the previous discussion has indicated, it may be the case that the strategy of storing entries in the lexicon is language-specific. While non-agglutinative languages tend to favour a full listing hypothesis, agglutinative languages seem to be in line with a somewhat weaker position. Over and above these language types there are the so-called *polysynthetic* languages, such as Eskimo or Chukchi, where entire clauses can be single words (Comrie 1981: 42). It seems unlikely that, despite their enormous memory capacity, humans store the 'words' of these languages in their entirety.

A final argument in favour of a minimal listing hypothesis is more philosophical in character. Sproat (1992: 122) argues that humans tend to work out structures whenever they are faced with the task of handling thousands of items. In Chinese, for example, an average educated reader knows roughly 6.000 to 7.000 characters. There is evidence that people do not memorise these arbitrary shapes. Rather, they are aware of some internal structure of these characters, since many words or complex characters are composed of individual ones.

Nevertheless, the issue has by no means been settled. This can be seen in the fact that both Butterworth and Henderson refer to the same speech error data, however, with opposing interpretations of the results and, consequently, with different conclusions. An interesting model was proposed by Caramazza et al. (1985). On the basis of their studies of dyslexia they suggested an addressed morphology model which makes use of two access mechanisms for reading morphologically complex words: a morphological parsing procedure and a holistic word address procedure. In such a model the access units are stored as decomposed forms with roots represented independently of affixes but with an address mechanism for permissible affixes. We will see that such a system where roots are connected with pointers or continuation classes is an interesting way of realising the morphological specification in machine-readable lexicons.

Having discussed the range of forms that may count as lexical items, we will now turn our attention to the representation format of lexical entries in dictionaries and in lexicons, to work out the parallels as well as the differences in content and representation formalisms.

2.2. The Specification of Dictionary Entries

Various aspects contribute to the overall specification of a dictionary entry. Depending on the dictionary type (monolingual, bilingual, dictionaries with a historical background, synonym dictionaries, etc.), specific aspects are emphasised or dropped. The Oxford English Dictionary (OED), for example, associates with each entry a collection of literature references illustrating occurrences of the entry in the past. Other dictionaries (e.g. Collins (COLL) and Advanced Learner's Dictionary (ALD)) put much emphasis on synonym information or on grammatical aspects, such as transitivity. While most existing dictionaries are more or less directly related to the OED, the Longman's Dictionary of Contemporary English (LDOCE) is a completely new, original work, which uses many findings of modern linguistics (Lipka 1992: 31). For example, it includes information about the entries' syllable structure, extensive typical contexts, and, most importantly, systematic and much more complex information about the syntactic possibilities of the items listed in the lexicon. In Appendix B and C, we illustrate how the conventions used in LDOCE can be exploited to generate machine-readable lexicons.

Despite the differences among dictionaries, a large number of parallels emerge. Generally, dictionary entries include the following aspects:

(a) access unit
(b) phonological specification
(c) grammatical aspects (morphology and syntax)
(d) meaning
(e) further aspects, e.g. history, examples in context, alternative spellings (depending on dictionary type)

(a) access unit

The access unit is the basis of consulting a dictionary. It has been mentioned above that an efficient lexicon stores roots. Dictionaries, however, employ stems or specific forms, such as verbal infinitives or the nominative forms of nouns, as access units. Their graphological structure guides the search process, where the input word is scanned for its letter sequence before the dictionary is entered. The search process itself (in case of a book dictionary) is a constant move backwards and forwards through the pages, until the entries that share the letter sequence with the input word are found.

(b) phonological specification

The phonological information of a dictionary entry is normally represented in terms of a code which is more or less closely related to the principles of the International Phonetic Association (IPA). A comparison of the dictionaries available, however, shows that different transcription systems are employed. While the OED employs a code which is a mere respelling of the character structure of the access units, COLL, ALD and LDOCE stick to standard transcription systems of the English language, based on Gimson (1962). For most lexical entries the phonetic code can be used for all senses of an entry and needs to be stated only once. However, there are entries whose pronunciation depends on the grammatical category. For example, words with primarily Romance origin, such as *contrast,* are assigned different stress patterns and have, as a consequence, a different segmental phonological structure depending on their grammatical category:

Verb [kən'trɑ:st]
Noun ['kɒntrɑ:st]

While most dictionaries for the English language confine their phonological information to segmental aspects, some languages also incorporate non-segmental information in dictionary entries. For example, the German standard dictionary, Duden, features hyphenation information by inserting syllable separators in the access unit:

Kon | trast

Among the English dictionaries, the LDOCE uses the same strategy. However, according to the hyphenation rules in English (Quirk, et al. 1985: 1613), the separators need not necessarily be interpreted as straightforward hyphenation possibilities but as information about phonologically natural syllable division points of a lexical access unit:[6]

flu · o · res · cent
struc · ture

(c) grammatical aspects

The grammatical information associated with a lexical entry can be subdivided into morphological and syntactic aspects. While morphological aspects normally denote the inflectional variants of a lexeme, for example, the past tense forms of verbs, syntactic aspects specify the syntactic context of an item. This means that each entry is first of all associated with a syntactic category. This seems to be trivial. However, a large number of entries are categorially ambiguous, that is, they may have more than one syntactic category. For example, many nouns have verbal counterparts (e.g. *fly*).

Thus, their lexical entries must consist of two parts, one part responsible for the description of the nominal interpretation, and one part dealing with the verbal interpretation. The most complex grammatical structure in this respect can be attributed to the entry *round,* which features in all open-class categories and can also occur as a preposition:[7]

(20)	a.	a *round* of drinks	Noun
	b.	he *rounded* me twice.	Verb
	c.	the *round* ball.	Adjective
	d.	he turned *round.*	Adverb
	e.	he went *round* the house.	Preposition

Secondly, each lexical entry must be associated with information specifying its syntactic neighbourhood. Let us consider the lexeme GIVE. The only information available in standard dictionaries concerns the transitivity status of this verb, that is, GIVE is a transitive verb. This information may suffice for the standard user of a dictionary. However, a more linguistically-oriented dictionary has to specify a much larger collection of syntactic aspects. These are indispensable for processes of sentence analysis and generation. For example, we need to incorporate syntactic information that prevents the following sentences from being generated.[8]

(21) a. * John gave.
b. * The table gave me a dollar.
c. ? The President gave capitalism to his country.

The syntactic category alone is not responsible for the ungrammaticality of the examples (21a) and (21b) and the oddity in (21c). Hence, the syntactic information must be more than a mere statement of the syntactic category and the transitivity status. In order to exclude sentences such as (21a) from the set of grammatical sentences, we must specify the number and the syntactic type of each obligatory argument of a verb. For GIVE this means that three noun phrase arguments must be present in the sentence whose main verb is GIVE. This information can be summarised in a syntactic frame such as:

GIVE, V: [NP, NP, NP]

Such a *subcategorisation-frame* defines the syntactic environment of a lexeme in terms of its phrasal arguments. Yet, this information is not sufficient to describe the ungrammaticality of (21b) and (21c). Here we need a more detailed lexical description of each argument of GIVE. For example, we would have to state that the first NP in (21b), i.e. the subject-NP, must be an element capable of initiating the causative process of abstract transfer (GIVE), and that, in (21c), the NP realising the direct object must be an element which has some sort of physical structure:

GIVE, V:	[NP-Subject]	[NP-Direct-Object]	[NP-Indirect-Object]
	[Actor]	[Physical Object]	[Person]
	[...]	[...]	[...]

Syntactic frames of this type have already been introduced in section 1.3.3. Traditionally, the definition of lexemes in terms of the lexical features of their argument structure has been referred to as *selectional restrictions.* Their main task is to determine the grammaticality of lexical entries when inserted into syntactic structures. Note that, despite these rather clear-cut examples, there are always cases where the description of the arguments of a verb has to be adjusted to specific interpretations:

(22) a. John gave his daughter to Fred.
b. The city lights gave the mayor's arrival a superb appearance.

(d) meaning

The description of the meaning of an entry is the most complex enterprise for the lexicographer. While in bilingual dictionaries the meaning of the entries is generally confined to the translation into the target language, monolingual dictionaries include a more or less detailed description of each facet of the entry in other words. The complexity of this description depends on the demands on the dictionary. Like the grammatical structure of lexical entries, it is this part of the lexical definition where dictionaries and lexicons differ enormously. In dictionaries, the representation of the meaning of an entry is a mere description in other words. Depending on the vocabulary, the user of such a dictionary can interpret the description more or less accurately. By contrast, meaning representations in the lexicon normally make use of primitives which allow the language processor to build up the meaning of an entry from scratch (see section 2.3.3.2. for a detailed description of such formalisms). Figure 19 illustrates the meaning specification of the nominal entry FLY in four standard dictionaries.

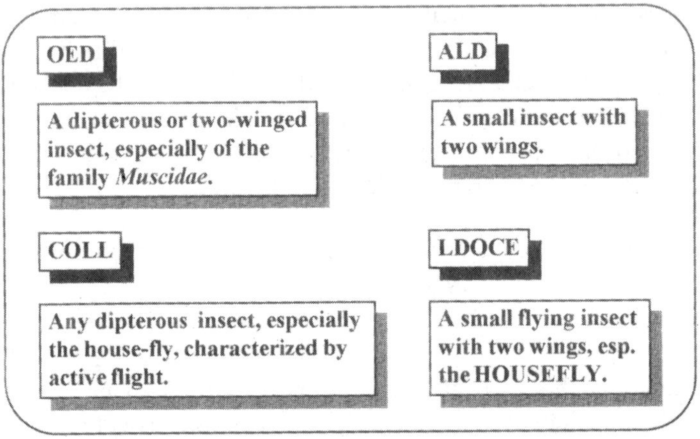

Figure 19. The meaning of the entry FLY (Noun) in four selected book dictionaries

(e) further aspects, e.g. history

Depending on the primary purpose of a dictionary, aspects such as historical background, etymology, examples of use, synonymical information, and various other aspects may supplement the information associated with the entries in the dictionary.

The main parts of information of the lexeme FLY as an entry in the OED may serve as a summary of the structure of a lexical entry in a dictionary:

Entry 1

1. Access unit FLY
2. Phonology (flaɪ)[9]
3. Grammar Sb (Substantive), Pl.: flies (flaɪz)
4. History flyȝe, fliȝe, flye, fly
5. Meaning

- Any winged insect, as the bee, gnat, locust, moth, etc.
  Example of use: (first occurrence in 1694):
  Here are divers sorts of Flies, as Butter-Flies, Butcher-Flies, Horse-Flies.
- A dipterous or two-winged insect, esp. of the family muscidae.
  Example of use (1841): Do what we can, summer will have its flies.

...

- fly on the wall: an unperceived observer ...
  Example of use (1983): The 'fly-on-the-wall' technique

...

- Angling: An insect attached to a hook as a lure in the mode of angling called fly-fishing.
- An artificial fly, i.e. a fish-hook dressed with feathers, silk, etc., so as to imitate some insects
  Example of use (1881): He tossed it [fish] into the basket and cast his fly again.

Entry 2

1. Access unit FLY
2. Phonology (flaɪ)
3. Grammar Sb (Substantive), Pl.: flies (flaɪz)
4. History flyge
5. Meaning

- I. The action of flying
- The action or manner of flying, flight (obsolete)
- A flying visit

...
- II. Something that flies in various senses
- A quick-travelling carriage

...

Entry 3

1. Access unit FLY
2. Phonology (flaɪ)
3. Grammar A (Adjective, slang) 4. History unknown
5. Meaning

- knowing, wide-awake, sharp
- of the fingers: dexterous, nimble, skilful

Entry 4

1. Access unit FLY
2. Phonology (flaɪ)
3. Grammar Verb, past: flew (flu:), past participle: flown (fləʊn)
4. History OE: fleogan, fliogan
5. Meaning

- Intransitive: To move through the air with wings
  Example of use (1796): On my approaching him, he [a butterfly] flew off.
- Transitive: To set birds flying one against the other; to let fly
  Example of use (1883): The pigeons are flown twice a day.

- Transitive/Causatively: To cause to rise and maintain its position in the air; to pilot
- Intransitive: To move or travel swiftly

This collection of senses of FLY in the OED illustrates the complexity of information associated with dictionary entries. The lexeme FLY consists of four main parts: two nominal entries with eleven senses for Entry 1 and eight senses for Entry 2, one adjectival entry with two senses, and one verbal entry with eleven senses. In addition to this, *fly* can occur in the modifier position of numerous compounds, e.g. *fly-back, fly-boat, fly-fish, fly half,* etc.

It has been mentioned above that a root lexicon closely interacts with a store that contains affixes and affixation rules. Standard dictionaries exhibit these components either in terms of a collection of the grammatical properties of an entry, or in terms of explicitly listing the variants of a lexeme. Alternatively, they may include an introductory chapter, where the general morphological rules and principles are listed.

2.3. The Specification of Entries in the Lexicon

When we produce language, we retrieve items from the lexicon on the basis of a pregenerated conceptual structure which has to be filled with actual words. When we perceive language, be it speech or print, we activate the mental lexicon on the basis of phonological or graphological patterns. In other words, each entry in the mental lexicon must be precisely specified for

- phonological aspects
- graphological aspects
- morphological aspects
- syntactic aspects
- semantic aspects

In order to understand or produce a word, these aspects have to be made available. We will see in chapter four that lexical processing in terms of language comprehension can be subdivided into

- word recognition, the identification of an item

– lexical retrieval, the retrieval of the content associated with an item

The differentiation of these two processes immediately evokes the question whether the strictly formal aspects of a lexical entry, i.e. phonological and morphological features, and the content-related aspects, i.e. syntactic and semantic features, can be kept apart. In other words, is it possible to recognise a word without retrieving its content from the mental lexicon, or, even more drastically, can we identify a word without understanding it?

2.3.1. Partitioned Lexical Entries

Levelt (1989: 182ff) discusses the structure of lexical entries from the point of view of producing language. He argues that the process of grammatical encoding, that is the process of generating a sentence structure which contains the content-related aspects of the words of the sentence, can be regarded as a process independent of the form-related aspects in lexical entries. For this reason, he suggests a subdivision of a lexical entry into form-related features and content-related features. The latter is referred to as *lemma.* Form-related aspects and lemma are linked by a pointer which can activate the formal aspects after the activation of the lemma. The picture shown in Figure 20 illustrates this conception of lexical entries from the view of language comprehension.

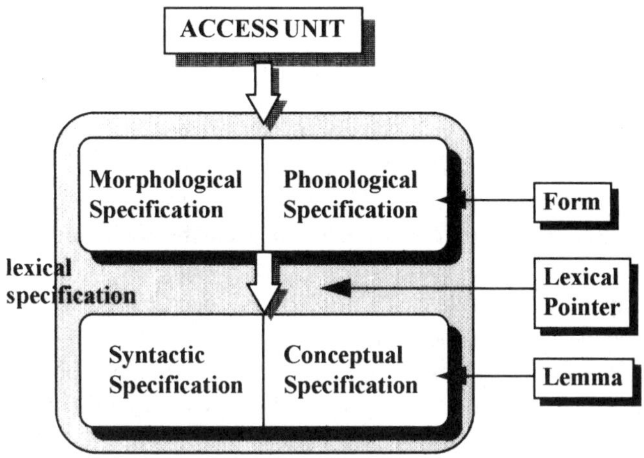

Figure 20. Partitioned lexical entries[10]

Even though this partitioning of a lexical entry into morpho-phonological form and lemma (the specification of meaning and syntax) is still very much an open issue (Levelt 187ff), a number of arguments support this subdivision. Language production phenomena especially provide evidence that the retrieval of formal aspects from the lexicon can be independent of lemma-related aspects.

One source of evidence comes from so-called *tip-of-the-tongue phenomena* (McKay 1970). Every speaker has had the experience that in fluent speech the intended word cannot be produced. Nevertheless, one knows that something has been retrieved from the lexicon, only the initial segment (e.g. the first consonant) or the number of syllables have not been made available. In other words, the target word is on the tip of one's tongue. One can conclude that in such cases the lemma has been accessed, i.e. the word's meaning and its syntax have been made available; the word's formal aspects, however, resist retrieval.

Other pieces of evidence have been drawn from speech errors where native speakers produce errors which are strictly form-related, such as (23), and which are related to lemma aspects, such as (24):

(23)	... put the freezes in the steaker.	(steaks / freezer)
(24)	... a very slice girl ...	(slim / nice)

In (23), all form-related aspects have been kept stable: morphological aspects such as plural markers have been positionally maintained (the intended plural *steak-s* has been transferred to *freeze-s,* resulting in a realisation of the plural morpheme as /ɪz/, and the agentive affix *-er* has been assigned to *steak*). In other words, the lemmas have been exchanged, while the form-related aspects have remained in their intended position. An error like (24), on the other hand, exhibits an example of a blend where two lemmas (SLIM and NICE), whose meanings are somehow similar, have been activated simultaneously. We will see below (section 2.3.2.1., example (26)) that phonological aspects, such as the syllable structure of the items involved, play a crucial role in constraining the formation of blends, yet the error in (24) relates to the lemma specification rather than to the formal specification of the items involved.

The way of partitioning the lexical specification of an entry is not undisputed. There is evidence from the study of language disorders that some patients maintained phonological and syntactic knowledge about lexical entries in the face of a severe breakdown of semantic knowledge (Emmorey/Fromkin 1988: 124), thus exhibiting a different way of partitioning the lexical specification of an entry. The modular structure of the lexical specification, however, remains unaffected. Even though access to the components of the lexical specification of an entry can be differently affected by brain damage, we will henceforth assume that there is partitioning, for the following reasons. First, it seems to make sense to modularise lexical information for research reasons, secondly, the insights from the study of speech errors strongly favour the partitioning of lexical entries, and, finally, computer implementations require some sort of partitioning for reasons of internal organisation and access efficiency (see section 5.3.4.1.).

2.3.2. The Specification of Form

In order to define the formal aspects of lexical entries, we have to differentiate between language production and language comprehension.

Assuming that lexical entries are subdivided into lemma and form (figure 20), the lemma triggers the formal specification via a pointer in the process of language production. Once the formal aspects are activated, they are used in general phonological processes, such as the phonological realisation of morphological aspects, e.g. past tense formation (25), and for the generation of a low-level articulatory program to be forwarded to the articulators (see figure 11).

(25)	chase + ed	→	/'tʃeɪst/
	move + ed	→	/'mu:vd/
	hate + ed	→	/'heɪtɪd/

The examples in (25) illustrate the intimate relationship between morphology and phonology. The addition of the -ed may not only lead to a different realisation of the past tense morpheme itself, depending on the root involved, but also to a resyllabification of the word concerned: *hated* now consists of two syllables and the final consonant of /'heɪt/ has become the intial segment of the second syllable /'heɪ - tɪd/.

In language comprehension, the formal aspects of lexical entries are employed as one key among others to activate the process of word recognition. Once the phonological properties are extracted from the sound wave, they serve as a basis for the lexical search process (see chapter three and four for more details).

In both cases, the collection of formal properties associated with an entry in the mental lexicon is far more complex than with dictionary entries, where the formal specification is a mere listing of the phonological code (see section 2.2.) and the specification of an item's syntactic category.

2.3.2.1. Phonological Specification

The phonological specification of an entry deals with segmental and non-segmental aspects. While segmental phonology is concerned with the structure of each segment of an entry, i.e. with the exact specification of vowels and consonants, non-segmental aspects relate to properties such as intonational contour or syllable structure.[11] Figure 21 illustrates the syllable structure of the lexeme WALK.

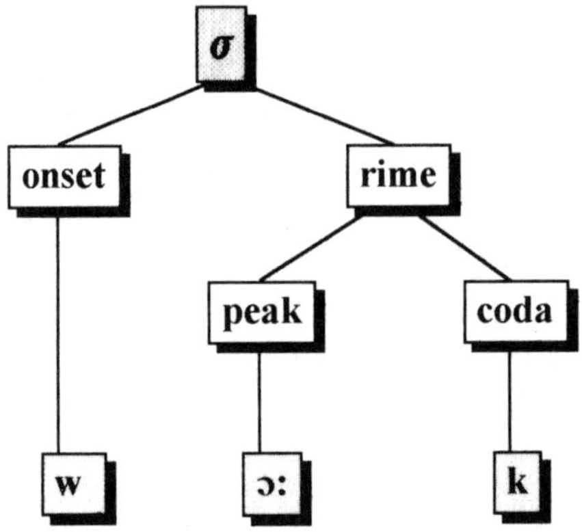

Figure 21. The syllable structure of WALK

A syllable, which is denoted by the Greek letter Sigma (σ), consists of an *onset* and a *rime* (alternative spelling: rhyme). Three arguments are generally used to support this onset-rime split (Durand 1990: 201ff).

The first argument is based on principles of stress assignment in Latin, where it is presupposed that a distinction can be drawn between *heavy* and *light* syllables. A heavy syllable contains a long vowel, a diphthong, or a short vowel plus consonant, and a light syllable a short vowel only. According to the structure of the rime, words such as *Romanorum* (Ro-ma-no-rum) consist of four heavy syllables. The structure of the onset is irrelevant in this respect. Given this concept, stress assignment proceeds along very simple lines: in words consisting of more than two syllables, the penultimate syllable is stressed if its rime is heavy (re-'la-tus, ro-ma-'no-rum). If the penultimate rime is light, the third syllable from the end is stressed (ex-'is-ti-mo).

Another argument comes from Spanish, where, according to Harris (1983: 9ff), the definition of syllable size is extremely complex, unless a split into onset and rime is introduced.

The third argument is based on exchange errors such as (26), where the rime of the syllables affected is respected and the onsets are exchanged.

(26) *if the fap kits* instead of *if the cap fits*

Similarly, blends such as (24) are sensitive to the internal organisation of syllables. The blend **slice* is made up from the onset of *slim* /sl/ and the rime of *nice* /aɪs/.

These errors illustrate that the native speaker has internalised a precise concept of the syllable and its internal subdivision into onset and rime. However, there are counter-examples:

(27) *cassy put* instead of *pussy cat*

Such an exchange error is insensitive to the division of a syllable into onset and rime; rather, it moves an entire syllable /pʊ/ into a syllabic frame which only maintains its final element /t/ (/kæ-t/ becomes /pʊ-t/).

The arguments employed for the subdivision of syllables into onset and rime can also be used for a further split of the rime into two parts: the *peak* or *nucleus,* and the *coda.* The peak is the head of the entire syllable. As a notational simplification, the peak is generally labelled with V, where V derives from vowel, but really means "high-sonorous element of the syllable". Even though high-sonorous elements are primarily vowels, there are syllables with peaks that are realised by less sonorous material such as syllabic consonants, for example the second syllable in *bottle,* /'bɒtl̩/. Non-peaks are denoted by C. Again, C derives from consonant, indicating that non-peaks are generally realised by consonants; however, it really means "low-sonorous element of a syllable".

In summary, C and V are place holders not for consonants and vowels but for the functional elements peak and non-peak. With this in mind, we can now associate the basic syllable structure with segmental phonological aspects, as in figure 22.

This kind of layered representation combines segmental and non-segmental aspects. It has become known as *autosegmental phonological representation* (van der Hulst/Smith 1982: 8ff) and proposes that the phonological representation consists of a set of layers, or *tiers,* where each tier constitutes an independent string of segments.

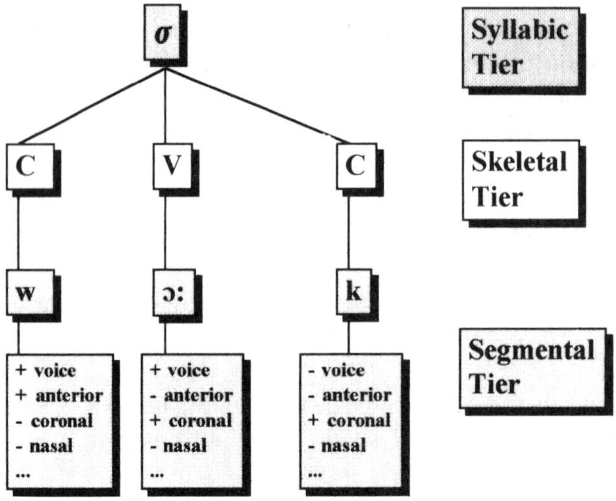

Figure 22. The phonological specification of WALK

The syllabic tier groups words into syllable units. Over and above a universal concept of the syllable, syllables are language-specifically defined on phonotactic grounds. In English, syllables can be realised by a vowel or a syllabic consonant. The lexeme *I,* which consists of a peak only, in this case the diphthong /aɪ/, is an example. Onset and coda may be represented by a number of consonants; in English syllables, maximally three consonants can occur in the onset and three in the coda, as in /'streŋkθ/.[12] Thus, the basic syllable structure in English can be represented as (C) V (C), where only the peak V is obligatory and the non-peaks (C) are optional.

The internal structure of each syllable, i.e. the subdivision into peaks and non-peaks, is represented at the skeletal tier. The relationship between the skeletal and the syllabic tier, that is the principles of syllable-building, or *syllabification,* is language-specific. While in the Romance languages, such as French, most words can be neatly split into syllables, Germanic languages like English frequently exhibit the phenomenon of *ambisyllabicity,* where consonants in intervocalic position make a liaison between adjacent syllables. In figure 23 the intervocalic nasal /n/ and the fricative /f/ are ambisyllabic.

The segmental tier represents a sequence of phones whose content specifies the articulatory program in speech production. Traditionally, the notation for phones is based on the International Phonetic Alphabet.

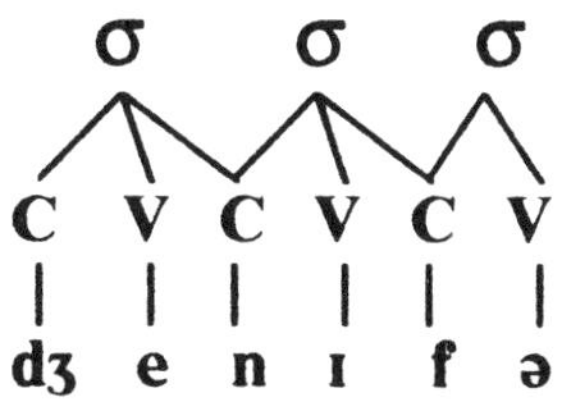

Figure 23. Ambisyllabicity in Jennifer

However, phones are not indivisible, as the following speech error suggests:

(28) /ə glɪə plu: skaɪ/ error: a "glear plue sky"; target: a clear blue sky, /klɪə blu:/

This phonetic error exhibits the exchange of voicing. This becomes more obvious if we decompose the initial consonantal phones of *clear* and *blue* into their phonetic properties:

(29)	Target		Error
	/k/ [voiceless, velar, plosive]	→	/g/ [voiced, velar, plosive]
	/b/ [voiced, bilabial, plosive]	→	/p/ [voiceless, bilabial, plosive]

Features which concern the status of the vocal folds (voiced/voiceless), or the place or manner of articulation, have long been used for the characterisation of speech sounds across languages. Today various features have been added; however, the number of features that distinguish the phonemes in a language is quite small, probably around 20. In figure 22, for example, the features *anterior* and *coronal* are used to represent the place of articulation, and the feature *nasal* denotes the involvement of the nasal cavity in the articulation process. For a detailed discussion of the content, the history, and the exact specification of these *distinctive features,* the reader is referred to the relevant literature, for example Hyman (1975) or Durand (1990).

It has been argued that the segmental tier can be split up into further sub-segmental tiers. The argument is quite simple: since some features spread over more than one segment (for example, voicing in *wonder* or nasality in *man*) the segmental tier should be used as a backbone for a number of additional feature tiers which are associated with it. In any case, the segmental tier represents – whether as a whole or supported by sub-segmental tiers – the exact phonetic specification of each vowel and each consonant.

The phonological specification presented thus far is by no means complete. Syllables in polysyllabic words can occur in varying degrees of stress, resulting in length differences, different degrees of loudness, or variations in pitch movement. These and other non-segmental aspects are attributed to the so-called *metrical tier,* where each syllable is associated with its basic stress pattern (figure 24).

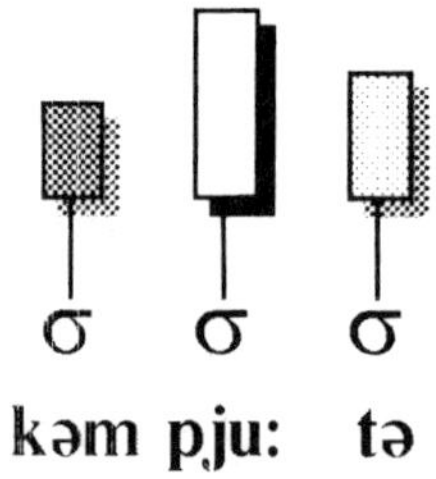

Figure 24. The metrical pattern of *computer*

The main word stress of *computer* is on the second syllable (*pu*). The first syllable (*com*), by contrast, has the minimum amount of stress.

We have seen that the phonological specification of a lexical entry is a collection of aspects relating to segments (vowels and consonants), elements above segments (syllable structure, stress), and sub-segments (features). With the multi-layered technique of representing these aspects, we can assign the phonological information to various tiers, which are hierarchically connected with each other.

The collection of the information associated with each tier, then, constitutes the phonological specification of a lexical entry. This, in turn, serves as the phonetic plan in speech production on the one hand, and is the primary source for the lexical look-up process in language comprehension on the other.

Recently, suggestions have been made to underspecify the information associated with the phonological specification of a lexical entry (Archangeli 1988; Lahiri/Marslen-Wilsen 1991). For example, the fact that initial voiceless plosives are aspirated in English need not explicitly be stated, since it is a fully predictable phenomenon. In such cases, the feature specification of voiceless plosives, such as /p/, /t/, and /k/, would contain the underspecified feature [α aspiration], where α means “unspecified”.

In addition to the phonological specification, each lexical entry must be specified for its graphological form for literate speakers of languages with a phonographic writing system. There are two general possible ways of establishing the spelling of an entry. Either the graphological form is represented in terms of an isolated orthographic code, or it is defined in terms of grapheme-to-phoneme conversion rules. That both formats are employed is supported by the fact that they can be differently affected by brain damage (see Emmorey/Fromkin 1988: 128 and 132 for a discussion).

2.3.2.2. Morphological Specification

Through processes of inflection, derivation, and compounding, the basic morphological forms of lexemes, or *roots,* can vary their phonological and graphological structure, their category and their syntactic behaviour, and, last but not least, their meaning.[13] In principle, we have two possible ways of dealing with such words. On the one hand, we can store them in the lexicon as so-called full forms, or we can opt for a much smaller lexicon, which stores only lexemes and generates these words by a collection of rules. It has been argued in section 2.1. that inflectional variants, some derivational variants, and semantically stable compounds should be rule-based, whereas the majority of derivatives and lexicalised compounds should be entries in the lexicon. The question arises, then, what kind of rules should be used to generate new words, what problems these rules have to solve, and what information must be stated in the lexicon to trigger these rules.

(a) phonological and graphological variation

If a root is combined with an affix, or with another root, phonological and graphological variants may be the result. Let us illustrate this on the basis of plural formation in English. If a noun is to be turned into its plural form, the plural morpheme, in English represented by {Plural} or by its most common realisation in spelling {-s}, is added. Note that morphemes, like phonemes, are only abstract units. They are head terms of a family of related elements. The symbol used for the head term of the family is chosen by means of notational convention; it is generally related to its function or to its graphological structure. Its actual realisation depends on the morpho-phonological context, i.e. the phonological or graphological structure of the root. The realisation of {-s} in pronunciation and in spelling, for example, depends on the final phoneme and on the final grapheme of the root to which {-s} is attached.

Let us look at the pronunciation first. If the root ends on -s, -z, -ʃ, or -ʒ, {-s} will be realised as /-ɪz/, as in *horses*; if the final phoneme of the root is voiceless, {-s} will be realised as /-s/, as in *cats*; and if the root in question ends on a voiced phoneme, the result will be /-z/, as in *dogs.*

The spelling of plural nouns is also sensitive to the phonological structure of the roots to which {-s} is added. If the root ends on -s or -ʃ, the letter -E- has to be inserted between lexeme and affix, as in *boss(e)s* or *watch(e)s.* This E-insertion rule of spelling is closely connected with another graphological rule that turns a final -Y into -I as in *fly* → *fli(e)s.*

Both phonological and graphological variation are subject to a number of additional rules, yet the principle should be clear: morphological processes are sensitive to the phonological structure of the roots and can result in phonological and graphological changes. To trigger such changes, the processor has to inspect the phonological and morphological structure of the root.

(b) syntax and morphology

The process of affixation, the addition of an affix to a root, is not only sensitive to the phonological and graphological properties of a lexical entry but also to its internal syntactic properties. Let us illustrate this on the basis of the highly productive rule of *er*-affixation to generate deverbal nouns, for example, *walk-er, sing-er, move-er,* etc. Obviously, this rule must observe the syntactic category of the root to which -er attaches, namely to verbs. Yet, not all verbal roots have an agentive noun. Take an ungrammatical word such as **rain-er,* for example. Here, the rule cannot apply, because the intransitive verb *rain* does not take an agentive subject, or, to use the framework of transformational generative grammar, *rain* has a subject position, which is not theta-marked.[14] Thus, the interpretation verb+er (= "someone who verbs") fails. In other words, morphological rules have to inspect not only the syntactic category but also more advanced syntactic properties of lexical entries, such as their transitivity status, the nature of their arguments, and their syntactic context.

Note that, in our example of *er*-affixation, etymological aspects also play a role. The phonological realisation of -er in most English dialects is /-ə/. Orthographically, however, -er can occur as -er, -or and -ar. The actual form depends on the type of root. Lexemes with neoclassical roots such as *accelerate, incubate, supervise,* etc., often use the -or variant (Quirk et al. 1985: 1550), while spelling variants in -ar, e.g. *beggar, liar,* are chiefly 16th and 17th century latinised versions of older variants in -er and -or (Marchand 1969: 281).

To sum up: the morphological specification of an entry must describe the conditions of affixation. As in dictionaries, the syntactic category must be inspected first. It serves as a basis for affixation and for lexical insertion in the generation of sentences. The statement of the syntactic category is slightly problematic. On the one hand, it is incorporated into the syntactic specification of a lemma. This is necessary for the linguistic level of processing to control the process of lexical insertion and to generate proper syntactic structures. On the other hand, the syntactic category can be recognised, or at least be narrowed down, without lemma activation. In nonsense sentences such as (30), we can precisely define the syntactic category of the words in italics without understanding them:

(30) The *glimsy blobs brated* the *belge.*

Clearly, the determiners indicate that the elements following are likely to be adjectives or nouns, and *brated* can be recognised as a verb from its morphological structure alone. In other words, at the level of morphology, the syntactic category can already be made available, thus easing the process of lemma activation in language comprehension.

In addition to the syntactic category, the morphological information must also indicate the precise affixational possibilities of a root. For example, the verbal root *walk* can productively form the following words: *walk, walk-s, walk-ed, walk-ing, walk-er,* whereas *go* only forms *go, go-(e)-s, go-ing*. The remaining forms are either unusual ?*go-er* or irregular *went.* The representation of the affixational properties in the lexicon is a matter of notational convention. One could either use numbers for specific root types or make use of special *continuation classes* to determine the morphological status of a lexeme. For example, we could assign the following morphological properties to verbal roots:

WALK	V,	V1
GO	V,	V2
RUN	V,	V3

where the continuation class V1 says that the root can be combined with -s, -ed, -ing and -er and V2 states that only -s and -ing forms are possible. V3, by contrast, denotes the possibility of generating -s, -ing and -er forms, but no -ed forms. Whether this information is encoded separately as a special class within the morphological specification of an entry, or whether it is incorporated into the syntactic category, is a matter of notational convention or preference.

2.3.3. Lemma Specification

It has already been mentioned that formal aspects and lemma are related by a *lexical pointer*. The term *pointer* has been used in the literature for a long time. While Collins/Loftus (1975: 408) used it as an alternative term for links in semantic networks, Levelt (1989: 165) introduced it as the indication of an address where the corresponding formal information of an entry is stored after the lemma has been accessed. That pointers, or more precisely *readpointers*, play a crucial role in the computational realisation of a lexicon will be shown in chapter five. In a machine-readable lexicon, readpointers are an essential tool not only to mark the position of lexical information on a storage device but also to enable the programmer to externalise the entire lemma information. Figure 25 illustrates the concept of pointers on the basis of language production, in particular on the basis of the retrieval of the form-based lexical specification associated with the lexical access unit FLY, whose lemma has already been inserted into the sentence structure "He saw a *fly*". The pointer is realised by the arbitrary value N3897 and it either evokes the retrieval of the lemma from the mind/brain (left-hand side) or from an external storage device on a computer (right-hand side).

In the mental lexicon, the activation of lemmas depends on the processing mode. In language production, lemmas are activated first, triggering the formal information via the lexical pointer; in language comprehension, the process is reversed. After the recognition of the formal properties of an item, the associated lemma is retrieved.

Two types of information are incorporated in the lemma: the syntactic information, which specifies a lexeme's syntactic category, its syntactic context and some additional parameters, and the semantic specification, which defines the meaning of an item. Some researchers also include the sociolinguistic and pragmatic information which is critical to lemma selection. Myers-Scotton (1993b: 2), for example, cites the information coupled with the lexemes MAYBE and PERHAPS, whose selection is based on sociolinguistic considerations and on degrees of formality.

2.3.3.1. Syntactic Specification

The formalisation of the syntactic specification of a lexical entry depends to a large extent on the syntactic framework employed. Nevertheless, the following aspects must be specified:

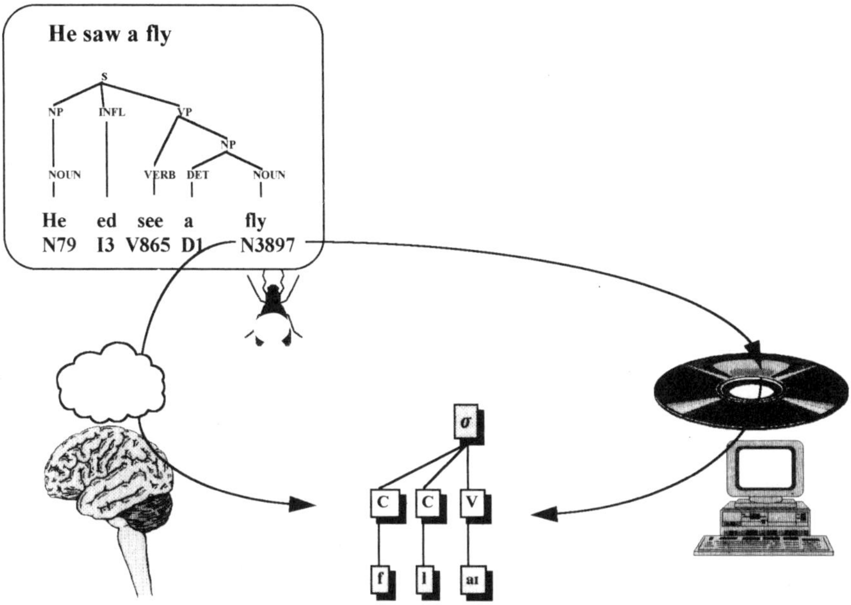

Figure 25. The concept of pointers

- the syntactic category of a lexeme
- the syntactic context of a lexeme
- syntactic idiosyncrasies

It has been shown in section 2.2. that standard dictionaries, such as the OED, merely list the syntactic category and, for verbs, the syntactic context in terms of its transitivity status. We have already seen that this is not sufficient for a lexicon based on linguistic principles, where the inclusion of the argument structure of lexemes in terms of selectional restrictions is necessary. Without any doubt a lexicon must incorporate information of this type.

(a) the syntactic category

That the syntactic category is syntactic as well as morphological in character has been explained above. Also, it has been pointed out that it may subdivide a lexical entry into several parts. As illustrated on the basis of the lexeme ROUND (see example (6), this chapter), this lexical entry can be split into at least five different components, based on its category.

(b) argument structure/subcategorisation

Only very rarely do words occur in isolation. Primarily, they are inserted into structures which are necessary to satisfy their contextual properties. For example, some verbs, traditionally referred to as transitive verbs, require objects, whereas other verbs, the class of intransitive verbs, must occur without objects. In English, prepositions normally precede noun phrases, adjectives may constitute heads of adjectival phrases or occur as the modifier of nouns, and so on. In other words, we can precisely define the syntactic context for each item in the lexicon in terms of its obligatory and optional complements. The representation of the syntactic context, however, is dependent on the theory and its notational conventions.

Let us illustrate the definition of the syntactic contextual aspects of a lemma on the basis of the verb *see*. Here are some examples:

(31) a. The man saw the woman.
 b. The man saw the woman in the park.
 c. The man saw the latest news.
 d. The man saw that the woman came.
 e. Yesterday saw a smiling President.
 f. *The man saw.
 g. *saw the woman.
 h. Oh, I see!
 i. *The table saw the woman.

The examples in (31) indicate that *see* requires two arguments, a subject-NP and an object-NP. In (31a) these arguments are "the man" and "the woman". Elements, such as "in the park" in (31b), are optional and do not play a major role in the lexical distinction of the lexeme SEE (Jackendoff 1990: 21). Note that (31d) features an object-NP which is actually realised as a *that*-clause; nevertheless its function is that of object. If one of the arguments is missing, as in (31f) and (31g), the resulting sentence is ungrammatical.

An objection which is often made mentions constructions of the type (31h), trying to use them as counter-examples. However, these are specific constructions which fail to meet the basic properties of major sentences, for example the ability to satisfy the substitution test. The fact that "*oh, they see!" is ungrammatical clearly indicates that (31h) is a special *comment clause* (Quirk et al. 1985: 1112ff). There are two possibilities of storing such comment clauses in the mental lexicon. Either they constitute separate entries or they are triggered as special items of a lemma as soon as a lemma's conceptual conditions are met. (The same applies to fixed phrases, such as "Merry Christmas!", or idiomatic expressions).

Ignoring the formalisation of these fixed expressions, we can establish the following syntactic context for SEE as a first approximation:

$$SEE : V; [SUBJ - NP, OBJ - NP]$$

This notation defines a category in terms of 'subcategories' and is thus called a *subcategorisation-frame* (also see section 2.2.). Essentially, it expresses the fact that SEE in its standard interpretation requires a subject-NP and an object-NP. Such a definition of a lemma's subcategorisation-frame alone is not sufficient to prevent sentences such as (31i) from being generated. Here, we need more specific information about the type of subject-NP required. We have already illustrated the technique of selectional restrictions, which define each argument in terms of lexical features such as [± concrete], [± human], etc. Another representation formalism makes use of *theta-roles,* a theory which is closely connected to the Chomskyan tradition of generative grammar. As already mentioned, this framework defines the argument positions of verbs in terms of a finite set of thematic roles such as agent, patient, theme, etc. However, there are verbs with argument positions that are not theta-marked, for example, *rain.* The system of theta-roles, then, replaces the selectional restrictions by a *theta-grid* of the following kind:

$$SEE : V; [SUBJ - NP(Agent), OBJ - NP(Theme)]$$

With this specification, which not only identifies the syntactic context of an item in terms of phrasal constituents but also associates with each constituent a thematic role, we can exclude sentence (31i). It clearly violates the theta-grid, since *tables* cannot act as agents. Sentences such as (31e), however, are problematic. They exhibit a tendency of language change in English, where agentive subjects are replaced by non-agentive subjects. Such subjects are semantically closely related to prepositional phrases, as their translation into languages such as German indicate.[15]

While the syntactic specification of SEE is relatively straightforward, there are numerous lemmas whose syntactic specification has to be split into several different argument structures.

(32) a. John believes my brother.
b. John still believes in communism.
c. John believes that Mary is his daughter.
d. John believes Jack to be his friend.

These examples indicate that the syntactic specification of the lemma BE-LIEVE must consist of four different theta-grids:

(32) a'. BELIEVE: V; [SUBJ-NP(Agent), OBJ-NP(Patient)]
b'. BELIEVE: V; [SUBJ-NP(Agent), in(NP(Theme))]
c'. BELIEVE: V; [SUBJ-NP(Agent), OBJECT(that-S(Theme))]
d'. BELIEVE: V; [SUBJ-NP(Agent), OBJECT( ), inf-S(Theme)]

All frames show that the theta-grid of BELIEVE has two arguments, where the first argument is always an agentive subject-NP. A very interesting case is exhibited in (32d). Superficially, this sentence seems to be similar to (32c). However, this example also features the direct object *Jack.* Clearly, *Jack* must be the object, since it is assigned the object-case. This becomes visible when we replace it by the respective personal pronoun which would have to be *him* and not *he.* Thematically, however, *Jack* is the agentive subject of "be his friend". Hence, we have the special case of an empty theta-position in the theta-grid of BELIEVE, which is filled during the process of sentence generation.

Recently, Jackendoff (1990) set up a modified subcategorisation system that unifies lexical entries with multiple argument structures. This system cuts across syntax and semantics and identifies the context of an item not only by a mere list of obligatory syntactic constituents but also in terms of optional conceptual arguments. As a result, this representation merges the various syntactic contexts of an item into a general structure with obligatory and optional variables. According to this view, the different syntactic contexts for *climb* in ((15), section 2.1.) can be represented as follows:

(33) a. Joe climbed for hours.
b. Joe climbed down the mountain.
c. Joe climbed down the rope.
d. Joe climbed through the tunnel.

$$[_{\text{Event}}\ \text{GO}([_{\text{Thing}}\ \ ]_j, \mathbf{[_{PATH}\{TO\ ([_{PLACE}TOP\text{-}OF([_{THING}\ \ ]_j)])\}]_{\{j\}}})]$$

The PATH-constituent (bold face) consists of two parts: a complex part and a reduced form. The reduced form dispenses with the contents of the curly brackets:

complex: $[_{\text{PATH}}\{\text{TO}([_{\text{PLACE}}\text{TOP-OF}\ ([_{\text{THING}}\ \ ]j)])\}]$
reduced: $[_{\text{PATH}}\ \ ]_j$

It fuses the various possibilities of (33) into a general structure. "The mountain" in (33b) can be conceptually defined as THING; hence "Joe went on top of the mountain". A phrase such as "down the rope", by contrast, expresses the conceptual category PATH and therefore satisfies the more general realisation of the PATH-constituent. Hence, there is no implication of "reaching the top of anything".

Such an extended subcategorisation system merges the principles of syntactic description with semantic aspects and thus captures many aspects of lexical relatedness. However, such a formalism is no longer strictly syntactic in character.

In addition to the regular syntactic properties, the syntactic specification of a lemma incorporates idiosyncratic information, such as the exceptional syntactic behaviour of an item in certain syntactic environments.

(34) a. The doctor weighs Mary twice a day.
b. Twice a day Mary is weighed by the doctor.
c. Mary weighs 60 kilograms.
d. *60 kilograms are weighed by Mary.

The lexeme WEIGH is a good candidate for the statement of such exceptional properties. Surely, it must be split into two lemmas, with the following theta-grids:

WEIGH: V; [SUBJ-NP(Agent), OBJ-NP(Patient)]
/ examples (34a) and (34b)
WEIGH: V; [SUBJ-NP(Agent), OBJ-NP(Theme)]
/ examples (34c) and (34d)

where the second interpretation requires that the object-NP is inanimate and expresses a measure. The fact that passivisation does not work with this interpretation of WEIGH has to be stated in the syntactic specification of the lemma.

In summary, the syntactic specification of a lexical entry determines its contextual properties. It specifies the principles according to which lexical items can be inserted into larger structures. However, very little is known how this information is utilised during speech comprehension and production (Emmorey/Fromkin 1988: 141).

That the syntactic specification cannot be separated from semantic considerations has been illustrated on the basis of Jackendoff's new system. The interaction between syntax and semantics, and the semantic specification itself, define the conceptual properties of the lexeme.

2.3.3.2. Semantic Specification

The representation of the meaning of a lexical item cannot work in the same way as in dictionaries for the following reason. Dictionaries are consulted to ascertain the meaning of unknown words. This requires some sort of linguistic sophistication, since dictionary entries define the meaning of one lexeme in terms of other lexemes, assuming that the meanings of the words used in the explanation are known or contained elsewhere in the dictionary. With this representation technique, standard monolingual dictionaries fail to meet two general demands on word semantics

- to establish a relation between word meanings and the world (referential relations),
- to establish relations among word meanings (sense relations).

In contrast to dictionary entries, these relations have to be built for every lexeme. This is often not the case in dictionaries, where the most common lexemes receive little attention and include quite arbitrary and useless meaning definitions.

(a) referential relations/semantics

The aim of referential semantics is to establish a relationship between the word that signifies something and the object signified by the word. This signifier-signified relationship is ideally a one-to-one relation where words are assumed to be labels for things. However, there are numerous difficulties with this view (Palmer 1981: 18ff). First, this *naming view* seems to apply only to nouns. Verbs, by contrast, do not identify what is named by them. Their meaning is a collection of complex properties, where the central meaning can hardly be isolated. Secondly, even if we maintain the view that nouns relate directly to their extra-linguistic objects, we run into trouble with nouns that do not refer to physical objects (*love, nonsense,* etc.) or nouns that refer to 'objects' that do not exist (*unicorn, goblin, fairy,* etc.). Further difficulties emerge with objects that *are* identifiable as single objects but can be denoted by various signifiers. *Morning star* and *evening star* undoubtedly denote the same object but can hardly be said to have the same meaning.

Due to these and many other difficulties, a reference relationship between word and object has been suggested that relates them through the mediation of *concepts* in the mind. In 1923, Ogden and Richards established this relationship as a triangle, where the relationship between word and object is only an indirect one. Figure 26 shows the Ogden/Richards-model, now known as *semiotic triangle.* It illustrates the relationship between a word and an object on the basis of one meaning of the lexeme FLY.[16] According to the semiotic triangle, the link between word and object is via the concepts in our mind, hence an indirect one. A direct link is impossible. The dotted horizontal line in figure 26, however, suggests that in some specific cases the connection between word and object is less indirect. Such cases can be found when words exhibit some sort of imagery, such as onomatopoeia or iconicity (Fromkin/Rodman 1981: 3).

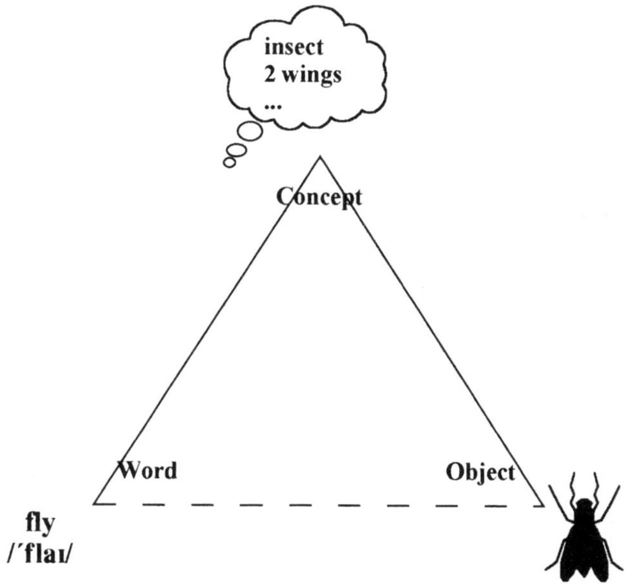

Figure 26. The semiotic triangle

Central to the semiotic triangle is the term *concept.* But what exactly is a concept? This is not the place to discuss this highly philosophical question, which has involved more than two generations of semanticists, who eventually have had to admit that they do not know (see, for example, the discussion in Palmer 1981: 25ff, or in Kempson 1976: 17ff). Most suitable is the view that concepts are mental information units of words. Since we cannot look into our mind, let alone into the minds of others, concepts will always be subject to speculation. However, it is clear that people must have a very large number of concepts, and that each concept must have a very complicated structure containing indefinitely large amounts of information (Collins/Loftus 1975: 408).

Even though there are no generally accepted frameworks for studying word meaning in linguistics, there are numerous approaches to defining word meaning. They have borrowed their ideas mainly from artificial intelligence (of which one branch is computational linguistics) and from psychology.

(b) sense relations

While referential relations deal with meaning in terms of our experience outside language, sense relations seek to establish relationships among the words of a language. Dictionaries state such relations. Yet, unless they are designed for specific purposes, they often do it in an unsystematic way. It seems that standard monolingual dictionaries supply the user with referential meaning. In doing so, they relate, via sense relations, a lexeme whose meaning is unknown to one or several lexemes whose meaning is understood.

In a systematic treatment of sense relations, one can distinguish two kinds: substitutional or *paradigmatic* sense relations, on the one hand, and combinatorial or *syntagmatic* sense relations, on the other (Lyons 1981: 91). Syntagmatic relations bring us into the area of grammatical meaning and sentence semantics. Even though we have little to say about the combinatorial possibilities of words, it should be mentioned that certain lexemes are highly restricted with respect to their collocational acceptability. Classic examples from English are adjective pairs such as *pretty/handsome* or *rancid/addled.* Surely, the semantic part of these lexemes has to include this information. It has to specify that PRETTY combines with WOMAN and HANDSOME with MAN, and, similarly, that RANCID collocates with BUTTER and ADDLED with EGG.

In establishing paradigmatic sense relations among lexemes, one can isolate three main types of relation, *hyponymy, synonymy* and *antonymy* (Palmer 1981: 85ff).[17] *Hyponymy,* also referred to as *inclusion,* defines a relationship between a more and a less general term, where the meaning of the more general term is totally included within the meaning of the less general term. For example, the relation between INSECT and FLY is one of inclusion, since FLY incorporates the meaning of INSECT. Hence, FLY is a hyponym of the superordinate term INSECT. Likewise, BEE includes the meaning of INSECT; consequently FLY and BEE have the same superordinate lexeme, they are *co-hyponyms.* On the basis of hyponymy relations, complex meaning hierarchies as shown in figure 27 can be established.

A large number of co-hyponyms do not have a superordinate term but are nevertheless subsumed under the heading of hyponymy. Lexemes that

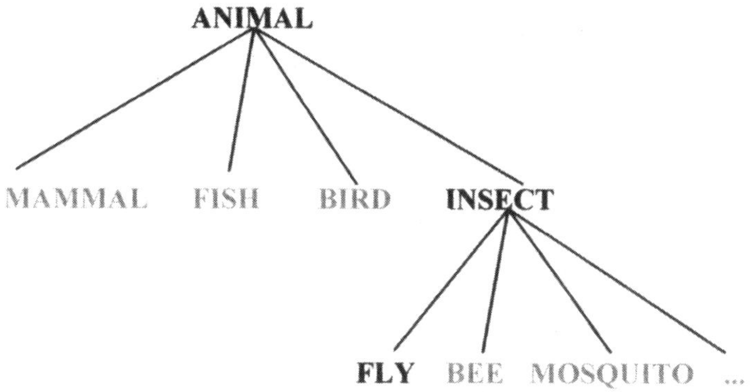

Figure 27. Hyponymy relations

denote colours, for example, have no superordinate term, since COLOURED normally excludes black and white.

In contrast to hyponymy, the relationship of meaning inclusion, *synonymy* defines a relationship of sameness of meaning. It has long been known that there are no real synonyms, i.e. that there are no two words that have exactly the same meaning. If this were the case, then it would be highly unlikely that both lexemes would survive. In looking at lexemes that are normally defined as synonyms, a number of differences between them can be worked out (Palmer 1981: 88ff):

- dialectal differences (e.g. AUTUMN and FALL)
- stylistic differences (e.g. NASTY, OBNOXIOUS, HORRIBLE)
- emotive differences (e.g. HIDE and CONCEAL)
- collocational/syntagmatic differences (e.g. RANCID and ADDLED)
- meaning overlap (e.g. MATURE, ADULT, RIPE, etc.)

For these reasons of meaning relatedness rather than meaning identity, synonymy is often defined as a relationship of 'similarity of meaning'.

The third sense relation, *antonymy,* is normally defined as 'oppositeness of meaning'. It is often referred to as the opposite of synonymy. However, the status of the two is very different. While real synonymy does not exist and is thus hard to define, antonymy is regular and can be precisely defined. Nevertheless, there are different kinds of oppositeness of meaning. The most important distinction concerns the exact relation between two antonymous lexemes. This relation can be binary, gradable or relational. *Binary antonyms* are pairs of lexemes where the meaning of one lexeme is clearly opposed to the other. ALIVE is certainly opposed to DEAD and MARRIED to SINGLE. *Gradable antonyms,* by contrast, are pairs which not only stand in binary opposition but represent different points along the scale according to which they differ. WIDE and NARROW, just like BIG and SMALL, may be seen in terms of the quality involved. Nevertheless, they are mutually exclusive. Interestingly, gradable antonyms follow the concept of *markedness.* This means that one lexeme of a gradable antonym pair is always selected as a default. Questions such as "how wide is it?" or "how big is it?" do not imply that the object in question is either wide or big. However, if we ask "how narrow is it?" or "how small is it?", it is implied that the object in question is actually narrow or small. Thus, NARROW and SMALL are the marked lexemes in their respective antonym pair. *Relational antonyms* are different from binary or gradable antonym relations. They exhibit a type of opposition which can be best described by converseness and typically express a relationship of transitivity. For example, the prepositional concepts ABOVE and BELOW form a converse pair since if A is above B, then B is below A. Likewise, verbal concepts such as GIVE and RECEIVE are converse. If A gives B to C, then C receives B from A.

Hyponymy, synonymy and antonymy, then, are the basic sense relations that hold between lexemes, which build a network of such relations. Lexemes do not stand in one sense relationship to one another, but they establish large webs of relationships to many other items. For example, WIFE is a hyponym of WOMAN, a hyponym of HUSBAND, and a synonym of SPOUSE. A fourth, often disputed type of sense relation establishes part-whole relationships, such as FINGER-HAND. This relationship of *meronymy* is controversial for various reasons. First, there are several types of meronymy, such as functional meronymy, where one concept is a functional part of the other (e.g. FINGER-HAND) or more general part-whole relations, where the part and the whole exist as a continuous entity (e.g. FLAME-FIRE). Secondly, there are diverging opinions as to whether meronymy should be treated as a semantic primitive in the sense of synonymy, antonymy, and hyponymy. However, since meronymy cannot be fully explicated by any of the three basic sense relations, it seems to makes sense to assign a basic status to this type of sense relationship. A functional part is neither synonymous with, nor a hyponym of the whole it is linked to.

All sense relations are employed for the definition of the meaning of dictionary entries, though not in a systematic way. The semantic specification of entries in the lexicon, by contrast, has to specify sense relationships in great detail, using adequate representation formalisms.

In addition to the representation of referential and lexical semantic relationships, one can distinguish different components of the meaning of an item. Flores d'Arcais (1986: 141) suggests a subdivision of meaning into sensory-related and knowledge-related aspects. This subdivision, which was supported experimentally, can be used to differentiate between those aspects of meaning which are primarily related to the form or colour of an object (sensory-related aspects), and those that deal with the function of an object (knowledge-related). However, the differentiation between form and function is mainly confined to physical objects and is problematic for items with abstract denotations.

2.3.3.3. Theories of Representing Word Meaning

In order to represent word meaning we have to find a formalism that incorporates the theoretical insights into referential and sense relations, that accounts for different aspects of meanings, and that is compatible with the data on language acquisition and the wide range of experimental data on word meaning. Whether such a formalism can be transferred to the specification of word meaning on machines is a matter of program design and implementation efficiency.

(a) feature theories

A common technique for establishing concepts is to break them into smaller parts. Depending on the theory used, these subparts of meaning are referred to as meaning atoms, lexical or semantic features, semantic primitives, or meaning components. Feature theories assume that lexemes can be represented as a semantic complex made up of such components. These components are not lexemes, but are part of a meta-language used for the semantic description of all languages. Conveniently English is used for this meta-language. In the case of the insect FLY, we could, as an approximation, make use of the following set of atomic semantic features:

[FLY: (ANIMAL), (INSECT), (2_WINGS), (6_LEGS), (NO_STING)]

Sometimes it has been suggested that the formalism of representing lexemes in terms of semantic features should, at least partly, make use of the concept of binarity, along the lines adopted in phonology or syntax. Thus, it seems suitable to state semantic features not in terms of simple meaning atoms, but as an ordered set of attribute-value pairs where each attribute, such as ANIMAL, is associated with a specific value. These values can be bivalent, such as (ANIMAL+), (STING-), etc., or numerical, such as (LEGS 6).

Hence, a mixture of bivalent and numerical values seems to be a more appropriate solution:

[FLY:(ANIMAL+), (INSECT+), (WINGS: 2), (LEGS: 6), (STING-)]

Additionally, there are attributes that have values that are neither bivalent nor numerical, but are truly atomic, that is they have a specific non-numerical value. For example, humans and some non-human individuals have names, buildings and many other objects are associated with precise locations, and so on. Such aspects have to be expressed by attribute-value pairs, such as (NAME: JOHN) or (LOCATION: LONDON).

Semantic features are not ordered hierarchically. The distinction (INSECT ±) is neither superordinate nor subordinate to the distinction (ANIMAL ±). The hierarchical character, however, can be captured by so-called default or redundancy rules of the type "if a lexeme has the feature (INSECT +), then it must have the feature (ANIMAL+)":

(INSECT+)→ (ANIMAL+)

The representation of lexemes in terms of semantic features is not confined to nouns. However, in order to express the complexity of verbal concepts on the basis of semantic features, for example, a simple list of semantic features is not sufficient. Consider one verbal sense of FLY:

[FLY: (TRANSFER+), (MOVE_WINGS-)]

This set of features expresses the fact that someone performs an action of flying without wing movement. It could semantically represent different sentences such as:

(35) a. John is flying to London.
(as a passenger on board a plane)
b. John is flying (the plane) to London.
(as a pilot)

The representation suggested does not take into account these differences in interpreting FLY. First of all, it does not include information about the reason for the action. While (35b) is a causative action, where the act of flying is caused by John as a pilot, (35a) expresses a non-causative action, where the subject (here: John as a passenger) has no influence on the action. Secondly, the representation format is unsatisfactory for there is no information as to the predication of the chosen features. Thus, we have to introduce a feature for causation, and variables for the arguments of the predicate to differentiate between the two interpretations of FLY:

(35) c. [FLY: ((CAUSE X)-) ((TRANSFER X)+) ((MOVE_WINGS Y)-)]
d. [FLY: ((CAUSE X)+) ((TRANSFER X Y)+) ((MOVE_WINGS Y)-)]

Now (35c) says that X transfers himself and is not the cause of the action, i.e. X flies as a passenger. (35d) represents the meaning "to fly as a pilot" and it expresses the fact that X (the pilot) causes the action and transfers himself and Y (the aeroplane), and that no wing movement is involved.

In general, then, we can say that, according to a feature theory, each lexeme is entered in the lexicon with a complex of semantic features or components. These can be ordered hierarchically by a set of redundancy rules and can be represented by a notation of attribute-value pairs which contains binary feature values, numerical values, and, in some cases, predicates and arguments.

A great advantage of feature theories is the possibility of providing a formal definition of sense relations. For example, a lexeme A can be defined as a hyponym of B, if all the features of B are contained in the feature specification of A. Furthermore, antonymy (in a general sense of incompatibility) can be defined as a relation between a set of lexemes, if they share a set of features but differ in one or more contrasting features (Kempson 1976: 86).

Using this definition, we can now specify hyponymy and antonymy relations, using feature representations. ANIMAL and FLY are in a relationship of hyponymy, since all semantic features of ANIMAL, for example, (HAS_SKIN +)(BREATHES +), etc., occur in the feature set of FLY. Likewise, we would define the main verbal senses of FLY as hyponymous, since they share a set of features but also differ in some of them.

Feature theories, which were introduced to linguistics through the work of Katz/Fodor (1963) and Katz/Postal (1964), are an adequate formalism for the representation of meaning. They are a suitable tool for the establishing of referential relations in general, and for the description of sense relations in particular. For this reason, they have been exploited in numerous linguistic models, especially in generative grammar. Nevertheless, there are problems with feature theories. These primarily concern the selection of features. For it is by no means clear which features should be chosen for which lexeme, and, even worse, the number of features necessary to distinguish lexemes from each other increases with the number of lexemes involved.[18]

(b) semantic networks [19]

Semantic networks have an even longer tradition than feature theories. They became known through work in biology and psychology, and it was as early as 1956 when the botanist Ritchens proposed this representation formalism (Hutchins 1986: 21ff). The psychological basis for semantic networks was laid in the 1960s, especially through the collaboration of the computer scientist, Collins, and the psychologist, Quillian. Semantic networks were primarily designed to show how to build human semantic structure and processing into a computer (Collins/Loftus 1975: 407); thus they can be viewed as psychological and computational models of human memory.

Originally, semantic networks were thought of as primarily representing nominal concepts. In the 1970s and 1980s, however, more and more complexities emerged and semantic networks were augmented by predicative knowledge, mechanisms for dealing with logical connectives, quantification, causalities, thresholds of activation spreading, hypothetical worlds, and further network-internal relations (Collins/Loftus 1975).

In a simple semantic network, concepts (objects and events) are represented by *nodes* and the interrelations between concepts by *arcs* or *links.*[20] The kind of relationship is specified by particular types of arcs. Figure 28 exhibits a fragment of a semantic network where, for reasons of simplicity, the relationships between the conceptual nodes are specified by just two arcs, the IS-A relation, which expresses a subset relationship, and the HAS-relation (sometimes called HAS-A or HAS-PROP-relation), which assigns attributes to conceptual nodes.

Semantic networks are a very popular representation scheme in artificial intelligence. One reason for their popularity is the elegance with which deductions can be made. In order to deduce that a fly has a head, all that is necessary is to trace up the IS-A hierarchy, assuming that attributes associated with higher nodes are also valid for lower nodes. This kind of reasoning, which is referred to as *property inheritance,* allows the inference that the concept FLY has all attributes of INSECT, and that both INSECT and FLY have all attributes of ANIMAL.

A second reason for the popularity of semantic networks in artificial intelligence and computational linguistics is the simplicity and elegance with which semantic networks can be implemented. Especially with LISP, one

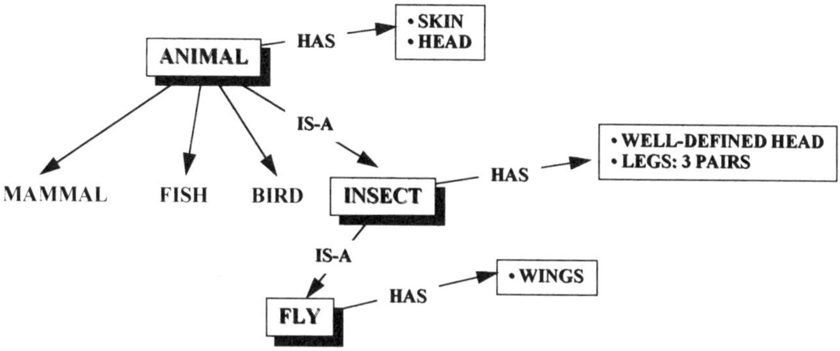

Figure 28. A simple semantic network

of the most powerful programming languages in artificial intelligence, semantic networks can be programmed very efficiently. LISP would represent a network such as in figure 28 as follows:

```
(ANIMAL
  (HAS  (SKIN HEAD))
  (IS-A (MAMMAL (...)))
  (IS-A (FISH       (...)))
  (IS-A (BIRD       (...)))
  (IS-A (INSECT     (HAS (WELL-DEFINED-HEAD LEGS-3-PAIRS))
        (IS-A       (FLY (HAS (WINGS)))))))
```

Another advantage of semantic networks is the ease with which relationships across the network can be built. In assigning the attribute WINGS to FLY we certainly want to distinguish between different types of WINGS, such as wings of flies, birds, or even aeroplanes. Thus, WINGS of flies are specific examples, or *instances,* of a more general concept WING with specific attributes. Semantic networks can capture this fact by establishing connections across the network. Figure 29 illustrates this possibility.

Semantic networks of the type discussed were not only developed as representation schemes for computational models but also as psychological models of human memory. Bischof (1976: 198ff) performed experiments based on the representation format in semantic networks. He showed that sentences such as "A fly has skin" are processed slower than "A fly has wings". This illustrates that information directly associated with a node is more accessible than information that has to be transferred to other nodes via property inheritance. This phenomenon has been termed *semantic distance.*

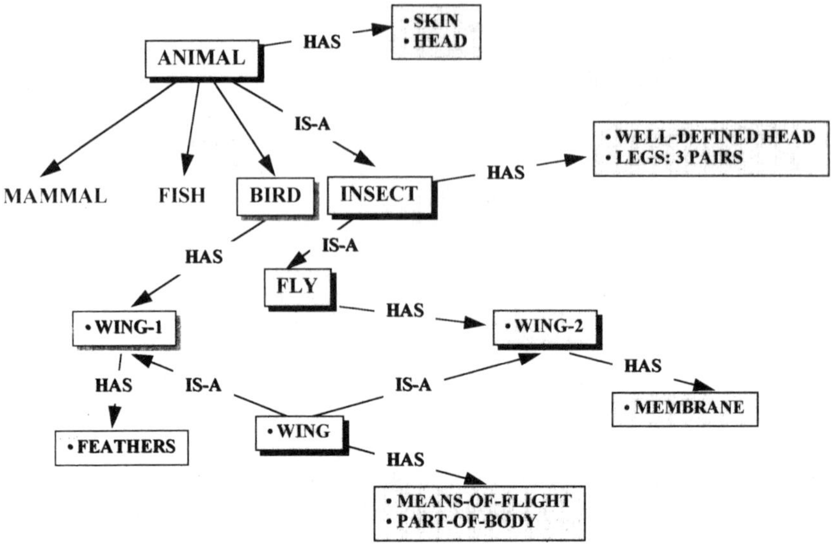

Figure 29. Relationships across semantic networks

To sum up, semantic networks are powerful tools for describing and implementing knowledge hierarchies and associations across concepts. Via property inheritance they avoid redundancies and a numerical explosion of semantic features for each concept. Hyponymical and meronymical relations are no problem for semantic networks; the hierarchical representation formalism itself establishes the semantic relationship of hyponymy, and the relationship of meronymy is expressed via the HAS-arc.

However, the popularity of semantic networks as a representation in Artificial Intelligence decreased in the 1980s, when they had become too complicated to be efficiently implemented on computer systems. The central problem is their size. Even if just a fraction of the entirety of human knowledge is to be represented as a semantic network, a gigantic database with a high number of links across the network will be the result. Also, as in feature theories, the choice of information associated with a node, and the degree of specification, is problematic. Is it necessary, for example, to go down to the last detail and associate information about the specific structure of the wings with the concept FLY, or is it sufficient to state that a fly has wings? However, the interest in network representations was rekindled by the end of the 1980s, due to several interlocking facts. Graphical user interfaces now made it possible to show networks dirtectly on the screen and, due to the increasing size and complexity of applications, graphic representations seemed a desirable alternative to rendered list procedures. Yet the semantic networks which have been constructed in this latter period have little similarity with the Collins/Quillian model, and it is debatable whether the term is still an adequate name for the networks that are nowadays subsumed under it. One major problem concerns the incorporation of predicative knowledge to express the meaning of sentences such as (20a) and (20b). Semantic networks as presented in figure 28 and 29 would have to be considerably extended to integrate predicative knowledge and the structure of predicative arguments. Such aspects of meaning require the introduction of variables, the integration of nodes that can represent situations and actions, mechanisms that represent sets of objects and attributes, and principles based upon logic. Sowa's conceptual graphs are an attempt at refining network structures by means of introducing such aspects (Sowa 1992)

Today's semantic networks are enormously complex structures. They establish numerous relationships between various types of conceptual nodes, they make use of principles of activation spreading and information strength, and they introduce thresholds for the accessibility of conceptual nodes. However, due to these augmentations and complications, which were introduced to handle experimental data, semantic networks have become less attractive. Today, they are still used in computer applications, but, as models of human memory, they are no longer exploited in their original form (Schade 1992: 15). The basic network structure and the principles of activation spreading, however, have survived and serve as the basis of connectionist models (see section 1.6.).

(c) prototype theory

When cognitive science emerged as a new field in the mid-1970s, the primary approach towards the representation of language in the mind was of an *objectivist* kind. According to this view, rational thought involves the manipulation of 'arbitrary abstract symbols'. These symbols function as internal representations of external reality, and the rules that manipulate them have no access to the meaning of these symbols (Lakoff 1988: 119). For example, the syntax of natural languages can be seen as a set of algorithmic principles that are applied to symbols, e.g. to words, without regard to their meaning. However, research in cognitive linguistics, cognitive anthrophology, and the philosophy of mind, indicated that the confinement of thought to arbitrary symbols whose internal structure cannot be utilised by the processes operating on them cannot be maintained empirically.

As an alternative, the *experientialist* position asserts that the mental processes underlying the use of language make use of *image-schemas*. These are meaningful symbols related to basic sensory-motor, emotional, social, and other experiences which interact to shape human cognition (Lakoff 1988: 120). In other words, meaningful conceptual structures are centered around bodily and social experience and some sort of innate capacity to structure them; or, to return to the syntax-meaning relationship, grammatical constructions are form-meaning pairs, and sentences are processed by general cognitive processes. Thus, experientialist cognition regards human thought as a result of innate human sensory-motor capacities, while objectivist cognition views human thought essentially as disembodied.

Before the terms objectivist and experientialist cognition emerged, the experientialist approach was generally referred to as *prototype theory*.[21] In contrast to feature theories and semantic networks, the theory of prototypes assumes that category membership is not a matter of necessary and sufficient conditions. Rather, category membership is centred around a representation of the prototypical member of the class a certain item denotes. Research, especially by Eleanor Rosch in the 1970s, has shown that some members of a category are judged to be more representative than others (see Rosch 1978, or Lakoff 1988, for a summary). Rosch tested the classical principles of categorisation (clear boundaries, shared properties, etc.) experimentally. Her results can be grouped into two types: prototype results and basic-level results.

prototype results

Some members of a category are judged to be more representative than other members. For example, ROBIN is a more representative member of the category BIRD than OSTRICH or PENGUIN, or FLY is judged to be more representative of the category INSECT than LADYBIRD. The most representative member of a category is called *prototype* or *prototypical member*.

In prototype theory, category membership is not defined by shared properties, that is by some sort of "checklist" which lists all the properties necessary and sufficient for class membership, but by a cluster of attributes that characterise the most representative member. None of these attributes may be necessary or sufficient for the definition of class membership; in fact, it may even be the case that no single member of the category has all the attributes in the cluster. For example, OSTRICH does not share all attributes of ROBIN, which is supposed to be a prototype of the class of birds, yet OSTRICH undoubtedly belongs to the same class. The prototype serves as a cognitive reference point (Lakoff 1982: 17); however, an object is not necessarily denied membership of a category just because it exhibits some differences from the prototype.

The prototype itself is not the meaning of a word. A prototype is located in a multi-dimensional space with dimensions corresponding to the attributes which may be different across a category. For example, in the case of the prototype BIRD, dimensions will be length, wingspan, colour, life-span, etc. A boundary around the space defines objects as birds. In many cases, the boundary is not sharp but fuzzy. In order to define this concept of fuzziness, it has been suggested that fuzzy-set theory be incorporated, on the basis of which graded category membership can be defined.

basic-level results

Certain categories are considered to be more "basic" than others: they are recognised more quickly, they are learnt earlier, and they are used more often; in summary, they are processed more easily than other categories. These *basic-level categories* are set-theoretically in the middle. They have both superordinate and subordinate categories. For example, FURNITURE is a superordinate, CHAIR a basic-level, and ROCKING-CHAIR a subordinate category. The idea behind the postulation of basic-level categories is that they

- serve as the basis for the interaction between category members
- serve as perceptual anchors
- provide mental images that can reflect the entire category

or, more generally, it is always the basic-level that guides the interaction of humans with objects. For example, we have a clear-cut mental image of the concept CHAIR, but none of FURNITURE. It is impossible to think of a piece of furniture that is not related to the concept CHAIR, TABLE, etc. Basic-level categories depend on the kind and the degree of interaction one has with objects. Hence, it is not surprising that basic-level categories are relative, varying across cultures (Lakoff 1982: 22).

Both prototypes and basic-level categories seem to be fundamental for the classification of category membership, and thus for the classification of meaning. Like network theories, prototype theory involves hierarchical relationships via the postulation of spaces with prototypical members in the middle. Consequently, the definition of sense relations is unproblematic for prototype theory. The primary difference between prototype theory and semantic networks concerns two central aspects: first, prototype theory assigns degrees of salience to the attributes used for the definition of category membership and, secondly, it postulates specific categories as more fundamental in a hierarchy than others.

(d) frames

One way of incorporating the notion of prototype into a theory of meaning representation uses the concept of the frame. *Frames* were originally proposed by Minsky (1975) as a basis for visual perception, understanding natural language dialogues, and other complex cognitive activities.[22]

The central idea behind a frame is that it makes possible the integration of new data into concepts acquired through previous experience. Two types of frame can be differentiated: frames that represent individual concepts and frames that organise knowledge about sequences of events. The latter ones are referred to as *scripts* and have been introduced by Schank/Abelson (1977).

In general, a frame consists of a declarative skeleton, with slots to which procedures can attach. Let us illustrate this on the basis of the nominal concept FLY (figure 30).

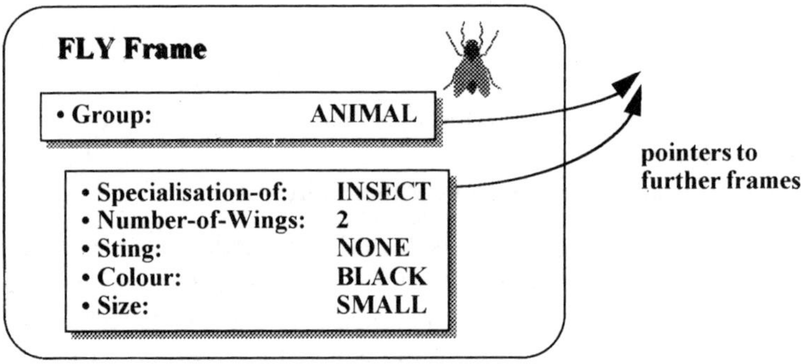

Figure 30. FLY as an object frame

Such an object frame contains several different kinds of knowledge. It always contains a Group slot, which specifies to which general class a concept belongs. The Specialisation-of slot is used to establish the superordinate concept of which the frame is a hyponym. Both Group and Specialisation-of slot are necessary for the general classification of a frame and essential to establish property inheritances among frames, much like the IS-A link in semantic networks.

In addition to these central slots, further slots supply places for knowledge, thus creating the opportunity for the inclusion of missing or incompletely specified knowledge. In figure 30, two value-assigning slots and two property slots that specify the particular object are associated with the frame. These slots contain *default values,* which remain unchanged unless there is contradictory evidence. For the concept FLY, the defaults include a numerical value for the number of wings, a binary value for the presence/absence of a sting, and specific properties concerning colour and size. The values of the size and the colour slot might be changed if an actual realisation of that frame is encountered, for instance, a big brown fly in the window.

Using the notation of defaults, frames can be considered as a formalisation of prototype theory. A prototype will then be defined as a frame in which all default slots are filled. The default value assigned to a variable is based on empirical evidence and represents distributions of possible values ranging from prototypical to less prototypical, rather than values. Thus, the conceptual representation of GIVE tends to require "giver" and "recipient" to be a person, and the element to be transferred of a physical kind. Less typical interpretations allow "givers" such as governments, institutions, or "recipients" such as inanimate objects. In allowing a range of defaults, we can choose from a set of alternatives. Under normal circumstances we will prefer values closer to the prototype, but we will accept deviant values if no other interpretation is possible (Rumelhart/Ortony 1977: 105). On this basis we can handle sentences such as (22a) and (22b).

(22) a'. John gave his daughter to Fred.
b'. The city lights gave the mayor's arrival a superb appearance.

As already mentioned, frames can be considered to be a mixture of declarative and procedural knowledge. They provide a general system for the presentation of knowledge plus a mechanism, the system of slots, that permits reasoning on the basis of seeking information of expectations, i.e. that flies are by default black. The declarative aspect is realised by the organisation of the static facts in a frame, e.g. that flies have wings, and the procedural aspect by procedures which fill or overwrite specific slot values.

The slot mechanism can be extended to set up frames for representing sequences of events. These *scripts* define sequences of events on the basis of prototypical expectations about the objects (properties) and the persons (roles) involved, and set up a fundamental sequence of events (scenes) that

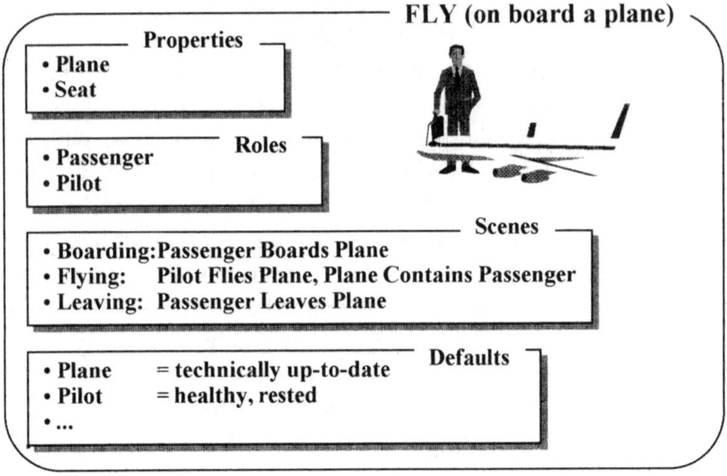

Figure 31. FLY as a Script

is necessary for the script to be realised. Figure 31 illustrates this on the basis of the script FLY (on board a plane).

Central to a script are the *scenes,* a system of a predefined sequence of events with one central event and a number of marginal scenes. In an actual story which activates a specific script the central event must be realised, whereas the marginal scenes may or may not be represented. The following simple stories may illustrate this:

(36) a. John flew to New York. He left the plane at nine.
b. ?John boarded a plane. He left it at nine.

While (36a) is clearly a story which satisfies the sequence of events in the FLY-script, (36b) is not. This is due to the absence of the central event FLYING.

Abelson (1981) extended the notion of script and differentiated between 'strong' and 'weak' scripts. While strong scripts involve expectations not only about the occurrence but also about the ordering of events, weak scripts only evoke the potential occurrence of specific events but do not strictly specify their position within the script.

In summary, frames and scripts are powerful tools of knowledge representation. They are capable of representing fundamental aspects of meaning as well as the basic sense relations such as hyponymy. Even though they face the same problems, like the formalisms presented above (feature selection, combinatorial explosion of features, in this case the number of slots), they have one central advantage: they allow reasoning on the basis of expectations and defaults and create the possibility of altering the meaning associated with a category.

(e) conceptual dependencies

A somewhat hybrid case, that is a mixture between semantic networks and frames, is Schank's (1975) *conceptual dependency theory* (short: CD-theory), which represents different predicative concepts and their arguments by a general underlying framework (Schank 1975: 37). According to this assumption every event has

- an ACTOR,
- an ACTION carried out by the ACTOR,
- an OBJECT as the goal of the ACTION,
- a DIRECTION as the basic orientation of the ACTION.

This simple system can be converted into a general framework which presents the relationship between ACTOR, ACTION, OBJECT and DIRECTION as a network of dependencies (figure 32).

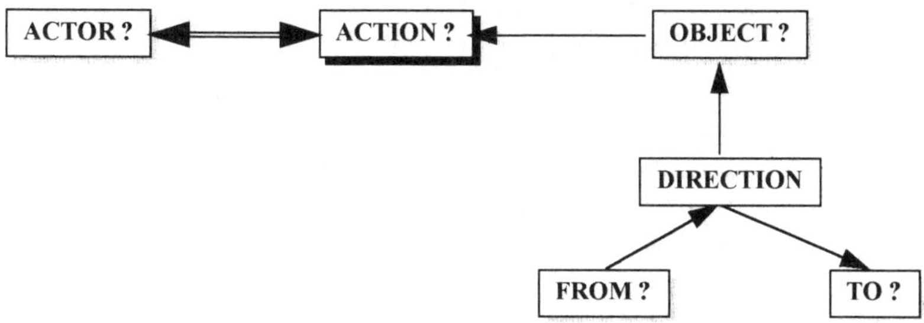

Figure 32. Conceptual Dependencies

An alternative presentation of the network presented in figure 32 is a bracketed construction such as:

(ACTION ? (ACTOR ?) (OBJECT ?)
(DIRECTION (FROM ?) (TO ?)))

The analysis of sentences, or, more precisely, predicative concepts, can now be reduced to a pattern-matching where, after the identification of the concepts in a sentence, each node of the network is matched against a corresponding CD-frame stored in the lexicon. Before we illustrate this matching procedure, we have to introduce the system of actions which is central to the conceptual dependency theory. The collection of action concepts is referred to as *primitive actions*. These can be differentiated into basic ACTs and instrumental ACTs. Whereas basic ACTs can represent an event on their own, instrumental ACTs are instrumental descriptions of basic ACTs or of further instrumental ACTs. CD-theory in its 1975 version introduced six basic ACTs and five instrumental ACTs:

Basic ACTs:

PTRANS = the physical transfer of objects, e.g. *go*
MTRANS = the mental transfer of information, e.g. *see*
ATRANS = the abstract transfer of objects, e.g. *give*
PROPEL = the application of force to objects, e.g. *throw*
INGEST = the act of ingesting objects, e.g. *eat*
MBUILD = the act of building information, e.g. *wonder*

Instrumental ACTs:

GRASP = the act of grasping an object
MOVE = the act of moving a (body) part
SPEAK = the production of noise
ATTEND = the drawing of attention to a stimulus
EXPEL = the act of expelling something from the inside

Using these primitive actions we can now assign a specific frame to each predicative concept. Let us consider the following sentences:

(37) a. John went to London.
b. The eagle flew to London.
c. John (the pilot) flew to London.
d. John (the passenger) flew to London.

Central to the meaning of all these sentences is the primitive action PTRANS, the concept of physical transfer. In all four cases, the actors are transferred from an unknown location to London. This can be expressed by the following general CD-frame, which is common to all four sentences:[23]

```
(PTRANS  (ACTOR X)     (OBJECT X)
         (DIRECTION    (FROM Y)     (TO Z)))
```

This CD-specification can be translated into the following conceptual specification: "An ACTOR X physically transferred an OBJECT X from location Y to location Z. Note that ACTOR and OBJECT (both X) are identical, indicating that the ACTOR physically transfers himself. Z stands for LONDON, whereas Y remains unbound, since we do not know the source of the action. Sentence (37a) can now be matched with the general CD-frame resulting in:

```
(37)    a'. (PTRANS  (ACTOR JOHN)  (OBJECT JOHN)
                     (DIRECTION    (FROM NIL) (TO LONDON)))
```

Unfortunately, this presentation applies to all four sentences, with the exception that in (37b) ACTOR and OBJECT are realised by "the eagle". In order to distinguish the meaning of the four sentences, instrumental ACTs have to be added, resulting in slightly more complex CD-representations for the remaining sentences:

```
(37)    b'. (PTRANS  (ACTOR EAGLE)  (OBJECT EAGLE)
                     (DIRECTION     (FROM NIL) (TO LONDON))
                     (MOVE          (ACTOR EAGLE)
                                      (OBJECT WINGS)))

        c'. (PTRANS  (ACTOR JOHN)   (OBJECT JOHN)
                     (DIRECTION     (FROM NIL) (TO LONDON))
                     (PROPEL        (ACTOR JOHN)
                                      (OBJECT PLANE)))

        d'. (PTRANS  (ACTOR JOHN)   (OBJECT JOHN)
                     (DIRECTION     (FROM NIL) (TO LONDON))
                     (PROPEL        (ACTOR PILOT)
                                      (OBJECT PLANE)))
```

In principle, each predicative concept can now be associated with a CD-frame along the lines presented above. In each CD-frame, some concepts have to be filled by variables, while others are realised by constants. Note, for example, that the difference between (37c) and (37d) is reduced to the presence/absence of the concept PILOT in the instrumental action PROPEL:

```
(PTRANS  (ACTOR X)     (OBJECT X)
         (DIRECTION    (FROM Y) (TO Z))
         (PROPEL       (ACTOR ?) (OBJECT PLANE)))
```

If the variable ? is filled by a concept identical with X, the interpretation is "fly as a pilot"; if not, the variable is automatically filled with PILOT, and the interpretation is "fly as a passenger".

With this mechanism, we can now translate every predicative concept into a CD-pattern and store it in the lexicon. Over and above the elegance of the presentation format, CD-frames allow the drawing of inferences, they can state sense relations such as hyponymy and antonymy, and they can be used to disambiguate sentences (see Schank/Riesbeck 1981, for further details).

However, it is not as simple as that. Even though CD-theory has been extremely successful and has resulted in a number of computer implementations, it soon became clear that events cannot be reduced to such a simple format and that additional mechanisms are required. For example, there are problems with quantification and metaphor which cannot be captured by the original CD-format. Furthermore, CD-theory in its original version concentrated on action verbs, but did not consider other dimensions of human actions such as problem-solving, reasoning, etc. Such *social* ACTs were introduced in later versions of CD-theory (Schank/Carbonell 1979: 331ff). Another problem with CD-theory is that it combines syntax and semantics in a way that it is difficult to extend or modify (Sowa 1984: 258).

Nevertheless, CD-theory is powerful enough to serve as the basis for the representation of meaning in a large number of domains. Also, other meaning representation formalisms can be integrated into the CD-scheme. Each concept, for example PILOT in (37d'), can be represented by lexical features, semantic networks, or by a frame. Moreover, CD-frames can be employed as the realisation of the scenes in scripts. The scenes of the FLY-script in figure 31, for instance, are all PTRANS-actions which can be established by analogy with the CD-frames presented above. Last but not least, CD-theory has been enriched with numerous reasoning procedures, such as inference mechanisms (Allen 1987: 214) and discrimination networks (Charniak et al. 1987: 149).

At least four further approaches to the formalisation of meaning deserve our attention:

- the theory of meaning postulates
- procedural systems
- production systems
- logic-based representations

The theory of meaning postulates was introduced as an alternative to feature theories. A meaning postulate, in general, is a rule or formula that regulates the interpretation of the sense of a lexeme by establishing equivalence or consequence relationships between the lexeme and related items. For example, the formula x $\mathrm{MAN}_1 \equiv$ x HUMAN BEING expresses the fact that MAN (in sense 1) is a synonym of HUMAN BEING (Hurford 1983: 188). Unlike feature theories, such as componential analysis, meaning postulates allow a full statement of semantic relations without making the further requirement that this be a complete characterisation of lexical meaning (Kempson 1976: 189). Since the relations expressed by meaning postulates can be readily captured by feature theories, which have already been discussed, we can dispense with a more elaborate treatment of meaning postulates.

The remaining formalisms have primarily been set up as computational paradigms and have influenced knowledge representation in artificial intelligence to some extent.

The essence of procedural systems, for example, is that meaning can be represented in terms of procedures as employed by AI-programming languages such as LISP. Production systems are also procedural in setting up a system of condition-action pairs, the so-called *production rules.* While strict procedural systems have not been used to a large extent, production systems have become the semantic backbone of numerous expert systems. This may be due to the elegance of implementing a manageable domain of knowledge using production rules. With the advent of new AI-programming languages, especially the arrival of PROLOG in the mid-1970s, the proponents of procedural approaches had to admit that representation formalisms based on propositional and predicate calculus could solve a number of problems which were previously highly problematic. Such logic-based systems had fewer problems with the definition of the scope of quantification, or the precise representation of predicates and their arguments.

In summary, the representation of the meaning of a lexeme is an enormously complex enterprise. Several representation formalisms are available, though none of them is capable of capturing all facets of meaning. While prototype theory and frames seem to offer the best results from a cognitive point of view, feature theories and formalisms based on logic are more formal in character and thus provide a more mathematical basis for the definition of meaning.

The reason for the enormous difficulty of providing a theory of word meaning lies in the complexity of meaning and knowledge in general. In the previous sections we have just discussed the formalisation of nominal and verbal concepts. The integration of, say, grammatical function words such as conjunctions, articles, etc., would extend each theory considerably.

In summary, then, all theories have their weaknesses. Only a combination of the formalisms available seems to provide a suitable solution.

2.4. Relations in the Lexicon

The complexity of the information associated with a lexical entry requires that the items in the lexicon, last but not least for reasons of storage efficiency, establish numerous relations across the lexicon. These relations concern all features that are associated with the lexical specification associated with an entry.

In section 2.1.4. we discussed the organisation of lexical entries as roots or as full-forms. In opting for a root lexicon we argued that the inflectional variants of a lexeme should not be listed. Thus, words like *fly, fly's, flies,* and *flies'* are not separate lexical entries but are generated on the basis of the lexeme FLY and its root. The relationship between a root and its productive morphological variants can be established by means of a morphological component. This has specific significance in computational linguistics, where computer systems with morphological components have been built to yield the syntactic analysis of texts. In such systems, the lexicon, or, more precisely, the formal specification of a lexical entry, closely interacts by means of morphological rules with a specific store that contains the productive affixes of a language. The entries in this *affix lexicon* can be organised by analogy with the main lexicon. They exhibit formal as well as lemma information. Let us illustrate this on the basis of the English plural morpheme{-s}:

access unit:	-S	
phonology:	/-z/ /-s/ /-ɪz/;	depending on the final root phoneme
spelling:	- s;	± E-deletion, ± I-to-Y conversion
morphology:	category: N,	attaches to nouns depending on the continuation class
syntax:	contexts: noun+s = plural ...	
meaning:	denotes more than one entity	

The main task of the affix lexicon is to associate with each lexical entry a list of affixes that specify the morphological possibilities of a root, and to define the lexical properties of each affix stored in the affix lexicon. It contains all those productive affixes required for the rule-based generation of words that are not stored in the lexicon, that is the inflectional affixes and those derivational affixes that are syntactically and semantically stable. The interaction between the affix lexicon and the main lexicon is achieved by means of a continuation class (see section 2.3.2.2.) and a small rule system that combines roots with affixes.

Such an affix lexicon considerably reduces the redundancies in the main lexicon, since the lexical information associated with an affix is only stated once, and all lexemes which share the same affixational pattern have the same continuation class in their morphological specification. That the separation of roots and affixes into two different stores is not only a matter of computational efficiency but can also be assumed for the mental lexicon was shown by MacKay (1979), who supported this idea on the basis of the analysis of speech errors.

Along similar lines we can organise an entry's lexical specification. Speech errors, comprehension experiments, and psycholinguistic models of word recognition suggest that the information associated with a lexeme is not stored in one place but in separate information-specific components or 'sub-lexicons'. Even though these subcomponents are assumed to be independent, they must interface and interrelate in a complex network (Emmorey/Fromkin 1988: 125). For example, instead of stating the syntactic properties of each lexeme within its syntactic specification, we can establish a pointer, which activates a particular syntactic frame that defines the syntactic behaviour of an entry. Nouns, for example, can be grouped into proper and common nouns, and the latter into count and non-count nouns (Quirk et al. 1985: 246ff). The division of nouns according to these categories has important consequences for their use. Non-count nouns, such as *furniture* or *music,* for example, must be seen as denoting an undifferentiated mass or continuum and do not occur with the indefinite article ("*a furniture", "*a music"). Also, the classification of nouns into different genders has important syntactic consequences, such as the selection of relative pronouns ("the man who.." vs. "the table which.."). Information about noun classes and gender type can be incorporated into syntactic frames which are activated when needed. The syntactic specification of a lexeme itself can be reduced to a pointer which triggers the relevant syntactic frame.

That the meaning of a lexeme consists of a collection of extremely complex aspects has been stated above. Also, it has been pointed out that meaning cannot be treated as an isolated bundle of information. As soon as the meaning of a lexeme is accessed, numerous additional connections are established. These connections concern the various sense relations from hyponymy to synonymy, and associative relations such as HOSPITAL and NURSE. That these connections exist has been shown by the analysis of speech errors or by priming effects (Levelt 1989: 184).

In summary, we can think of a lexical entry's specification as a skeleton on the basis of which the various properties can be triggered. Figure 33 illustrates a fragment of the maximally possible relations in the lexicon established by one nominal sense of FLY.

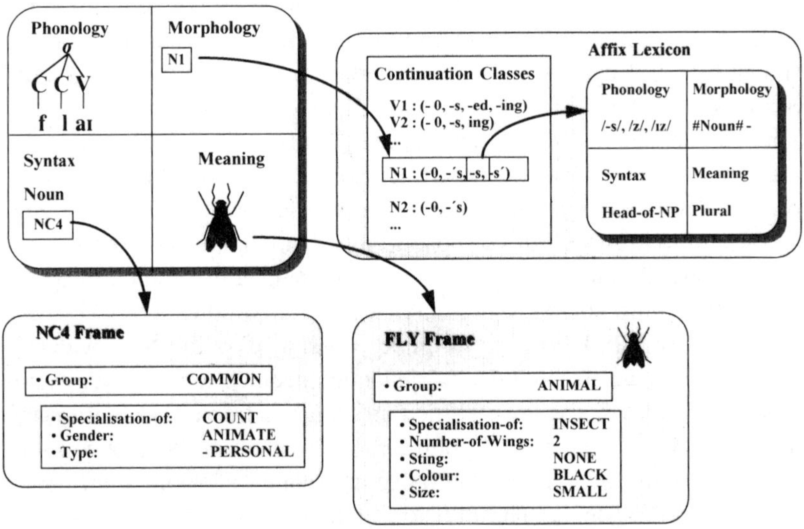

Figure 33. Relations in the lexicon

2.5. Summary

This chapter has illustrated the enormous complexity of information associated with lexical entries. We have seen that there is a fundamental difference between dictionary entries and entries in the lexicon, because dictionary entries contain just a fragment of the information required for natural language processing. It has been shown that for an efficient language processor each lexical entry has to be specified for the following aspects:

- phonology
- morphology
- syntax
- semantics

plus a set of relationships across the lexicon.

Figure 34 summarises the structure of a lexical entry on the basis of four senses of the lexeme FLY. Instead of using a specific formalism, such as a frame, for the representation of the meaning of each sense, symbols have been incorporated into each sense of FLY. That the morphological and syntactic specification is to be handled by a pointer has been mentioned above. For reasons of illustration, however, the verbal senses of FLY have been connected with more explicit morphological and syntactic information.

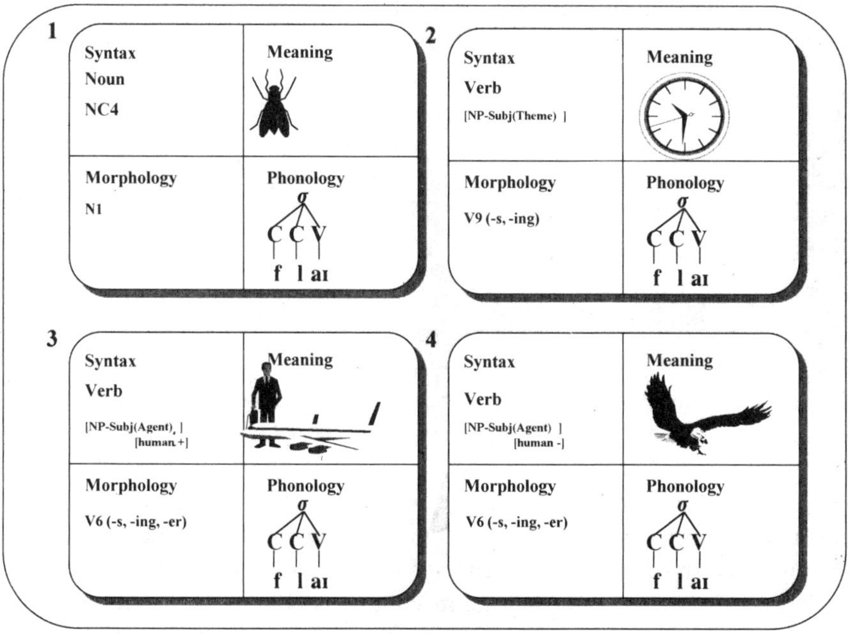

Figure 34. The lexeme FLY, a fragment

The four senses of the lexeme FLY as presented in figure 34 can, by and large, handle the interpretation of FLY in the following sentences:

(38) a. There were ten flies in my bedroom last night.
Sense 1 of figure 34

b. The coach is flying.
   Sense 2 of figure 34
c. John is flying to New York.
   Sense 3 of figure 34
d. The eagle is flying over the field.
   Sense 4 of figure 34

Sentences (38e) to (38i), however, can only be analysed if further senses of FLY are included in the lexicon, or if techniques are made available capable of handling special interpretations such as (38h) and (38i).

(38) e. The plane is flying to New York.
f. John is flying the plane.
g. The plane is flying.
h. The soldiers are flying the flag.
i. What a fly person!

While the information associated with the entries in the mental lexicon is normally confined to the aspects stated above, machine-readable lexicons can, depending on their purpose, additionally include

- etymological information
- synonymical information
- examples of entries in context
- statistical information

These aspects may be required for specific computational applications, such as machine translation. For example, machine translation systems often rely on passages which have already been translated or on statistics about syntagmatic relationships. This information can be triggered via additional pointers contained in the specification of the entries in a machine-readable lexicon. (We will return to this issue in chapter five).

The whole lexicon, whether the machine-readable or the mental lexicon, is a multi-pointered structure, with several thousands of entries packed with information. Each lexical entry can establish numerous associations across the lexicon and is capable of retrieving information from additional stores which are specialised for morphological, syntactic or semantic aspects. Despite the enormous amount of information associated with a lexeme and the complexity of the lexicon itself, words, can be recognised effortlessly at an extremely high-speed. How this is achieved will be discussed in the following chapters.

3. Pre-lexical Processing

"The usual goal of reading or listening is to derive meanings from visual patterns or sound patterns. If this goal is to be achieved, incoming perceptual information must activate stored knowledge about words that are presented."
(Garnham 1985: 43).

The representation of an item in the mental lexicon is referred to as *lexical entry*. Each lexical entry can be subdivided into an access unit and the corresponding lexical specification, which defines the entry's phonological, morphological, syntactic and semantic/conceptual structure. The central task of lexical processing is to gain access to an entry's lexical specification.

Prior to lexical processing, the language processor has to perform a preliminary analysis of the input. In reading, for example, lexical processing involves using information from written language, while, in speech, lexical access is achieved on the basis of the acoustic representation of the input signal. A third type of information that can be utilised in gaining access to the lexicon can be referred to as logographic. Think, for example, of symbols such as & or $, which are available on a standard typewriter. These symbols represent just a fraction of the set of logograms that are used today. Figure 35 illustrates some of these logographic symbols.

Figure 35.. Logographic symbols in modern society

The symbols shown in figure 35 may represent simple lexical entries, they may trigger complex concepts, or they can even evoke complex actions. A symbol such as ✂, for example, is normally understood as "cut here".

Hence, as a first approximation, we can define three different input channels to the mental lexicon:

– the acoustic/auditory input channel
– the visual input channel for graphological information
– the visual input channel for logographic information

The question arises whether the two input channels for visual information are distinct, or whether they can be merged into one more general input channel.

To postulate two separate visual input channels implies that processing written information is different from processing general visual input. There are good reasons to believe that this is not the case. First, not all languages have a writing system, and, furthermore, many writing systems are logographic in character, i.e. the words are written as complex visual patterns, rather than as units decomposable into graphemes (see section 3.1.2.). To maintain the idea of a distinct channel for written information, one would have to confine this channel to a few languages, and define one general visual input channel for all others. This seems totally implausible. Instead, it seems suitable to merge the graphological and the logographic input channel into one general channel responsible for visual information and assume that written information is processed according to general principles of visual perception. In fact, there are good reasons to believe that the processing of written information makes use of a number of principles employed in general vision (see section 3.3).[1]

In addition to these modes, the lexicon can be activated by questions such as "what has two wings, no sting, six legs, and is black and small?", i.e. by a collection of questions that constitute the semantic information associated with a lexical entry. This mode of processing, however, arises only in language production where, at the stage of grammatical encoding, lexical items have to be selected that express particular meanings (see figure 11, chapter one). In language comprehension, by contrast, particular items have to be identified from sensory input.

Figure 36 illustrates the central levels of processing lexical information. It suggests that at the lowest level, the pre-lexical level, two perceptual devices are used, one responsible for the perception of speech and one for the perception of visual information, including the processing of written input.

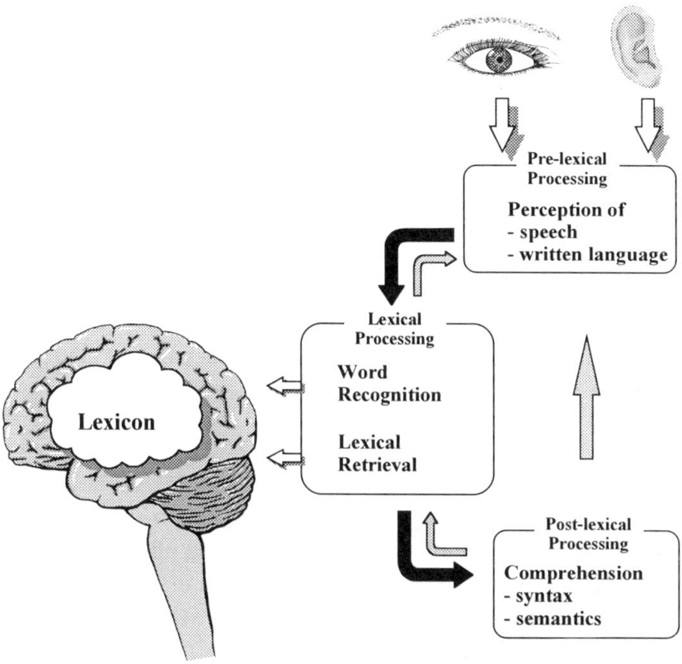

Figure 36. Pre-lexical, lexical, and post-lexical processing

The flow of information between pre-lexical, lexical, and post-lexical processes can be defined in various ways. On the one hand, we could think of an autonomy model, where the flow of information is strictly serial and bottom-up. In such models decisions at lower levels are not determined by information coming from higher levels; for example, the pre-lexical level is insensitive to any information from the lexical level. The black arrows in figure 36 illustrate such an information flow. On the other hand, one could assume an interactive model that allows information flow between the processing levels in a top-down fashion, i.e. levels further removed from the input influence lower levels. The additional possibility of top-down information flow is expressed by the grey arrows in figure 36. We will see that both models are possible. Also, it will be shown that both models involve massive parallelism at each level, that is many facets of information can be dealt with at a time.

The following sections focus on the acoustic/auditory and the visual processes that are performed prior to lexical processing. We will discuss how the sensory input is analysed, how the relevant features necessary for lexical processing are extracted, and we will present the most influential hypotheses concerning this pre-lexical phase. Having postulated two general input channels, we will also have to address the question whether these channels interact or not.

3.1. The Nature of the Input Signal

The input signal is a highly complex string of information. It features numerous possibilities of variation, it often occurs against a considerable portion of background information, it may be distorted, and it is full of redundancies. Let us look more closely at these aspects.

(a) variation in the signal

Both speech and written input can be varied considerably. In speech, there are two major sources for this variability - variations in the physical properties of speakers and variations in the physical conditions under which specific sounds occur (Lahiri/Marslen-Wilson 1991: 247). More particularly, speech sounds can be produced at different pitch levels, they may involve different degrees of loudness, they can be varied concerning their individual length, they are influenced by their acoustic/phonetic neighbourhood, etc. Furthermore, different dialects make the identification of the contents of the speech signal specifically difficult. In fact, the degree of variation is constrained only by the articulatory production machinery itself, i.e. by the fundamental properties of the vocal organs.

Like speech, the written signal (logographic or phonographic) is highly variable.[2] Characters can be written using several writing techniques (handwriting, print) and the shapes of the individual characters can be varied considerably (specific character types, specific sizes, different colours, etc.). Figure 37 illustrates the multitude of variants of one single character of the Roman alphabet.

Further sources of variation can be attributed to the use of different sizes and typefaces[3], different writing styles (handwriting versus print), and the possibilities of using case-changes. Table 2 illustrates a number of such variants.

(b) background information and distortions

The input signal rarely occurs in isolation. Speech, for example, is normally surrounded by a good deal of noise, which may even be higher in intensity

Figure 37. Variants of the grapheme "A" (taken from Kurzweil 1990: 241)

Table 2. Word-based orthographical variants

No.	Example	Font/Style
1	`word`	Courier, normal, lower-case
2	`WORD`	Courier, normal, upper-case
3	word	Modern, Sanserif, normal, lower-case
4	Word	Modern, Sanserif, normal, capitalised
5	*word*	Times Roman, italics, lower-case
6	**Word**	Times Roman, bold-face, capitalised
7	`wOrd`	Courier, normal, lower-case, internal case-change
8	WoRd	Times Roman, normal, two internal case-changes

than the speech signal itself. This may lead to distortions of various kinds. Some fragments of the input signal may be missing, others may be disrupted by background noise, etc.

The same problem can be found in the written signal. Characters can touch each other, they can be broken, they can be surrounded by additional material, and so on. Even well-printed documents contain a surprisingly large number of such defects. Figure 38 illustrates them.

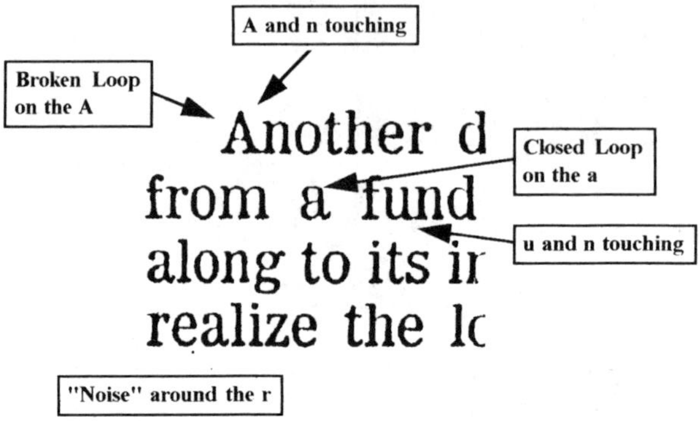

Figure 38. Typical defects in print (after Kurzweil 1990: 240)

(c) redundancies

In many cases the input signal contains a number of overlapping features where one feature would be sufficient for the identification of the input. In speech, for example, the difference between a voiced plosive [b] and its voiceless counterpart [p], is not only characterised by the degree of voicing but also by the intensity of the accompanying friction noise.

In order to cope with these complications of the input signal, enormously complex operations have to be performed at the pre-lexical level. These concern, among others,

- sensory and filtering operations
- the recognition of patterns in the signal
- the identification and isolation of processing units
- the detection and correction of perception errors

The entirety of these operations is referred to as *perception.* It is the first of several processes of *comprehension,* which is generally defined as 'understanding language' and involves several overlapping processes, from perception, via lexical processing, to parsing and conceptual interpretation. Thus, the term 'perception' indicates that at the pre-lexical level no understanding of the input signal is achieved. However, the term 'perception' is sometimes also used for the whole process of understanding, including higher levels of processing. Furthermore, there is disagreement over the extent to which the levels of comprehension are interlinked or dependent on one another (Aitchison 1992: 83). We will use the term 'perception' in its narrow interpretation henceforth, i.e. as the level of processing which is confined to the identification of spoken and written input.

3.1.1. Perceiving the Speech Signal

Speech perception begins with a highly complex, continuously varying, acoustic signal and ends with a representation of the phonological features and segments encoded in that signal. The central task of speech perception is thus to convert the acoustic input into a code on the basis of which lexical processing, in particular word recognition, can be initiated.

Ideally, speech perception involves a one-to-one correspondence between the acoustic signal and the phonological patterns; in other words, we ideally perceive the speech signal as a string of phonemes. Unfortunately, such a correspondence is impossible for various reasons. First, it would exceed the resolution capacity of the auditory system, since too many phonemes per second would have to be analysed by the hearing mechanism. Secondly, phoneme-sized portions, if they can be manifested, are not separated sharply but they are interwoven with each other horizontally. A cross-section of the acoustic signal at a given interval will typically yield information about more than one phoneme. Hence, the auditory system cannot rely on phoneme detection but has to react to much smaller events. These specific events are referred to as *acoustic cues*. Let us illustrate the function of these cues on the basis of vowels.

Vowels can be acoustically characterised by bundles of frequencies and resonances (see below). Since vowels are normally voiced, the vocal folds vibrate, producing a fundamental frequency, generally referred to as F0.[4] This frequency serves as the input to a complicated amplification and resonance system in the vocal tract. As each vowel requires a certain configuration of the articulators (tongue, lips, velum, uvula), a specific acoustic profile emerges, with certain resonance properties, depending on the position of the articulators. This profile consists of a pattern of frequencies produced by the resonance chambers of the vocal tract. Depending on the vowel, these resonance frequencies, or *formants,* may be more or less intensive. They can be displayed on spectrograms, where they occur as dark bundles of energy.[5] The arrangement of formants serves as the basis for the recognition of vowels. Figure 39 illustrates the relationship between the shape of the vocal tract and the frequency values of the most important formants, F1 and F2, and the respective spectrograms for the vowels [i] and [ɑ].

It should be mentioned, though, that the formant pattern of a particular speech sound does not result from the position of the articulators alone, but from the shape and size of the entire vocal tract. Nevertheless, in the case of F1 and F2, it is true that the vertical section of the vocal tract is responsible

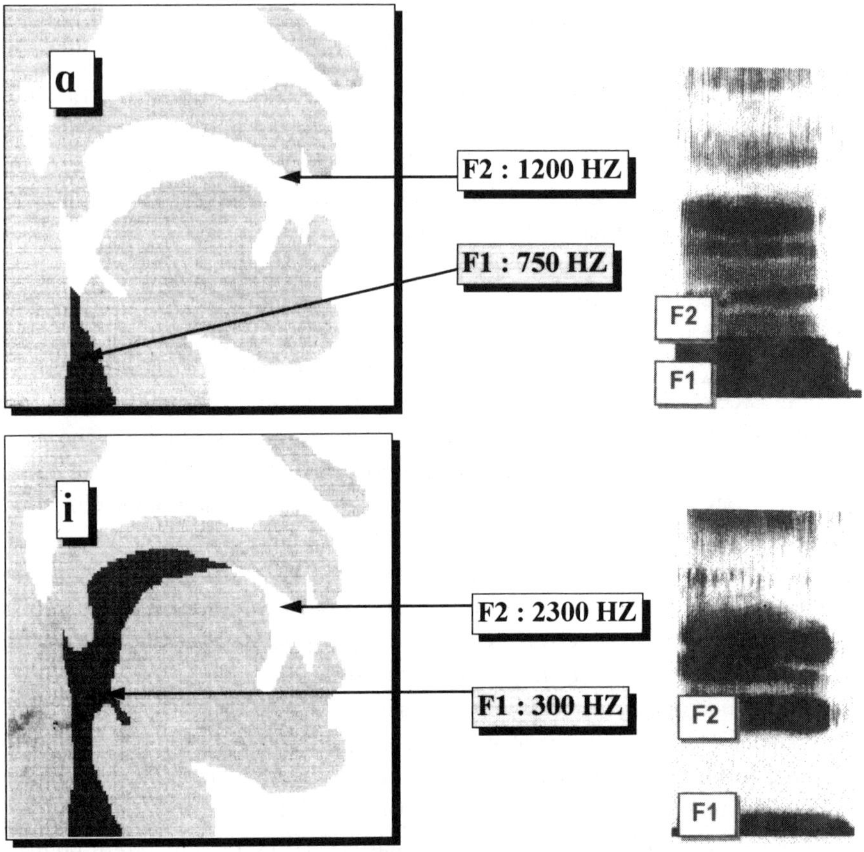

Figure 39. The acoustics of vowels, after Miller (1981: 44); spectrograms from Borden/Harris (1980)

for F1, and the shorter, primarily horizontal section, for F2. Miller (1981: 44) illustrated this relationship between front and back cavity using an artificial model of the vocal tract. Depending on the point of constriction, that is the position where the tongue is close to the palate, and on the lip position, the values of F1 and F2 differ. If the result is a small but open oral front cavity, as in [i], F2 is very high; if the constriction occurs in the back of the mouth and the lips are close together, as in [u], F2 has a low value. Such acoustic defaults can be postulated for each vowel. Needless to say, the frequency values of F1 and F2 are not the only cues for vowels. Additional cues, such as formant amplitude, frequency values of formants other than F1 and F2, or formant band-width, play a crucial role for the identification of vowels.

Like vowels, consonants are perceived on the basis of specific acoustic cues. These concern burst frequencies[6], portions of silence, degree of voicing, etc. An overview of the main acoustic cues for the perception of speech sounds can be found in Pickett (1980: 170ff).

Knowing that speech is perceived on the basis of specific acoustic cues, one could assume that each speech sound can be characterised by a collection of such cues. However, two central problems emerge, inter-speaker variation and the influence of the acoustic environment.

(a) inter-speaker variation

That vowels are discriminated primarily on the basis of their formant structure is undisputed. Yet, there are enormous physiological differences across speakers, particularly between men, women and children, resulting in different formant frequencies. Consider, for example, the different lengths and shapes of the vocal tracts of speakers, which cause the fundamental frequency to vary. Minute changes of the fundamental frequency, which serves as an input to the entire system, may alter the resulting formant pattern of a vowel, and, secondly, slight positional and configurational variations of the articulators may lead to slight deviations from the standard formant pattern. In fact, all speakers are capable of an infinity of such modifications.

(b) the acoustic context

Speech sounds do not occur in isolation. Vowels, for example, are normally embedded within a skeleton of consonants, to form syllables. However, these consonants influence the vocalic formant patterns, leading to variations of F1 and F2. In other words, the acoustic cues of speech sounds cannot be defined in isolation. Vowels do not have a fixed formant pattern but are influenced by their environment; consonants, in turn, interact with the acoustic properties of vowels. Hence, the acoustic definition of vowels in terms of formant defaults alone misses the point, since formants are variable, depending on the environment.

Taking into account these two sources of variation, we would have to assert an infinity of acoustic patterns for each speech sound. Considering the neural memory capacity available, however, we would soon reach our storage limits. Hence, our perceptual mechanism cannot rely only on specific patterns of acoustic cues but must also use a specific perceptual strategy.

Theoretically, one could assume a speech perception mechanism which operates in a continuous mode, capable of drawing fine distinctions between frequency values, duration times, etc. However, numerous experimental results suggest that this is not the case and that many speech sounds are perceived in a discontinuous or categorical manner.

This phenomenon of *categorical perception* has long been known. Its central idea is that the speech perception mechanism is especially sensitive for specific cues in the speech. These cues are not perceived along a continuum but as fixed categories. Let us illustrate this phenomenon on the basis of the acoustic cue for place of articulation (F2-transition), and for the voiced-voiceless distinction, *Voice Onset Time* (VOT).

(a) F2-transition

The formant pattern of vowels in isolation differs enormously from that of vowels embedded in a consonantal context. If a consonant precedes a vowel, this leads to a transition of F1 and F2. While the transition of F1 is difficult to define for different consonants, the transition of F2 seems to follow certain patterns. In order to show such patterns, phonetic recognition experiments are performed where human subjects are confronted with clusters such as [bɑ], [dɑ] and [gɑ]. These clusters are generated using a speech synthesiser, where all acoustic properties can be controlled by the experimenter. For example, the transition from [bɑ] to [dɑ] and from [dɑ] to [gɑ] can be gradually altered, keeping all acoustic aspects stable except one property which the experimenter feels to be important for the experiment. In the case of our consonant vowel clusters, it has been found that a variation of F2 will lead to the perception of a different consonant. Figure 40 illustrates the experimental technique and the gradual shift of F2 from a low to a high value.

Thus, the frequency value of F2 for [ɑ] cannot be treated in isolation, but the preceding consonant has to be considered as well. If the vowel [ɑ] is preceded by the labial consonant [b], F2 emerges from a low-frequency region; if the velar consonant [g] precedes, F2 originates in a high-frequency region. The question arises whether we perceive the differences between [b], [d], and [g] in a continuous fashion, or whether we are sensitive to specific frequency values, where we can discriminate [b] from [d], and [d] from [g].

When listeners are confronted with the synthesised clusters [bɑ], [dɑ] and [gɑ], as shown in figure 40, in random order, they can identify the stimuli with great consistency. However, in a few cases (stimuli 4 and 5 and stimuli 9 and 10), subjects express some uncertainty. These stimuli represent the borderlines between labial [b] and alveolar [d], on the one hand, and between alveolar [d] and velar [g], on the other (Liberman, et al.; 1957). In an additional discrimination test, one can present the listener with pairs of synthesised consonant-vowel clusters, e.g. [bɑ] and [dɑ], and a third cluster, which is identical either with the first or with the second. The subject's task is to find out with which cluster the third stimulus is identical. The identification ability depends, of course, on the difference between stimulus 1 and stimulus 2. If they are different (e.g. stimuli 1 and 8 in figure 40), then no difficulties should emerge in relating stimulus 3 to either of them. In cases of great similarity (e.g., stimuli 9 and 10 in figure 40), however, all three stimuli will sound the same and the discrimination ability is poor.

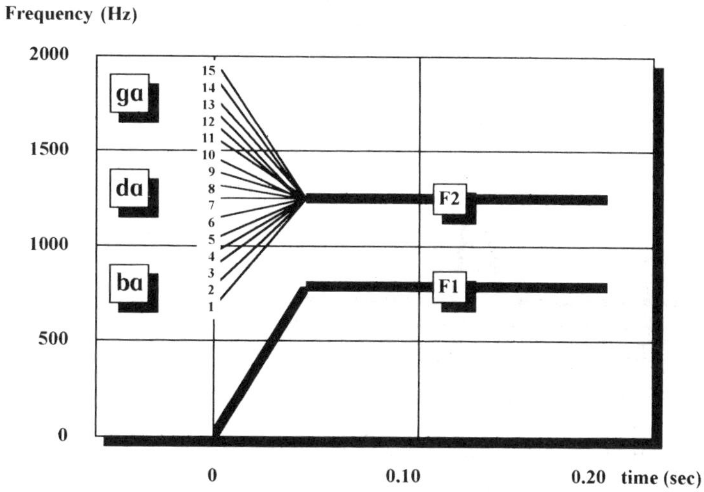

Figure 40. F2-transition in speech synthesis (after Miller 1981: 68)

To summarise, stimuli which belong to different categories are identified best, whereas identification is poor among those stimuli identified as belonging to the same category. In other words, the listener is unable to hear the acoustic differences among stimuli that he identifies as belonging to the same category, but, if two stimuli belong to different categories, listeners can discriminate very well. Thus, perception does not seem to rely on continuous information but on categories, i.e. the phenomenon of categorical perception.

(b) Voice Onset Time (VOT)

Similar results can be obtained by varying the Voice Onset Time that allows listeners to discriminate between clusters such as [bɑ] and [pɑ]. Again, listeners are presented with synthesised clusters and are asked to identify the stimuli. Keeping all acoustic properties stable, one can start off with [bɑ] and delay the initial portion of voicing in small steps, to arrive at [pɑ].

The results obtained are similar to the F2-transition experiment. Once again, small differences in onset time are not perceived. Within a category, all onset times sound alike, whereas, at category boundaries (in this case approximately at 0.03 seconds), small differences are heard. Figure 41 illustrates the results.

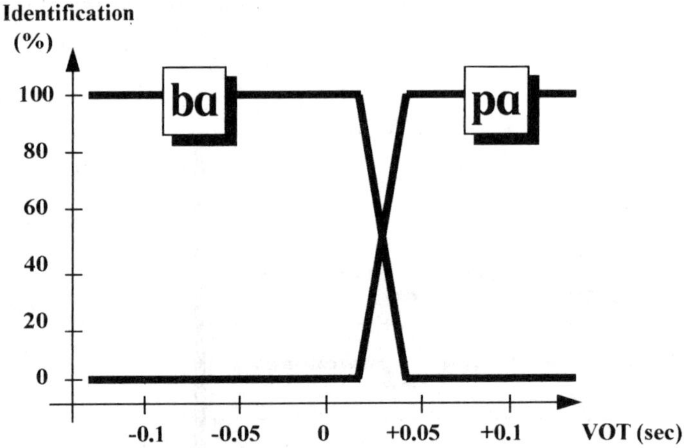

Figure 41. The perception of VOT

VOT, then, is another crucial factor in speech perception. Like the transition of F2, a gradual delay of VOT does not lead to a differentiation between voiced and voiceless consonants; rather, a categorical value of 0.03 seconds serves as the key factor.[7] If VOT is less than 0.03 seconds, the consonant is heard as voiced, if VOT is more than 0.03 seconds, the consonant is perceived as voiceless.

The phenomenon of categorical perception, which some scientists believe to be innate (Miller 1981: 69), supports the idea that there must be some specialised mechanism for the perception of speech. However, there are also categorical perceptual effects in non-speech as well as continuous low-level processes in speech. The difference between the fricatives [fɑ], [θɑ], [sɑ], and [ʃɑ], for example, is mainly a matter of the frequency of noise and not one of categorical perception (Garman 1990: 199). Also phonemes have allophones with different phonetic properties in different phonetic contexts. Take, for example, the degree of aspiration in the realisation of /t/ in the following contexts: *tan, cat, atlas, batting.* Recently it has been suggested that such allophonic variation be used as an indicator for the position of a phone in the phonetic string (Church 1987a: 55ff).

To sum up, a number of specific sub-phonemic cues, some of which are perceived categorically, constitute the basis for speech perception. On the basis of these cues, we convert the acoustic input into a phonological representation. In other words, the result of speech perception is a string of phonetic patterns that can be forwarded to higher levels of analysis.[8]

3.1.2. Perceiving the Written Signal [9]

The examples presented in figure 37, table 2, and figure 38 suggest even greater variations in written signals than in speech signals. While the nature of the speech signal is highly constrained by the articulatory production machinery, the production of written language can be considered to be much more flexible. From this observation we can conclude that categorical perceptual differences, such as VOT or F2 transition, which result from the specific articulatory limitations of the speech production mechanism, have no equivalent in written language. Hence, abstracting invariant forms from the various realisations of a letter or letter combinations is quite different from the equivalent problem with the speech signal (Henderson 1982: 221). This also means that the analogy between phonemes and allophones, on the one hand, and graphemes and allographs, on the other, is misleading.

Despite the variability of the written signal, the human visual recognition system is capable of correctly identifying written language with great precision. How is this achieved? Even though there are many aspects of visual perception that are not yet understood, some understanding of the processes central to human vision has been achieved. These insights come from psycholinguistic studies, on the one hand, and from studies into computer vision, on the other.

Human vision is an even more complex process than listening. This is due to the different neuro-physiological foundations of the systems underlying both processes. While the auditory system is essentially a serial device, the eye accepts information in parallel (Foss/Hakes 1978: 327). Parallel in this sense means that the visual information is not spread out over time, but that much of the information is available at one instant. The acoustic signal, by contrast, is spread out over time, so that at any given time interval only a fraction of the signal is available for further analysis. There are many aspects of visual perception that are not yet understood; however, two aspects seem to be central to the process of human vision (Kurzweil

1990: 225ff). First, visual data generally undergoes a process of filtering. Whenever we perceive a visual stimulus, we need to smooth the data so that small defects are ignored. Second, changes in the visual information are of paramount importance. These two observations remind us of the basic principles of acoustic perception, where the signal is filtered to cope with variations and distortions, and where changes, for example in VOT or formant transitions, receive a high degree of attention. Because of this similarity, it is not surprising that in vision, just as in speech perception, the recognition of patterns in the sensory signal is assumed to be fundamental.

The generation of patterns from visual input is essentially a process of edge and depth detection and the building of hypotheses on the basis of visual knowledge. Whenever a visual signal is processed, the visual system picks up the image with a system of specialised cells. After a filtering process, the two images, one recorded with each eye, are fused. Because of the spatial difference between the eyes, we can detect depth, and we can determine the relative distance between objects. Once the edges of the objects are detected, an iconic representation or pattern is built, which is eventually mapped on to more general visual frames. In this last process a great deal of general knowledge influenced by expectation is used. Thus, massive parallel processing, especially during the first phases of visual analysis, is fundamental for visual perception.

While in most cases visual perception involves three-dimensional input, reading, i.e. the analysis of written language, primarily uses two-dimensional input. Although there are cases where three-dimensional characters have to be identified, for example in outdoor advertising, these are examples of minor importance. Moreover, unlike general visual images, characters have a highly conventional structure: they are normally perceived in their entirety, they do not move, they do not have other objects lying on top of them, nor do they change during the perception process. They consist of a limited number of dark-light patterns in terms of lines and edges.

It has long been known that the human perceptual system makes use of specific perceptual units in the analysis of written language. In phonographic alphabetic writing systems, words are composed of a small set of basic visual elements, the graphemes. Hence, it is legitimate to ask whether the perceptual analysis of written language in these languages is not based, in some sense, upon letter recognition. Such a *letter-mediated approach* would be enormously economical, since the recognition device would have to rely on a limited set of perceptual patterns. Alternatively, one could assume a *holistic approach,* where elementary visual features are employed to address the lexicon directly.

3.1.2.1. The Holistic Approach

A holistic strategy of perceiving the written signal does not rely on letters as mediators between the visual information and recognition; rather, it says that the information uptake by-passes the level of letter identification and that the extracted features are directly mapped on to the stored pattern descriptions for individual words (Henderson 1982: 230). In other words, the written form of a lexical entry is stored as a complex pattern, which can be conceived of as a word-shape representing the individual characters within it, or, even more complexly, in terms of its general spatial orientation. The stored word forms correspond to their perceptual counterparts, which are characterisable on the basis of their subsegmental properties. The process of written word recognition is, then, a process identical with general visual perception. The only difference is the two-dimensional nature of the written signal.

Such a conception of holistic word representation makes sense if we consider logographic writing systems, where characters represent words. However, even alphabetic writing systems make use of a large number of words that are invariable and are written in the same way whenever they occur. Words used in the domain of public relations and advertisement are good cases in point (figure 42). Such words have distinct envelopes, are highly logographic in character, i.e. they can hardly be decomposed into their individual letters, and are thus recognised as holistic patterns.[10]

Figure 42. Words as visual patterns

The holistic view raises the question as to what type of whole-word units or global features can be extracted from the visual input.

(a) word envelope cues

In the simplest case the entire word is employed as a perceptual cue. This overall visual shape is called *word envelope.*

(b) transgraphemic features

A second possibility postulates holistic patterns that expand over several letters. Typical examples of such patterns can be found in print defects, where due to the use of specific fonts or different degrees of saturation, two or more adjacent letters touch each other (see figure 38).

According to Henderson (1982: 232ff) both global features are problematic to a considerable degree. The main source of experimental evidence comes from studies into the *word superiority effect,* that is the superior perceptibility of words compared with non-words or single letters. In other words, the presence of a single printed letter in a brief display is easier to determine when the letter is presented within the context of a word than in isolation (Feldman/Ballard 1982: 207).

If word envelope cues or transgraphemic features play a role in the perception of written information, two effects should be established experimentally. First, both global cues should constitute a source of information to discriminate between words and non-words,[11] and, secondly, font or case-changes within words (see No. 7/8 in table 2) should disrupt the perceptual process because the resulting contours would be less familiar. It has been shown that it is not as simple as that. The disruption of perception involving words with case-changes, for example, can be observed. However, this effect also occurs with regular non-words, such as *mav/MaV/mAV,* for which no stored patterns exist (Henderson 1982: 237). This equal behaviour of words and non-words, involving mutilations of their visual configuration, is fatal for the holistic approach to written word recognition.

Further problems concern the processing of orthographical variants, which arise through morphological processes. Assuming a minimal listing hypothesis for the conception of the lexicon (see section 2.4.), the processing of orthographical variants as holistic patterns should be problematic, since the input may vary considerably from the assumed stored pattern. Variants such as *dying, carries,* and *hating* illustrate this point. Their underlying patterns *die, carry,* and *hate* can only serve as a general guideline for their identification; only by reference to higher levels of linguistic processing can the exact analysis be carried out. This in turn means that the holistic view presupposes an interaction between pre-lexical and lexical processing, or that a full listing hypothesis receives further support.

3.1.2.2. The Letter-Mediated Approach

The possibility of storing words as graphological structures can only apply to those languages that employ a phonographic writing system, and to those speakers of these languages who can write, hence, to a minority of all cases. Furthermore, if words are stored as graphological structures, then the graphological structure must be somehow related to the phonological structure, since phonographic writing systems by nature establish a sound-symbol relationship. However, the graphological specification cannot be accessible during pre-lexical processes, since it is part of the lexical specification of an entry itself. A possible solution to this dilemma is the assumption of a processing system where several levels operate in parallel and allow top-town interaction. On the basis of such a model, one could retrieve the graphological information of an item by means of top-down interaction between pre-lexical and lexical processing. In a strictly serial model, by contrast, we have access to the graphological representation only after a word has been identified on the basis of its visual properties.

In assuming a model that mediates between visual information and recognised structure by means of letters, we can speculate whether the mediation process is based on physical letter forms or on abstract graphemes. Even though experimental evidence is not conclusive (Henderson 1982: 275), it seems that both representations are employed. In building such representations, two sources of information interact: information of a graphotactic kind, that is the subject's knowledge of the position of letters to identify, and knowledge about the geometrical shapes of the individual letters.

Whatever model we assume, we do not know very much about the representation format of the graphological forms in terms of graphemes at present. By analogy with the non-linear presentation of the phonological specification of lexical entries, we can assume a similar multi-layered model for graphological information, consisting of a syllabic, a skeletal, and a segmental tier.

3.1.2.3. The Computational Approach

Recently, new insights from studies into computer vision have enriched our understanding of visual perception. The central aim of this branch of artificial intelligence is to study human strategies of visual pattern recognition in order to develop practical computer applications, such as robotic vision systems. One branch of computer vision which deserves special mention in our context is concerned with the development of machines capable of reading printed information. Even though the analysis of hand-written characters is possible, the degree of variation across humans is too high to obtain safe results using machines.[12]

A reading machine consists of a camera or a scanner that records a portion of written text, and an Optical Character Recognition (OCR) component that recognises the characters and extracts the graphological information.

Research into computer vision has provided evidence that, as in speech perception, the signal first undergoes a process of clearance, and, secondly, the visual perception mechanism looks for specific low-level cues. What are these cues, then, in OCR? Let us illustrate the central assumptions on the basis of some selected printed (not hand-written) characters of the Roman alphabet.[13]

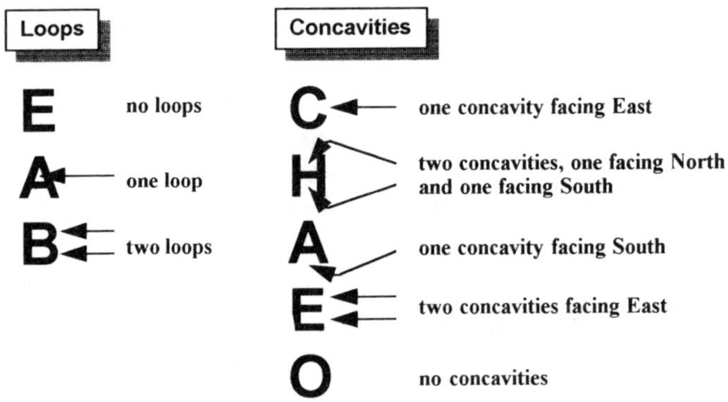

Figure 43. Cues in written language

The general assumption in OCR research is that the characters of the Roman alphabetic system can be identified on the basis of a number of geometrical cues. One such cue, for example, concerns loops, that is areas of white that are totally surrounded by black. Another cue deals with concavities, i.e. with concave regions facing in a certain direction. Figure 43 illustrates these cues on the basis of some selected Roman Sanserif characters.

Thus, two cues, the number of loops and the direction of concavities, are central for the identification of Roman Sanserif characters. In a real system, however, the classification of characters is much more complicated than suggested. Clearly, two cues alone are not sufficient for the process of OCR. Further cues concern the position of horizontal and vertical lines, the shape of edges, and so on. In addition to this, defects such as shown in figure 38 complicate the recognition process. Especially, characters that are not neatly separated from each other by spaces, or characters whose typical features are distorted, for example by bold face print, confront the recognition system with enormous problems. A strategy of recognising such patterns incorporates transgraphemic or even word envelope patterns, i.e. holistic patterns as outlined in section 3.1.2.1.

Nevertheless, the general conception should be clear. By a combination of specific cues, the characters of the Roman alphabet can be identified. Table 3 illustrates the actual values of the two cues discussed for the identification of the first eight upper-case Sanserif characters of the Roman alphabet.

Table 3.. Cues for Roman characters

Character	Loops	Concavities
A	1	South
B	2	East
C	0	East
D	1	none
E	0	East, East
F	0	East
G	0	East, North
H	0	North, South

To summarise, modern OCR-systems combine the insights derived from studies into human visual perception. They rely heavily on low-level features to detect the relevant graphemes; at the same time, they make use of holistic patterns such as transgraphemic features or word envelope shapes.

3.1.3. The Nature of the Input Signal; a Summary

The input signal, whether spoken or written, is extremely complex. Aspects such as variation, distortion, background information, and redundancy make the perception process an enormously complex enterprise. Nevertheless, we succeed in recognising the input with great precision and ease.

In speech perception, it seems, we rely on a number of acoustic spectral cues, of which some are perceived categorically while others are processed in a non-categorical or continuous fashion. Additionally, aspects of allophonic variation as suggested by Church (1987a) may also contribute to the perception of the speech signal. Phonemes do not play a major role in the analysis of speech. Only in computational models of speech recognition are phonemes, and even combinations of them, of major importance.

Even though the nature of visual perception is different from speech, it also involves the identification of a number of basic patterns. These concern sub-graphemic geometrical aspects, such as curve and edge identification, as well as larger units. Especially in the case of orthographical defects and specific word shapes, it seems likely that higher patterns such as trans-graphemic properties and word envelopes are employed in the perceptual process.

In the following sections we discuss the most influential theories of perceiving speech and written information.

3.2. Theories of Speech Perception

Every model of speech perception has an input and an output and a number of intermediate processing levels. Each level also includes an input and an output and contains a number of rules that manipulate the input. Many of these rules are inaccessible to direct exploration. For this reason, the internal structure of speech perception models is speculative, or it emerged from rather fragmentary experimental studies of the following kind (Lobacz 1984: 11):

- the identification of phonemes in monosyllabic nonsense words
- the use of synthesised stimuli
- the use of distorted stimuli
- the study of pathological cases
- the study of retention and recall of preselected syllables or lexemes
- the study of language acquisition

In the construction of a model of speech perception we are confronted with two general options:

- serial vs. parallel
- active vs. passive

While a serial model of speech processing assumes a strict hierarchy of processing levels, a parallel model asserts that some, or even most operations are carried out in parallel. Since today's models rely on massive parallelism, strictly serial models will be ignored by and large.

The second choice concerns the process of matching the input against one's own knowledge. Active and passive theories have in common that they consider speech perception as a process which is generally sensory in character. The message is sensed and filtered before further operations are triggered. Also, both theories involve some sort of mapping process where the relevant acoustic information is mapped on to the acoustic-phonetic features of the language. The primary difference between active and passive theories of speech perception is in their reference to speech production. While active theories posit a working relationship between perception and production, where the result of the acoustic analysis is constantly matched against one's own production model, passive theories are exclusively sensory and model perception and production as independent of each other. In passive theories, the analysis primarily consists in matching the input against stored prototypes.

Additional models postulate a certain degree of sensitivity to specific acoustic aspects or postulate a correlation between vocal tract characteristics and acoustic changes. Figure 44 provides an overview of the most influential models of speech perception.

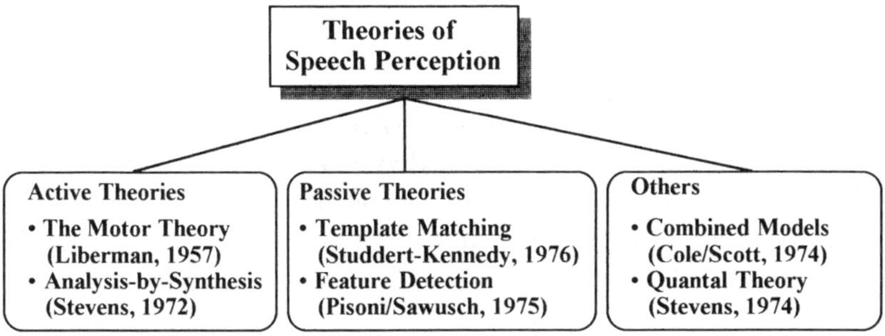

Figure 44. Theories of speech perception

3.2.1. Active Theories of Speech Perception [14]

Active theories of speech perception emphasise the role of low-level knowledge in the analysis of the speech signal, i.e. articulatory knowledge, knowledge of vocal tract outputs, and knowledge of the influence of the phonetic context. In other words, the hearer "acts" not only when he produces a linguistic signal, but also when he receives it (Lobacz 1984: 27). The central assumption of active theories is that the process of speech perception involves some sort of speech production. The reference to speech production can be of a physiological kind, where the listener constantly refers to his articulatory knowledge, or it can be of an auditory kind, where the listener makes use of an auditory model of his own speech production. The two possibilities have resulted in distinct active theories of speech perception.

Active theories were developed from efforts to find a one-to-one correspondence between phonemes and the acoustic signal. They have been strongly influenced by the problem of the complex relationship between acoustic cues and perceived phonemes, and by the problem of segmenting the speech wave into higher linguistic units, e.g. into syllables or words.

As pointed out in section 3.1.1., the speech signal contains a certain number of acoustic cues; however, they do not correspond to one phoneme or to specific classes of phonemes. Even the often cited examples of categorically perceived cues such as F2-transition, Voice Onset Time, or the relationship between F1 and F2 are problematic in this respect. Let us reconsider the phenomenon of F2-transition to illustrate this point. The difference between [di], [dɑ], and [du] is perceived on the basis of the origin of F2 and the corresponding burst frequency. Yet, the same F2-transition that characterises [d] before vowels is employed to identify the consonants in consonant-vowel clusters such as [pi], [kɑ], or [ku]. Hence, discrete acoustic events cannot be associated with separate phonemes, for different acoustic events can be perceived as the same phoneme, and the same acoustic event may result in the perception of different phonemes (Borden/Harris 1980: 205). Further arguments against such a one-to-one correspondence were posited in section 3.1.1., where we mentioned that such a direct mapping would exceed the resolution capacity of the auditory system, and that the horizontal overlap of acoustic features contradicts such a relationship between acoustic events and phonemes.

Furthermore, acoustic cues do not occur in isolation but are conditioned by the context and transmitted in parallel. For example, the distinction between [dɑ] and [kɑ] is not only drawn on the basis of the transition of F2 but also by the preceding portion of Voice Onset Time. The parallel occurrence of acoustic cues, their high degree of encodedness in the speech signal, and the fact that acoustic cues constitute only one aspect of the enormously complex process of speech perception suggest that a direct mapping of the acoustic signal to phonemes or other linguistic units is impossible. Hence, speech perception is not a direct process of translating acoustic information to phonemes but a process that employs a mechanism that mediates between the two. According to the active theories of speech perception, the listener's speech production competence serves as the mediator.

Speech perception theories do not allow rigorous experimental testing. Nevertheless, a number of arguments in favour of active theories have emerged. One of the strongest arguments is their ability to explain the phenomenon of categorical perception. As pointed out above, the perception of certain speech sounds is discontinuous, despite an enormous variation of the acoustic signal. Interestingly, the corresponding articulation is also discontinuous. Even though the acoustic cues can be varied along a continuum, which corresponds to various articulatory movements, it turns out that, in actual speech, articulation is often accomplished by discontinuous or categorically different articulatory movements. Bilabial plosives such as [b] and [p], for example, are produced by an oral closure, and alveolar plosives such as such as [d] and [t] by a front closure using the tip of the tongue (Liberman et al. 1967). Hence, we can explain the categorical perception of these sounds by assuming that they are perceived by reference to their production, which itself is categorical.

Another argument in favour of active theories of speech perception is *coarticulation.* This is a phenomenon of speech production where the articulation of adjacent speech sounds overlaps (Ladefoged 1975: 48ff). Take, for example, the realisation of the phoneme /k/ in *key* as compared with *caw.* In both cases, the articulation of the initial consonant is highly influenced by the subsequent vowel. In *key* the place of articulation is much farther forward than in *caw,* where the [k] is produced at the back of the mouth fairly low down on the soft palate. Also, the [k] in *caw* is accompanied by a considerable amount of lip rounding, whereas the [k] in *key* is produced with spread lips. In other words, long before its actual production we anticipate the articulatory characteristics of the vowel in consonant-vowel clusters. This phenomenon is known as *anticipatory coarticulation.* According to active theories, coarticulation is not only confined to speech production, but it is also exploited in speech perception. The initial segments of words such as *key/caw* are not only specified by their burst frequency and their Voice Onset Time, but they also anticipate the following speech sound. By referring to their own production, listeners are capable of performing this anticipation. Experimental evidence comes from shadowing tasks, where shadowers start before they have heard the stimulus in its entirety (Pickett 1980: 195).

Active theories have had a considerable influence on research in speech perception. Two models deserve special attention:

- the motor theory of speech perception, Haskins Laboratories
- the analysis-by-synthesis model, Massachusetts Institute of Technology

While the motor theory defines speech perception by reference to articulatory patterns, the analysis-by-synthesis model makes reference to neurally generated auditory patterns.

(a) The motor theory of speech perception

The *motor theory* goes back to Liberman and his colleagues, who undertook extensive research into speech perception from the 1950s onwards. Essentially, the motor theory claims that the listener's articulatory knowledge is employed to mediate between the acoustic input and the phonological analysis. The basic idea is that somewhere in the nervous system the neural signals corresponding to the sensory input are mapped on to internally generated neural signals that would be the result of the articulation of the sensory input (Moore 1977: 224). Early versions of the motor theory (e.g. Liberman et al. 1957) assumed that the patterns which are internally generated by the listener are produced as covert articulations. In later versions, this view was given up, since there is evidence that speech can be perceived without any measurable articulatory response on the part of the listener. In the 1963 version of the motor theory, Liberman et al. suggested that speech perception is performed by reference to the respective neural commands rather than by covert articulatory movements.

The following arguments led Liberman et al. (1967) to the assumption that speech perception proceeds via production. First, they claimed that every listener is also a speaker and it seems unlikely to assume two separate processes, one for encoding speech and one for decoding it. More economically, one could assume that there is only one process, with an appropriate link between sensory and motor components. A second argument comes from observations of muscular activities from the speech musculature. These have resulted in the assumption that speech perception is much more closely related to the patterns produced by articulatory processes than to the acoustic signals that produce them.

(b) The analysis-by-synthesis theory of speech perception

Another theory that seeks to explain speech perception in the face of so few invariant acoustic cues that lead to phonemes is the *analysis-by-synthesis theory*. This model goes back to Stevens (1972). Even though it can be considered as a more detailed and slightly modified form of the motor theory, there are differences. According to this model, the patterns generated by neural activity are not only subject to preliminary analysis, but they are also held in a temporary store from where they can be passed on to higher levels of analysis. Furthermore, the reference to the listener's production system is not articulatory but auditory. The analysis-by-synthesis theory relies on a system of matching where the input is compared with an auditory pattern generated by the listener's production system. Hence, this theory is less physiological than the motor theory. Also, the analysis-by-synthesis model allows interaction with other levels of comprehension in such a way that information about the phonological, syntactic, and semantic properties of the utterance enters into determining the final phonological representation of what is heard (Foss/Hakes 1978: 94). Basically, there are two versions of the analysis-by-synthesis model. In Stevens' original version the emphasis lay on the phonetic processing of the information, i.e. the reference to the production model was made in terms of phonetic and acoustic aspects. Other versions of the analysis-by-synthesis model, for example Chomsky/Halle (1968), Klatt (1979), included phonological knowledge or even higher level knowledge in the synthesis process that evaluates the nature of what was heard.

Figure 45 summarises the general conception of an active theory of speech perception, where the reference to the production system is simply labelled as "neural pattern". Note that, in the case of an unsuccessful match between the auditory pattern and the neural pattern, the analysis is carried out again, or, and this can hardly be illustrated, the interlocutor is asked to repeat:

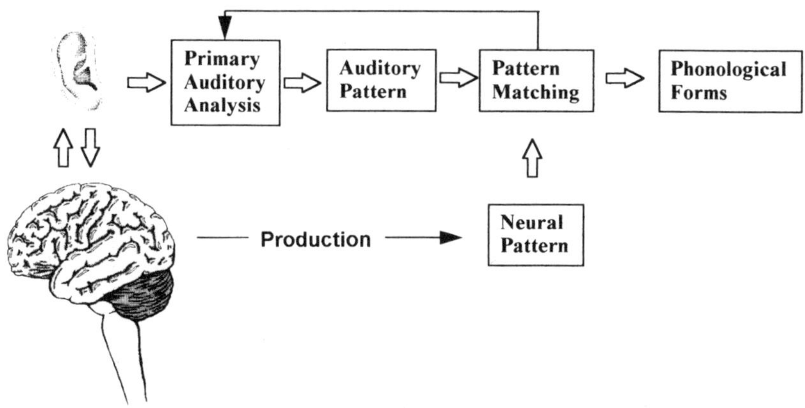

Figure 45. The architecture of active theories of speech perception

Both active theories of speech perception outlined hold much promise but also raise numerous questions. Basically, they rely on a comparison of neural patterns. One pattern is the result of the acoustic analysis, the other is encoded as a set of neural commands which would result in the articulation of a phoneme or a larger unit (motor theory), or it is some kind of stored representation corresponding to the acoustic pattern (analysis-by-synthesis).

How these patterns are generated by the brain and how they are compared is difficult to explain. In addition to this, all arguments proposed in favour of active theories can also be interpreted against them.

Categorical perception, for example, which is normally taken as an argument for active theories of speech perception, can also be explained on different grounds. First, categorical perception is not confined to speech (Foss/Hakes 1978: 82ff). Also, categorical perception can be affected by the degree of encodedness, that is by the degree of overlap of acoustic cues in speech sounds. Consonants, for example, are much more encoded than vowels, because several acoustic cues can be relevant for their identification. Hence, each individual cue can be assumed to receive relatively little attention in memory. Vowels, by contrast, are relatively unencoded. Thus, each of their acoustic cues can be retained in memory for a much longer time, so that additional analyses can be made. Perhaps one of the most crucial pieces of evidence against active theories has been presented by Lenneberg (1962). He described a case of a patient with an organic defect that prevented him from acquiring the motor skills necessary for speaking. Nevertheless, the patient could understand speech perfectly well. According to the active theories, which refer to the listener's speech production ability, such a case should be impossible. Another argument posited against active theories can be taken from studies into language acquisition that have shown that children understand spoken language before they can speak. Hence, they cannot rely on any articulatory knowledge. Of course, modern versions of active theories assume that it is not the articulatory process itself that is the mediator but the neural commands corresponding to it. Hence, in theory, it is not necessary for a listener to speak.

To sum up, all arguments put forward in favour of active theories of speech perception can be interpreted in other ways, allowing an alternative model of speech perception.

3.2.2. Passive Theories of Speech Perception

Passive theories of speech perception put much more emphasis on the sensory side of the perceptual process and relegate the role of speech production to a minor, if not completely negligible role. This does not imply that reference to production does not occur at all, but that it does so only under specific circumstances, when the perceptual task is extremely difficult, as, for example, in phonetic transcription tasks. Two influential passive models of speech perception have emerged:

- the theory of template matching
- the theory of feature detectors

Both models postulate the use of stored neural patterns in the analysis of speech, which are possibly innate. According to the theory of template matching, these patterns are rudimentary at birth and are tuned to the requirements of language processing as language is acquired. The theory of feature detectors presupposes specialised feature detectors realised by neural receptors, which generate the auditory pattern necessary for higher levels of analysis.

(a) the theory of template matching

A *template* can be defined as a rudimentary pattern which serves as the basis for more detailed construction processes.[15] The input to a template matching system is assumed to be segmental and the range of variations will be stored as fixed patterns. The realisation of /k/, for example, is hypothesised as a pattern of the form X[k]Y, where X and Y are variables ranging over the whole class of preceding and following elements, including a zero realisation in the case of initial and final /k/ (Garman 1990: 226).

The theory of template matching emerged from experimental work in the analysis of bird song. It was found that birds are born with a general ability or template of song characteristic for their species. This ability is refined as they grow older. According to the propagators of this theory, human infants proceed similarly during the process of language acquisition. They are born with a number of templates tuned to the requirements of speech. These templates are adapted to the requirements of speech during the acquisition process. Adult speakers have at their disposal a system of elaborate templates which are matched with the incoming signal and are used to translate it to phonetic structures (phonemes, syllables, words). The phenomenon of coarticulation can be neglected in a theory of template matching, since phones that require coarticulation are stored among the set of templates. The main problem for a template matching theory, however, is the amount of storage capacity required for the enormously high number of patterns.

(b) the theory of feature detectors

That the speech signal is often not sufficiently distinct to allow its properties to be unambiguously identified has been stated more than once. In normal fluent speech various parts of the incoming signal are often obscured. Syllables are reduced, formant structures lack clarity, and frequency intensities are insufficient. Interestingly, the process of identifying the phonological features encoded in the speech signal is not affected by any variability in the signal. As in print, certain features can be distorted or even be absent; yet, if a sufficient amount of information can be collected, the identification process can proceed.

Research on vision has revealed so-called *feature detectors* in the form of special neural receptors, for example, one for horizontal lines, one for vertical lines, etc. By analogy, one can assume a number of such feature detectors for the analysis of speech. There is some controversy about the exact nature of these detectors. Obviously, one group of detectors must be responsible for sub-phonemic acoustic stimuli, for example, one for F2-transitions, one for Voice Onset Time, and so on. Another group of detectors may concern linguistic-phonetic parameters such as place and manner of articulation. Pisoni/Sawush (1975) suggest a combination of both detector systems. At the lowest level, a system of acoustic-phonetic feature detectors processes the variant and invariant acoustic cues in the signal; at a second level, the results of stage one are interpreted in terms of distinctive phonetic features. The intermediate analysis results are stored in short-term memory, from where they are retrieved on request.

Feature detectors, whatever their exact nature, are informationally encapsulated. They respond to specific properties of a stimulus, but remain unaffected by others. Their processing units satisfy the requirements of the connectionist framework (see section 1.6.). Hence, it is not surprising that feature detector models are essentially connectionist.

According to Pisoni/Sawusch (1975), there are two types of feature detector, acoustic and phonetic. Acoustic feature detectors perform a preliminary analysis of the input and map their results on to a second system, the phonetic feature detectors. The overall result of the analysis is a rough feature matrix which can be forwarded to lexical processing.

Meanwhile, experimental evidence has been collected to support the existence of feature detectors. It comes from experiments applying a method of *selective adaptation* where presumed feature detectors are fatigued due to a repeated presentation of acoustic cues (Foss/Hakes 1978: 90ff; Lobacz 1984: 53).

Last but not least, the theory of feature detectors claims that humans possess an innate linguistic capacity in the form of special neural receptors that are tuned to universal distinctive features (Borden/Harris 1980: 207). Such arguments are not only in line with findings from studies of visual perception, but are also in agreement with general assumptions about the innate character of basic linguistic capacity in humans. The bulk of evidence for these assumptions comes from studies of infant speech perception. It has been found that infants as young as one month react to speech stimuli like adults and can discriminate the acoustic cues of voicing and place of articulation of consonants (Pickett 1980: 201). It seems that the theory of feature detectors is the most promising of the models of speech perception (see also section 3.4.).

The architecture of passive theories of speech perception can be outlined as in figure 46. As in active theories, an auditory pattern is generated from the incoming signal. However, this pattern does not emerge by reference to the speech production system, but it stems from a specialised recognition device which is realised either by stored templates or by a collection of feature detectors.

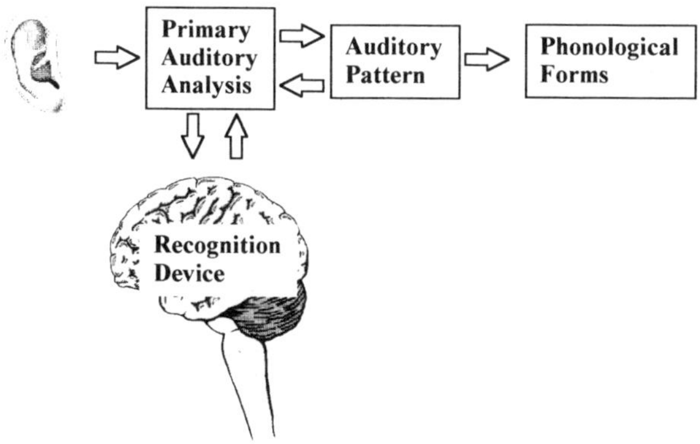

Figure 46. The architecture of passive theories of speech perception

3.2.3. Speech Perception; a Summary

Even though active and passive theories of speech perception have been most influential, there are alternative views. Cole/Scott (1974), for example, argued for a combination of active and passive theories of speech perception. They postulated a model where perception is guided by invariant cues and by cues which are conditioned by the phonetic environment (e.g. formant transitions). In addition to this, they suggested a third aspect employed in speech perception, the waveform envelope, which gives us information about fluctuations in amplitude as a function of time.[16] There is evidence that the waveform envelope, over and above its importance in determining non-segmental features of speech, provides information about segmental aspects. In other words, time/amplitude variations may also play a role in speech perception. That the ability to extract waveform information is not confined to speech has been discussed at length in Moore (1977: 125ff).

Another model of speech perception has become known as *Quantal Theory*. Basically, this model postulates a discontinuity between articulatory changes and acoustic results. There are regions in the vocal tract where large articulatory changes may have little or no effect on the acoustic output, but there are also areas where small articulatory changes may lead to enormous acoustic differences. In these critical areas, slight articulatory adjustments may cause a quantal leap in terms of acoustic results. It has been suggested that this discontinuity is taken advantage of in the perception of speech, where the perceptual mechanism seems to be sensitive to such quantal aspects. Hence, a theory of speech perception must take into account the inherently quantal nature of places of articulation. Even though the quantal theory is different from the active theories discussed, it underlines the active character of speech perception in postulating a relationship between acoustic changes and articulatory movements.

Whatever model of speech perception is proposed, it is clear that the human listener makes use of a variety of features contained in the speech signal to arrive at a hypothesis of what was actually heard. Many different cues are available. That these cues are not constant but differ from utterance to utterance has been pointed out above. Furthermore, acoustic cues have a multi-dimensional nature: several different cues may classify a given phoneme, but just one or two of them might be sufficient for its identification. Hence, we can observe a high-degree of redundancy in the speech signal. This redundancy can be used to overcome distortions of the signal, poor articulation on the part of the speaker, interference with non-speech noise, etc. In order to cope with such a mass of sensory information, any model of speech perception must use a parallel processing strategy (see section 1.5. for processing strategies). Especially if some sort of feature detection system is used in the front-end acoustic analysis, all feature detectors have to operate in parallel to normalise the acoustic signal and prepare it for a matching process with a stored pattern (Kurzweil 1990: 266ff).

Another demand on speech perception models is the possibility of having access to higher levels of analysis. Phonotactic knowledge, i.e. knowledge about the combinatorial possibilities of phonemes, for example, is an important factor that decides whether a stimulus can be identified or not.

Also, knowledge about the syntactic and semantic properties of a given sensory input supports the recognition result.

In summary, then, it seems that speech perception is a massively parallel process which incorporates knowledge from other levels. By and large, the passive analysis of the incoming signal seems sufficient for the identification of phonological properties. Among the passive theories mentioned, feature detector systems are most promising.

Feature detector systems are not only supported by experimental studies of human speech perception but have also been used as the basis for computer systems with *Automatic Speech Recognition* (ASR) capability, that is for systems capable of processing spoken input. Basically, an ASR-system uses an analog to digital converter to capture speech data. These digitisers accept input from an amplified audio source (Watson 1991: 62).

While less advanced ASR-systems employ direct matching techniques to identify a small vocabulary of words created by an individual speaker, speaker-independent systems rely on low-level feature detection techniques. These include more sophisticated techniques, such as multiple feature detectors and expert managers.[17] The heart of the system, however, comprises a set of sub-phonemic feature detectors.

Of course, ASR-systems cannot refer to their own production knowledge, since they have none. Humans, by contrast, may utilise their own production model in speech perception. Especially if errors are made in the identification of the speech signal or if difficult perceptual tasks have to be performed, they can be overcome by incorporating the listener's knowledge of his own production, thus, by a more active perceptual analysis. Furthermore, additional low-level aspects, such as the waveform envelope or quantal aspects of speech production, may be incorporated.

3.3 Theories of Character Recognition

On the basis of the discussion so far, it is clear that a theory of character recognition is passive in character. By analogy with speech perception, one could hypothesise about an active theory of character recognition. However, visual perception, whether by man or by machines, is exclusively sensory, so that there cannot be any relationship between the incoming signal and a visual production mechanism. Thus, we are left with passive models of character recognition.

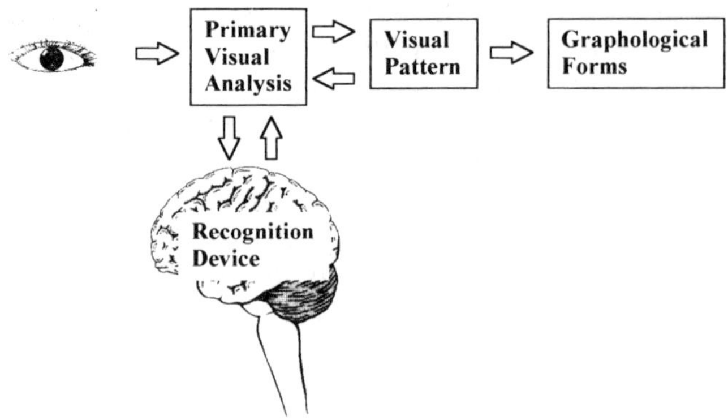

Figure 47. A model of the perception of written language

Figure 47 illustrates the general architecture of a model of the perception of written language.

In speech perception, we are confronted with two variants of a passive model: one that makes use of templates, and a feature detection model. The central difference between the two models in speech perception concerns the status of the stored patterns on the basis of which the recognition device operates. Templates are generally whole-object patterns, whereas features are sub-phonemic in character. As outlined above, feature detection models have proven to be very successful as a basis for OCR-systems. Whole-object template theories, by contrast, are usually dismissed as models of visual perception. Templates are incapable of accounting for the vast number of shape and size variations objects exhibit. Even though many of the problems of general visual perception can be ignored in OCR (due to the conventional structure of characters), whole-object templates will still be high in number. For these reasons, we are left with feature detection models that rely on feature detectors for recurring parts of shapes.

3.4. Feature Detector Models

The heart of a feature detector model is a multi-layered network of recognition devices where evidence for the symbols in the input stream is collected. At the lowest level a system of feature detector units analyses the fundamental characteristics of the input signal, at higher levels this information is interpreted in terms of abstract linguistic units, i.e. in terms of phonemes, graphemes, words, etc. Feature detector models belong to the class of restricted connectionist models (see section 1.6.), which allow their processing units to exchange information in both directions and incorporate the notion of excitatory and inhibitory connections between the processing units. Figure 48 sketches the general architecture of the recognition device, irrespective of the nature of the incoming signal, i.e. speech or written input.

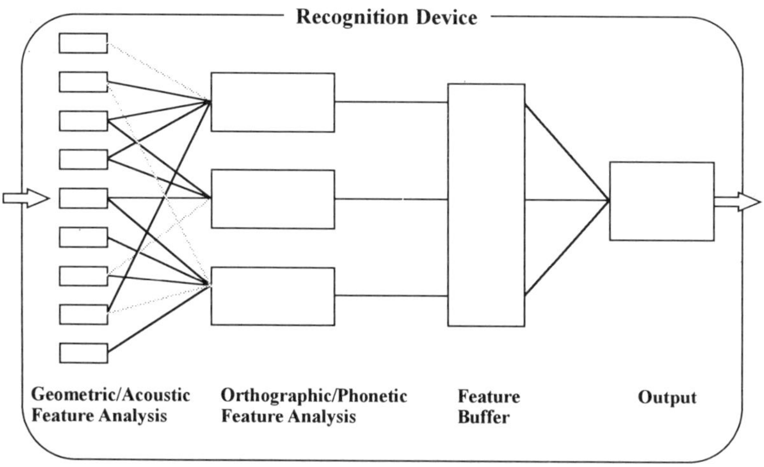

Figure 48. The architecture of a feature detector model
(excitatory connections = grey, inhibitory connections = black)

Let us illustrate the process of feature analysis and feature interpretation on the basis of OCR. At the lowest level of analysis (the level on the left-hand side in figure 48), geometric features that concern the general shape of the symbols, i.e. horizontal lines, edge location, pixel position, colour saturation, etc., are analysed. The phonographic alphabetic characters P, B and R, for example, will not be distinguished at this level; only a set of feature detectors indicating the presence, the location, and the shape of lines, edges, curves, etc., will be active. At the next level of analysis, however, a distinction can be drawn on the basis of sub-graphemic orthographical features, such as loops and concavities. For P, one loop and one concavity will be detected, whereas R has one loop and two concavities. The evidence collected at this point is dropped into a feature buffer, where it remains for a short interval, until further information comes in to combine the features into characters. Figure 49 illustrates the process of OCR on the basis of an 8-dot pixel matrix featuring the phonographic alphabetic Sanserif letter P.

The process of feature combination is heavily influenced by higher levels of analysis. The discrimination of P from R in a word such as PLAY, for

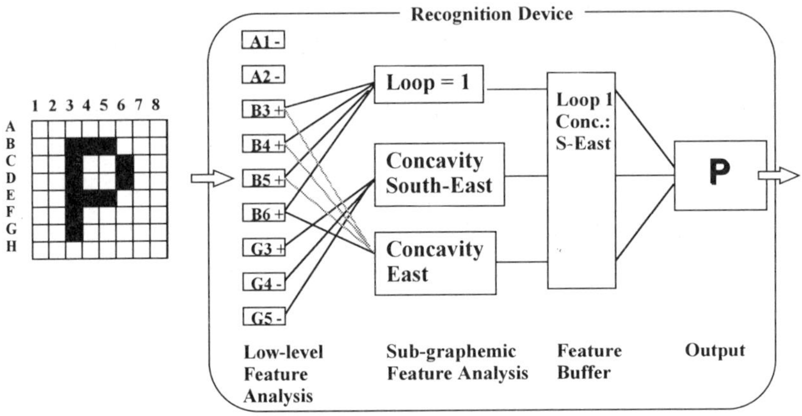

Figure 49. An OCR-feature detector system illustrated[18]

example, is phonotactically and graphologically influenced by the fact that initial clusters such as *RL are impossible in English.

In summary, the recognition device of a feature detection model has to be seen as a process consisting of multiple stages of perceptual analysis, ranging from the identification of the signal itself, via the location of edges and shapes, to the generation of graphological patterns which can be forwarded to higher levels. Also, high-level processing, for example, the integration of the linguistic context, interacts with these early phases of analysis. Especially if we fail to identify characters, or if the recognition result contradicts our expectations, higher levels are consulted. Needless to say, a feature detector system requires massive parallel processing, especially in the early stages of analysis, where the low-level feature detectors have to operate simultaneously.

Feature detector models are much more economic than template systems. They require relatively little storage space; only a limited number of feature detectors have to be represented. However, they need extra processing for a feature managing system that organises the parallel operation of the detectors and supervises the assigning of features to larger structures.

In view of the writing systems presented in Appendix A, the process of extracting information from print heavily depends on the writing system employed. While the characters in logographic writing systems such as Chinese primarily represent words, the characters in phonographic writing systems essentially establish a symbol-to-sound relationship. This in turn means that words in Chinese are more likely to be identified as holistic patterns, whereas words in languages with phonographic writing systems can be perceived in two ways: as complex transgraphemic or holistic visual patterns (figure 42), or as graphological structures, e.g. new words or non-words.[19]

In summary, we can assume a model for the identification of the written signal that is passive on the one hand, and is closely related to the principles of general visual perception on the other. The recognition device seems likely to be realised by a system of feature detectors, which, especially during the initial phase of analysis, involve massive parallel processing. Whether the written input is processed in terms of graphemes or as holistic word-shaped patterns is not entirely clear. However, it seems that a good deal of written information is identified as holistic patterns. Graphological forms, if relevant at all, are significant only after the identification of the written signal in a serial processing model, or they have to be made available by means of top-down interaction with higher levels of processing. Hence, the perception of written input can in general be characterised by analogy with general processes of visual perception: most languages employ writing systems that only allow a strategy of holistic pattern recognition on the basis of the spatial characteristics of the written input, and, even in languages with writing systems that permit a symbol-sound correspondence, holistic perception strategies are used.

Despite the tendencies to perceive written input holistically, we have to discuss the possibility of analysing phonographically represented written input by reference to speech. That is, we have to find out whether the processes of perceiving written input are completely encapsulated, or whether there are possibilities for the two modes of pre-lexical processing to interact. Clearly, speech perception must be independent of the perception of the written signal, otherwise numerous listeners who cannot read and write would suffer from severe processing impairment. However, we can speculate whether the identification of written language is exclusively restricted to visual perception, or whether an optional link to the input channel for speech perception can be established. In other words, do we use the speech perception mechanism, especially the result of it, when we read?

3.5. Speech Perception and Reading

There are two ways of comprehending language, one way, which essentially says that reading is not mediated by a process of mapping graphemes to phonemes, and another, which says that the input channels for spoken and written input converge. The first strategy is referred to as the *direct access view,* because printed information makes contact with the lexicon without any speech processing intervening. The second strategy is called the *indirect access view.* It defines reading as a process via access to the respective phonological forms.

Here, we are on the borderline between pre-lexical processing (the contents of this chapter) and lexical processing. If reading is direct in character and no cross-modal links between speech and written input are established, we do not have to speculate about the level at which the written signal makes contact with the speech signal. However, if there is evidence for the indirect access view, the question arises whether the convergence occurs prior to the phase of lexical processing or not.

It can be shown that both strategies are used, and also that both strategies are significant in the process of learning to read. Let us look at the phases in learning to read English first. Harris/Coltheart (1986: 87ff) discussed learning to read in terms of four central phases:

(a) the sight-vocabulary phase

At a relatively early age (between four and five years), the child is able to read a small vocabulary using a direct procedure. Words which are used in advertisements, such as shown in figure 42, are good cases in point. These words are taught or simply picked up by the child. A proposal which is often made is that children in this early phase recognise words in terms of their overall shape, hence on the basis of a holistic pattern. In view of the experiments Harris/Coltheart describe, this position cannot be maintained. They showed that the child has access to the individual letters, but not on the basis of a procedure that converts them to sound representations. The lack of availability of the phonetic code can be manifested by the fact that the child at this age cannot read unfamiliar words or non-words.

(b) the discrimination-net phase

At this stage the child decides on what was perceived on the basis of fragmentary cues in the written signal and behaves as if he has to select from a group of related word candidates. One such cue can be the initial letter, another word-length, etc. Still the child does not read by converting letters into sounds, but, in contrast with the sight-vocabulary phase, he no longer relies on the overall shape of a word.

(c) the phonological recoding phase

Before this phase, the child is completely unable to read non-words aloud. Yet, as the child's vocabulary expands, reading on the basis of discrimination techniques will become increasingly complicated, and letter-sound rules will begin to emerge, enabling the child to read words aloud which he has never encountered before.

(d) the orthographic phase

The use of a phonological recoding strategy, hence an indirect strategy of reading, has numerous disadvantages. One problem concerns the handling of homophonic material. Homophones such as *sale* and *sail,* which have identical phonological representations but different graphological structures, cannot be discriminated. A second problem concerns the unstable relationship between spelling and pronunciation in English (see Appendix A2). A reliance on a phonological recoding strategy will lead to severe problems with words such as *dough, cough,* and *rough,* which involve exceptional spelling. For this reason, a direct access view seems to be more suitable, where the child recognises words directly on the basis of their spelling, without further reference to their phonological code.

While the first two phases of learning to read are insignificant for adults, both the direct access view and the indirect access view bear some significance for adult language processing. The direct access view asserts that readers go directly from the written representation of a word to its lexical representation, without reference to the phonological representation. Evidence for such an assumption comes from logographic writing systems, and from logographic symbols used in all writing systems (see Appendix A1 for examples). These symbols do not specify the sounds of the words. Hence, it is unlikely that the reader "pronounces" these symbols. Further evidence comes from deep dyslexic patients who are able to read words but have difficulty with non-words, showing an inability to utilise grapheme-to-phoneme conversion rules (Emmorey/Fromkin 1988: 128).

Indirect access models, by contrast, claim that readers convert the written representation into a speech-related code, in other words that the phonological system is involved in reading. Foss/Hakes (1978: 329ff) discuss two variants of this view: the *subvocalisation* hypothesis, and the *phonological recoding* hypothesis. While subvocalisation essentially says that reading is talking to oneself, phonological recoding says that the written information is converted into an abstract phonological representation during the reading process. The bulk of evidence for the indirect view comes from reading unfamiliar words. Such words can be non-words, words which involve errors, homophones, and words which involve exceptional spelling. Let us illustrate the experimental findings using exceptional words. In a word decision task originally conducted by Meyer et al. (1974), subjects were presented with the following pairs:

(39)	set - wet	candle - handle	bribe - tribe
(40)	few - sew	lemon - demon	mint - pint

While the pairs in (39) follow the rules of English pronunciation, they do not in (40). In experiments where subjects had to decide whether both members of each pair were words or not, it took longer to process the examples in (40) than in (39). According to a direct access view this should not be the case, since all words involve a direct mapping to graphemes. The longer reaction time for the examples in (40) suggests that an additional operation is involved, a conversion into a phonological code. This and many other experiments have obtained evidence that the phonological character of a word affects visual processing.

Further evidence comes from the *pseudo-homophone effect* (Taft 1986: 305). Pseudo-homophones are non-words that are homophonic with real words, for example, *brane.* In lexical decision tasks, where subjects have to decide whether a stimulus is a word or not, pseudo-homophones take longer to respond to than non-homophonic non-words, e.g. *brate.* It would seem that this is due to the conversion of the pseudo-homophone into a sound representation which accesses an existing lexical entry for *brane* but not for *brate.*

Evidence against an indirect access view comes from studies into word-length, where words consisting of three phonemes were contrasted with four-phoneme-words. If phonological recoding occurs, then words with more phonemes should take longer to process. This was not found to be so. Another problem with the indirect view comes from an experiment conducted by Kleitman (1975), where the relationship between the following and other pairs had to be judged:

(41)	blame - flame	vs.	rough - dough
(42)	nasty - hasty	vs.	shadow - fallow
(43)	mourn - grieve	vs.	depart - couple

Note that the relationship between these pairs is different. While the pairs in (41) represent a relationship of a phonological kind in that they rhyme or do not rhyme, the examples in (42) are graphologically related in that the letters after the initial segment are identical, or not. The pairs in (43), by contrast, are related in meaning, or not. In all three cases, response times of around one second were measured. In addition to judging the relatedness of the items presented, the subjects had to shadow (to repeat verbatim) a rapid series of digits while they were performing the decision task. This led to a much larger increase in cases such as (41), i.e. in cases of phonological similarity, than in the remaining cases. Thus, shadowing had a large interference effect when a phonological decision was required, as in (41), but not when graphological decisions had to be taken, as in (42). These findings are in line with a direct access and not an indirect access view.

What shall we do with all these findings? Shall we assert a direct access model of written word processing that relegates those speakers that use a phonographic writing system to a handful of specialists, or should we assume a model that is essentially indirect and ignores the fact that all those speakers whose languages use a logographic writing system are not capable of establishing symbol-to-sound relationships?

A compromise along the lines of Foss/Hakes (1978: 341) seems to be the best solution. Such a *dual access* hypothesis makes use of both strategies of analysing written input. It takes into account that phonological recoding not only occurs, but is necessary in phonographic systems in order to read unknown or difficult information, but it also recognises that the central strategy is a direct one which generates a graphological form without reference to the phonological representation. Figure 50 illustrates such a combined view. The theory is that there are two routes to the lexicon when words are visually presented: a direct route for visual information and an indirect, slower, phonological route. The latter converts the visual information into a sound representation which is used when the visual route is too slow or fails to find access to the lexicon. The dotted line represents the process of phonological recoding and illustrates the specialised character of this mode.

That all sorts of processes may interact in identifying the written signal of a phonographic writing system can be illustrated by innovative letter combinations such as XTC.[20] Normally this input should be rejected, since at first reading neither a graphological nor a phonological representation exists. Graphological as well as phonotactic rules of English are violated. However, by referring to higher levels of processing, such as syntax, semantics, and even conceptual knowledge, we identify XTC as a name. Similar cases in point are car model designations such as MAZDA GLX, FORD GTI, etc., where we infer that GLX is part of a name on the basis

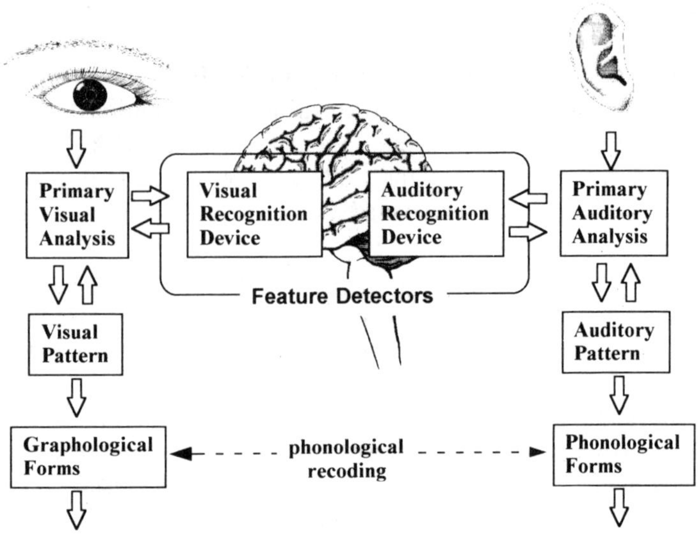

Figure 50. A combined view of perception

of constructions like "This is a MAZDA GLX". In the case of our band name, XTC, something interesting happens: assuming that XTC is not only a weird combination of three characters, we refer to our lexicon, retrieve the phonological representation of each character, /'eks/, /'ti:/, and /'si:/, and combine them to form /'ekstəsɪ/. This newly coined word can now be forwarded to other levels of processing.

3.6. The Segmentation Problem

Thus far, we have been primarily concerned with input identification, i.e. with the recognition of speech sounds, letters, letter combinations, and even entire words, on the basis of a set of features that are used to analyse the input. However, one of the most crucial problems of pre-lexical processing concerns the segmentation of the input string into individual units. These units can be located at a fairly low level (features/phones), or they can be attributed to higher levels (syllables/words). Hence, we are confronted with a problem that crosses the borderline between pre-lexical and lexical processing. In order to initiate lexical processing, low-level processes must segment the input stream into specific units that can be forwarded to higher levels.

While in visual processing words can in most cases be relatively easily separated from each other, auditory processing involves numerous segmentation problems.[21] One such problem is that the acoustic input string is not neatly divided into linguistic units. Neither individual phonemes nor words can be separately identified from the acoustic input. One essential problem for this lack of segmentation is the high degree of encodedness of speech sounds: the overlap of acoustic cues and the lack of a one-to-one correspondence between acoustic cues and phonemes make the acoustic segmentation process an almost insurmountable problem. Further segmentation complications can be found at higher levels. In section 1.3.2. we pointed out that these problems occur at the level of words as well as at the level of sentences. Despite the fact that the spoken input signal is not conveniently divided into word-like segments, words can be identified from the input. Hence, we must be able to overcome the segmentation problem. How can this be achieved?

According to Altmann (1990: 3ff), there are two central lines of reasoning. One says that segmentation primarily employs phonetic/phonological strategies, while the other asserts a high-level segmentation strategy based on syntactic and semantic aspects.

(a) phonetic/phonological segmentation

One variant of this strategy could be to initiate lexical processing at each phoneme boundary. Such a strategy would soon overwhelm the recognition system, since the number of potential word candidates arising at each new phoneme would be too large. A second variant assumes that lexical processing starts at the onset of a sentence and, after the identification of the first word, at the onset of each subsequent word. Again, this would involve a large number of hypotheses about each word. Shillcock (1990: 24) discusses the two-word utterance "recognise speech", which allows numerous hypotheses about the first segment (*reckon, recog-nice, reckon nice, wreck a nice, wreck an ice*, and many more). Secondly, as Shillcock (1990: 32ff) points out, there is evidence that this strategy is not an adequate reflection of human processing. On the basis of a cross-modal priming task, where written primes influence spoken targets, and vice versa, he showed that the lexical item *bone* in *trombone* is activated despite the fact that the sequence *trom-* is not a valid word.[22] If a strategy of segmentation at each word onset were used, lexical processing should not begin at the offset of *trom-,* and the embedded sequence *bone* should not trigger lexical processing.

A further phonetic-based strategy postulates that segmentation is based on the syllable, rather than on word or phoneme boundaries. Depending on the language, syllables can be differentiated into strong syllables with unreduced peak vowels, and reduced syllables, whose peak vowel is quantitatively less prominent. While some researchers do not draw a distinction between strong and reduced syllables in segmenting the input stream, others favour the onsets of strong syllables only as the basis for the initiation of lexical look-up. That the syllable in general plays an important role as a perceptual unit of processing will be illustrated in section 3.7.

(b) high-level segmentation

The central assumption of a high-level segmentation strategy is that the process of lexical look-up is initiated by phonetic/phonological properties. The choice between alternative interpretations, however, is determined by higher levels such as the semantic content of the utterance or the lexicon. Assumptions of this kind have been backed up by computer systems with ASR-capability (Automatic Speech Recognition, see section 3.1.3.). ASR-systems rely on results drawn from higher levels of processing to disambiguate the various segmentation possibilities (Kurzweil 1990: 226ff).

That such a reference to higher levels is unlikely becomes obvious on the basis of studies in language acquisition. As Mehler et al. (1990: 237) point out, such segmentation routines cannot be used in infant speech. Infants lack high-level knowledge, such as syntax, semantics, pragmatics, and, last but not least, lexical knowledge.[23] At the onset of the acquisition process infants have no lexicon. Nevertheless, they succeed in segmenting the input string and eventually build up their lexicon from scratch. Thus, constraints derived from higher levels cannot be the answer to the segmentation problem.

To sum up, the segmentation problem can only be solved in terms of a pre-lexical unit which is based on phonetic principles. Studies in language acquisition, especially in infant speech processing, suggest that this unit corresponds roughly to the syllable. Interestingly, the significance of the syllable can be experimentally supported by studies in written language using phonographic alphabetic writing systems.

3.7 Pre-lexial Units

The central argument of postulating a pre-lexical unit based on the syllable is the unavailability of obvious cues that facilitate the segmentation process. Despite the absence of such cues, children are capable of acquiring their lexicon, even though they have little or no information about the phonological properties of the words. Hence, they must possess some sort of information, perhaps innate, about the properties that distinguish one word from another. After careful evaluation of computational and psychological models of speech processing, Mehler et al. (1990: 237) suggest that this information is based on the syllable.

While computational models postulate processing units without clear linguistic status, e.g. vectors, spectral templates, formant transitions (see Klatt 1989), psychologically motivated models represent words in terms of linguistic units such as features, phonemes, syllables, morphemes, etc. Depending on the degree of linguistic reality postulated, psychological models can be separated into models with strong and with weak linguistic reality. Models with *strong linguistic reality* commit themselves to processing units that are isomorphic to linguistic units. *Weak linguistic reality,* by contrast, means that the processing units assumed are similar to the ones used in linguistics, without reference to the internal linguistic structure of such units.

In the past, most studies of the nature of the processes underlying speech comprehension have concentrated on adult speech. Meanwhile, empirical data is available which allows us to model speech processing and acquisition strategies in infancy. The studies of Mehler and his group (Mehler 1981; Mehler et al. 1990; Segui et al. 1990) deserve special attention in this respect. One central claim of their research is that infants process speech differently from non-speech. Also, they recognise individual voices, for instance their mother's voice, soon after birth. Hence, they are equipped with a machinery that allows them to process and represent speech.

There are two possible ways of coping with the incoming material. While *fine-grained models* rely on a smooth and almost continuous transduction of the incoming signal, based on very small units, *coarse-grained models* say that the information flow is discontinuous and relies on larger units. The difference between these two models can also be seen from a different angle: coarse-grained models collect acoustic information before addressing higher-levels, whereas fine-grained models prefer an information uptake that is essentially continuous. In other words, coarse-grained models assume a pre-lexical level that mediates between low-level and lexical processing.

According to Mehler et al. (1990: 241) there are various reasons to prefer a coarse-grained model. These reasons concern the inability of fine-grained models to filter out phonotactic violations, and their difficulties in coping with temporal normalisation, that is, with the adaptation to different speech rates. Since any processing unit that makes contact with the lexicon must be phonetic in character, and there is no a priori knowledge about phonemes, morphemes, or words, only one candidate remains: a syllable-like unit with weak linguistic reality.

Syllables are useful in many respects: they are specific linguistic units, they may correspond to words, they have a structure which is general enough to be used for the acquisition of the phonotactic principles of a language, and they are large enough to cope with the temporal problems of speech processing, reducing the number of units emitted per time unit. What about other phonetic properties? In section 3.1.1. we mentioned that allophonic characteristics are also employed as mediators between the speech signal and the lexicon (Church 1987a). In fact, such information can be used to solve the juncture problem, as in "fast team" versus "far steam" (see section 1.3.2.). However, before such information can be exploited, the notion of a word with its boundaries must be available. Hence, a larger, syllable-like unit, seems to be a much better candidate.

Nevertheless, we must acknowledge that there is no direct evidence for the use of the syllable in infant speech processing. The arguments for a syllable-like unit are primarily based on theoretical grounds. Empirical data is scarce, but it is consistent with the syllable-hypothesis. In a series of French target identification tasks (Mehler 1981; Mehler et al. 1981) it was found that responses to syllable-like targets such as /'kʌ/ were faster in words such as *carotte* than in *carton.* Vice versa, the target /'kʌr/ was identified better in *carton* than in *carotte.* However, these findings cannot be generalised across languages. French is a typical example of a *syllable-timed* language, i.e. a language that organises syllables at roughly regular intervals of time. English, by contrast, is a *stress-timed* language, with a tendency for stresses to recur at regular time intervals (Ladefoged 1975: 222).[24] In section 2.3.2.1. we noted that, in addition to the lack of the prominence of the syllable in stress-timed languages such as English, these languages also exhibit the phenomenon of *ambisyllabicity,* where segments may cross over syllable boundaries (see figure 23, chapter II). Hence, it is not surprising that, in English experiments using the same monitoring technique, the syllabic effect disappears. Targets such as /'bʌ/ and /'bʌl/ were identified at the same speed in simple stimuli such as *bal-cony,* as in ambisyllabic material such as *ba(l)ance.*

That the phonological structure of the language plays an important role in the identification of syllables was supported in a number of syllable-detection tasks by Segui et al. (1990), who found that aspects such as syllable complexity, and the structure of the syllable onset, heavily influence the strategy of segmenting spoken input.

On the basis of these and other considerations, Mehler et al. (1990: 254) developed SARAH, a model that links word recognition and the acquisition of the lexicon. SARAH (Syllable Acquisition, Representation, and Access Hypothesis) not only postulates the syllable as an essential device in establishing a contact with the lexicon, but it also relates infant speech processing to adult speech processing.

SARAH assumes that infants (the initial state) are equipped with three basic routines in order to facilitate the acquisition of a lexicon. Central to this state is a syllabic filter, which segments the input stream into syllable-like elements. It also excludes illegal syllabic sequences such as ['pst] and non-speech sounds from further analysis, and it is sensitive to variations in the speech rate. The phonetic analyser is responsible for the extraction of the elementary phonetic properties relevant for the recognition of syllables. Using syllabic representations, the word boundary detector identifies the onset and offset of words. Figure 51 illustrates the basic components of SARAH.

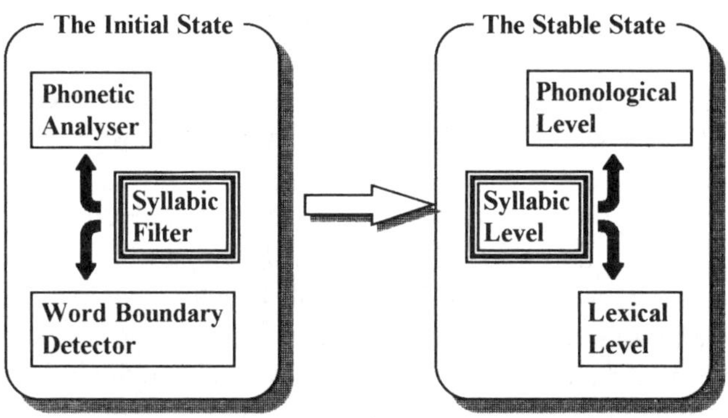

Figure 51. SARAH (based on Mehler et al. 1990)

According to SARAH, the acquisition of the spoken forms of words is a transition from the initial to the stable state. At the syllabic level of the stable state, the input is segmented into syllables. Since the number of syllables in a language is limited, Mehler et al. (1990: 255) assume some sort of syllable database where the language-specific syllabic frames are stored. On the basis of these syllabic frames, the lexical level is activated, i.e. the syllabic code is used to access the lexicon. Phonemes do not play a major role, but they can be derived at the phonological level by reference to the syllabic frames. That phonemes play only a subordinate role in pre-lexical processes is described at length in Lobacz (1984: 64ff) and has been experimentally supported by a series of phoneme monitoring tasks (Cutler et al. 1987).

Such a model incorporates many aspects of psycholinguistic research. However, more research is needed to specify the exact nature of the syllable-like unit. At present it is not clear whether this unit is related to the syllable as defined in phonological theory (section 2.3.2.1.), or whether diphonic clusters such as CV structures, triphones such as CVC, or other units are employed. However, there is enough evidence to assume that the syllable is a fundamental unit in speech processing.

Syllables have traditionally been defined by reference to phonology. Even though the processing of written language based on a phonographic writing system is a highly specialised process confined to a minority, we may speculate whether the syllable plays a similarly important role in the identification of the written signal in phonographic languages.

Taft (1979) put forward the idea of a syllable based on orthographic and morphological considerations as a lexical access unit of written language. He referred to this unit as *BOSS* (Basic Orthographic Syllable Structure). Essentially, the BOSS is defined as the first syllable of a word's root, which includes all consonants following the first vowel (Lima/Pollatsek 1983: 311). Taft (1986: 298) illustrates the structure of the BOSS on the basis of *blemish,* whose BOSS is *blem-,* and *blend* whose BOSS is not *blen-* but *blend.*

The BOSS-hypothesis rests on two assumptions. First, morphologically related words are accessed via an identical entry in the lexicon, and, secondly, words are accessed on the basis of their first syllable. In addition to this, written word recognition is defined as a left-to-right parsing process in which the information is collected in terms of individual letters. Starting with the initial letter, parsing stops at the BOSS, the underlying access code.

The BOSS-hypothesis is not undisputed. On the basis of lexical decisions tasks, Lima/Pollatsek (1983) have collected evidence against the BOSS and rejected the BOSS as the sole unit of visual lexical processing. Also, aspects of general visual processing suggest that the analysis of written language on the basis of a letter-by-letter analysis involves numerous problems (see section 3.2.3. and figure 51). One problem is that the graphological specification of a word does not become available before a word's recognition, since it is part of the lexical specification itself. How, then, can the graphological representation evoke lexical processing? Taft (1986) accounted for these problems by a revised hypothesis which he called the *Activate and Check* model. According to this model all those lexical entries that share the same amount of information (e.g. DIFFICULT, DIFFERENT, DIFFIDENT, etc.) are activated on the basis of the sensory information available. The Activate and Check model combines the processing of low-level information with information from higher levels. Still, lexical entries are activated by the orthographically defined first syllable, or BOSS. (We will return to the implications of this model in section 4.3.1.).

To sum up, the listener starts out analysing the input stream. Even though there is relatively little known about how this is done, the input is processed and matched against the lexicon. A few researchers have argued that this is a direct process, where the matching process does not require further chunking (Klatt 1981). The majority of researchers, however, propose an intermediate stage, where the information is translated into a mediating unit. There is evidence from language acquisition as well as from studies in adult language that this unit is a syllable with weak linguistic reality. Both auditory and visual processing seem to rely heavily on a unit which is larger than the phoneme but smaller than the word. The exact nature of this syllable-like unit, however, is not entirely clear. Also, this unit has a different status across languages. Experimental evidence suggests that the relatively undisputed status of the syllable in the Romance languages becomes less clear in the Germanic languages, where the listener is confronted with less clear-cut syllable boundaries. Whether this language-specific character can also be found in the orthographic syllable has not been studied yet.

Aitchison (1987: 179) attributes this somewhat dubious status of a processing unit to the complexity of natural languages and the ways of processing them. Perhaps, she argues, there is no single way in which humans analyse speech. Since languages involve different organisational principles (e.g. syllable-timed vs. stress-timed), and speech may occur in several different modes (e.g. TV-news, foreign speech, party noises, etc.) and at different speed ranges, the analysis techniques may also vary. Hence, we might not be confronted with one unitary unit of processing but with several, depending on the type of input.

3.8. Summary

In the previous sections we have shown that the phase of pre-lexical processing is highly complex. Two input signals are central to this early phase of language processing: speech and written language. It has been shown that, despite numerous attempts at describing the nature of the processes underlying the identification of these signals, one view seems likely: the analysis of both input signals is sensory and does not involve any active mechanisms. Furthermore, we have argued that a system of sub-segmental feature detectors is central to passive theories of perception. In the case of speech, these feature detectors are concerned with specific acoustic cues in the signal, in the case of written language, with edges, lines, and loops in the written input. Whether there is a cross-modal link between speech and written language, i.e. between graphological and phonological information, is not entirely clear. If it exists, it is confined to a few languages and can thus be defined as a highly specialised possibility of processing.

The results generated by feature detector systems are helpful in analysing the input into speech sounds in terms of speech, and into letters or larger units in terms of written input. However, they are not directly forwarded to the lexicon. Larger units, such as the syllable and its orthographical counterpart, the BOSS, seem to be suitable candidates for the initiation of the lexical look-up process. Figure 52 provides an extended model of the stages of word processing integrating the most important perceptual units.

In the introduction to this chapter we defined two possible ways of modelling the comprehension process. According to an autonomy model, little or no interaction between the processing levels occurs. An interactive model, by contrast, will allow level interaction in a top-down fashion, where higher levels influence the decisions taken at lower levels. We have seen that there are numerous arguments for an interaction between pre-lexical, lexical and post-lexical levels. However, there is also evidence for a strict serial ordering of processing. Cutler et al. (1987: 173), for example, claim that information flow is always bottom-up and lexical processing can only ever take place after pre-lexical processing.

Even though this debate is still an open issue, the model presented in figure 52, whether interactive or not, will serve as a framework for the next chapter, where we will discuss the principles of word recognition and lexical access.

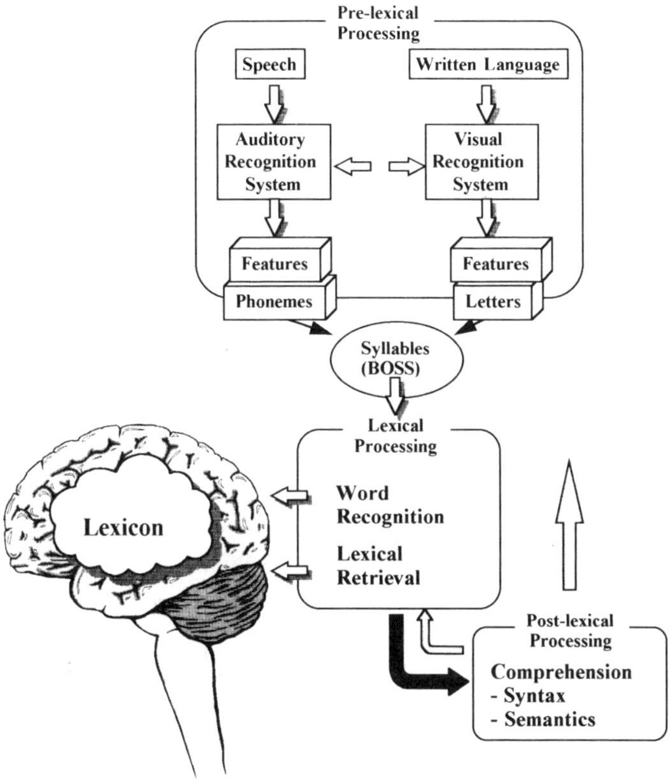

Figure 52. Pre-lexical processing and lexical processing revisited

4. Lexical Processing

"The goal of lexical processing is to make available stored knowledge associated with a word so that this can be used to develop a meaningful interpretation of an utterance."
(Tyler/Frauenfelder 1987:7)

Lexical processing can be subdivided into two stages. At stage one, the input, regardless of whether it is visually or orally presented, is matched against the collection of access units contained in the lexicon, until there is only one remaining candidate and the input has been identified. This process is called *word recognition.* At stage two, the various properties associated with the access unit identified are made available. This stage is called *lexical retrieval* (see section 1.3.2.). Figure 53 illustrates the stages of lexical processing on the basis of the nominal sense of the lexical entry FLY.

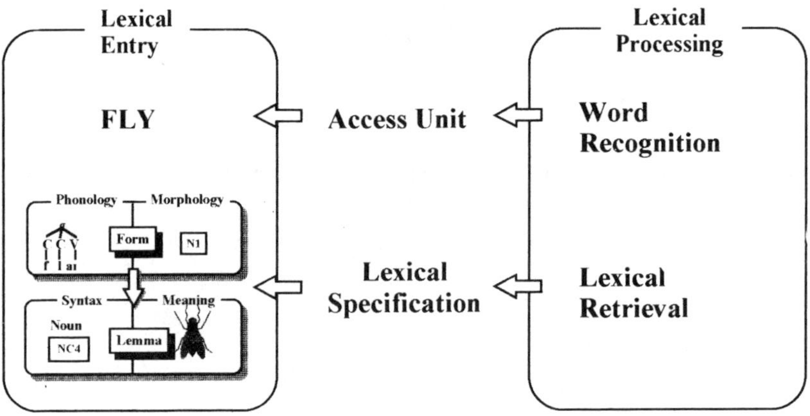

Figure 53. Lexical processing and the relationship between word recognition and lexical retrieval

The relationship between word recognition and lexical retrieval, or, more particularly, the question whether they are two separate processes or not, varies according to the theory used. There is agreement that some form-based information is made use of during the initial phase of lexical processing. This is necessary to match the lexical access unit with the sensory input. However, there is disagreement about the availability of the remaining aspects of an entry's lexical specification. While some approaches, for example Marslen-Wilson's (1978/1987) cohort model, claim that for known words all lexical information is available upon initial lexical contact, models such as Forster's (1976/1979) search model postulate a temporal sequence between word recognition and lexical retrieval (see sections 4.2.1. and 4.5.2. below).

That the various aspects of an entry's lexical specification can be retrieved independently of each other has been discussed in section 2.3.1., when a distinction was drawn between form and lemma specification. These arguments concern the processing of unknown words, tip-of-the-tongue phenomena, subconscious activation of lexical entries, and speech errors.

For example, we can store and use the form of the unknown or newly encountered word *phonon* without knowing its meaning. While the phonological, graphemic and morphological properties of this item are available, the meaning is beyond our judgement. Nevertheless, *phonon* will be entered into the lexicon, even if its lexical specification is fragmentary. By contrast, we can retrieve the lemma of a lexical entry without its form. For example, we may be able to visualise the shape of an animal or the properties of a specific person; yet, we are unable to produce its name. In such cases, we fail to access the formal properties of an entry. The consequence is that we cannot retrieve the item's full phonological code and are thus unable to pronounce it. In other words, the item is "on the tip of our tongue". Hence, it seems plausible to subdivide the level of lexical retrieval into two further stages, the level of form retrieval and the level of lemma retrieval.

The primary task of this chapter is to outline the phases and strategies of lexical processing. Among others, the following questions will be addressed:

- How is the result of pre-lexical processing used in lexical processing?
- What is the exact nature of the access unit?
- How does the access unit make contact with the lexicon?
- What are the central stages in lexical processing?
- What strategies are used to facilitate word recognition and lexical retrieval?
- To what extent are word recognition and lexical retrieval related?
- Is word recognition an isolated process or is it affected by other processing levels?
- What experimental data is available to study word recognition and lexical retrieval?

In discussing these and many other issues, an attempt will be made to set up a model of lexical processing which incorporates the experimental results of word recognition and lexical retrieval and which can be integrated into other levels of language processing. As a result, we will present a number of lexical processing models and some possible architectures of the mental lexicon.

4.1. Experiments and Experimental Findings

In order to study the phases and strategies of lexical processing, a variety of experimental techniques have been used. The most popular method of investigating lexical processing is the *lexical decision task*. Within this experimental paradigm subjects are presented with visual or auditory input and have to decide as quickly as possible whether the input is a word of their language or not. On the basis of their reaction time important conclusions with regard to the strategy of lexical processing and the architecture of the lexicon itself can be drawn. Lexical decision tasks are considered to be an appropriate way of studying lexical processing, since the subjects only have to access the meaning of the input. No other processing is required. However, it has been pointed out recently that lexical decision tasks can easily be contaminated by post-lexical effects such as the context, or by general conceptual aspects.

Lexical decision tasks can be supplemented in various ways. Instead of simple button presses, with which subjects accept or reject the input as a word, they can be asked to read the input or repeat it orally. This variant of a lexical decision task is generally referred to as a *naming task*. Another variant of decision tasks presents stimuli in pairs, where the first word, the so-called *prime*, inhibits or supports the identification of the second. The prime *bread*, for example, leads to a quick response if the target is *butter*, but it does not evoke a quick response if *car* is the target. Techniques which preactivate lexical processing, using certain triggers, are called *priming tasks*. They help to answer questions about the relationship between lexical entries and about strategies of lexical retrieval. Further techniques which are used in conjunction with lexical decision tasks are *masking techniques*, where some sort of stimulus follows the target. When a word is presented visually, the subject's ability to report the word is influenced if the word is followed by another stimulus (a backward mask) and not simply by darkness. Backward masks are normally presented in two varieties: brightness masks, where a homogeneous bright field follows the stimulus, and pattern masks, where the subsequent stimulus contains contours.

Another class of experiments that can be employed to study lexical processing is the class of *monitoring tasks*, where subjects have to identify the first occurrence of a given stimulus within an input string. In *phoneme monitoring*, for example, a specific phoneme has to be identified, in *rhyme monitoring* the occurrence of a word that rhymes with another word has to be recognised, and so on. The examples in (44) illustrate some variants of monitoring tasks:

(44)
a. The canary is on the *b*ranch.
phoneme monitoring, target: /b/
b. The young girl was chased by the *cat*.
word monitoring, target: *cat*
c. The young girl was chased by the *cat*.
rhyme monitoring, target:
"a word that rhymes with *hat*"
d. The young girl was chased by the *cat*.
semantic monitoring,
target: "an animal"

Another technique which is used in exploring lexical processing is the *shadowing technique*, where subjects have to repeat an input string verbatim. By inserting deviant words (words that are contextually unusual or words that do not exist) in the string which has to be shadowed, interesting results about word recognition and lexical retrieval can be obtained (see below).

The primary aim of all these experimental techniques is to work out the strategies of lexical processing. To achieve this goal, various stimuli can be presented to the subjects. Figure 54 provides an overview of these stimuli.

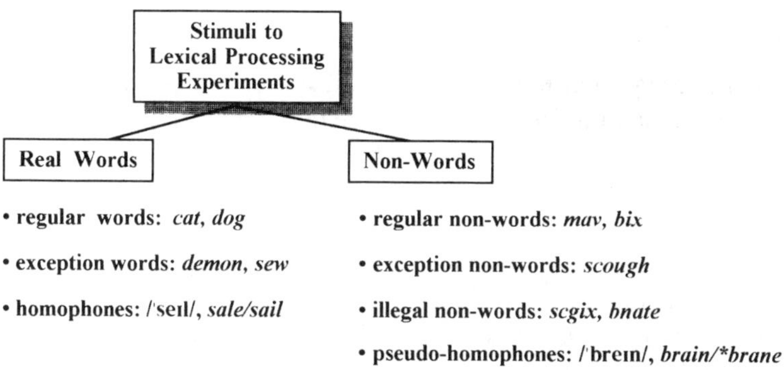

Figure 54. Stimuli to lexical processing experiments[1]

The fundamental question which lexical processing tasks seek to answer is: how do subjects react to stimuli as listed in figure 54? Are there certain correlations between input type and reaction time, and how can we explain these observations? The following major experimental findings are now well-established:

(a) the frequency and recency effect

One of the most reliable findings in word recognition literature is that the ease of recognition of a word is influenced by the frequency of its occurrence in the language (Norris 1986: 1). Hence, it has been concluded that the entries in the mental lexicon are organised according to a principle of frequency of occurrence. The exact nature of this organisational principle is unknown. One might, for example, assume some sort of "stack" principle, where high-frequency words are positioned before low-frequency words and are thus processed faster. Such assumptions received support from a series of lexical decision tasks where Forster/Chambers (1973) and Chambers/Forster (1975) found that high-frequency words are recognised earlier than low-frequency words. However, the frequency difference between words seems to be a short-lived effect. This was demonstrated by Scarborough et al. (1977), who showed that the response time to infrequent words decreases when they are presented again. Hence, the frequency effect may be neutralised by a recency effect. According to Henderson (1982) there are two possibilities to accommodate these findings. Either high-frequency words are stored before low-frequency ones, or they are stored more often. In any case, the frequency effect is a fundamental factor in the organisation of lexical entries.

(b) the length effect

In spoken word recognition the temporal extension of the signal does not allow the identification of the input as a whole. Thus, length effects may play a role and we can assume that short words will be recognised faster than long words, since less information has to be collected. However, an early portion of a long word may be sufficient for its identification, because there are no competing candidates. Long words such as *hallucination* /həlu:sɪˈneɪʃn/, for example, may evoke fast responses, since they can be unambiguously identified after a relatively short portion (*hallu-*, /həlu:-/), and do not allow alternatives after this point. In such cases, the length effect can be dismissed. For this reason, the question whether word-length affects processing has been traditionally addressed within studies into visual word recognition. It has been shown that, despite some drop in clarity, all letters of a given word are simultaneously available for processing (Foss/Hakes 1978: 326).

As we saw in section 3.1.2., there are two positions concerning the identification of written input: the holistic view and the letter-mediated view. According to the holistic view there should be no length effects. If length effects exist, they can be attributed to a grapho-phonological recoding strategy, especially in naming tasks, where subjects have to read aloud given stimuli. Garman (1990: 251ff) mentions a number of experiments showing that there is virtually no length effect in written word processing and that phonological recoding seems to be confined to exceptional cases.

(c) the regularity effect

The regularity effect concerns the mapping of letters to sounds. Thus, this effect is confined to written word processing. As we mentioned in section 3.5. (examples (39) and (40)), the experimental finding is that words whose graphemic structure is in line with the graphemic-to-phonological conversion rules of a language are processed faster than words which have a unique pronunciation and violate the grapheme-phoneme correspondence rule. The central assumption of this effect is that, in the case of such "irregular" words as *sew* and *demon*, a specific grapheme-to-phoneme route is made use of.

However, we could posit a completely different explanation, which does not view the regularity effect as an isolated aspect, but as an effect which is influenced by other variables of lexical processing. Take the "irregular" words *sew* and *have*. In terms of grapheme-to-phoneme correspondence, both have a large number of "regular" neighbours: *new, few, dew*, etc., and *gave, shave, behave, brave, wave*, etc., respectively. However, the pronunciation of *sew* can be seen as more difficult than *have*. This is due to the relationship between *sew* and *have* and their respective "regular" counterparts. While the deviation of *sew* /ˈsəʊ/ from the grapheme-to-phoneme conversion rule "ew" → /ju:/ may be viewed as relatively large, the relationship between *have* /ˈhæv/ and the corresponding conversion rule "ave" → /eɪv/ is much closer. Hence, we could redefine the regularity effect as one of degree of consistency with the grapheme-to-phoneme conversion rule.

As outlined above, another variable that affects the pronunciation of words is the frequency effect. Even though there is no experimental data available, we may assume that the pronunciation of the relatively infrequent word *sew* is complicated by high-frequency words among the "regular" neighbours, such as *new* and *few*. The pronunciation of *have*, by contrast, may to be less difficult, since it is a high-frequency word itself.

Hence the regularity effect is a highly specialised effect. It is confined to written input, it concerns a relatively small group of words, and it is likely to be influenced by other variables of lexical processing.

(d) the lexicality effect (word/non-word effect)

A common input to lexical decision tasks is non-words. As illustrated in figure 54, there are numerous variants of non-words, ranging from stimuli that could graphemically as well as phonologically be actual words to items that fail to become word candidates due to their illegal graphemic or phonological structure. The lexicality effect simply says that non-words are processed differently from real words. However, a distinction must be drawn between types of non-words. While regular non-words, such as **mav*, take fairly long to reject, illegal non-words, for example ***thlib*, produce very fast responses. They are probably rejected without any access to the lexicon.

Numerous explanations have been offered to account for the difference of response to real words and to regular non-words and the finding that it takes longer to reject a regular non-word than to accept a real word. The central assumption is that the processing of regular non-words involves a search procedure that scans the entire lexicon and thus prolongs lexical search until there is no successful match with an existing access unit. Again, this effect may be seen as matter of gradience. It has been shown that the difference between the response to real words and regular non-words relates to the degree of similarity between the two: the greater the similarity, the larger the difference. Similarly, there are differences in response time among illegal non-words. Partially illegal non-words, such as ?**sajf*, are rejected less rapidly than fully illegal items such as ***sjmf*. Garman (1990: 253) refers to this constraint as *legality effect*.

(e) the homophone effect

Phonological representations that may have more than one graphemic counterpart are called homophones. In lexical decision tasks three types of homophones have been used:

(45)	a.	real homophones:	/ˈseɪl/	→ *sail/sale*
	b.	pseudo-homophones:	/ˈbreɪn/	→ *brain/*brane*
	c.	non-word homophones:	/ˈzeɪn/	→ **zain/*zane*

Basically, the homophone effect concerns pseudo-homophones, i.e. pairs with a real word and a regular non-word. We already pointed out, in section 3.5., that in lexical decision tasks it takes longer to reject pseudo-homophones than non-homophonous material. Also, it takes longer to accept the less frequent member of a homophone pair, for example *buoy* in /ˈbɔɪ/. These findings are normally used as an argument for a phonological recoding strategy in reading. It says that, whenever we process a pseudo-homophone such as **brane*, we are in fact confronted with two words: with the pseudo-homophone, and with the real word. The graphemic structure of **brane* results in the real word *brain*, which in turn leads to a rejection of the pseudo-homophonous non-word.

(f) the word superiority effect

Words have a superior perceptibility compared with single letters. This statement by Henderson (1982: 222) underlines a fact which has long been known. In fact, the respective experiments date back into the 19th century. Nevertheless, there is sufficient evidence available based on modern experimental paradigms.

Harris/Coltheart (1986: 155ff) report on masking experiments where words of four letters were more accurately reported than single letter items. These results suggest that words, even though they are visually more complex, are perceived more rapidly than single letter targets. Harris/Coltheart also report on masking experiments carried out by Johnston and McClelland in 1973. They presented four-letter-stimuli, such as COIN, followed by a word-stimulus or by a one-letter-stimulus. The word-stimulus was either the word COIN itself or a stimulus with a different initial letter, for example JOIN. The one-letter-stimulus used either the initial letter of the original stimulus, here C, or a different letter which could result in a real word, e.g. J. To present these additional stimuli, both masking techniques were employed: brightness masking and pattern masking. While with brightness masks no word-superiority effect was recorded, performance was much better when a pattern mask was realised by a word than by a letter. These findings suggest that two levels of input identification are made use of in visual processing: the level of letter detection and the level of word detection. How these two levels can be integrated into a model of word recognition will be discussed in section 4.2.1.2.

(g) the contextual effect

An additional source of information utilised in word recognition is the context. Words are recognised more rapidly in an appropriate context than in isolation. The contextual effect has mainly been established on the basis of priming tasks where subjects responded much faster to stimuli which exhibited a good match with a previous prime than to stimuli that did not match with a given prime. Further evidence comes from phoneme restoration experiments, where a portion of the acoustic signal is spliced out and replaced with a non-linguistic signal, e.g. with a cough. The result of such experiments is that listeners report hearing an intact word with an additional noise in the background. The only explanation for the ability to identify this incomplete information is the integration of the context. That contextual effects exist is beyond any question; however, there is some debate about the type of context that affects processing (syntax, word-semantics, general knowledge).

A somewhat different 'contextual effect' is sometimes referred to as the 'lexical effect' (Connine 1990: 286). Basically, it means that, apart from the sentence context, lexical knowledge is used directly in lexical processing. We will see below (section 4.2.2.) that such lexical knowledge may be used after the identification of the stimulus to manifest or refine decisions about what was heard prior to that. For example, in the case of distorted input – let us say the input is the item *?lug* with the first element missing, we will be biased towards an identification of the missing element as /p/, since no other lexical access units with this structure are contained in our lexicon.

That the contextual effect exists is beyond any doubt. For this reason, the proper handling of contextual aspects provides a yardstick for judging the psychological adequacy of word processing models.

That all these experimental findings cannot be dealt with in isolation has been pointed out above. They influence each other. For example, the regularity and the frequency effects are often a matter of degree, and they are affected by various processing levels, ranging from low-level to high-level processing. Also, it seems that, by and large, a number of experimental findings are irrelevant for auditory lexical processing and are confined to the highly specialised mode of processing written phonographic information. Table 4 illustrates the relevance of the experimental findings for visual and auditory lexical processing.

Even though we have to be careful about putting too much emphasis on certain experimental effects, any model of lexical processing has to explain at least those effects relevant for the auditory processing mode and has to be modelled accordingly.

Table 4. Experimental effects in word recognition Annotations: ✓ = relevant, X = irrelevant

	Visual Lexical Processing	Auditory Lexical Processing
the frequency and recency effect	✓	✓
the length effect	(X)	(X)
the regularity effect	✓	X
the lexicality effect	✓	✓
the homophone effect	✓	X
the word superiority effect	✓	X
the contextual effect	✓	✓

4.2. Modelling Word Recognition

Up to this point we have primarily been concerned with processes that occur prior to the activation of the lexicon. It has been shown that a number of these issues are at present beyond our judgement. Nevertheless, we have collected a certain amount of material to approach one of the most important questions of lexical processing: how do we make contact with the lexicon?

Generally, there are two types of model characterising the process of word recognition. One kind of model grew out of research into engineering and artificial intelligence, where attempts were made to provide a machine solution to the problem of language processing. A second kind of model was shaped to account for psychological data on the perception of language. Both approaches must be judged in terms of different criteria: while machine-based models are primarily interested in language recognition and should thus be judged in terms of their actual performance, psychological models seek to account for the details of human processing performance. McClelland/Elman (1986: 3) refer to this distinction as *computational* and *psychological* adequacy.

The ideal model of word recognition, then, is computationally and psychologically fully adequate. It will not only sufficiently explain the experimental effects discussed, but it will also incorporate a phonetic/phonological segmentation strategy. Such a model will in some way or another incorporate the idea of a syllable-like pre-lexical processing unit, as outlined in section 3.7. However, since there are controversial positions about the status of such a unit, its incorporation into a model of word recognition is desirable but not a crucial issue.

The overwhelming amount of processing relates to auditory input. For this reason, psychologically adequate models of word recognition primarily have to address the phenomena of speech analysis and have to explain at least those three experimental effects that are related to speech (see table 4):

- the frequency/recency effect
- the lexicality effect
- the contextual effect

Additionally, any model should also say something about a word's *recognition point*. In section 4.1. results from lexical decision tasks were presented, suggesting that the length effect does not play a major role in lexical processing. Words are identified irrespective of their length, and, more importantly, some long words are recognised faster than their short counterparts. Hence, recognition is not a function of a word's length. However, depending on the availability of alternative word candidates, length effects can be observed and should thus be accounted for in models of word recognition.

Last but not least, any model of word recognition should have an architecture that allows interaction with other levels of processing.

In the following sections we will discuss the main implications of two of the leading models of spoken word recognition. The first is the *Cohort model of spoken word recognition*, essentially a psychological model; the second, *TRACE*, grew out of computational efforts to model human speech understanding.

Both models belong to the class of interactive models of comprehension allowing the top-down flow of information, where higher processing levels influence lower levels (Cutler et al. 1987: 142). There are alternative, less interactive models, where the flow of information is serial and bottom-up. The implications of such modular approaches will be discussed in section 4.2.3.

4.2.1. The Cohort Model of Spoken Word Recognition

The *Cohort model* assumes that there is a separate active processing element associated with each item in the lexicon (Norris 1986: 103). Each of these processing elements is a discrete, computationally independent, element representing a bundle of phonological, morphological, syntactic, and semantic properties, and it is sensitive to acoustic input (Lahiri/Marslen-Wilson 1991: 255). As soon as there is a match between the input and the perceptual specifications of these elements in the lexicon, syntactic and semantic specifications associated with the respective lexical item are brought into operation.

The Cohort model goes back to Marslen-Wilson/Welsh (1978). It was set up to account for a number of experimental effects which were observed using the shadowing technique. In a series of shadowing tasks, listeners had to reproduce in their own speech the text read from a novel. Unknown to the subjects, certain words in the original text were deliberately mispronounced and became regular non-words. Here is an example:

(46) target word: /'trævədɪ/ (**travedy*)

There are two possible ways of coping with such distortions: either they are simply repeated, or they are fluently restored to become a real word, e.g. *tragedy*. Interestingly, fluent restorations occurred, even though a number of conditions had to be met. First, the phonemic deviation from the target had to be slight, e.g. a change of voicing, secondly, the distortion had to be located in a syllable other than the initial one, and, thirdly, the real word had to be predictable from the context.

From these and other findings Marslen-Wilson/Welsh concluded that word recognition has to be defined as a process that narrows down an initially large set of possible candidates until only one remaining element is left. At the earliest possible stage of lexical processing, we start off with a set of all elements that share the initial sequence of the input. This set is referred to as *word-initial cohort*.[2] In the first version of the cohort model, the word-initial cohort consisted of all elements sharing the first sound; later (Marslen-Wilson/Tyler 1980), the initial cohort was established on the basis of the first CV-cluster.

Once the initial set of potential word candidates has been built, a process of candidate elimination begins. As each successive phoneme arrives, all those members of the initial cohort whose next phoneme fails to match the incoming signal will be eliminated. With more phonetic information arriving, the subsequent cohorts will gradually shrink, until there is only one remaining candidate. At this point a word is recognised. In other words, any input can be uniquely identified when the cohort has been reduced to one single element. Figure 55 illustrates the first version of the Cohort model.

The Cohort model can be viewed as an on-line interactive model of spoken word recognition. As soon as the first sound, or perhaps the first CV-cluster, has been perceived, lexical processing begins without any further delay. In other words, processing occurs instantaneously, or, *on-line*. That the model must be able to incorporate information from other levels becomes clear if we consider contextual effects. For this reason, the reduction of the initial cohort is not only a matter of phonetic input but also

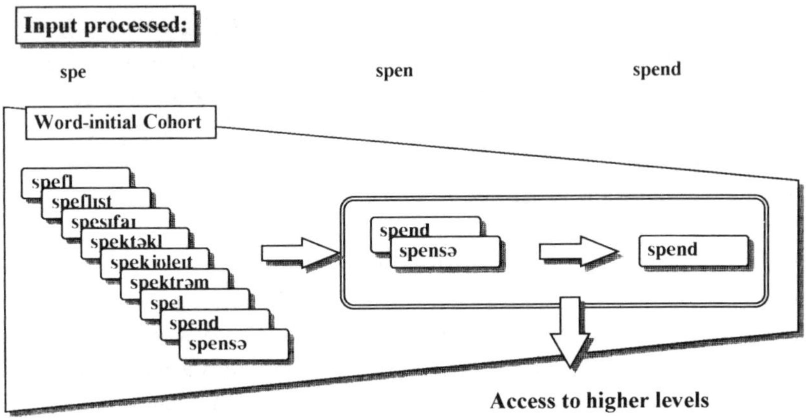

Figure 55. The Cohort model of spoken word recognition, version I Target to identify: /'spend/, *spend*

one of the interaction with other levels. This on-line interactive character of the Cohort model neatly fits into a more general model of natural language comprehension by Marslen-Wilson, the *on-line interactive parallel model* (see Tyler 1981, for a good summary).

An interesting implication of the Cohort model is the possibility of identifying words even before they have been completely spoken. A word such as *trespass*, for example, can be unambiguously recognised after the /p/, since there is no other candidate in English that begins with /'tresp/. According to the Cohort model, the initial cohort will have shrunk to only one candidate at this point. To identify this candidate, no additional information is required, and the word can be recognised, even though a number of additional phonemes have not yet been heard. The point at which a word can be unambiguously identified is referred to as the *acceptance* or *recognition point* (Harris/Coltheart 1986: 160).

Let us return to the experimental effects. The lexicality effect can be explained very efficiently. A word will be rejected if the remaining cohort is empty. The difference in reaction time for regular non-words, such as **mav* or **bix*, versus illegal non-words, such as ***scgix*, or ***bnate*, can be attributed to their recognition points, or, to be precise in these cases, to their rejection points, i.e. the position in a word which shrinks the remaining cohort to zero. While regular non-words often have to be heard in their entirety and require the entire lexicon to be inspected before the word can be rejected, illegal non-words often exhibit relatively early rejection points. An obvious prediction, then, is that non-words with late rejection points will take longer to process than non-words with early rejection points, an effect which we referred to as 'legality effect' in section 4.1. (d). On the basis of non-words with late rejection points, such as **thousiding*, and non-words with early rejection points, such as **vleesidence*, this prediction has turned out to be true. Note that, along similar lines, the length effect can be explained. As already mentioned, length does not play a crucial role in spoken word recognition. On the basis of the Cohort model, this is obvious: it is not the length of a word in terms of its phonemes or syllables that influences word recognition but the occurrence of the recognition point. Despite its length, a long word such as *hallucination* can be identified very quickly since its recognition point /u:/ occurs relatively early in the word.

The two remaining experimental effects cannot be directly derived from the model. That the context plays an important role in word recognition is an established fact. To incorporate the context, the Cohort model permits access to higher levels as soon as the initial cohort has been built. Frequency and recency effects, by contrast, were not explicitly mentioned in the 1978 version of the Cohort model. However, if we assume an internal order of each cohort according to high-frequency and low-frequency words, we can easily incorporate this effect.

Even though the Cohort model accounts for a large body of data, it involves a number of problems. Consider the following elements, one with a distorted beginning, and the other with an element missing, perhaps through the influence of surrounding noise.

(47) dwibble /ˈdwɪbl/, ?ate /ˈ?eɪt/

In both cases, we are nevertheless capable of relating these elements to existing words, perhaps, *dribble* or *gate/Kate, date, bait.* However, the Cohort model, which defines spoken word recognition as a serial or 'left-to-right' process of successive candidate elimination (Rickheit/Strohner 1993: 197), cannot cope with distorted input, since in such cases no initial cohort would emerge. In order to establish the word-initial cohort, the system requires undistorted acoustic signals, especially at the beginning of the word.

Further problems with the Cohort model concern the processing of novel words (the Cohort model assumes a fixed number of words in one's lexicon), and segmentation. It was mentioned above that segmentation is a huge problem in general. For the Cohort model, however, segmentation is essential. In order to recognise words, word boundaries have to be precisely identified, before initial cohorts can be built and final decisions can be taken.

As a reaction to these problems, Marslen-Wilson (1987) set up a second version of the Cohort model. Even though this model does not provide an answer to the segmentation problem, it incorporates the possibility of handling distorted input. Figure 56 illustrates the Cohort model, version II.

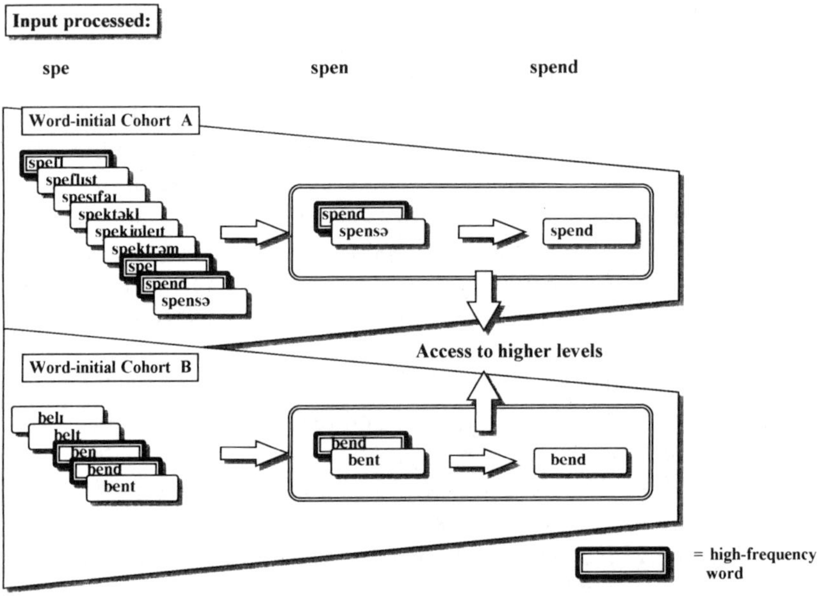

Figure 56. The Cohort model of spoken word recognition, version II Target to identify: /ˈspend/, *spend*

The new Cohort model is innovative in two respects: first, it explicitly integrates the idea of word frequency, and, secondly, it permits deviant words to enter the cohort.

To incorporate the frequency effect into the Cohort model, Marslen-Wilson made use of the idea of *activation levels*. On the basis of a series of lexical decision and priming tasks, Marslen-Wilson (1987) found that the response to high-frequency words seems to be enhanced in some way, especially early in the word. High-frequency words are now associated with an activation level which is higher than that of low-frequency words, and which takes longer to drop below the level of competing low-frequency candidates. In other words, the items in the cohort are not simply switched on or off. Rather, they represent different activation levels, which may rise and fall during the recognition process.[3]

That the human spoken word recognition system is capable of handling deviant input, especially if it is embedded in an utterance context, has been stated above. Again, activation levels are used to solve this problem. The selection of potential word candidates is no longer an all-or-none matching process but it depends on the relative degree of matching with the sensory input (Marslen-Wilson 1987: 95). Hence, candidates that do not fully match the input may also participate in the selection process. In figure 56 the possibility of processing deviant input is represented in terms of a second cohort, which contains a set of alternative candidates.

The processing of deviant input is highly dependent on the results of pre-lexical processing. The more abstract the result of pre-lexical processing, the more difficult the processing of deviant input. Take the target input /'ben/ and the competing candidate /'pen/ as an example. If phonemes serve as the input to a model of word recognition, it is very difficult to integrate disrupted input in the analysis process. Depending on the initial phoneme identified, for example /b/, the corresponding cohort will be built. The competing cohort, i.e. all items beginning with a /p/, will not receive any attention. This is due to the abstract nature of the phoneme as a holistic unit. By contrast, if the input is specified as a set of feature values, the model has less difficulty in processing minimal pairs such as /'ben/ and /'pen/. Despite a failure of feature match in terms of the feature [±voicing], both items will receive sufficient attention along the feature parameters, such as [labial], [plosive], etc. To sum up, we are confronted with two possible models. On the one hand, the decision between competing candidates could be taken at the pre-lexical level, in which case the output of this processing stage could be phonemes. On the other hand, the pre-lexical level candidate selection could be performed at the lexical level. In this case, a less abstract pre-lexical result is required. The advantage of this latter model is its delay of committing itself to final decisions about the input. This delay permits the integration of additional aspects such as the context.

In 1991 Lahiri/Marslen-Wilson became more precise concerning the phonological specification of the access unit. Instead of a linear string of input segments, they postulated – in line with current phonological theories – that every linguistic item has a single underlying non-linear phonetic description, which is only minimally specified (Lahiri/Marslen-Wilson 1991: 252). Hence, the phoneme only plays a subordinate role in a revised theory of the Cohort model.

That contextual effects exist is well-known, but how does the utterance context influence word recognition? In the 1978 version of the Cohort model, an all-or-none technique was asserted, according to which all those candidates drop out of the cohort that do not fit the specifications of the context. The revised model adopts a view which Marslen-Wilson (1987: 97) characterises as 'selection and integration'. Central to this view is the observation that the context does not function to exclude candidates from the cohort. Words that occur in syntactically or semantically anomalous contexts do not cause a break-down of the recognition process. Here are some examples:

(48) a. John buried the guitar.
b. John drank the guitar.
c. John slept the guitar.

The contextually inappropriate word *guitar* is implausible in (48a), semantically anomalous in (48b), and violates the subcategorisation of *sleep* in (48c), but it can be readily perceived and is only slightly more slowly responded to than in normal contexts, so long as it can be unambiguously identified in the input signal. This indicates that word recognition follows a principle of bottom-up-priority. If the sensory input clearly differentiates one candidate from a set of competitors, the context is irrelevant, even if it is completely anomalous. If several candidates emerge from the sensory input, the context may facilitate word recognition. Yet, if the context itself provides the system with alternatives, only those candidates will emerge that also fit the bottom-up input. Hence, the context only has facilitatory effects but does not inhibit word recognition. How do we model these findings?

Again we can employ the system of activation levels, perhaps by increasing the activation level for those candidates that fit the current context, and postulate a model where access and selection are clearly autonomous and strictly bottom-up. Alternatively, we can assume a model where different sources of information interact on-line to compute the final output, hence a system which compensates for the lack of top-down contextual influences by massive parallelism. The contextual effect, with its bottom-up-priority, suggests that this interaction is fairly unconventional. The process of selection can be seen as an autonomous process as long as the signal is heard in isolation. However, if words occur in contexts (fluent conversational speech), there need not be a phase of form-based selection; rather, selection becomes a by-product of the integration of the input into higher level representations such as the utterance context or the discourse. In other words, the 1987 Cohort model defines a phase of access and selection as the basis for on-line comprehension processes. However, this phase is only partial to a system that is not concerned primarily with the identification of word-forms, but with the uncovering of meaning.

To sum up, the Cohort model still defines word recognition as a process of successive candidate elimination. Central to the revised version of this model is the integration of activation levels, the specification of bottom-up input in terms of sub-phonemic feature values, and the exclusion of top-down contextual influences. The idea is that, in the process of word recognition, potential candidates are activated and deactivated as a result of their match with the phonological input. Additionally, their activation levels can be altered by word-frequency aspects and by the context. The primary difference between the 1987 version of the Cohort model and its predecessor is that word recognition is no longer an all-or-none process that is defined by the presence or absence of different candidates.

4.2.2. The TRACE Model of Spoken Word Recognition

The TRACE model of spoken word recognition is a computational simulation of speech processing which unites the principles of pre-lexical processing (chapter three) with the main aspects of word recognition.[4] It belongs to the class of restricted connectionist models (see section 1.6.) and consists of a number of simple processing units allowing information exchange in both directions (bottom-up and top-down). According to the connectionist framework, the interaction between the processing units can be excitatory or inhibitory.[5]

The central idea of the TRACE model is that word recognition depends on a number of cues that are available during the information uptake. Consider the first phoneme of the word *cup* (/ˈkʌp/) in (49):

(49) He prefers to drink from a tea *cup*.

There are various cues to the identity of /k/ in (49). First, there are acoustic cues, such as F2-transition, VOT, the preceding portion of silence, etc., which identify the speech sound [k] itself. Secondly, there are phonological aspects, such as the phonological environment. As soon as we know the remainder of the word *cup*, we know that the phonotactic possibilities are restricted. ***kgup*, for example, can be excluded on the basis of such considerations. Finally, the integration of the syntactic and semantic context puts further constraints on the set of potential word candidates.

The primary purpose of the TRACE model is the integration of multiple sources of information, ranging from acoustic to semantic. Essentially, the

TRACE model makes use of a large number of processing units at different processing levels. Information processing takes place via excitatory and inhibitory connections between the processing units. As soon as a processing unit exceeds a threshold activation value, it may influence other units via its outgoing connection. At each point in time the system presents a hypothesis about the input which depends on the activation values of the processing units and the strength of the connections within the system. Let us look more closely at the processing units, the processing levels, and the representation of the temporal nature of the speech signal in the TRACE model.

(a) processing levels and processing units in the TRACE model

The TRACE model consists of three processing levels and a large number of processing units at each level.

The feature level

At the feature level, seven banks of feature detectors analyse the acoustic properties of speech sounds. Table 5 provides an overview of the five main acoustic-articulatory feature detectors used in the TRACE model, on the basis of a feature classification by Hyman (1975: 32ff).

Table 5. The classification of the main acoustic-phonetic features in the TRACE model

Feature	Acoustic Definition	Articulatory Definition	Example Phonemes
vocalic	presence of sharply defined formant structure	glottal excitation plus free air passage	vowel phonemes, liquids (l, r)
consonantal	low total energy	obstruction in the vocal tract	consonantal phonemes, liquids (l, r)
acute	energy in upper frequencies	medial obstruction	back vowels, dental/ alveolar consonants
diffuse	energy concentration in a narrow region	forward constriction	low vowels
voicing	F0 energy concentration	voiced/voiceless	vowels vs. consonants (voiced/voiceless)

In addition to these primarily phonetic features, the features *power*, as a further distinction between vowels and consonants, and *burst amplitude*, for the identification of word-initial plosives, are used. The activation values for each feature are represented in terms of numerical values, ranging from 8 (high excitation) to 1 (low excitation/inhibition).

For example, our target phoneme /k/ would fully excite the feature detector 'consonantal' and would inhibit the feature detector 'vocalic'. According to McClelland/Elman (1986: 15), /k/ can be associated with the following activation values:

– power	4
– consonantal	8
– vocalic	1
– diffuse	2
– acute	3
– voiced	1
– burst	4

The bank of feature detectors in figure 57 illustrates the situation for the first phoneme of /'kʌp/. Ideally, we should represent each feature value by a different colour, for reasons of representational simplicity. However, in figure 57 excitatory connections are double-lined and black, semi-excitatory connections are single-lined and black, and inhibitory connections are grey. Additionally, the feature detectors that receive the highest activation values relevant for /k/, 'consonantal', 'power', and 'burst', have been marked with double-lined boxes.

The phoneme level

At the phoneme level, there is a set of phoneme detectors, one for each phoneme and one for the presence of silence. Each phoneme is specified phonetically on the basis of a feature matrix. The phoneme /k/, for example, is associated with the feature specification values as given above ([power 4], [consonantal 8], etc.). The connection strengths between the feature level and the phoneme level exactly match this specification (see figure 57, where a selection of 6 phoneme detectors is represented).

The word level

At the word level, the TRACE model represents a list of words, ideally the entire set of the words of a language. The actual word list of the TRACE model, however, does not meet this criterion. Word detector units receive their excitation/inhibition from the phoneme level. The strength of the connection depends on the temporal nature of the input signal (see below).

Figure 57 gives a first account of the three processing levels of the TRACE model, on the basis of the first phoneme of the input /'kʌp/.

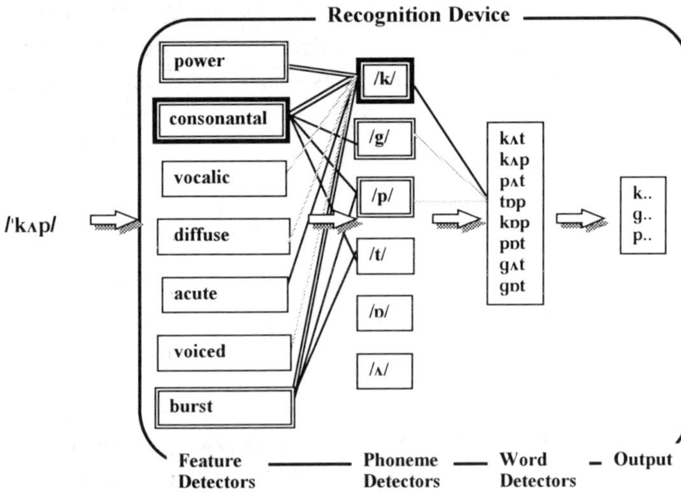

Figure 57. Processing units and processing levels in the TRACE model (a fragment)

While the excitatory and inhibitory connections between the feature level and the phoneme level depend on the acoustic analysis of the input, the types of connection between the phoneme and the word level are due to the integration of the temporal nature of speech. McClelland/Elman refer to this notion as *time slices* (see below).

(b) temporal overlaps/time slices

One of the primary properties which distinguishes speech from written information is the extension of the speech signal in time. However, as we have seen in section 3.1., the speech signal does not contain neatly segmented acoustic cues which can be attributed to specific phonemes. Rather, the identification of phonemes depends on the acoustic environment. For example, the locus of F2 is influenced by the preceding plosive. Furthermore, many acoustic cues overlap in time. As already mentioned, this makes a one-to-one association between acoustic cues and phonemes impossible. In other words, there are no separable packets of phonetic information in the speech signal like the separable bundles of information in the written signal. This high degree of encodedness makes the processing of acoustic information especially difficult. Hence, we have to incorporate the notion of the phonetic context and the possibility of feature overlap into the speech recognition device. For this reason McClelland/Elman (1986) introduced the idea of successive *feature replication* and *time slices*. This means that every bank of feature detectors is replicated for each of several moments in time.

At the feature level, we have 24 time slices, at the phoneme and at the word level 8. The greater number of time slices at the feature level is due to the lack of a one-to-one correspondence between features and phonemes, and the lack of clear acoustic boundaries between phonemes. For example, the feature 'diffuse', which has a higher value for /ʌ/ than for /k/ (according to McClelland/Elman 7 versus 5), cannot be associated with the beginning of each phoneme; rather, it gradually builds up its activation value. By means of several time slices at the feature level, one for each 25 msec, the TRACE model can incorporate this fact. Figure 58 illustrates the phenomenon of temporal overlap on the basis of three selected feature detectors and 24 time slices, where the overlap occurs within time slices 8 and 9, for the transition from /k/ to /ʌ/, and within time slices 15 and 16, for the transition from /ʌ/ to /p/.

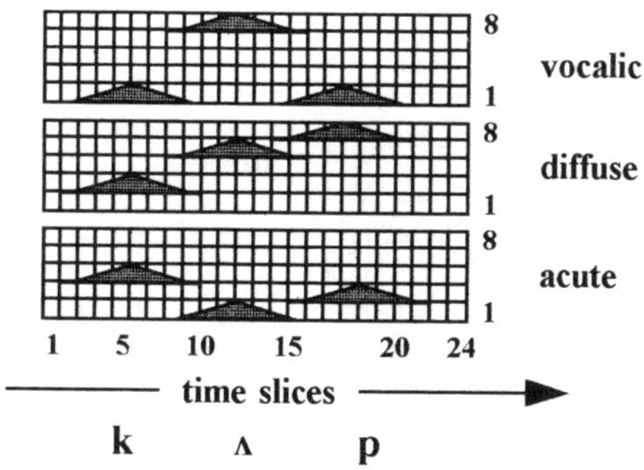

Figure 58. Feature detectors and time slices in the TRACE model

The 24 time slices at the feature level correspond to 8 time slices at the phoneme level, or, vice versa, each phoneme time slice spans three time slices at the feature level. Once phonemes have been isolated, they activate the word level by means of a one-to-one correspondence, that is, each incoming phoneme triggers one or several word candidates. Hence, the number of time slices at the phoneme and at the word level is identical. However, the strength of the connections is determined by the information contained in a series of overlapping slices at the phoneme level. The unit for /'kʌp/ at the word level, for instance, will receive excitation at the phoneme level from /k/ in time slices neighbouring slice 4 (figure 59), and from /ʌ/

and /p/ and their respective slices. The connections are strongest at the centre of each slice.

Figure 59 illustrates a fragment of the entire system, showing three feature detectors over 24 time slices, three phoneme detectors over 8 time slices, and three word detectors over 8 time slices.

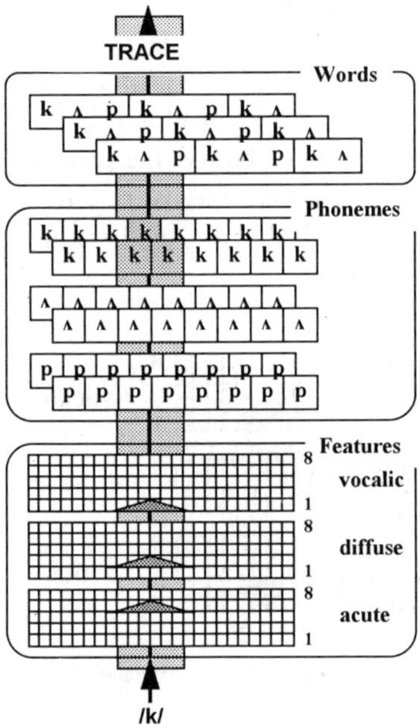

Figure 59. Feature replication over time slices in the TRACE model, example input /k/

To summarise, the system of time slices and feature replication enables the TRACE model to use information from overlapping portions of speech to identify successive phonemes. In figure 59, for example, there are excitatory connections to three replications of /k/ at the phoneme level (shown in grey), as a result of the temporal expansion of the processing units at the feature level. Likewise, there are two opportunities to identify the initial portion of the word /'kʌp/ at the word level, due to the temporal nature of phoneme identification.

(c) activation patterns

As already mentioned, processing takes place through the excitatory and inhibitory interaction of the processing units at the processing levels. The entirety of connections established constitutes an activation pattern, which is the result of the activation value at each processing level. This overall pattern is referred to as the 'Trace' and lends its name to the model. In figure 59 the 'Trace' is drawn as a slim grey rectangle, with the central activation value expressed by the upward arrow. The idea of the 'Trace' goes back to the HEARSAY speech understanding system, a model which made use of independent knowledge sources, such as phonetics, syntax, and semantics (McClelland/Elman 1986: 12). These knowledge sources "looked" at the speech signal and made independent hypotheses about syllable structure, words, phrases, etc. The hypotheses about the nature of the input were recorded on a data structure accessible by all knowledge sources. This data structure was referred to as *blackboard* (Barr/Feigenbaum 1981: 326).

To sum up, the TRACE model processes speech input at three processing levels. Each processing level features several processing units, which overlap and are replicated over time. Due to their activation values, the units build a general activation pattern, called the 'Trace'. Figure 60 exhibits the entire system, using our example input /'kʌp/. Note that, due to its multi-dimensional character, it is extraordinarily hard to visualise the TRACE model in its entirety. For this reason, connections have been omitted in figure 60 and the 'Trace' itself has been drawn by a simple vertical arrow, one for each input phoneme.

(d) processing utterances

Before processing begins, the activation values of all processing units are set to their resting values. Processing itself can be defined as a left-to-right procedure where the input updates the information in successive time slices, one slice at a time. As each time slice is filled with information, interactions between the processing levels occur on the basis of excitatory and inhibitory connections. Thus, processing is a constant building and refinement of hypotheses about the nature of the input on the basis of three processing levels and the connections between them.

An important feature of the TRACE model is its ability to cope with distorted input. How is this achieved, and how does the TRACE model arrive at a final decision about the input? McClelland/Elman (1986: 24ff) illustrate the processing steps and the technique of handling ambiguous in-

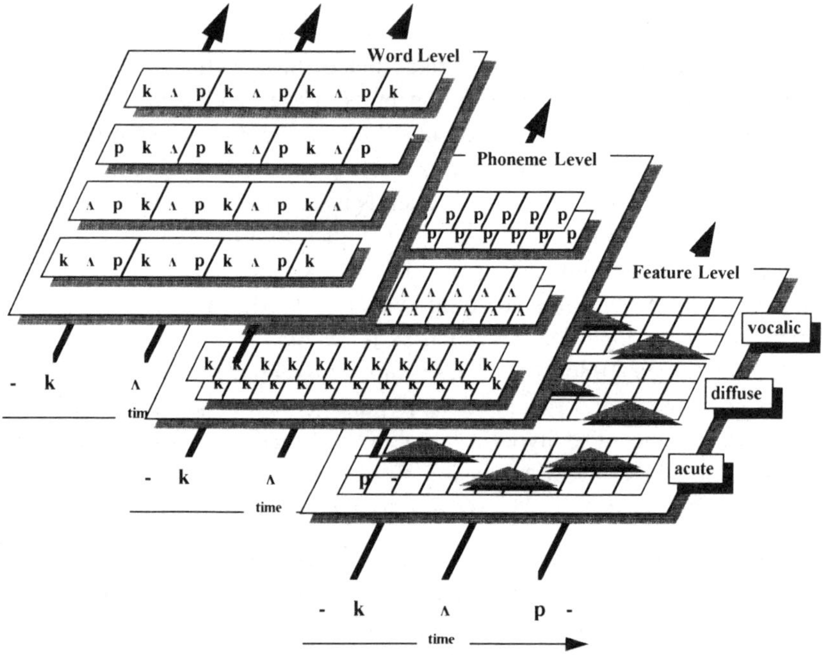

Figure 60. Processing in the TRACE model (after Elman/McClelland 1986)

put, that is input which may evoke several hypotheses. As a demonstration, they chose all those words contained in TRACE's word detector lexicon which begin with *bl-* and *pl-*, i.e. *plug, plus, blush, blood,* etc. They simulated processing on the basis of the target input *?lug* (/?lʌg/), where the first phoneme was distorted and could be identified as being either /p/ or /b/. In such a case, the system receives a feature specification as input where, due to distortions, the feature [voicing] is not specified and can be interpreted as /p/ or /b/.

Processing starts at the feature level, building activation values for /p/ and /b/. The only activation value difference between these two phonemes concerns the feature values 'voiced' (/p/ = 1, /b/ = 7), and 'burst' (/p/ = 8, /b/ = 7); all other activation values are identical for both phonemes. As soon as the activation values build, hypotheses at the phoneme level and at the word level unfold. At this early moment, phoneme detectors for /p/ and /b/, as well as word detectors for words beginning with *p-* and *b-*, are active. The next portion of input, the [l], activates /l/ and /r/ at the phoneme level (/l/ and /r/ are very similar and only differ in the features 'acute' and 'diffuse'), and words starting with *pl-*, *bl-*, *pr-*, and *br-*. A decision about the first phoneme, /p/ or /b/ cannot be taken yet; however, because of the greater number of words in the list of word detectors beginning with *pl-*, there is a slight advantage for /p/ as the initial element. As processing continues, more and more information emerges, and more precise hypotheses about the input are established. However, it is only after the /g/ has come in that the model is capable of deciding whether the input is closer to /'plʌ?/ or /'blʌ?/. In our case, /'plʌg/ wins the competition and via feedback to the phoneme level, /p/ will eventually dominate /b/.

Hence, the TRACE model can simulate the lexical contextual effect (see section 4.1. (g)), where the contents of the lexicon itself influence phoneme identification in a top-down fashion. Interestingly, this top-down effect does not occur during but after the information uptake. This might seem surprising, since most aspects of word processing have been defined as on-line effects. However, as Aitchison (1987: 186) points out, such an off-line effect is not surprising at all. She reports on observations that sure identification, especially with short words, often happens after words have been spoken.

A second top-down effect on speech processing that can be simulated by the TRACE model concerns the influence of phonotactic knowledge on phoneme identification. Even though the TRACE model has no phonotactic knowledge, it can simulate the lexicality effect, i.e. the distinction between types of non-words (see figure 54). Unlike conventional symbolic models, the TRACE model does not generally reject illegal non-words. Rather, illegal non-words receive less activation. A "word" such as **/'tli:/ (***tlee*), for example, has no lexical status at the level of word detectors and is only partially activated. A real word, such as /'tri:/ (*tree*), by contrast, receives full activation. This in turn leads to an interesting hypothesis: the model should be able to cope with phonotactically ill-formed material if enough top-down support can be built. For example, the item ***bwacelet* (**/'bweɪslɪt/) should be identified as *bracelet* (/'breɪslɪt/), even though /bw/ is phonotactically impossible. The TRACE model can simulate this effect. McClelland/Elman (1986: 35) illustrate this phenomenon on the basis of the input *?luly* (/'?lu:lɪ/), which during the initial stages of processing seems to favour an interpretation as /'plu?/. Later, when the item *truly* begins to dominate at the word detector level, the phonotactically inappropriate interpretation of the initial consonant cluster as /'tlu?/ will be preferred, leading to a reduced activation of ***tluly*, and to the possibility of an eventual interpretation of the originally illegal input as *truly*.

To sum up, the TRACE model of spoken word recognition combines bottom-up and top-down information and supports the on-line character of speech perception. Also, it simulates some sorts of off-line effect by delaying the final decision in cases of uncertainty. Furthermore, it takes account of numerous effects that influence phoneme identification, such as phonotactic rule knowledge or the influence of lexical knowledge, and even some aspects of categorical perception.[6] But what about the other effects which have been established experimentally?

As already mentioned, the lexicality effect, i.e. the rejection of non-words, is no problem for the TRACE model. Non-words are handled in terms of reduced activation values. It has been pointed out above that this leads to a very interesting offshoot, the possibility of processing illegal non-words and words whose phonetic structure is distorted.

Two further effects, the word frequency effect and the predictability of words by means of the sentence context have not been incorporated into the TRACE model. However, the integration of contextual influences on word recognition can be achieved by supplying activation to word units from even higher levels of processing. That such information is necessary can be demonstrated with the following example:

(50) /ðɪ ɒbtl wəz ˈfʊl əv ˈwɔ:tə/ (The ***obttle* was full of water)

Despite its distortion, which results in an illegal non-word, we can recognise the second item in (50) as /'bɒtl/ (*bottle*). However, without the context this would be a very difficult enterprise. Processed in isolation, the distorted item would, perhaps, lead to a reduced activation of the real word in the TRACE model; a recognition of it as *bottle*, however, is likely to fail. Hence, we need the sentence context as an additional source of information. The integration of the sentence context into the TRACE model leads to a very interesting consequence. A central idea of the TRACE model is that activation accumulates over time. For the integration of the context this would mean that some effects only become available if a certain amount of time has elapsed (Connine 1990: 282). An alternative would be to postulate a word recognition model where contextual information is used in a non-interactive fashion and only influences the final decision, i.e. the output of the model.

4.2.3. Non-interactive Models

Both the Cohort model and the TRACE model are interactive models of spoken word recognition. They assume that word recognition is a process of constantly activating and deactivating information at various levels of processing each action influencing the other's results.

An alternative to interactive models can be seen in Fodor's (1983) modularity hypothesis. According to this view, first, language processing is independent from other cognitive activities, and, secondly, the natural language faculty in the mind consists of a number of highly specialised components or 'modules' (see section 1.2.). At first sight this seems to be totally in line with the processing levels in the TRACE model or the various components of the Cohort model. However, one primary difference is the degree of encapsulation of the components. While interactive theories allow top-down feedback, for example, from the word level to the phoneme level, non-interactive models involve representations that are not directly influenced by decisions taken at higher levels. Especially, representations computed at lower levels are not directly affected by information from higher levels, such as lexical knowledge, phonotactic knowledge, etc.

Probably the most influential modular model is the *Search model* proposed by Forster (1976/1979). It assumes that higher levels have access to the results of lower levels, but do not directly intervene in processing decisions. For example, information about the sentence context is not accumulated over time; rather, it is used as a corrective function which might overturn decisions taken at lower levels once the perceptual information has been processed. However, there is a problem. If we consider the word recognition device of the Search model in isolation, we are confronted with a recognition device that does not make any claims about internal levels, and is thus neither interactive nor modular. (We will return to the Search model in section 4.5.2., where we will reconsider the relationship between word recognition and lexical retrieval).

Hence, we have two possible ways of accounting for the contextual effect, an interactive strategy, which collects information from the sentence context over time, and a non-interactive or modular strategy, which serves as a corrective device after the perceptual information has been processed. Connine (1990: 283ff) argues for a modular approach. She used the IFSP (Identification-Function Shift Paradigm) technique to illustrate that the sentence context does not accrue over time, but is confined to specific endpoint stimuli. Let us look more closely at the results, using the IFSP. In this experimental paradigm, listeners have to choose from a set of items, such as *bath/path*, where the initial phoneme varies between /p/ and /b/. The stimuli are presented in semantically biased sentences, such as (51):[7]

(51) a. She put the towel in the ____.
b. She walked the horse along the ____.

While in (51a) *bath* is more likely as a response, (51b) is semantically biased towards an interpretation of the initial phoneme of the target item as /p/. Not surprisingly, reaction times are faster if the stimulus is consistent with the sentence context. However, as Connine (1990: 285) reports, this effect was confined to endpoint and midpoint stimuli, whereas no such effects were observed in the category boundary region, i.e. the region where the perceptual mechanism has difficulties in deciding between voiced/voiceless distinctions (the area around the VOT-boundary). These results are in sharp contrast with the predictions of interactive models, where the sentence context would provide sufficient information about the nature of the input. Hence, the conclusion can only be that the contextual effect is an important argument for non-interactive models of word recognition, at least at the sentence level.

In section 4.1. we mentioned a second context effect, the influence of lexical knowledge on word recognition, the 'lexical effect'. However, in contrast to the sentence context, lexical knowledge is used directly in word recognition. Experiments that focus on this effect normally use stimuli similar to the ones employed in IFSP. The interesting difference is that one stimulus of the two endpoint pairs forms a word, the other does not, e.g. *type/*dype*, or **tice/dice*. Irrespective of whether the stimulus difference occurs within the categorical boundary region or not, response times are generally faster for words than for non-words. The only explanation for these findings is that lexical knowledge is constantly used for the interpretation of the perceptual input.

Hence, contextual effects argue for interactive as well as for non-interactive models. While the lexical contextual effect is interactively made use of, the sentence context is integrated to choose between alternative interpretations in a modular way. According to these findings, lower processing levels, such as the feature level, the phoneme level, or the word level, apply interactively. Higher levels, by contrast, are more encapsulated and less likely to interact with lower levels (We will return to this issue in section 4.5.4.).

4.2.4. Spoken Word Recognition; a Summary

Thus far we have considered word recognition as a process distinct from the level of lexical retrieval. More precisely and strictly speaking, this means that the decision as to whether something is a word or not does not involve the retrieval of the lexical specification associated with a lexical access unit from the lexicon. In modelling this process, we are confronted with two highly-interactive models, the Cohort model of spoken 'word recognition', and the TRACE model of 'speech perception'. The terminological distinction between 'word recognition' and 'speech perception' exactly captures one basic difference between these two models. While the Cohort model does not make precise claims about processing the acoustic/phonetic details of the input, i.e. about pre-lexical processes, the TRACE model is a direct successor of the feature detector models introduced in section 3.2.2. and 3.4. It combines the most important aspects of pre-lexical processing, through the presence of a set of sub-phonemic processing units, with the details of word recognition.

Another important difference between the two models concerns their ability to account for a number of aspects of human speech perception and word recognition. The TRACE model makes much stronger claims in this respect. It is not only capable of simulating a number of effects and structures associated with human word recognition (McClelland/Elman 1986: 71) but it also claims to be computationally adequate. However, there is a huge problem for the TRACE model. It concerns the theoretical as well as the psychological validity of the level of phoneme detectors. As outlined above, the recognition device generates a string of phonemes as input to the lexical level. The phoneme, however, important as it may have been in the past, has a much less dominant status in today's linguistic theory. In section 2.3.2.1. we discussed the non-linear phonological approach which considers the phonological specification of a lexical entry as a collection of segmental and non-segmental phonetic aspects. The TRACE model incorporates only a fraction of these aspects. Although there may be a representation that roughly corresponds to a phoneme-like unit, it is just one level among others. In order to achieve linguistic and psychological adequacy, a model must account for all levels of phonological representation, ranging from sub-segmental features via phoneme-like structures, to metrical aspects and syllable structures. Since the TRACE model fails to do this, it can, at least at present, not be attributed the status of psychological adequacy.

The Cohort model makes no claim with regard to computational adequacy. However, it seeks to be psychologically adequate by emphasising its ability to account for a number of effects observed experimentally. The phoneme plays only a subordinate role in the Cohort model. Lahiri/Marslen-Wilson (1991) argue on the basis of experimental evidence from two different languages, English and Bengali, that the listener does not have available a surface form, i.e. a phonetic representation of a given word form. Rather, the input is interpreted on the basis of an underspecified abstract phonetic representation of the speech input.

Table 6. The Cohort model and the TRACE model compared

Type of Knowledge/Effect	Cohort Model	TRACE Model
phonotactic knowledge	implicit	implicit
lexical knowledge	via elements in the cohort	via word detectors
sentence context	via higher level knowledge	via higher level knowledge
length effect	via recognition point	not represented
lexicality effect	via cohort structure	via activation levels
– regular non-words	– long search	– reduced activation level
– impossible non-words	– no or short search	– reduced activation level
frequency effect	via internal cohort structure	not represented
categorical perception	not represented	via activation levels
handling of distorted input	via parallel cohort	via activation across levels
phoneme as processing unit	implicit, in terms of abstract phonological representation	explicit, in terms of phoneme detectors
syllable as processing unit	implicit in initial cohort	not represented

Table 6 summarises the realisation of various knowledge sources in the Cohort and the TRACE model and the possibility of integrating experimental observations and structures.

The primary advantage of the Cohort model can be seen in its excellent account of the length effect and its elegant technique for narrowing down the set of possible word candidates. Furthermore, it makes an attempt to incorporate as many theoretical linguistic and psycholinguistic insights and theories as possible. The disadvantage of this model lies in the fact that some aspects, especially those which were integrated in version II as a reaction to the deficiencies of the first version, are fairly abstract in character. For example, the frequency effect and the possibility of coping with distorted input have been solved via abstract activation thresholds. This is not surprising, since Marslen-Wilson's (1987) innovations were primarily a reaction towards McClelland/Elman's (1986) TRACE model. For this reason, the use of activation thresholds reminds us, of course, of the activation levels used in the connectionist framework.

Due to these activation levels and the multitude of connections across the network, the TRACE model has no problems in handling distorted input. Furthermore, it provides the possibility of provisional input identification, it is capable of changing preliminary guesses, etc. Also, the integration of the temporal factor of speech processing enables the TRACE model to incorporate aspects such as the phonetic context or categorical perception. Thus, viewed as a coherent theory from pre-lexical to lexical processing, the TRACE model seems to be well equipped to cope with natural language input.[8]

One aspect which neither of the two models has been able to solve is the problem of segmenting the input stream into processing units. In section 3.6. we argued on the basis of data from studies in language acquisition that some sort of syllable structure is central to pre-lexical processing. Since both models incorporate the stage of pre-lexical processing (the TRACE model more explicitly than the Cohort model), they should be able to use syllabic structures to some extent. The TRACE model certainly does not; as far as the Cohort model is concerned, it builds the initial cohort around some sort of syllabic structure, i.e. around the initial CV-cluster, which is typically defined as the universal syllable structure.

Over and above the Cohort and the TRACE model, there are further models of word recognition. Norris (1986) subsumes Morton's (1979) Logogen model, Forster's (1976/1979) Search model, Becker's (1976) Verification model, and his own alternative, the Checking model, under models of word recognition. However, as we will see below, terminology is not consistent in this field. According to our suggestions, these models should be treated as combined models of word recognition and lexical access rather than as isolated word recognition models (see section 4.5.4.).

Up to this point we have treated the process of word recognition primarily on the basis of processing words which are morphologically simple. The recognition of morphological variants, i.e. inflected and derived forms, has not been mentioned. Henderson (1985: 45ff) discussed the possibilities of word recognition and morphological decomposition on the basis of the example *unlucky*. Basically, there are three possible ways of processing such a complex item:

Strategy 1:
Enter the lexicon via the root *luck*, with which, among others, the derivative *unlucky* is connected.

Strategy 2:
Break down the item *unlucky* into *un-*, *luck,* and *-y*, using a set of morpheme detectors.

Strategy 3:
Process the item on the basis of its root *luck,* and use a set of decomposition rules to work out the internal structure of the item *unlucky*.

The first strategy would allow the access units of the entries in the lexicon to reflect morphological structure; however, it would unnecessarily complicate lexical processing because word recognition would imply an intermediate step of searching lists of alternative forms associated with roots. Strategy 2 implies that each morpheme, free morphemes as well as bound morphemes, is defined only once in the lexicon. The system of morpheme detectors, however, would establish an enormous processing load, since the morpheme detectors would be active not only for composite forms such as *unlucky*, but also for quasi-decomposable forms like *inflammable*. The third strategy makes use of a root lexicon, as defined in section 2.1.1., and a separate affix lexicon, where each affix is fully specified for its combinatorial possibilities. According to such a strategy, *un-* would be analysed as a potential prefix in words such as *unlucky*, as well as in words like *undulate*. In the case of *unlucky*, *luck* passes the test as a root, while the *un*-prefixing rule fails in the case of *undulate*, since neither *dul-* nor *dulate* are separate access forms.

To find out which of the three strategies is most likely to be used, Henderson (1985) discussed the results of a series of mainly written word recognition experiments. Unfortunately, experimental evidence is not conclusive. As already mentioned in section 2.1.4., the type of strategy used depends on the representation of the access units in the lexicon. At present we cannot say with absolute certainty whether a full-listing hypothesis or a minimal listing hypothesis is to be preferred. Hence, it is not surprising that Henderson's (1985: 68) conclusion leaves the issue open and highly hypothetical. It may be, Henderson summarises, that polymorphemic words are represented in the lexicon even if a decomposition rule exists. Moreover, there may be differences between inflectional and derivational morphology.

For these reasons it is not surprising that the most influential models of spoken word recognition make no specific claims about the processing of complex words. Consider this last sentence as an example: it contains almost 50% of complex words about which little or nothing is known.

4.3. Models of Written Word Recognition

While the speech signal is extended in time, the written signal is extended in space (Elman/McClelland 1986: 4). Consequently, the temporal factor only plays a subordinate role in written word recognition, and, whatever model is employed, aspects such as temporal overlap, time slices, etc., can by and large be ignored.

As we pointed out in section 3.1.2., it is likely that the process of written word recognition makes use of two recognition strategies: the letter-mediated approach, where the processor relies on letters as mediators between the visual information and recognition, and the holistic approach, which makes use of transgraphemic features or full words (see section 3.1.2.1.). Despite their differences, both approaches are similar, since they employ a general strategy of pattern recognition. The patterns to be identified concern the geometrical shapes of letters and letter combinations, as well as entire words.

In the following, we will have a closer look at two influential models of written word recognition: the *Word Detector* model of written word recognition (Johnston/McClelland 1980), and the *Activate and Check* model (Taft 1986). While the Word Detector model is a computational model based on the insights of connectionism, the Activate and Check model can be viewed as a variant of the Cohort model of spoken word recognition.

4.3.1. The Activate and Check Model

The idea behind the Activate and Check model is that written word recognition proceeds in a 'left-to-right' fashion. However, in contrast to the temporal 'left-to-right' character of spoken word recognition, where the set of potential word candidates is progressively reduced as more information comes in, the visual interpretation of a 'left-to-right' processing strategy says that larger and larger units are used as attempts are made to find a match within the lexicon (Taft 1986: 298). Hence, recognising the word *blend* involves successive attempts to match the incoming information with the access units in the lexicon; in this case, an attempt will be made to identify successively larger units such as *ble-*, *blen-*, *blend* as words, where only the last attempt will be successful. In other words, units smaller than the access units in the lexicon are insufficient to retrieve a word from the lexicon. This assumption is in sharp contrast with the Cohort model of spoken word recognition, where word recognition is initiated on the basis of a fraction of the input. In the case of the spoken input *blend*, it is likely that word recognition occurs once /'blen/ has been processed.

However, this does not mean that written word recognition is only performed on the basis of entire words. There are cases where the Activate and Check model facilitates word recognition using information smaller than words. Hence, we need a processing unit large enough to constitute a word but small enough to deal with cases where fragmentary information is sufficient for word recognition. This unit is an orthographically defined syllable, the *BOSS* (Basic Orthographical Syllable Structure). In numerous word recognition experiments, Taft (1979; 1986) collected experimental evidence that the contact between the written input and the lexicon is established via the BOSS. The general structure of the BOSS is fairly simple; it is centred around the first vowel of a word and includes all consonants prior and subsequent to it. Here are some examples:

(52)	a. Word: lexicon	BOSS:	#lex#
	b. Word: structure	BOSS:	#struct#
	c. Word: English	BOSS:	#Engl#
	d. Word: blend	BOSS:	#blend#
	e. Word: blemish	BOSS:	#blem#

The examples (52d) and (52e) are of special interest. *Blend* will only be accessed via its full representation, since there is no BOSS smaller than the entire word (*ble-* or *blen-* do not constitute a BOSS). The recognition of *blemish*, by contrast, can be facilitated on the basis of a letter string smaller than the entire word, since its first four letters constitute a BOSS.

These assumptions about accessing words via an orthographical syllable which may or may not correspond to an entire word were based on a series of lexical decision tasks by Taft/Forster (1976). Yet, they are inconsistent with the Cohort model of spoken word recognition, where no difference of word recognition between the spoken counterparts of (52d) and (52e) would be expected. The Cohort model simply predicts that /'blen/ and /'blem/ would initiate word recognition in the same way. For this reason Taft (1986) proposed a modification of the Cohort model to satisfy the needs of written word recognition. On the basis of a lexical decision task where he compared spoken and visually presented input (words and regular non-words) he defined a fundamental difference between spoken and written word recognition. In speech, word candidates become activated by the first few phonemes regardless of whether these phonemes constitute a syllable or not, whereas, in written language, words become activated only via their orthographically defined syllable (BOSS).[9] Table 7 illustrates these differences between the Cohort model and the Activate and Check model on the basis of a few words (the word recognition points have been marked with an asterisk and the successively larger units, such as "BLE", represent graphemic and phonological codes).

Table 7. Spoken and written word recognition

Model	"B"	"BL"	"BLE"	"BLEN"	"BLEND"
Cohort	–	–	blemish blend blench blenheim bless	blend blench blenheim	blend*
Activate & Check	–	–	–	–	blend*

Model	"B"	"BL"	"BLEM"	"BLEMI"	"BLEMISH"
Cohort	–	–	blemish*		
Activate & Check	–	–	blemish*		

Model	"D"	"DI"	"DIF"	"DIFFE"	"DIFFER"
Cohort	–	–	differ diffuse difficult	differ*	
Activate & Check	–	–	differ diffuse difficult	differ diffuse difficult	differ*

In principle, the Activate and Check model can be considered as a variant of the Cohort model (or vice versa), since it establishes sets of possible word candidates on the basis of the incoming information, just like the Cohort model. The only difference is that word recognition is a process of 'activating and checking' those lexical entries whose access code is the BOSS of the visually presented word. The Cohort model, by contrast, establishes sets of word candidates (cohorts) by the first few phonemes.

Like the revised (1987/1991) version of the Cohort model, the Activate and Check model is an interactive model of written word recognition, since it allows top-down information to influence low-level decisions. More precisely, lexical information, i.e. knowledge about the orthographical structure of possible word candidates, is allowed to guide lower levels of word identification.

How does this model incorporate the experimental findings discussed in section 4.1?

The representation of the frequency effect is not explicitly mentioned in the literature. However, just as Marslen-Wilson (1987) proposed an inherent order based on word frequency for the revised version of the Cohort model, one could group the set of candidates activated via a BOSS according to their frequencies of usage. On the basis of different activation levels (the notion of activation levels is implicit in the Activate and Check model), one could assume a priority-based ordering of possible word candidates. Thus, the frequency effect should not cause a major problem for this model.

The lexicality effect (word vs. regular non-word) is reinterpreted in the Activate and Check model. According to standard experimental findings, regular non-words take longer to process than real words. Taft (1986) found that this is not generally the case. In comparing visual stimuli whose first part (a CVC cluster) was part of a polysyllabic real word (e.g. FUT – FUTURE), part of a monosyllabic real word (e.g. DUS – DUST), or part of a regular non-word (e.g. BUP – *BUP-), he found that there was no difference in reaction times between items such as DUS/BUP, but a significant difference between stimuli such as FUT, on the one hand, and DUS/BUP on the other. This suggests that a stimulus such as FUT activates the lexicon, while DUS/BUP do not. Taft's explanation should be clear by now. It is irrelevant whether a stimulus is part of a word or a non-word; rather, it is of major importance whether the stimulus constitutes a BOSS. Hence, it is the BOSS that initiates word recognition (FUT is a BOSS, but DUS/BUP are not).

Like the frequency effect, the contextual effect is only implicit in the model. Via the possibility of top-down information flow, the 'lexical contextual effect', i.e. the knowledge about the access units available, influences the result of the initial stages of processing. How the general context affects word processing is not explained.

Models of written word recognition have to account for at least two further aspects: the possibility of phonological recoding and the homophone effect (see sections 3.5. and 4.1. (g)), on the one hand, and the processing of irregular words (see section 4.1. (c)), on the other. These aspects are related. The idea is that homophones (*sail/sale*) and pseudo-homophones (*brain/*brane*) make use of two routes to the lexicon, a direct visual route and a slower phonological route. The latter involves the conversion of the graphemic structure into phonemes. It is employed whenever the visual route fails to find an access unit to the lexicon (as in the case of **brane*). Similarly, phonologically irregular words, such as *sew*, whose phonetic realisation is different from the general letter-to-sound conversion rules, may involve phonological recoding. Interestingly, the Activate and Check model does not support a strategy of phonological recoding, at least not on the basis of the model-specific experimental evidence. If phonological recoding took place, then a unit smaller than a potential BOSS, such as BLEN-, would have to be converted into /'blen-/ and should establish a cohort such as in table 7. Taft (1986) suggests two explanations for the lack of the recoding effect. First, it could be that the homophone and the regularity effects are not all-or-none effects but a matter of degree. In section 4.1. (c) we discussed such a possibility of defining the regularity effect as one of degree of consistency, using grapheme-to-phoneme conversion procedures. A second possibility is that the code resulting from a phonological conversion procedure involves some sort of abstract representation which reaches the lexicon via a specific route. That such additional routes are problematic and highly expensive from the perspective of processing efficiency has been discussed in chapter three. In any case, the main point of the Activate and Check model is that there are two different routes to the lexicon, one for visual and one for spoken material.

The Activate and Check model is based on two fundamental, but highly problematic assumptions. First, it supposes that the visual input is undistorted and can neatly be segmented. Secondly, it assumes a letter-mediated approach where each input unit can be analysed into its individual letters. Both assumptions have to be taken with great care. In section 3.1. (figures 37, 38, table 2) we have illustrated that undistorted input is the exception rather than the rule. Furthermore, we have seen in section 3.1.2.1. that there are good arguments to assume an additional strategy of interpreting visual input holistically. Such a strategy, however, does not receive any attention in the Activate and Check model. Also, graphotactic knowledge, i.e. knowledge about the combinatorial possibilities of letters, is not explicitly incorporated in the Activate and Check model.

In summary, then, the Activate and Check model provides an interesting account of a number of experimentally observable effects. Also, it incorporates an orthographically defined version of the syllable, which has been shown to be an important unit of word processing. It is an interactive model, allowing top-down information flow, especially for selection among a set of lexical access units. Its main problems concern the nature of the input itself, the reliance on a letter-mediated approach, and the lack of graphotactic knowledge. Finally, the BOSS itself may come under attack. Most importantly, it is not clear whether it can be defined universally, or whether it is a language-specific unit confined to English. If we compare the situation with the process of spoken word recognition, we know that the syllable effect differs across languages and has to be interpreted very carefully (Segui et al. 1990).

4.3.2. The Word Detector Model

A completely different model of written word recognition has been defined within the connectionist framework (Johnston/McClelland 1980). This *Word Detector model* can be viewed as the counterpart of the TRACE model of spoken word recognition (section 4.2.2.). It consists of a number of processing levels and processing units at each level. The connections between the processing units at each level can be of an excitatory and an inhibitory kind. The primary difference between the TRACE model and the Word Detector model concerns the low-level detector banks, and the presence of a level of grapheme detectors instead of phoneme detectors. Figure 61 illustrates the architecture of the Word Detector model.

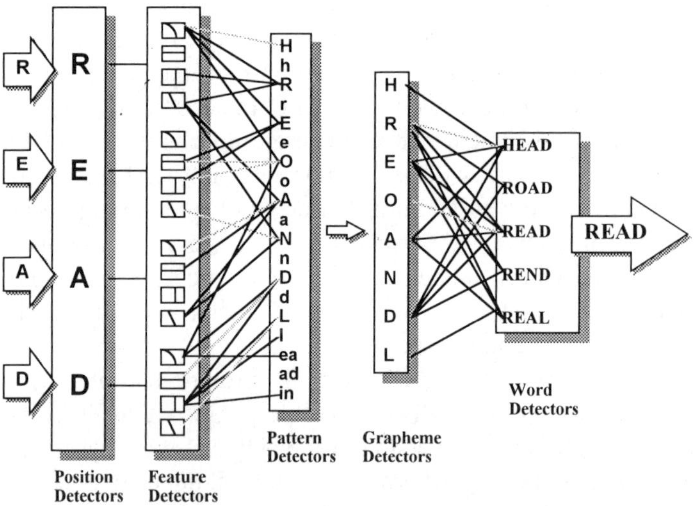

Figure 61. The Word Detector model of written word recognition[10] (not all connections have been drawn) grey connections = inhibitory, black connections = excitatory

Let us look more closely at the processing levels of the Word Detector model.

At the first level, the level of position detectors, a process of filtering is performed, where each letter, or, more precisely, each individual pattern is simply segregated from its background. The primary result of this level is that each letter in the input stream is associated with a number indicating its position in the input stream. As shown in figure 38, there are numerous cases, for example ligatures, where a segmentation of the input into individual letters is impossible. In such cases, patterns larger than one letter are processed as transgraphemic units (see section 3.1.2.1.). Hence, the result of analysis at the position detector level is a sequence of unanalysed geometrical shapes labelled with their ordinal positions.

The next three levels constitute the heart of an OCR-feature detector system. In section 3.4. we discussed the ingredients of such a practical computer application (see figure 49). The primary task of an OCR-system is to convert the input stream into individual letters without reference to word recognition.[11] Hence, the levels of feature, pattern and grapheme detectors correspond to the levels of low-level feature analysis, sub-graphemic feature analysis, and the feature buffer in an OCR-system.

If we compare the TRACE model with the Word Detector model, one interesting difference emerges. Normally we should expect that the level of phoneme detectors of the TRACE model corresponds to a level of grapheme detectors in the Word Detector model. However, the story is not as simple as that. This is due to the different temporal nature of written input and the resulting segmentation procedure. While McClelland/Elman (1986) approach the segmentation problem in speech by a system of temporally overlapping processing units, the segmentation problem in written word recognition can – due to its different temporal character – not be solved in such a way. Rather, it must be captured by introducing an additional level of (orthographical) pattern detectors.

In addition to the 52 letters of the Roman alphabet (upper and lower case) and a number of language-specific letters (e.g. umlauts), the level of pattern detectors should also have a set of transgraphemic patterns at its disposal. In practical OCR-systems, for example, the program will identify such transgraphemic patterns and store them together with their individual letter interpretations. Since printed documents may be written using different fonts, modern OCR-systems allow for the possibility of storing several thousand transgraphemic patterns per font-type. The proportional font-type 'Times New Roman', for example, requires a large number of such patterns, e.g. "rm", "in", "im", etc., where the two adjacent letters cannot be clearly kept apart. Hence, the level of 'orthographic pattern detectors' constitutes the heart of the Word Detector model. It contains the upper and lower case individual letters of a language, a number of special characters, in German, for example, ä, ö, ü, and ß, a small set of logographic characters, e.g. $, &, §, etc., a large set of transgraphemic patterns, and, last but not least, a number of fixed images or holistic patterns (see figure 42, chapter III). In addition to this, there is a detector for space, which prevents stimuli such as READ from activating READY. The analysis result of this level is graphemes, or, in the case of practical computer applications, ASCII-values.

While true OCR-systems are primarily interested in the recognition of individual letters, the Word Detector model involves an additional stage of word detectors, i.e. the system's internal list of access units. This stage is identical with the level of word detectors in the TRACE model of spoken word recognition, which has been discussed at length in section 4.2.2. Again, all processing units at the level of letter detectors have links to all the words at the word detector level.

How does this model handle the experimental findings?

Essentially, we can replicate the basic findings in association with the TRACE model. Due to the permitting of top-down information flow, phonotactic and lexical knowledge can influence lower level decisions. For example, real words receive full activation at the level of word detectors, whereas regular non-words do not. Again, this leads to the interesting assumption that distorted input can be processed, if enough top-down support is available, and, moreover, that even graphotactically ill-formed material will evoke some activation at the word detector level. Hence, the 'lexicality effect', i.e. the identification of non-words, is not problematic for the Word Detector model.

While the 'word frequency effect' is not incorporated in the model, the 'contextual effect' can be represented via access to higher level information.

4.3.3. Written Word Recognition; a Summary

The primary difference between a connectionist model such as the Word Detector model and the Activate and Check model concerns the incorporation of the syllable effect. Unfortunately, the Word Detector model does not make any claim about processing units other than letters or holistic patterns. Of course, it allows for the possibility of dealing with transgraphemic structures; however, these only accidentally correspond to orthographically defined syllables. This is one major shortcoming of the model. The primary advantage of the Word Detector model is its ability to process distorted or ill-formed input. Furthermore, Word Detector models can, at least to some extent, cope with the high degree of variability in the written signal (fonts, styles, case, see figure 38). Table 8 summarises the main differences between the two models.

Table 8. The Activate and Check model and the Word Detector model compared

Type of Knowledge/Effect	Activate and Check Model	Word Detector Model
phonotactic knowledge	not represented	implicit
lexical knowledge	via top-down effects	via top-down effects
sentence context	via higher level knowledge	via higher level knowledge
length effect	via BOSS structure	not represented
lexicality effect	via BOSS availability	via activation levels
frequency effect	implicit	not represented
homophone effect	no	no
phonological recoding	no	no
handling of distorted input	no	via activation across levels
letter-mediation	yes	yes
holistic patterns	no	yes
syllable as processing unit	yes: BOSS	not represented

4.4. Word Recognition; a Summary

In the previous sections we have discussed two fundamentally different approaches to word recognition: the connectionist approach and the conventional symbolic approach.[12] Table 9 summarises this situation.

Table 9. Word recognition models

Approach	Spoken Word Recognition	Written Word Recognition
Connectionism	TRACE model	Word Detector model
Conventional Computation	Cohort model	Activate and Check model

Irrespective of the processing mode (speech vs. written input), some interesting parallels between the models of each framework, and across the two frameworks, emerge. For example, connectionist as well as conventional symbolic approaches make use of the notion of activation thresholds. In connectionist models, the emergence of specific recognition results is dependent on excitatory and inhibitory connections across the system. In conventional symbolic models, by contrast, specific elements among the set of potential word candidates receive a higher activation level due to the integration of other processing levels, e.g. via the context. Furthermore, both frameworks assume that a word to be processed is first of all a member of a set of candidates. This set may be realised by a cohort, a list of words sharing the same BOSS, or a list of word detectors. In any case, word recognition can be viewed as a process of narrowing down an initially large set of candidates to a single or, in the case of ambiguity (distorted input, illegal input), a few remaining ones.

The primary difference between the connectionist and the conventional symbolic view lies in the feasibility of handling distorted or illegal input. While the Cohort and the Activate and Check model make use of rather abstract notions, for example the postulation of a parallel cohort, connectionist models can explicitly account for input ambiguities via reduced activation levels. By contrast, the conventional symbolic models seem to be more in line with psychological insights. The simulation of the syllable effect, even though it is problematic across languages (Segui et al. 1990), is a good case in point.

Another important difference between the two types of model concerns the integration of learning processes. While connectionist models can relatively easily simulate self-adaptation via training, conventional models have nothing to say about learning processes. How learning can be achieved in terms of connectionist models is explained in Watson (1991: 72ff) on the basis of a simple OCR-program written in LISP.

Thus, we are confronted with two different approaches; one is computationally highly adequate, and one relies fully on psychological insights. It remains to be seen which one will eventually be more successful. Considering the development of the debate between the advocates of the two models (Marslen-Wilson and McClelland), however, we can expect more and more similarities to emerge, which will eventually result in a system architecture that merges both approaches.

4.5. Modelling Lexical Access

In section 1.3.2. we suggested that the term 'lexical access' should avoided where possible. One reason for our suggestion was the inconsistency with which the term is used in the relevant literature, especially if we look at word processing models. For example, a model such as the Cohort model is sometimes referred to as a model of 'word recognition' (e.g. Norris 1986; Harris/Coltheart 1986; Aitchison 1987), other researchers define it as a model of 'speech perception' (McClelland/Elman 1986; Connine 1990), and yet others subsume it under the heading of 'lexical access' (Garman 1990). Likewise, a model such as Forster's Search model (see section 4.5.2.) is often discussed under the heading of 'word recognition' (Norris 1986; Aitchison 1987), as well as 'lexical access' (Garman 1990).

To keep terminology tidy, we classify models of word processing into three different types:

- models of pre-lexical processing
- word recognition models
- lexical access models

Those models that make no claim about word recognition have been defined as models of pre-lexical processing. They are primarily interested in defining the low-level processes involved in the perception of spoken or written input. Such models, e.g. feature detector models, have been discussed in chapter three.

All those models that discuss the possibility of recognising words, i.e. the access units associated with a lexical entry, without specific reference to a lexical entry's specification, have been defined as word recognition models in this book. The most prominent models, the Cohort model, the Activate and Check model, the TRACE model, and the Word Detector model, have been discussed in this chapter.

The last group of models treated in this book contains all those integrated models that seek to combine word recognition and lexical retrieval. Such models are generally called *lexical access models*. According to our suggestion in section 1.3.2., they should be referred to as *lexical processing models*.

Sometimes it is very hard to draw the borderline between pre-lexical processing, word recognition, and lexical retrieval. The TRACE model and the Word Detector model, which should be referred to as models of word recognition according to our terminology, can also be seen as a models of pre-lexical processing, since they combine pre-lexical processes, such as feature identification, with aspects of lexical processing, such as lexical look-up. The Cohort model and the Activate and Check model, by contrast, cut across the processes of word recognition and lexical retrieval, since they interactively integrate strictly lexical processes, such as narrowing down the set of potential word candidates, with higher level processes, such as semantic aspects of an entry's lexical specification.

In summary, it is hard to provide a strict classification of the models that describe the processing of lexical information into models of pre-lexical processing, word recognition, and lexical access. However, in terms of a negative definition, i.e. in terms of what a model does not do, a distinction is possible.

Figure 62 illustrates our terminology and the most important models of each branch.

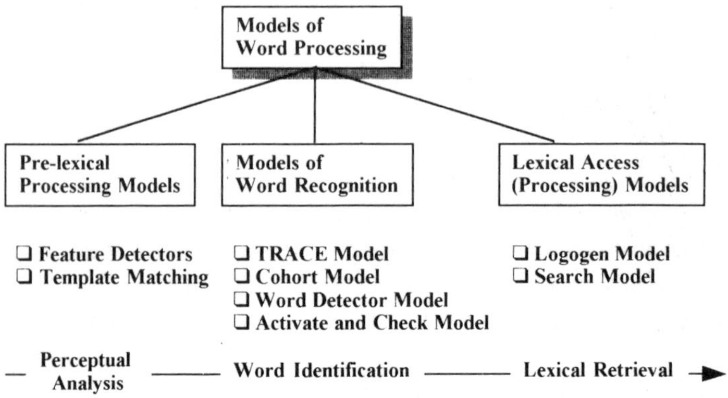

Figure 62. Word processing, from perception to lexical retrieval

Even though the three main branches of word processing are difficult to keep apart, there are two further important differences between them. They concern the number of input channels and the ability to explain the observable experimental effects.

While pre-lexical processing models and models of word recognition are always defined with regard to either speech or written input, lexical access models incorporate both input channels. They are not specifically concerned with low-level analysis processes and the exact description of the operation of each input channel. Rather, they assume more or less abstract recognition devices, on the basis of which word recognition can be carried out. In other words, lexical access models presuppose that visual or auditory recognition processes are peripheral and have already taken place. The primary interest of lexical access models is thus not the description of word recognition processes but the exact definition of top-down influences on word recognition, especially the influence of the sentence context, and the possibility of observing cross-modal effects, i.e. the possibility of mutual influences between, and top-down influences on, the input channels. To find out whether cross-modal effects exist, experiments have to be carried out where the input modes are mixed. In spoken word recognition experiments, for example, stimuli will have to be presented visually; in reading tasks, primes or target information will have to be given auditorily. In other words, the stimulus information crosses the processing modes. We will see below whether cross-modal effects exist.

In section 4.1. we discussed a number of experimental techniques and their results with regard to word recognition. Also, we introduced a distinction between those effects that are of special interest for spoken word recognition and those that are primarily relevant for visual processing (see table 4). A further distinction can be drawn between those experimental effects that are exclusively relevant for the process of word recognition and those that affect higher levels. For example, the length effect (long words are recognised more slowly, unless the recognition point is early in the word) and the word superiority effect (letters are identified more rapidly if presented in the context of a word rather than in isolation) only concern the process of word recognition. The contextual effect (words can be identified faster when placed in an appropriate utterance context), by contrast, goes beyond the level of word recognition and is thus central to lexical access models.

4.5.1. Indirect vs. Direct Lexical Access

A central question of lexical access concerns the number of stages involved (Garman 1990: 260ff). In *indirect* or *search models*, lexical access is achieved by a search procedure that sequentially activates several stages of lexical processing. These stages can best be described by drawing a parallel with a library. In trying to locate a book on a specific shelf, one first consults the main catalogue to find the book's signature. This signature serves then as a pointer to indicate the book's precise position. Indirect access proceeds in a similar way. Once a word has been recognised at stage one, we know its location in the master file, or, to maintain the analogy with the library, in the main catalogue, and lexical access can proceed to stage two. At this stage, the lexical specification associated with the access unit can be retrieved. Maintaining the parallel with the library, stage two will involve getting the book from the shelf. Figure 63 illustrates the general architecture of an indirect access model.

In a direct access model such a differentiation between stages of lexical look-up is not necessary. The input signal (spoken or written) can be directly matched with the lexicon and invoke lexical retrieval. Figure 64 illustrates the central stages of direct lexical access.

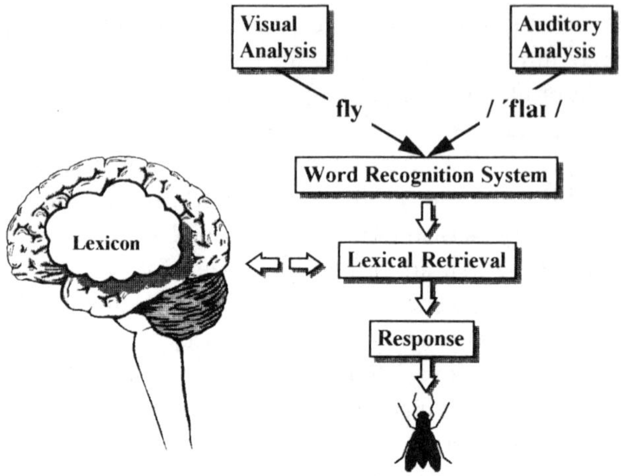

Figure 63. Indirect lexical access

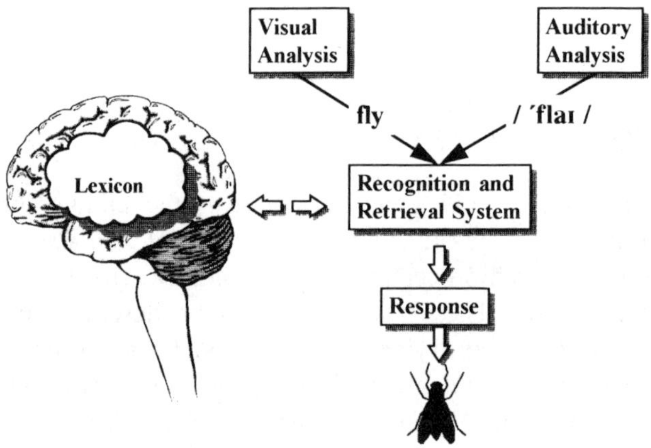

Figure 64. Direct lexical access

There are different views about the terms 'indirect' and 'direct'. Foss/Hakes (1978: 329ff) reserve them for their discussion about the relationship between reading and listening (see section 3.5.). The direct access hypothesis of reading says that printed information reaches the lexicon directly without the intervention of phonetic processes. By contrast, indirect access hypotheses (subvocalisation and phonological recoding) claim that the processing of written information involves the conversion of print into subvocal speech. Hence, the terms 'direct' and 'indirect' in this interpretation are reserved for the relationship between the oral and the written input channel to the lexicon.

Even though the terms 'direct' and 'indirect' make sense in their application to the process of written word recognition, they have been reserved in this book for the discussion of the general architecture of lexical access models. Concerning the process of written word recognition, we maintain the terms 'phonological recoding' (indirect) and 'no phonological recoding' (direct), as above.

4.5.2. The Search Model of Lexical Access (Indirect Access)[13]

The Search model of lexical access goes back to Forster (1976). Essentially, it is a two-stage model where the first stage is completed before the second stage begins (Garman 1990: 266). Hence, concerning its operational principles, it is a serial rather than a parallel model. At stage one, the level of word recognition, the search is carried out. Since words can be accessible in their written and their spoken form, and, in language production on the basis of their conceptual specification, the search can be carried out in three ways, orthographically, phonologically, and semantically. At stage two, the specification associated with the lexical access code is made available (lexical retrieval). Figure 65 illustrates the basic architecture of the Search model of lexical access.

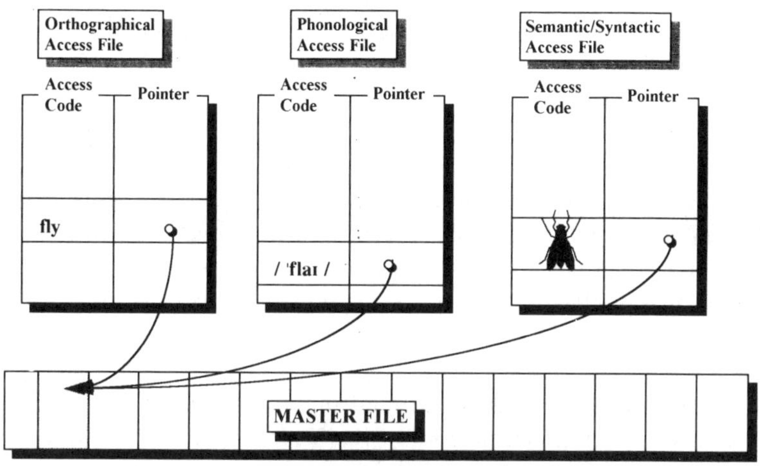

Figure 65. The Search model of lexical access

The central assumption of the Search model is that the mental lexicon can be subdivided into two general stores: one big store which contains the lexical specification of each entry, the so-called *master file*, and a system of three peripheral *access files*, one organised according to the orthographical properties of words, one according to the phonological properties of words, and one according to the conceptual, or semantic/syntactic properties of words. The file systems are connected by means of a pointer system, which allows the retrieval of an entry's specification once it has been identified in an access file. This two-level system accounts for the intuition that the mental lexicon must permit diversity of access but unity of storage (Garman 1990: 267). The separation into access files and master file, and the use of lexical pointers, guarantee that, irrespective of the input mode, we always access the same item in the master file.

Since the Search model contains a component whose main task is to identify whether an item is a word or not, it must account for the main experimental effects which are related to the level of word recognition. Furthermore, it should explain higher-level effects, such as how the utterance context guides the identification of lexical items. Let us look at the integration of the effects of word recognition first.

The frequency effect (high-frequency words are processed faster than low-frequency words) is accounted for by the internal organisation of the items in the access files, where an abstract system of so-called 'bins' associates a pointer to the master file with each item. Whenever the input signal reaches the mental lexicon, the appropriate area or 'bin' of the relevant access file is activated. Within each bin, the access units are organised according to their frequency of usage, with high-frequency words at the top of the stack, and low-frequency words at the bottom. The exact nature of this fairly abstract organisational principle, however, is not clear.

In the Search model, the lexicality effect (words are processed faster than regular non-words, see figure 54) follows from the fact that for regular non-words the phonotactically or graphotactically legal stimulus will activate the appropriate bin but will eventually result in a fruitless search where no pointer to the master file can be generated. For illegal non-words, which are rejected very quickly, no entry route into any access file, and thus no bin, can be established.

Further effects of word recognition (word superiority, length effect) cannot be explained within the framework of the Search model. This is due to the fact that this model makes no claims about the relevance of processing units (phonemes, letters, syllables, holistic patterns) at the early stage of word recognition. Let us therefore turn to experimental effects that relate to higher levels.

The main experimental effect at these levels concerns the influence of the utterance context, in terms of experimental observations, the priming effect. The fact that a stimulus such as *doctor* facilitates the recognition of the item *nurse* is accounted for by a system of cross-references in the master file. Thus far, little has been said about the internal organisation of this store, except that it contains the lexical specifications of all items in the lexicon common to all modes of language processing. However, the master file must not be seen as a mere assembly of lexical specifications; rather, it is a highly complex system of inter-relationships between them. These inter-relationships, or cross-references, can be thought of as a gigantic network. Alternatively, one can assume that the master file does not contain very much information about the lexical specifications associated with the access units, but acts as a kind of backbone that is linked to the general conceptual system, where all kinds of knowledge are represented (Matthei/Roeper 1983: 190). In any case, the integration of the contextual effect into a model of lexical access will always be a fairly abstract technique.

One question, which the Search model implicitly answers, concerns the impossibility of permitting cross-modal priming effects. Due to the strict separation of access files, the facilitation of spoken word recognition by written primes, and vice versa, should not exist. In fact, this assumption has been confirmed experimentally (see Harris/Coltheart 1986: 141ff, for a discussion). Thus, Forster seems right in strictly separating the access files from one another.

4.5.3. The Logogen Model of Lexical Access (Direct Access)

The most prominent model of direct access is the Logogen model. Like many other models it has undergone drastic revision due to a number of experimental observations. The first version of the Logogen model originated with Morton (1969); the revised version was proposed by the same researcher (Morton 1979).

The essential characteristic of the Logogen model of lexical access is that words are recognised by a set of logogens, one corresponding to each word in the language. Essentially, a *logogen* is a kind of word detector (Greek: *logos* = *word*, *idea*) that collects evidence for the occurrence of a specific word on the basis of a set of feature counters (Norris 1986: 95). Figure

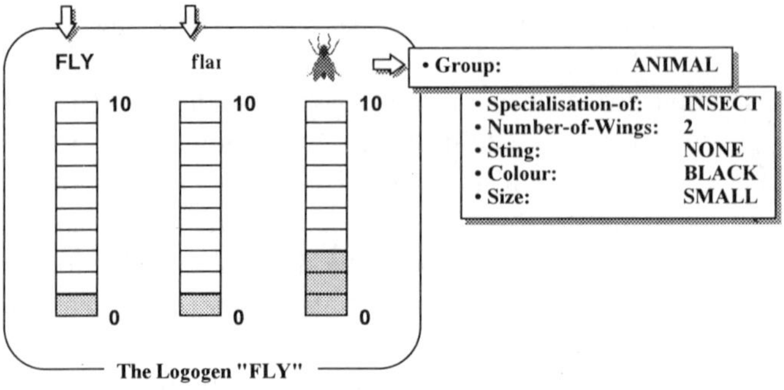

Figure 66. The basic structure of a logogen

66 illustrates the basic internal structure of a logogen and the conceptual information associated with it.

Each logogen is sensitive to perceptual (visual and auditory) and semantic input features, that is, it accepts three types of evidence: visual, auditory, and semantic/conceptual. All logogens have thresholds, or activation values. In figure 66 the thresholds have been illustrated by three banks of arbitrary numerical values ranging from 0 to 10. Whenever the logogen has collected enough evidence, i.e. as soon as a certain overall activation value as a sum of all numerical banks is reached, the logogen 'fires' and the word has been recognised.

In contrast to the Search model, the Logogen model is a one-stage system, where the process of word recognition does not occur prior to lexical retrieval but simultaneously with it. Figure 67 provides a sketch of the architecture of the first version of the Logogen model.

Essentially, the Logogen model consists of two sub-systems: the logogen system, which contains logogens for each word in the language, and the response buffer, from which a written, spoken, or semantic response can be generated.

The principle of direct lexical access is realised via a pathway from the entries in the logogen system to the cognitive system (the overall knowledge base). In figure 66, the availability of semantic/conceptual information is realised via a pointer to the frame containing the conceptual characteristics of FLY. The direct relationship between the logogen system and the conceptual specification of a lexical entry explains the facilitation of word recognition on the basis of the utterance context. For example, if the word *insect* occurs prior to the word *fly*, the logogen for *fly* will collect some evidence, even before the word is actually perceived. In other words, if a

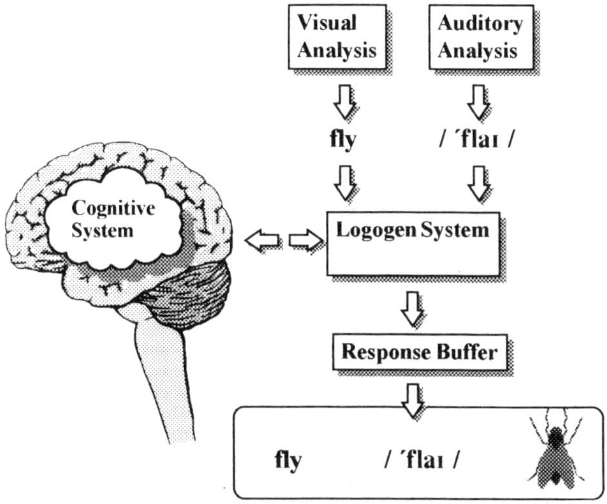

Figure 67. The Logogen model of lexical access, first version

logogen is activated by the semantic features of a related word, then fewer perceptual features will be required for the recognition of the target. In figure 66, this facilitatory effect is exhibited by the arbitrary activation value 3 for the semantic/conceptual part of the logogen.

Over and above the integration of contextual effects, the system of activation thresholds accounts for the frequency effect on word recognition. Assuming that logogens have different initial resting values, all those logogens that correspond to high-frequency words simply have a higher initial value than low-frequency words. In figure 66 the initial values for the visual and auditory recognition system have been preset to value 1 to illustrate the incorporation of word frequency effects.

One necessary organisational principle of logogens is the assumption of a rapid decay of the activation values once they have reached their threshold value. If this were not the case, the identification of subsequent words would be inhibited. Imagine the system has just processed the word *fly* and the activation of that logogen remains high. In such a case, a visually similar word, such as *flu*, might cause the logogen for *fly* to be more highly activated than the correct stimulus *fly* (see Harris/Coltheart 1986: 140ff for a discussion of the activation and deactivation of thresholds).

Unfortunately, an essential prediction of the original version of the Logogen model turns out to be wrong. Because each word is associated with only one logogen, which combines visual and auditory aspects, different processing modes will always activate the same logogen. In other words, the Logogen model permits cross-modal priming effects. That this is not generally the case (only visual word recognition is facilitated by prior reading aloud) has already been mentioned (Harris/Coltheart 1986: 142). Thus, the model had to be altered in such a way that different logogens, one per word for each processing mode, visual and auditory, come into action. Figure 68 outlines this revised architecture.

According to the revised version of the Logogen model, the mental lexicon is no longer considered as a unified whole but it is divided into a semantic/conceptual system, and a visual and auditory recognition system. Both the visual and the auditory input systems have direct encapsulated links to the cognitive system. This subdivision guarantees that priming effects occur only within but not across processing modes. Whether the input logogens can also be directly connected with the output system (the response buffer in the original version) is not clear. For this reason, these connections have been drawn in grey in figure 68.

While the frequency effect and the influence of the context can be explained relatively easily, there are two major problems, even for the revised version of the Logogen model. One problem concerns the processing of non-words, i.e. the lexicality effect. In fact the Logogen model has nothing to say about non-words. All input logogens can only recognise words. This certainly contradicts the experimental findings about non-words. According to the Logogen model, both regular non-words and illegal non-words would be rejected at the same speed, since neither of them would cause an input logogen to respond.

A further problem concerns the status of the input signal. Like the Search model of lexical access, the Logogen model is totally unspecific about the exact nature of the input. No claim is made as to whether the building of activation potentials starts on the basis of phonemes, graphemes, syllables, etc. However, as we saw in section 4.5., lexical access models are not primarily interested in lower levels of word processing. Their main purpose is to describe those lexical processes that are affected by higher levels, such as the influence of the sentence context.

4.5.4. Lexical Access Models; a Summary

The major difference between the Search model and the Logogen model concerns the treatment of the level of lexical retrieval. While in Forster's Search model lexical retrieval is a completely autonomous subcomponent of a strictly bottom-up non-interactive processing system, Morton's Logogen

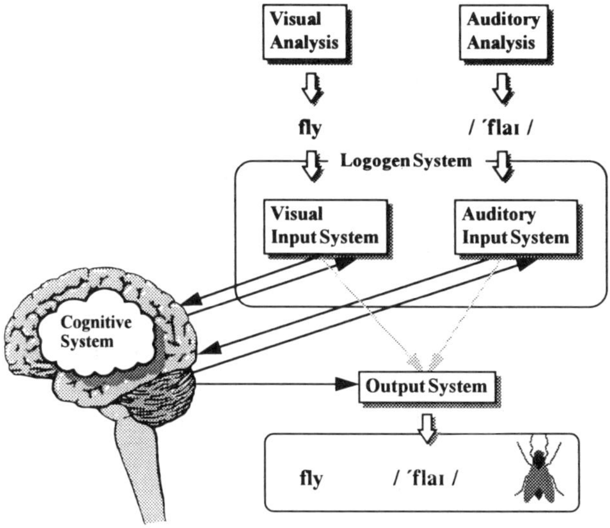

Figure 68. The Logogen model of lexical access, revised version

model integrates lexical retrieval within word recognition and thus allows top-down processing effects to occur.

As outlined, neither model makes any precise claims about the phase of word recognition, or the use of specific processing units, such as phonemes or syllables. Rather, they make an attempt to integrate the findings of word processing and higher levels of lexical processing. Thus, it is not surprising that both lexical access models have nothing to say about typical word recognition effects, such as the length effect or the lexicality effect. Low-level processes, such as feature detection, temporal overlap, etc. are beyond the scope of these models. The primary purpose of lexical access models of the type discussed above is to explain two central effects on word recognition which can, by and large, be attributed to levels higher than word identification processes: the contextual effect, and the word frequency effect.

While both models attribute the frequency effect to some sort of internal structure of their word recognition devices (internal bin ordering vs. logogen activation values), the explanation of contextual effects clearly outlines their different system architectures.

As shown in section 4.1., there are two types of context that affect word processing: the sentential or utterance context, and the lexical context. While the lexical context, i.e. our knowledge about the availability of words in the lexicon, concerns the level of word recognition, the sentential context applies to higher levels of processing. In section 4.2.3. we argued on the basis of Connine's (1990) experimental results that the lexical contextual effect clearly supports an interactive architecture of word recognition processes, that is, an interaction of feature levels, phoneme levels, and word detection levels. But what about the sentential context?

The conventional view of sentential contextual effects on lexical processing is that the context somehow exerts control over the speed of word recognition. In the Logogen model, this is achieved by incrementing the feature count of logogens, whereas in the Search model, the sentential context has no direct influence on word recognition. According to Forster's (1981) 'error checking view', context effects exclusively take place after recognition and serve as a corrective device after input identification.

Both views are problematic. The explanation of contextual effects in the Logogen model, for example, is mainly based on priming effects. However, as Norris (1986: 96) points out, there is a growing body of experimental evidence that the context provided by sentence fragments influences lexical processing. To incorporate these findings into the Logogen model would require each logogen to become enormously complex, perhaps three- or several-dimensional, since any logogen would now have to accept activation potentials not only from conceptually related individual words, but also from phrases, clauses, or entire sentences. By contrast, the Search model's claim that contextual effects can be defined as independent from the search process faces strong opposition from experimental observations involving degraded stimuli. Norris (1986: 99) discusses an experiment showing that the influence of the sentence context increases with degraded or difficult stimuli. This clearly suggests that sentential contextual effects are employed interactively. On the other hand, we discussed more recent experimental findings by Connine (1990) indicating that word recognition and higher levels do not interact with each other.

Thus, we are in a dilemma concerning a decision about the interaction between word processing and higher levels of lexical processing. Either we can dismiss both models of lexical access and propose an entirely new model, or we can opt for a combination of both architectures. Such a combination has been developed by Norris (1986), who refers to his integrated model as the 'Checking model'. This model, whose architecture is illustrated in figure 69, claims that the stages of word processing operate simultaneously in a somewhat cascaded fashion. Using the terminology suggested in section 1.5., the Checking model employs an incremental processing strategy (see figure 14, chapter I).

Norris' model postulates the following stages of processing. At stage one, the perceptual characteristics of the input are identified. As in the Logogen or in the Search model, no further claims about the exact nature of the processes involved and the units employed at this level are made. Level two is responsible for the identification of words. At this level each word candidate is tagged with an index of the amount of perceptual evidence in its favour. This index resembles the threshold associated with the logogens in Morton's model. Over and above the perceptual value, words also have an indication of their frequency of occurrence. In figure 69 the indices are given as Perc-Val$_N$ for the perceptual and Freq-Val$_N$ for the frequency index. If words are perceived in isolation, they will be recognised when the weighted combination of both indices exceeds a preset recognition value.

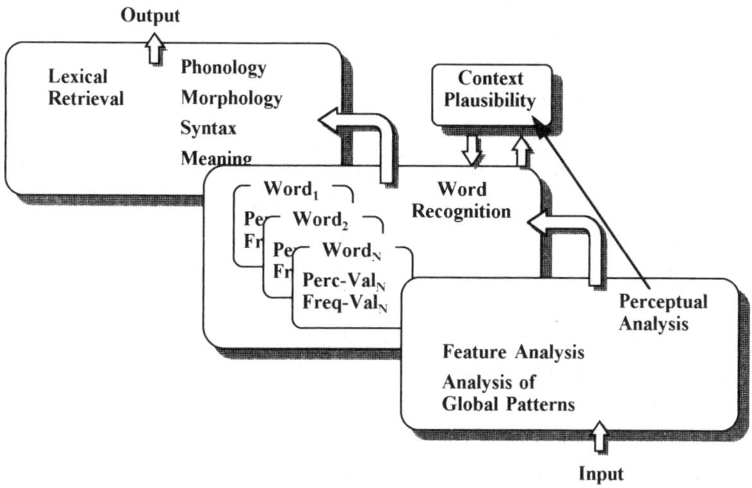

Figure 69. The system architecture of the Checking model

Up to this stage, there is almost no difference between the Logogen and the Checking model. At this point we are confronted with the identification of an item from a set of potential candidates, where each item in the set is weighted according to its frequency and its perceptual characteristics. However, in contrast to the Logogen model, each item in the candidate set can now be accessed and checked to evaluate its contextual plausibility. One essential assumption about this checking process is that it does not start before the candidate set at the level of word recognition is reduced to a manageable size.

To test the contextual plausibility, the additional contextual level receives the most recent output from the level of word recognition, i.e. the candidate set in question, and the most recent output from the level of perceptual analysis, i.e. information derived from the inspection at the level of word recognition. In other words, the system is capable of processing two or more fragments of the input, a possibility which is typical for incremental processing systems. As a result of the contextual checking process, the recognition values will be reduced for plausible words and increased for implausible words at the level of word recognition.[14]

The Checking model bears a number of resemblances to the Logogen model. However, while the Logogen model integrates information from all sources, the Checking model is clearly non-interactive in character. All that the Checking model requires is a system that can identify a set of words from its perceptual characteristics. Additionally, the system requires a temporal store that keeps track of the perceptual and the contextual evidence in favour of a word candidate. Since the checking process does not involve all words of the language but only operates on a limited set, the assumption of such a store should not be problematic.

The most significant feature of the Checking model is that it is, at least as far as the interpretation of contextual effects is concerned, a bottom-up system. This architecture is in sharp contrast with the interactive principles of direct lexical access, and the possibility of integrating higher levels into word recognition models, as suggested in the Cohort model. According to Norris' (1986) and Connine's (1990) discussion of experimental results, such a non-interactive architecture receives a good deal of support. Hence, it may be argued that the integration of the sentential context is established using a non-interactive strategy. The sentence context, it seems, does not interact with lexical processing; rather, contextual information is retrieved from a temporal store by a mechanism which keeps track of the contextual characteristics of the input. This store contains the lexical and higher level information about the items in the context and helps to increase or decrease the contextual plausibility of an item to be identified. In other words, Connine's (1990: 283) position that sentence-context effects are modular in character and influence the output of the perceptual mechanism is more likely than a position that fully integrates lexical processing with higher levels of analysis.

4.6. Summary

Lexical processing is an enormously complex mental activity. It involves the recognition of words and the retrieval of the lexical specification associated with them. In the previous sections, a number of frameworks which attempt to model these activities have been introduced. Not all of these models can be associated exclusively with either of the two activities. Rather, almost all of them cut across word recognition and lexical retrieval, and, even worse, include aspects of pre-lexical processing. Furthermore, it has been shown that terminology is fairly fluid in this area. What some researchers consider to be a process of lexical access, others treat as word recognition, and yet others subsume aspects of pre-lexical processing under word recognition or lexical access. We have tried to remove this terminological vagueness to some extent in section 4.5. Nevertheless, there are difficulties. Take the Checking model, for example. It is meant to be a model of lexical access, but seems to concentrate on recognition processes and even lower levels.

Despite these terminological deficiencies and despite the fact that no model of lexical processing is conclusive, a number of interesting insights about lexical processing should have emerged. Let us look at word recognition first.

Basically, all word recognition models assert the following:

- Input to the lexicon is mode-specific. Despite a number of parallels between spoken and written word recognition (e.g. the status of the processing units: BOSS/syllables), there are fundamental differences, for example the temporal character, that distinguish these two processes. Hence, models of word recognition must be defined in a mode-specific way.
- Any model of word recognition must be able to handle all those experimental effects which are attributable to word recognition, for example, the lexicality effect.
- Word recognition seems to be level-interactive in character. It has been shown above that aspects such as the lexical contextual effect are processed by an interactive integration of several levels of word processing (feature, phoneme, word level).
- Word recognition is highly likely to be a process of selection of an item from a set of rivalling candidates. The items in the set are activated by processing units which are larger than individual letters or phonemes. The set itself may be seen as a list where each item is associated with a preset value. In order to recognise a word this value has to be reached.

Having outlined a number of important aspects of word recognition, we have tried to define the basic properties of lexical access, i.e. the integration of word recognition and lexical retrieval). However, we have found that lexical access models have almost nothing to say about how the lexical specification associated with a lexical access unit is retrieved from the lexicon. Primarily such models are interested in looking at the interaction between the levels of lexical processing, that is, whether word recognition and lexical retrieval are serial or parallel processes. Unlike word recognition models, lexical access models are not mode-specific. Here are some claims about the levels of lexical processing:

- Word frequency effects can be relegated to the level of word recognition and represented via internal orderings of the set of potential word candidates or via increased initial activation values associated with the access units.
- The sentence context influences word recognition. However, there are various arguments that support a non-interactive function of the sentence context within a model of lexical access, rather than an interactive one.

At present, we are confronted with numerous approaches to lexical processes. In modelling word recognition, conventional symbolic and connectionist models compete for predominance; with regard to the more general process of lexical access we can choose from interactive and non-interactive architectures. Nevertheless, more and more parallels emerge between all these frameworks. These parallels concern the reliance on a recognition system that operates with activation values. Irrespective of the processing mode, the selection of a word from a set of alternative candidates can be best defined by associating a value with each item. These values can be affected by other levels of processing.

The second parallel within all the models is the availability of a set of alternative candidates at the early stage of lexical processing. This is remarkable and distinguishes the mental lexicon from ordinary databases, where search does not narrow down existing sets but examines individual candidates sequentially.

It is hard to unify all models discussed and merge them into a generalised model of the mental lexicon and word processing. However, if we remain abstract enough about the definition of the contributing processes and unspecific about the internal structure of each module, a general conception of the mental lexicon and word processing can be set up. Figure 70 outlines the basic architecture of such a model, which attempts to integrate the main models of word recognition outlined in this chapter.

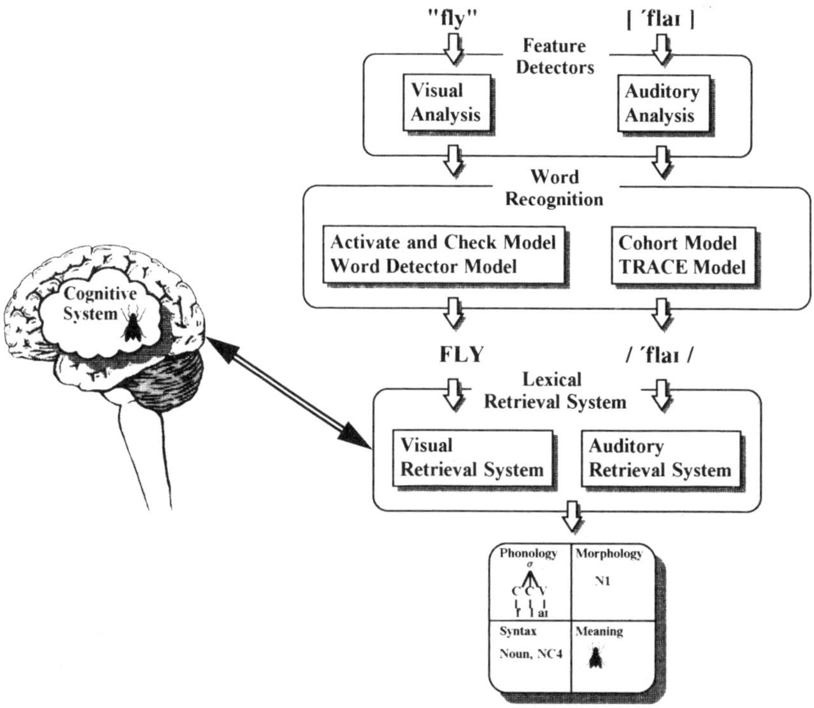

Figure 70. A general conception of word processing

This unified model consists of three general levels: the level of pre-lexical processing, the level of word recognition, and the level of lexical retrieval. In chapter three we argued for a realisation of pre-lexical processes by a system of feature detectors. These feature detectors are an integral part of connectionism and can thus easily be combined with the connectionist approaches to word recognition, e.g. with the TRACE model or the Word Detector model, and merge the pre-lexical level and the level of word recognition into one general level. Since conventional symbolic models, by contrast, are less specific about low-level processes, the level of feature detectors has been maintained. Whether the level of word recognition has access to the cognitive system is not clear. The question boils down to the debate about the interaction between the components of lexical processing. Since sentential contextual effects seem to favour a non-interactive strategy, the link between word recognition and the cognitive system has been shown in grey.

The lexical retrieval system, however, interacts with the cognitive system. In figure 70 no specific claim about the internal nature of the retrieval system has been made, though Morton's (1979) differentiation between a visual and an auditory system has been maintained to account for the lack of cross-modal priming effects.

Before we turn to the realisation of the principles of human lexical processing and the possibilities of transferring the basic architecture of the mental lexicon to machines, we have to sort out a final issue concerning the mental lexicon. Even though this book is primarily interested in language comprehension, we will briefly outline the difference between language production and language comprehension. More specifically, we would like to know whether we make use of the same mental lexicon in both modes, or whether it is possible to use two different lexicons.

At present, it seems that only one general store, i.e. one general cognitive system, which contains the lexical specifications associated with each access unit, is employed. There are suggestions, however, that at lower levels, i.e. at the level of pre-lexical processing, the lexicon behaves differently for both modes. Klatt (1981) defined two different 'access lexicons'. While in speech production a phonemically represented access lexicon is used, speech perception seems to employ an access lexicon that makes use of many more aspects. This model has become known as LAFS (Lexical Access From Spectra) and it integrates low-level acoustic cues, segmentation strategies, non-segmental aspects, etc.[15]

For the purpose of this book, the differences between production and perception are of minor importance. The general conception of the mental lexicon, however, seems clear: it is a gigantic store containing thousands of lexical specifications. These specifications can be retrieved via access units which have to be identified by a complex and highly interactive recognition device.

In the next chapter we will relate human and machine-based lexical processing, investigating possible ways of converting aspects of the mental lexicon to a machine-readable lexicon. In using an actual implementation, we will see what kind of human processing strategies can be exploited by machines and which ones lead to undesirable results.

5. Machine-Readable Lexicons

> *"While computers have a superiority in certain 'idiot savant' types of thinking, our thinking is today significantly superior to that of our machines. Yet the intelligence of our machines is improving at a very rapid pace. Within a matter of years or decades it appears that computers will compete successfully with human intelligence in many spheres."*
> *(Kurzweil 1990: 21).*

The central issue of this chapter is to relate the mental lexicon to machine-readable lexicons, trying to establish parallels and pointing out differences where possible. Ideally, the implementation of a machine-readable lexicon and a powerful lexicon access algorithm would be a straightforward transfer of the insights of pre-lexical and lexical processing to a computer program, i.e. a simulation of the strategies of human processing by the machine. Yet there is absolutely no guarantee that human processing strategies are the most efficient ones. Even though human language processing is more robust than anything that we can currently build (Sproat 1992: 110), a direct conversion of natural techniques to develop an artificial mechanism may turn out to be impossible, on the one hand, and undesirable, on the other.

Let us use a parallel to illustrate this point. When humans thought about the invention of mechanical flying-devices, they first tried to imitate nature by employing nature-like movable wings. The use of such devices, however, has proven disastrous. Today we know that, among others, one fundamental problem of natural flying with movable wings concerns the supply of bodily energy. In order to keep the wings in motion an enormous amount of energy has to be used and supplied, far too much to be carried along by artificial flying-devices. The static wing, by contrast, which has only few parallels in nature, has emerged as more successful for mechanical flying-devices. It makes use of some general insights into the principles of flying, for example, the Bernoulli effect, but abandons a variety of natural aspects in favour of artificially realisable techniques.

It will be shown that, by and large, this parallel holds for the relationship between the human mind and present computer architectures. These still adhere to the *von-Neumann architecture*, with its single central processing unit, separate memory, and step-in and fetch-it instruction sets. In recent years, however, computer designers have realised that, despite an increase in performance up to over 500 MFLOPs[1], the addition of several add-ons will not lead to much further progress in computational performance. The use of techniques such as virtual memory, caching techniques, or multiple-processor architectures; the use of alternatives to the MOS-Technique (MOS = Metal-Oxide-Semiconductor); and the integration of highly-specialised and, to some extent, intelligent software, has improved but not revolutionised computational performance.

One central deficiency of the von-Neumann architecture is its inability to perform several tasks in parallel. Massive parallelism, however, is essential for human cognition, especially for the processing of natural language.

A key breakthrough in computer technology is the widespread abandonment of the long cherished von-Neumann architecture. The only real alternative is massively parallel computer systems that replace this architecture with thousands of small processors working simultaneously. With this parallel architecture, it is believed, most of the problems that seem insurmountable today will soon be solved.

However, at present we have to be content with a computer architecture that is essentially serial in character. Hence, we have to employ alternative techniques enabling the computer to process natural language. These techniques might not resemble their natural counterparts but make an efficient use of presently available machines. With increasing machine intelligence and advances in computational engineering, it is hoped that many of these techniques will soon be replaced by more efficient ones and that today's differences between human and machine language processing can be overcome.

The main problem for today's computer architectures is to cope with data that requires massive parallel processing. Let us look at an actual example on the basis of written word processing. Using a root lexicon, the analysis of the word *racing* is an enormous problem. Since only RACE is represented as an access unit, an algorithm is required that internally reanalyses *racing* as RAC+E#ING. The central problem of such an internal reanalysis is to decide whether the rule of E-insertion can be applied before the affix -ING or not. To do this, the algorithm has to solve, among others, the following essential problems:

Step 1:	Is RAC a potential word?	No.
Step 2:	Could -ING be an affix?	Yes.

Step 3:	Is RAC#ING a legitimate environment for E-insertion?	Yes.
Step 4:	Is RAC+E a potential word?	yes.
Step 5:	Is -ING a legitimate affix of RACE?	Yes.

While the first two steps can be performed relatively easily, step three involves a highly complicated operation. Since the application of the rule of E-insertion partly depends on the phonological structure of the environment (Quirk et al. 1985: 102), the algorithm must have access to this part of the lexical specification of the item in question. Hence, in the case of RAC#ING, the algorithm must make an attempt to identify RAC+E as a word (step four), retrieve its phonological form, and return to step three to justify the insertion of -E at the word boundary.

Ideally, these operations are carried out in parallel, where each operation has constant access to the results of its neighbour. Figure 71 illustrates this possibility.

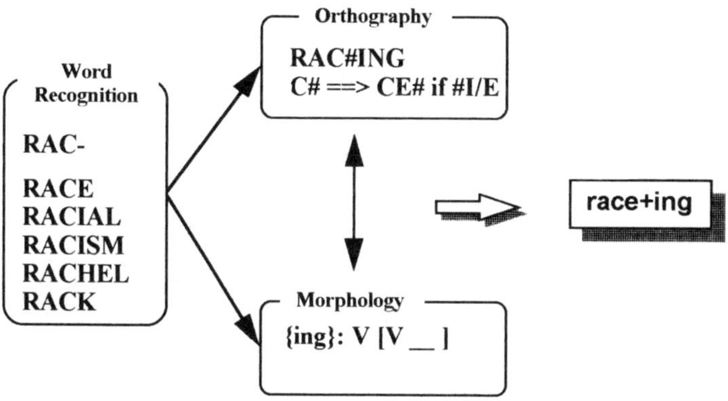

Figure 71. Parallel word processing[2]

Such a parallel architecture would have numerous advantages. It would avoid a number of superfluous processing operations. For example, we would not wastefully activate the morphological level on the basis of -CING. This would be possible, since RA- is not a word. A sequential algorithm would test this option of analysing -CING as an affix, or it would try an orthographical alternation rule. In a parallel architecture, the system has constant access to all levels of information and would thus straightforwardly reject -CING as a potential affix. However, true parallelism is impossible on today's machines.

One technique to simulate parallelism employs an incremental processing strategy. Now the three modules are also all operative at the same time, i.e. they are active in working memory and constantly exchange data. However, only one module can actually process information at a time. Thus, processing is an operation that accumulates or 'increments' specific values over time. Figure 72 illustrates the main steps of incremental word processing.

In the case of *racing*, the level of word processing activates the morphological component. At this level an attempt is made to analyse -ING as an affix. Since this attempt is successful but the level of word recognition is not (RAC is not a word), the third module, the orthographical analyser, comes into operation. Now three components are active. Since the orthographical analyser has a context-sensitive rule that inserts -E before -I(NG), the level of word recognition is reconsulted, seeking an item RAC+E. As a result, part of the lexical specification associated with RACE becomes available. On the basis of this information, the morphological component accepts the remainder, -ING, as a legitimate affix for the verbal interpretation of RACE.

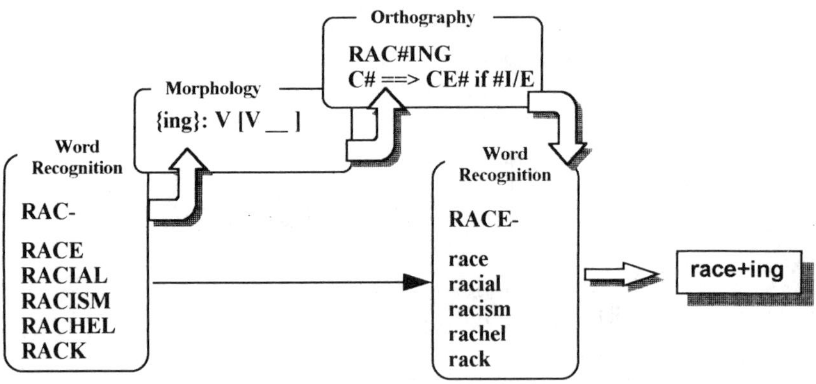

Figure 72. Incremental word processing

Essentially, the difference between parallel and incremental processing boils down to the availability of processing results. In a fully parallel system all results are available at the same time, in an incremental model they are not. Nevertheless, a dynamic data exchange is possible between the modules in a multi-dimensional way.

Other techniques of simulating parallelism make use of the possibilities of multitasking, allowing several programs to be loaded into working memory and dynamic data exchange between them; or they simulate connectionist frameworks, using techniques which are essentially serial in character (see Watson's LISP-code of a speech recognition system 1991: 61ff). True parallelism, however, cannot be simulated on today's standard computer architectures.

It will be shown in this chapter that, despite the architectural differences between the human brain and serial computers, there are still a number of parallels between mental and machine-readable lexicons whose realisation may lead to an enormous increase in computational efficiency, even on conventional machines. These parallels, as well as the differences, can be discussed with regard to the fundamental design and contents of both mental and machine-readable lexicons, and with regard to the strategies for processing lexical information.

5.1. Central Issues of Machine-Readable Lexicons

According to Ritchie (1987: 227) a distinction can be drawn between *lexicon use* and *lexicon construction*. 'Lexicon use' refers to the general functionality of the lexicon module within a natural language processing system, that is, to all those aspects that have been discussed in the previous chapters with regard to the mental lexicon. An important operation in this respect concerns the processing of lexical information. Since this aspect of lexicon use exhibits important differences between man and machine, we will dedicate extra attention to it. 'Lexicon construction', by contrast, deals with the implementation, the generation, and the administration of a machine-readable lexicon. This aspect is of less relevance for the mental lexicon, unless we want to inspect where and how the mental lexicon is stored in the brain, how existing entries are administered, and how new entries are built.

5.1.1. Machine-Readable Lexicons and Natural Language Processing

The central criterion that distinguishes a lexicon, whether mental or machine-readable, from a dictionary is its status within a natural language processing system. That the mental lexicon is an integral part of natural language processing, positioned somewhere between low-level processes and higher levels, such as conceptualising, is undisputed. The function and the use of machine-readable lexicons, however, depends on a number of variables.[3]

(a) The status of machine-readable lexicons in natural language processing systems

The exact position and thus the function of a machine-readable lexicon within a natural language processing system depends on the design and the application area of the entire system. For example, if a machine-readable lexicon is confined to the analysis of natural language, one can dispense with a number of routines and principles that generate words from lexical entries. Furthermore, in natural language processing systems that handle only written information, the machine-readable lexicon need not be interfaced with low-level analysis processes that filter out the processing units contained in the acoustic input stream.

Thus, the function and the use of a machine-readable lexicon, as well as the structure of its lexical entries, depend on its general application, i.e. on questions such as

- Is the lexicon interfaced with a parser?
- Is the lexicon connected with a morphological component?
- Can the lexicon be used interactively, e.g. for teaching or man-machine communication?
- Is the lexicon exclusively non-interactive, as, for example, in a retrieval system?
- How much information must be contained in an entry's lexical specification?

In view of these facts it is not surprising that current computer systems, developed with particular applications in mind, contain machine-readable lexicons which are adequate for the intended purpose but cannot be generalised to other systems (Boguraev/Briscoe 1989a:11).

(b) Interfacing machine-readable lexicons with other modules

There is no doubt that the mental lexicon is central to a natural language processing system and is interfaced with the other modules. The analysis of natural language using a computer provides us with a number of interfacing options. Like the general function of a machine-readable lexicon, these options depend on the application of the overall system.

For example, if the lexicon's primary task is the retrieval of information from textual data, it must have access to techniques of disambiguation. Ideally, this would be a syntax module and a knowledge base. In a retrieval system, however, disambiguation on the basis of the analysis of sentences and the integration of general knowledge is far too costly and time-consuming. For this reason, one might opt for the alternative of interfacing the lexicon with a small morpho-syntactic module responsible for the disambiguation on the basis of local context (see section 6.2.).

Another possible way of interfacing the lexicon with other components is the integration of generation routines within the analysis process. In an Intelligent Language Tutoring System (see section 1.1.3. (c)), for example, one would like to provide orthographical error detection routines that not only recognise orthographical mistakes but also generate the correct orthographical structure from deviant input. For example, if a word, such as *developing*, is accidentally spelt as **developping*, the system should correct it and inform the user about the correct orthographical structure and, in this case, about the principles of consonantal doubling.

(c) the flow of information

As already mentioned, truly parallel natural language processing systems cannot be implemented at present. Thus, it is not surprising that the degree of interaction between the modules of such a system is different from that of their mental counterparts. One important difference concerns the occurrence of top-down information flow during the processing of lexical information, especially during the early phases of processing. However, in computational systems with an incremental processing strategy, top-down effects are extremely hard to implement, since a sufficient amount of low-level information must be available before top-down processing can occur.

Thus, machine-readable lexicons exhibit three important differences with regard to their function within natural language processing systems. While their status and the degree of their interaction with other modules depend on the application, the flow of information between the lexicon and other modules is restricted by present computer architectures.

5.1.2. The Processing of Lexical Information in Machine-Readable Lexicons

By analogy with the human strategies of processing lexical information we can draw a distinction between pre-lexical processing, lexical processing, and post-lexical processing, i.e. the integration of higher levels.

(a) pre-lexical processing

The most important difference between human pre-lexical processing and pre-lexical processing by machines concerns the general ability of performing these tasks. In contrast to the human ease of carrying out these operations, machines are still only rudimentarily capable of coping with spoken and written input with the same accuracy as humans. Even though enormous progress has been made in research into OCR (optical character recognition) and ASR (automatic speech recognition), at present machines cannot flexibly deal with spoken and written input as humans do. Moreover, it will not be until the early decades of the 21st century that machines will be able to process spoken and written input in real-time (Kurzweil 1990: 483).[4]

Despite these differences, the general architecture of the low-level processing component is very similar to its human counterpart. Irrespective of the mode, it makes use of a system of feature detectors that identify geometrical shapes, prestored acoustic patterns, etc., and generates some sort of abstract output. In the case of OCR, this is a graphological form, which is internally represented as an ASCII-value; ASR-systems, by contrast, generate, depending on their degree of sophistication, more holistic patterns, such as syllables, words, or even phrases. Watson (1991: 62) outlines the basic structure of an ASR-system in terms of its hardware requirements and presents a relatively simple speech recognition algorithm that can be trained to recognise a few words on the basis a of neural network, programmed in LISP.

Unlike humans, machines are today not designed to handle both spoken and written input simultaneously. Thus, any machine model of pre-lexical processing is mode specific. For this reason, cross-modal information exchange, such as phonological recoding (see section 3.5., figure 50) cannot occur. Figure 73 illustrates the components of machine-based pre-lexical processing presenting both input channels. In contrast to their mental counterparts, however, both input channels to the machine-readable lexicon are fairly limited in their operational flexibility.

(a1) Optical Character Recognition

The processing of written input is restricted to printed information. Handwritten text from different persons cannot be processed.[5] Furthermore, standard OCR-software cannot analyse written documents with total accuracy. Due to the lack of top-down information flow, i.e. the availability of sophisticated phonotactic and lexical information, numerous letter patterns are recognised incorrectly or are marked as impossible to identify. Figure 74 illustrates the phases of OCR on the basis of an actual example. It exhibits the input to a standard OCR-system for a microcomputer and its analysis result.

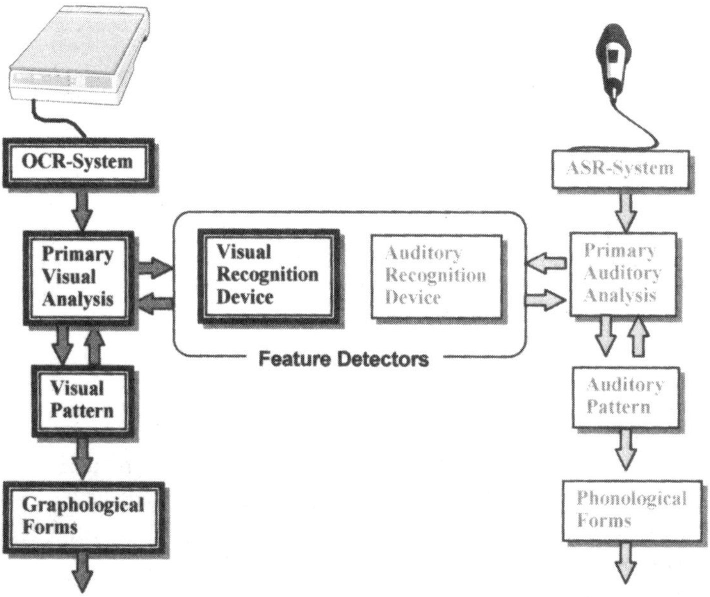

Figure 73. Pre-lexical processing by machines[6]

Note that the OCR-result in figure 74 contains three mistakes (indicated in bold face print). In the case of *de@ine, the program introduces a user-defined symbol @ to mark the erroneous analysis. In the other bold face examples the mistakes have slipped through unnoticed. A mistake, such as *de@ine, could be avoided if the OCR-system had at its disposal more sophisticated top-down routines that mediate between low-level analysis and lexical knowledge (Since **deine* is not a word in English, it would have been rejected in favour of alternatives).

(a2) Automatic Speech Recognition

Computer systems with ASR ability are even less advanced (for this reason, the ASR side in figure 73 is shown in grey). At present ASR-systems cannot handle spoken input in a flexible way and are constrained in various ways: they normally have to be tuned to the vocal characteristics of their interlocutor by means of a series of training sessions, they can only cope

Original Text, before OCR (TEXT.TIF; 76.442 Bytes)

when initiating a telephone call to another host. This prevents you from having to include that prefix when you define the route to each host. Then, if the dialing prefix changes, you can change easily the dialing prefix without redefining the call sequence for each host.

ASCII Text, after OCR (TEXT.ASC; 294 Bytes)

```
when initiating a telephone call to another host. This
prevents you from having to include that prefix when you
de@ine the route to each host. 'Men, if the dialing prefix
changes, you can change easily the dialing prefix without
redefining the call sequence for each host-
```

Figure 74. OCR on a microcomputer (original text enlarged)[7]

with a limited patternised vocabulary, and they cannot freely segment spoken input and thus rely on the insertion of a brief pause between each word uttered by the speaker. In summary, ASR-systems are confined to specific speakers and process input in a fairly unnatural way (see Kurzweil 1990: 276, for the state of the art).

Neither OCR-systems nor ASR-systems can compete with their human counterparts. Even though the general principles underlying mental pre-lexical processing can be realised on machines, there is one general deficiency: the lack of top-down information flow on machines. As long as OCR- and ASR-systems are encapsulated and have limited or no access to higher levels, they will lack the power and flexibility of their human counterparts. For this reason, this chapter primarily deals with lexical processing.

(b) lexical processing

The primary goal of a machine-readable lexicon – and we are talking about large-scale lexicons here – is to provide the lexical specification associated with an access unit as quickly as possible. Hence, the most important aspect of lexical processing in real-time systems is efficiency of lexical look-up.[8]

There are various possible ways of speeding up a machine-readable lexicon. On the one hand, the organisation of the access units themselves can influence the efficiency of access. In the worst case, we could arrange all lexical access units in terms of a sequential list and use a linear search strategy, in which case access speed would be dependent on the length of the list and on the position of an item in the list. Alternatively, we could arrange all access units in terms of a gigantic binary tree, where the access speed would no longer be a matter of position but a function of the number of branching nodes on the search path. Both ordering principles have advantages and disadvantages. They will be discussed in section 5.2.4.

Another possible way of accelerating lexical look-up in a machine-readable lexicon concerns the structure and the implementation of the lexical specification of an entry. It will be shown that many aspects, such as the conceptual specification, can be externalised, leading to a higher performance during the word recognition phase.

Finally, we could think of realising human effects on word recognition. The frequency effect, for example, could be a candidate in this respect. If we arrange the access units in a machine-readable lexicon in such a way that high-frequency words are accessed first, we might improve the performance of the entire system. We will discuss the implications of adopting such techniques in section 5.2.5.2.

(c) higher levels

The interfacing of a machine-readable lexicon with higher processing levels, such as a syntax parser or a knowledge base, depends on the system's application. In a machine translation system, for example, a desirable option could be to make use of context-based word excitation, that is, to integrate the sentence context into the analysis. Words that have already been processed prior to the target word could be used to build hypotheses about the interpretation of the syntax and the meaning. There are two ways of integrating contextual information, a strategy of local context analysis, and a principle of global context analysis (see section 5.2.5.2.). It will be shown that both techniques ideally involve massive parallel processing.

5.1.3. The Administration of Machine-Readable Lexicons

The administration of a machine-readable lexicon involves two important aspects:

- the construction and manipulation of a machine-readable lexicon
- the use of a machine-readable lexicon as an independent module

While the first aspect is basically related to the question of where and how one can get a machine-readable lexicon and its content for a natural language processing system, the second is concerned with aspects such as database management and user engineering.

(a) the construction and manipulation of a machine-readable lexicon

The question of where one gets the actual content of a machine-readable lexicon is not trivial. Theoretically, one might think of converting a dictionary, such as the OED, into a machine-readable format. There are several problems with that. Standard dictionaries tend to have in them information which is not at all the kind of information required for natural language processing systems (see sections 2.2. and 2.3. for a discussion of these issues). Primarily, the information contained in a standard dictionary is too crude to be used in a machine-readable lexicon. For example, the phonological information is generally confined to segmental aspects and ignores non-linear aspects such as the subdivision of words into syllables and of syllables into onset and rhyme. Furthermore, as shown in section 2.2., the syntactic information is often a mere statement of an item's word-class plus a definition of its transitivity status in terms of intransitive and transitive. That this is by no means sufficient for what is needed for interfacing a machine-readable lexicon with other modules of a natural language processing system has been pointed out in section 2.3.3.1.

Despite these and other inconsistencies, for example punctuation in standard dictionaries (Carroll/Grover 1989: 123), hand-crafting the entries in a substantial machine-readable lexicon is often not feasible. Thus, one could envisage getting the raw data from a standard dictionary (in book form via a scanner, in which case one has to deal with the problems of OCR; or in a machine-readable format via CD-ROM or tape) and pre-processing it into a crude approximation of what is actually needed. For example, one could translate a verbal entry such as "Verb, transitive, about" into a subcategorisation-frame of the kind V: [___ NP+about], or, even simpler, V17, where V expresses V and 17 the arbitrary reference number in a list of subcategorisation patterns. However, after the application of such a conversion procedure one would still have to go through the data by hand to resolve ambiguities and to correct false analyses. In other words, editing has to be done manually (see Appendix B and C for details about these issues).

Another issue that is closely related to the construction of machine-readable lexicons using computational tools is testing. Before the newly-generated machine-readable lexicon can be used in an actual application, it must be exhaustively tested with actual material. Particularly, if the system is capable of performing morphological analysis, a whole lot of data has to be run over to see what actually happens. In Appendix C2 a small testing routine is introduced to illustrate this problem.

(b) the use of a machine-readable lexicon as an independent module

Any machine-readable lexicon is a large-scale database that has to permit the following operations (Lipschutz 1987: 73):

(A) search, locating the position of a data element
(B) insertion, adding a new data element
(C) deletion, deleting an existing data element
(D) editing, manipulating the contents of a data element
(E) unification, merging one or several data elements into one
(F) sorting, sorting data elements

While the search operation is performed without human interference, the insertion of entries in the database, the deletion of data elements, and the manipulation of items, requires human assistance.

The question of permitting lexicon manipulation is closely tied up with the purpose of the system, i.e. is it a system open for changes or not? One possible way of carrying out these tasks is to confine them to experts, i.e. to those people who have created the entire database. Alternatively, one could develop a number of user-friendly tools that interactively guide the user through the various stages of manipulating the contents of the database. Depending on the structure of the machine-readable lexicon, these tools can be more or less complex (see section 6.3.).

(c) memory management

A large-scale machine-readable lexicon requires an enormous amount of computer memory. Even though technology has made almost unbelievable progress, and computer memory has become less costly over the past three decades, it has to be efficiently used.[9] For a standard machine-readable lexicon with several thousands of access units coupled with highly complex lexical specifications, computer memory of several megabytes would have to be reserved. Thus, in most cases, machine-readable lexicons are far too large to be loaded into RAM. The availability of the entire lexicon in RAM would drastically reduce the overall performance of a natural language processing system,[10] since a number of additional tasks (e.g. parsing, semantic analysis) would simply become too slow. For this reason, it seems suitable to externalise as many portions of a machine-readable lexicon as possible. For example, one could think of a system that loads all access units into RAM and stores the lexical specifications on external storage devices (e.g. on disk or tape). As soon as an access unit is recognised, the lexical specification associated with it will be read and loaded into RAM. Such a possibility will be introduced in section 5.2.1. Another possibility is to split the lexicon into several parts, one that contains high-frequency words, one that contains less common words, and one for phrases and idioms. In any case, machine-readable lexicons have to be properly managed to avoid an excessive use of working memory.

5.2. The Implementation of a Machine-Readable Lexicon

Having outlined some general issues concerning the use and the administration of machine-readable lexicons, we will now turn to the central question of this chapter, the implementation of a machine-readable lexicon. This involves dealing with two fundamental aspects. First, we will discuss the structure of the lexicon itself, defining its entries and their internal make-up. Secondly, we will investigate the possible ways of accessing such a database. In both cases, our suggestions are highly dependent on a number of variables.

The structure of the lexical database, especially the internal structure of the lexical entries, depends on the application area of the lexicon (machine-translation, dialogue systems, etc.) and on the possibility of allowing human interference (can the entries be edited by the user?). Furthermore, we can influence the size of the database. In section 2.1. we introduced three possible ways of listing the access units in the lexicon: full-forms, morpho-graphemes, and roots. It has been shown that a full-form lexicon is larger and contains more redundancies than a root lexicon or a lexicon that uses morpho-graphemes as access units.

Likewise, the complexity of the access algorithm is a function of the structure and the application of the lexical database itself. If, for example, a full-form lexicon is chosen, we can dispense with a morphological component and complicated morphological access procedures. However, abandoning a morphological component also means that helpful operations, such as error detection and correction at word boundaries (e.g. consonantal doubling, as in *swim*#(m)-*ing*), cannot be performed without additional information in the lexical entries.

In any case, before implementing a machine-readable lexicon one has to know precisely the application area of the lexicon and the tasks the lexicon has to fulfil within the overall system.

5.2.1. Entries in Machine-Readable Lexicons

The entries in machine-readable lexicons can be constructed by analogy with the mental lexicon, where each entry consists of an access unit coupled with its lexical specification (see figure 20). Using Levelt's (1989: 182ff) partitioned structure of lexical entries, the following two main organisational principles emerge for the entries in the mental lexicon:

- access unit and lexical specification can be separated
- the lexical specification can be split into form and lemma

For reasons of system performance and memory management, the subdivision of lexical entries into several parts is even more important for a machine-readable lexicon than for the mental lexicon. We have already seen in section 5.1.3. that one essential demand on the implementation of a machine-readable lexicon is the most economical use of a machine's working memory. Should we not segregate the access units from their lexical specification in a large-scale machine-readable lexicon, we will have to load the entire lexicon into the machine's working memory and will soon reach the limits of memory capacity. A split of each lexical entry into access unit and lexical specification is much more economical. Now only the access units are loaded into working memory, whereas the lexical specifications are stored in a separate file on an external storage device. The link between each access unit and its lexical specification is established by means of a pointer.[11] Hence, such a split is not only psychologically motivated as suggested in chapter two, but it is also an important organisational principle for a machine-readable lexicon.

In the following we will propose a further subdivision of the lexical specification, for exactly the same reasons (system performance and memory management). Let us illustrate the arguments for this suggestion on the basis of an actual example.

(53) Thousands of matches were lit in the audience.

Imagine the word *matches* has to be processed using a root lexicon. This involves three essential steps:

- the identification of the word and its components (word recognition) (MATCH as a root, -E- as a result of orthographical alternation, and -S as an affix)
- the retrieval of the syntactic properties of the word (verb or noun)
- the generation of the meaning ("game" vs. "lighter")

The first step, the process of word recognition, has to find whether the item *matches* is contained among the set of all access units. In a root lexicon, this is not the case, since inflected forms have no direct representation. Hence, the processing algorithm must be coupled with a number of morphological routines that identify MATCH as potential root and -(E)S as a suitable affix. To do this the system requires two additional pieces of information:

- the phonological code of the root /'mætʃ/ (after -tʃ E-deletion is permitted)
- information about the affixational possibilities of the root (e.g. -S is a possible affix)

One essential property of a machine-based word processing algorithm is that it collects information about possible word candidates letter by letter. As the letter "h" is reached, i.e. the system has already processed "m-a-t-c" but could not identify it as a potential word, "m-a-t-c-h" will be correctly identified as a word. But what about the remainder, "es"? At this point the system must have access to the formal information of the lexical specification of MATCH, that is it must know that MATCH can be a count noun, allowing plural formation, or a verb that can occur in the 3rd person singular. In both cases -(E)S would be permitted as a suitable continuation of the stem MATCH.

The lemma information is not required yet. All those aspects that are not directly related to the morpho-syntactic structure, for example the subcategorisation-frame of the verbal interpretation, or the noun class of the nominal meaning of MATCH, are so far not relevant. All that is required at this moment is the information about the entry's morphological continuation class (see section 2.3.2.2.). The retrieval of syntactic aspects or even further parts of the lemma information will only reduce the available memory and slow down the system's performance.[12] All the machine has to examine at this point is whether -(E)S is a possible continuation of MATCH or not.

This system of loading the various aspects of an entry's lexical specification when required can be made even more efficient from a computational point of view. Since most morphologically-determined orthographic alternations (E-insertion, consonantal doubling, E-deletion, I-to-Y change, and

Y-to-IE change in English, see Quirk et al. 1985: 100ff) depend on the phonological structure of roots/stems and affixes, we can provide a further subdivision of the formal specification of the entries in machine-readable lexicons. Let us return to our example (53).

In order to identify *matches* as a legitimate English word, the morpho-syntactic information (i.e. the syntactic category) alone is not sufficient. Before we identify the remainder, -(E)S, as a legitimate continuation of MATCH-, the -E- has to be deleted. The application of this orthographical rule, however, is not dependent on the morpho-syntactic category of an entry but it operates solely on the basis of phonological information. With the information that E-deletion is possible after /tʃ/ as in *match*, the -E- can be deleted and -S can be identified as an affix.

The application of orthographical alternation rules depends on the morphological possibilities of the words involved. In English there are many invariable words that do not undergo any orthographical changes, e.g. conjunctions, articles, pronouns, etc. The recognition of these words requires neither morpho-syntactic nor phonological information. Variable words, that is words that can undergo inflectional processes, can be subdivided into two groups. One group of inflected forms is orthographically fully regular, e.g. *walk-s*, *go-ing*, etc., and can be identified solely on the basis of the morphological specification. The phonological specification is not required. Only the second group of inflected forms, e.g. *carri-(e)s*, *rac(e)-ing*, etc., involves orthographical alternation. Hence, we can distinguish three groups of words: invariable words, orthographically regular words, and orthographical variants. Table 10 summarises this situation.

Table 10. Words and orthographical variation

Type	Example Alternation	Morphological Change	Orthographical Change
1 invariable	Conj: AND	no	no
2 variable/no change	Noun: TABLE, *table-s*	yes	no
3 variable/change	Noun: FLY, *flies*	yes	yes

On the basis of this distinction we can now control the processing algorithm in a highly efficient way and thus enormously increase the overall system performance. Type 1 words do not require any formal information during the process of word recognition, whereas type 3 words can only be processed on the basis of their entire formal specification. Type 2 words, by contrast, only need their morphological specification but no information about their phonological structure.[13] Hence, we can implement the lexical retrieval algorithm in such a way that it only loads those formal aspects that are required. In other words, we suggest a further separation of the formal information into phonological and morpho-syntactic specification, and a retrieval routine that loads these aspects at request. The link between the phonological and the morpho-syntactic specification can be established by a pointer.

A further step in the analysis of (53) involves disambiguation. The word *matches* is ambiguous in two ways: on the one hand it is categorially ambiguous, i.e. it is either a noun or a verb; on the other hand, it is semantically ambiguous, i.e. as a noun it has two different interpretations (see section 1.1. for a classification of ambiguity). The categorial ambiguity can be resolved on the basis of the local context, since the pattern "of ___ were" clearly suggests an analysis of *matches* as a noun. The selection of the correct meaning of the noun *matches*, by contrast, can only be performed on the basis of an integration into the conceptual characteristics of the context. Interestingly, only the resolution of semantic ambiguity requires the activation of the entry's lemma, whereas the analysis of *matches* as a noun can be carried out exclusively on the basis of an entry's morpho-syntactic properties (see section 6.2. for an illustration of such a disambiguation technique). Thus, for reasons of processing efficiency, the activation of an entry's lemma should be postponed as long as possible.

That an entry's lemma information is amazingly complex has been shown in section 2.3.3. Aspects such as the syntactic argument structure or the conceptual representation of an entry not only require complicated representation mechanisms but a large amount of memory. Depending on the application area of a machine-readable lexicon, additional facets of information may have to be included in an entry's lemma specification. In machine translation programs, for example, one might want to associate lexical entries with passages of text that have already been translated. In other applications, such as tutoring systems, visual and auditory information about the entry, or examples that illustrate the entry's use in context, may be desirable. Since all these additional aspects are not constantly needed in a natural language processing system, they do not have to be available in working memory but should be loaded at request.

Figure 75 illustrates the highly-pointered structure of a lexical entry in a machine-readable lexicon, where the pointers have been drawn as arrows.

To sum up, each lexical entry can be subdivided into an access unit and its lexical specification, which in turn is subdivided into various aspects. Hence, a machine-readable lexicon ideally consists of two general file systems: the access file that contains the set of all access units and the data file system

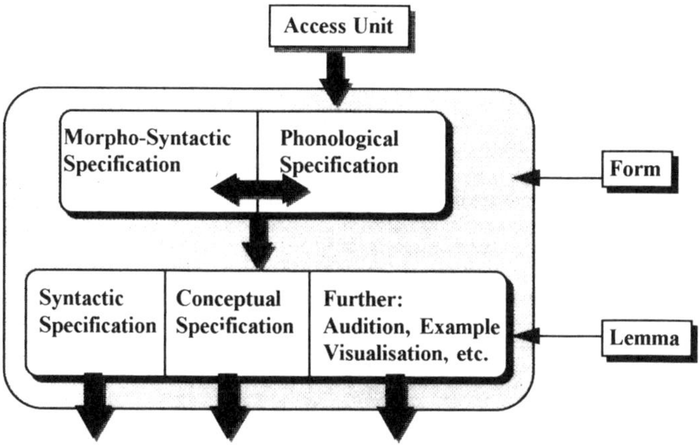

Figure 75. The structure of an entry in a machine-readable lexicon

with the lexical specification for each access unit. The connection between both systems is established by a pointer associated with each access unit. The various aspects of lexical specification can also be externalised on the basis of additional file and pointer systems.

5.2.2. Access Units

The organisation of the access units in a machine-readable lexicon involves a number of interesting options which are dependent on the application of the system within which the lexicon operates, on general aspects of memory management, and on the language to be processed.

The first question concerns the type of access unit to be listed in the mental lexicon and principles of condensing this information as much as possible. A second aspect deals with the structure of the access file itself and the implementation of an efficient access and retrieval algorithm.

(a) selecting the right access unit

In section 2.1. we introduced two possible ways of listing the access units in the mental lexicon: the 'minimal listing hypothesis', which only lists roots in the lexicon, and the 'full listing hypothesis', according to which words are processed on the basis of their full forms. Also, we mentioned the possibility of using a third structure, the so-called 'morpho-grapheme'. Figure 76 replicates these findings.

Access units in machine-readable lexicons

❑ Roots	WALK	CARRY	SWIM	HATE
❑ Full Forms	WALK WALKS WALKED WALKING	CARRY CARRIES CARRIED CARRYING	SWIM SWIMS SWIMMING	HATE HATES HATED HATING
❑ Morpho-Graphemes	WALK	CARRY CARRI	SWIM SWIMM	HATE HAT

Figure 76. Access units in machine-readable lexicons

Again, the selection of the access unit structure depends on the application area of the natural language processing system in general, and the machine-readable lexicon in particular. In an indirect machine translation system with a limited semantic domain, such as the TAUM-Meteo system, for example, only a limited number of words have to be processed.[14] In such a case one might opt for a full-form lexicon and eliminate a morphological component, together with a complex morphological processing algorithm. Machine translation systems that are not domain-specific, for example the EUROTRA (European Translation) project, may become too complex if full-forms are entered into the lexicon. Especially for languages which exhibit a high degree of synthesis, i.e. languages with a rich morphology, full forms may lead to a wasteful usage of memory. Let us compare the relationship between the number of entries in a full-form and a root lexicon for English and German on the basis of the inflectional variants of a regular verb, such as *play* (Ger. = *spielen*).

(54) a. plays, play (present tense/basic/imperative forms)
b. played, playing (past tense/participles)

(55) a. spiele, spielst, spielt, spielen, spiel (present tense/basic/imperative forms)
b. spielte, spieltest, spielten, spieltet (past tense forms)
c. spielend, gespielt (participle forms)

While English generally allows four inflectional variants of each regular verb, German permits 11 inflectional variants. Thus, the listing of full-forms in an English lexicon would only increase the number of verbal entries by a relatively small factor, whereas the listing of all these 11 forms would have disastrous consequences for a German full-form lexicon. In other words, for languages with a high degree of inflectional morphological variation, full-form lexicons are out of the question. Too many redundancies and too much replication of identical information would unnecessarily enlarge the lexicon and, as a consequence, burden the memory with superfluous material.

Despite their economy, root lexicons have to cope with an enormous problem. It concerns the processing of orthographical variants as a consequence of affixation. Here are some selected examples:

(56) English: *carries* (carry-s), *making* (make-ing), *swimming* (swim-ing), *watches* (watch-s)

(57) German: *atmete* (atem-te), *redete* (red-te), *Blumen* (Blume-en), *müssen* (muß-en)

To process these forms, a root lexicon must be accompanied by an algorithm capable of handling morphological processes and orthographical alternation. The use of morpho-graphemes offers an interesting alternative for the organisation of the access units in machine-readable lexicons, even though there are no psychological arguments in favour of such a structure. In a lexicon with morpho-graphemes, we would store abstract access units in those cases where affixation processes lead to a change of the orthographical structure of the basic forms. In English this would be forms such as CARRI and CARRY, in German, RED and REDE (= talk). This would allow us to continue using a root lexicon, only in those cases where affixation leads to orthographical changes we would have to increase the number of access units. In contrast to the relationship between the number of access units in an English full-form and in an English root lexicon, however, the size of the lexicon only increases by a small factor, since, according to our calculation in section 5.2.1., only 20% of all actual word forms are orthographical variants of a given root.[15]

(b) condensing the lexicon

Many languages allow alternative spelling due to dialectal or etymological influences. In English this is most obvious if we consider British English (BrE.) as opposed to American English (AmE.) forms:

(58) a. BrE.: economise, colour
b. AmE.: economize, color

To maintain our premise of efficiency we could, by analogy with the use of morpho-graphemes, establish access units that resemble both variants. In the case of the "s/z" alternation, for example, we could make use of an arbitrary symbol, such as "?", which allows to process both *economise/economize* on the basis of the common form ECONOMI?E. In addition to this, we have to implement a simple context-sensitive orthographical rule that unifies "?" with either "s" or "z". The "ou/o" alternation could be realised along the same lines, representing pairs such as *colour/color* by the abstract common access unit COL%R.

In some cases, the story is not that simple. Take the phenomenon of umlauting in German. Here are some examples:

(59) a. Fuß, Fußes, Füße, Füßen (Noun: foot/foot's/feet/feet's)
b. fuße, fußte, fußend (Verb: base on, based on, basing on)

In order to maintain the idea of a root lexicon, both the noun and the verb should be traced back to the same access unit: FUß-. To account for the actual forms in (59a) and (59b), the vowel of the access unit has to be replaced by an arbitrary symbol as in the "s/z" alternation in English. Thus, both the verb *fuß-* and the noun *Fuß* can be represented by a common form, e.g. *F&ß*. The orthographical rule that turns "&" into "u" or into "ü", however, must not only be context-sensitive concerning the orthographical environment, but it must also have access to the morpho-syntactic information associated with the access unit (note that only the noun *Fuß-* can participate in umlauting processes). Such a condensing principle enormously cuts the total number of access units. However, it is extremely difficult to implement and requires a number of additional routines. It remains to be seen whether the advantages (economy and memory usage) compensate for the complexity of the additional program code.

5.2.3. The Structure of the Access File

As outlined above, a machine-readable lexicon consists of two basic components or files: the access file and the data file. Both files, or, more particularly, all access units and their lexical specifications are linked by a pointer system. The central task of the access file is to identify whether an item is a word or not. Hence, one essential demand on the access file is to allow high-speed access. To satisfy this premise various techniques of data organisation and file structuring are available. Let us look more closely at the possible ways of arranging the data elements, in our case the access units, and their conversion into an adequate file structure.

5.2.3.1. Data Structures

According to Rembold (1987: 115ff) any data structure (D) is defined by the type of relations (R) existing between the individual data elements (E), where R is defined as a finite set of binary relations which hold between any two data elements.

$$D = (E, R)$$

Even though we can imagine a large number of relationships between the data elements, only four fundamental data structures are known:

(a) linear order

The linear data structure is characterised by a total order among all individual data elements, where any two data elements can be compared with regard to their relationship to one another:

Figure 77. Linear order

(b) partitions

In a partition the relationship between the data elements is a relation of equivalence, i.e. a reflexive (data elements can refer to themselves), transitive (data elements can refer to other data elements), and symmetrical relationship (reference is bilateral).

(c) graphs

In a graph a single relationship between any number of data elements can be established. To express this relationship in terms of a diagram, nodes and arcs are used.

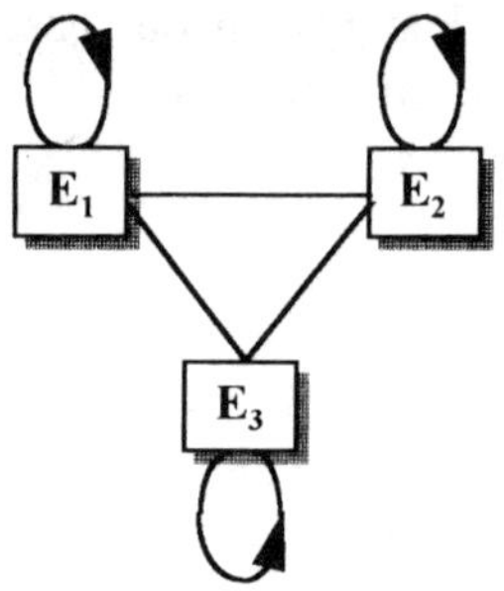

Figure 78. Partitions

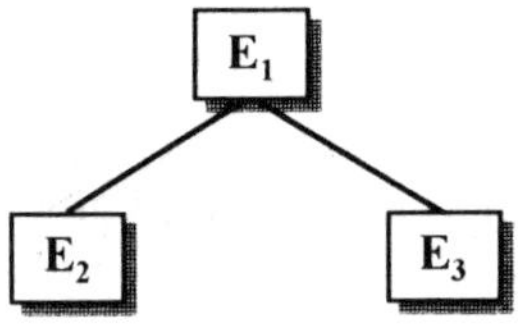

Figure 79. Graphs

(d) associations

Associations are multi-dimensional relations between data elements. In contrast to graphs, the data elements are not related via a single relationship but by a finite set of binary relations. The most common realisation of this data structure is the relational database.

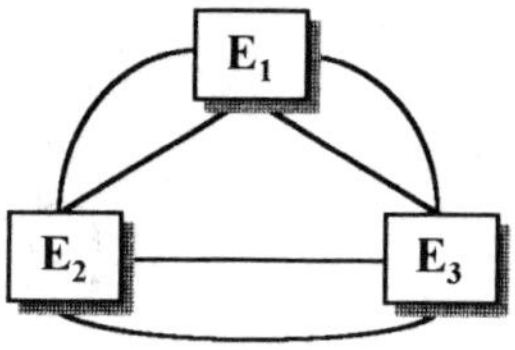

Figure 80. Associations

5.2.3.2. File Structures

Any data structure has to be converted into a file and must satisfy two criteria: search efficiency and efficient data management. Salton/McGill (1987: 13ff) define the following file structures in this respect: *linear lists* and *sequentially ordered files*. A further technique for organising data structures in terms of files makes use of a system of *indices*.

(a) linear lists

One possible way of organising data uses a simple linear list, where all data elements occur as a simple unordered sequence. While such a file can easily be managed (new data elements are inserted at any free location or they are simply appended to the end), search is not very efficient because access time is dependent on the position of a data element in the list and the length of the overall list. Figure 81 exemplifies a linear list on the basis of a small lexical database with a new entry inserted at the end.

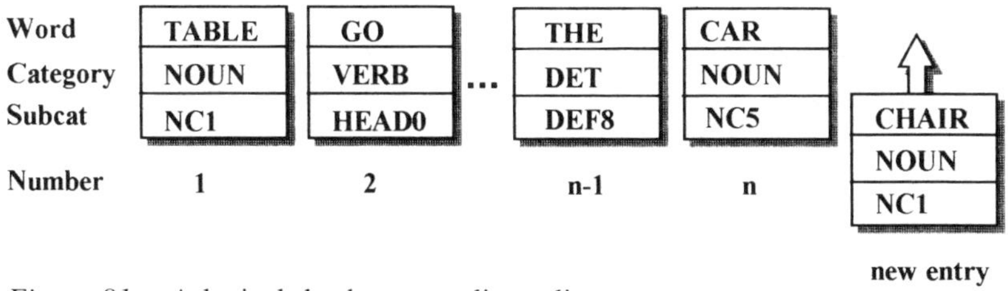

Figure 81. A lexical database as a linear list

The use of a specific file structure depends on the possibility of permitting fast data access. Using a linear list, the simplest strategy to search a data element is a *sequential search*, where the algorithm starts at the beginning of the database and inspects each item until the target is reached. The number of steps taken correlates with the position of the target item in the database. Figure 82 illustrates the simple sequential search on the basis of a linear list and the target element WOOD.

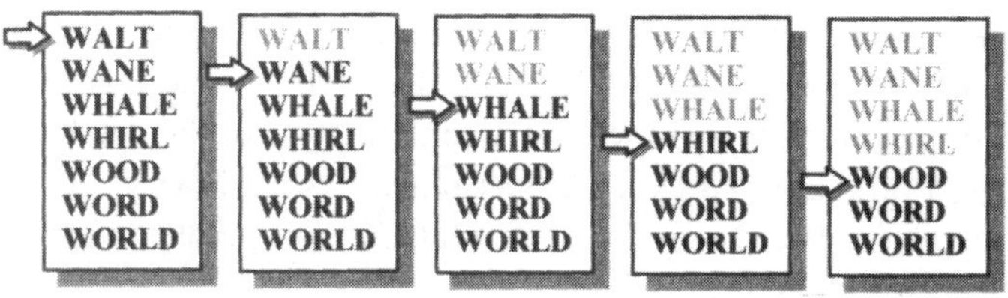

Figure 82. Sequential search

(b) sequentially ordered files

In a sequentially ordered file the data elements are ordered on the basis of specific keys. In standard database applications, for example in address registers, keys, such as surname, residence, age, etc., are common. The use of such keys increases the search efficiency at the expense of more complex data and file management procedures. A new data element can now no longer be inserted at any position, since this would disrupt the internal order of the file. Rather, data insertion consists of two complex operations: the identification of the position, and the reorganisation of the file. Figure 83 exhibits a file which has been sequentially ordered according to word-classes, and illustrates the problem of inserting new data elements.

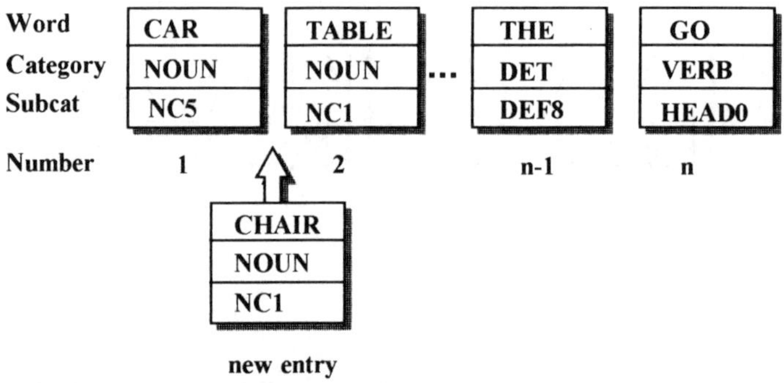

Figure 83. A lexical database as a sequentially ordered file

Sequentially ordered files normally make use of the so-called *binary search*. Using this technique, the algorithm starts in the middle of the database and continues search either in the middle of the upper half or in the middle of the lower half. By a comparison of the target element with the respective element in the database, it divides the number of data elements into halves until the target is found. The binary search is only possible if the database has been sequentially ordered on the basis of specific keys, as suggested above. Without an internal order the comparison between target and data element and the subsequent division of the database into two halves would be impossible. Figure 84 illustrates the binary search on the basis of the target WOOD and a sequential file with alphabetically ordered head words as key elements.

Obviously, the binary search is much more powerful than the sequential search. While the sequential search has to inspect each data element until the target can be found, the binary search takes into account only those elements that belong to that half of the database which satisfies the comparison between target and data element. An actually existing system that makes use of the binary search is the VIRTEX-project (Verbs-into-Russian-Translation-Experiment). However, its strategy of database access, which uses a communication between dBASE and LISP on the basis of

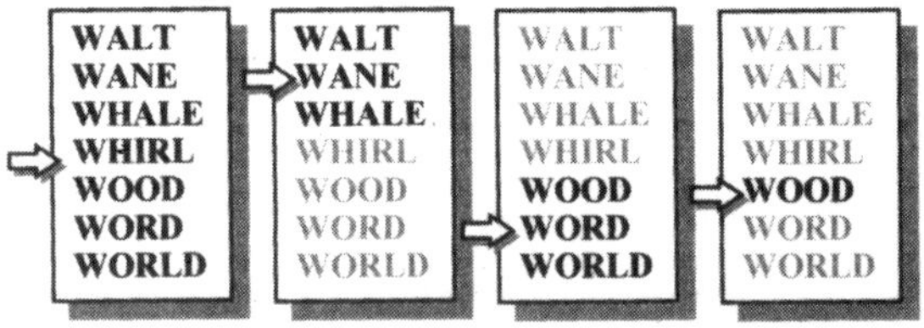

Figure 84. Binary Search

temporary files (Küster 1991: 102), seems to be a very complicated and time-consuming method.[16]

(c) files with indices

An index is a pointer that permits access to specific segments of a database. The use of indices is a highly efficient means of accelerating data search. Let us illustrate this on the basis of an example. Imagine we would like to sort all entries in a lexical database alphabetically. To do this we could generate a temporary file that contains the results of the sorting operation. However, now we have two databases: our original file and the alphabetically ordered file. Both have the same number of entries and are identical in size. We could, of course, delete the original file and use the temporal file as our new database. However, if alternative sorting criteria are applied, e.g. sorting according to word-classes, the same problem arises. Depending on the number of keys (headword, word-class, subcategorisation, etc.) we might eventually end up with a large number of files, sorted according to different criteria but all equal in size.

An alternative way is to generate additional files that keep only the sorting results while the main file of the database remains unaffected. In the case of sorting the entries alphabetically, the additional file would be a mere list which only contains all headwords in alphabetical order, but not all entries. This list is much smaller than the main file. The connection between the main file and the additional file is established via indices, where each element in the new file is associated with an index that points to the position of the entire entry in the main file. In standard database systems indices are pointers to a position on an external store, e.g. a harddisk.

Figure 85 displays our lexical database as an indexed system. It consists of three index files (I:1, I:2, and I:3) and the main file. The index files are internally ordered according to headwords (I:1), word-classes (I:2), and subcategorisation types (I:3). The indices themselves are represented as

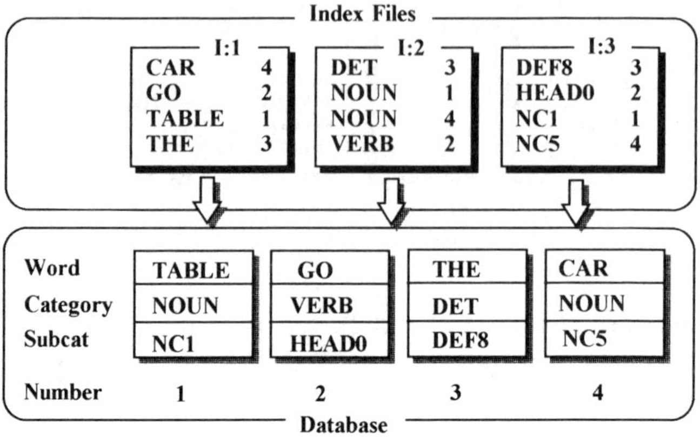

Figure 85. A lexical database with index files

simple numerical values displaying the position of the entry in the main file. In such an indexed database, search begins in an index file and is continued in that part of the main file to which the index establishes a relationship. Looking up all nouns, for example, would involve a search in index file I:2 and establish a connection to data elements 1 and 4 in the main file. The use of several index files also permits the combination of search targets, such as, "look up all nouns of the subcategorisation type NC1". In such a case, search would be carried out in I:2 and I:3, leading to a retrieval of data element 1.

While search in an indexed database is extremely efficient, file administration is problematic. The insertion of a new data element, for example, not only involves manipulation of the main file, but the index files have also to be updated. Hence, as efficient as such a file structure may be for general information retrieval, it is equally problematic for database systems that require permanent changes.

5.2.4. Discrimination Networks

Selecting an adequate data structure for a machine-readable lexicon and converting it into a suitable file structure requires a precise definition of its tasks and demands. One central problem of a machine-readable lexicon is its enormous size. Several tens of thousands of entries are the rule rather than the exception. Such a size excludes linear data and file structures, as well as sequential search strategies, from further consideration.

Another problem has to do with the selection of the access units. If we opt for a full-form lexicon, or for its variant, the morpho-grapheme lexicon, the processing of orthographical variants, such as *racing,* is not problematic. In a root lexicon, however, the situation is different. As long as orthographical alternation is flanking, as in *watch+es*, search will be relatively easy. The algorithm will identify the root WATCH and analyse -ES as an orthographical variant of the affix -S. The fact that a number of orthographical changes occur before the root boundary complicates the story. The processing of items such as RAC(E)-ING requires the activation of orthographical and morphological procedures during database search and the possibility of comparing several data elements at a time. In order to insert an "E" after "RAC", the algorithm must inspect all elements with the initial letters "RAC" and examine the morphological properties of all those candidates that allow E-insertion. Suitable data structures to represent this phenomenon are graphs or associations. They allow a single data element to be succeeded not only by one but by several data elements. Hence, the comparison between a target and a whole group of potential candidates can be made.

To allow fast data access, we have the choice between variants of binary search, in the case of sequentially ordered files, or the use of indexed systems. A reasonable format for the organisation of the access units of a machine-readable lexicon that is based on graphs and allows fast data access is the *discrimination network* (Charniak et al. 1987: 149ff).[17]

The idea of organising the access units of a machine-readable lexicon in terms of a discrimination network is not new. Kay (1977: 159ff) introduced this structure under the heading of 'balanced binary-branching search tree'; Karttunen (1983: 177) acknowledged the high access efficiency of this structure and used it in the morphological analyser system, KIMMO. A general discussion about the search efficiency of tree structures can be found in Smith (1991: 106ff).

In principle, a discrimination network is a gigantic tree that tries to match incoming information with its nodes, using a letter-by-letter strategy. Figure 86 represents one possible realisation of a linear list as a simple discrimination network.

Such a structure has at least two advantages. First, it allows extremely fast data access. Search is no longer a function of the position of an element in the database but it depends on the number of branching nodes on the search path. Using a top-down, breadth-first search strategy, looking up the item WOOD requires only four steps (WA, WH, WO, and WOOD). Secondly, a discrimination network can easily be converted into an adequate

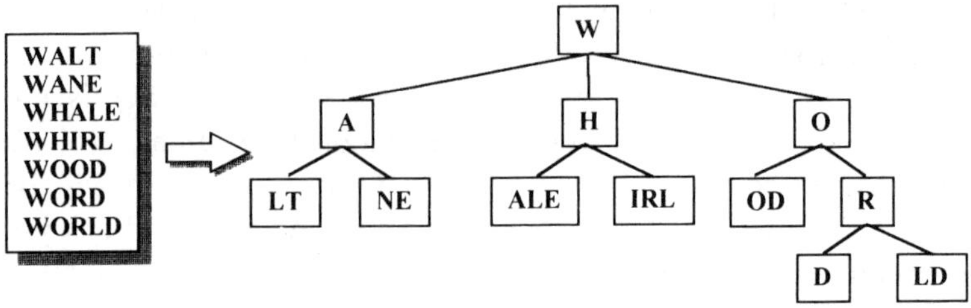

Figure 86. A simple discrimination network

code for an AI programming language. In LISP, for example, the network of figure 86 looks like this:

(W (A (LT NE))
  (H (ALE IRL))
  (O (OD)
    (R (D LD))))

However, discrimination networks are problematic in various ways. One problem concerns their generation and administration. In order to generate such a network, a complicated compilation algorithm has to be written that converts a linear list of access units into a tree structure. Secondly, database operations such as inserting, unifying, or deleting data elements can only be performed on the basis of very complex routines that rearrange the tree structure. Imagine the item WHAT has to be inserted into the discrimination network as shown in figure 86. In such a case the entire WH-branch has to be manipulated, leading to the following new structure (changes in bold face):

(W (A (LT NE))
  (H (A (T LE))
    (IRL))
  (O (OD)
    (R (D LD))))

A further problem concerns the management of working memory. In order to use a discrimination network we have to load it into the machine's working memory. For very large lexical databases, however, this might be problematic. Hence, we have to think about efficient storage management routines to implement discrimination networks (see section 5.2.5.1.).

The most problematic aspect can be referred to as the *multiple-access-phenomenon*. It relates to the fact that, using a root lexicon, a multitude of input structures can be analysed as potential root-affix combinations, even though they are not. Let us illustrate this phenomenon on the basis of the following simple discrimination network.

```
(CA
    (R *
          (E *)
          (RY *)
          (T *)))
```

It contains five branching nodes, four of which represent actual words: *car*, *care*, *carry*, *cart*. These terminal nodes have been associated with an asterisk. Whenever such a node in the network is reached, the processing algorithm has to look at the remainder of the input. Imagine the word *cars* has to be analysed. In such a case, the system will correctly identify CAR as a word candidate, retrieve the formal specification from the lexicon, and analyse *-S* as the plural affix. However, if *carry* is to be processed, the system will perform exactly the same operations: analyse CAR as a potential root and inspect -RY as its affix on the basis of the formal specification of CAR. Since the latter step fails, the algorithm will proceed and eventually identify CARRY as an individual unit. However, it has already wastefully analysed the formal specification of CAR.

There are various possible ways of avoiding multiple-access. One strategy is to associate with each node in the tree a list of affixes in terms of letters. Even though multiple-access will still occur, processing will be accelerated, since the lexical specification is no longer required. A similar technique makes use of external transition networks. In such transition networks, the continuation possibilities are represented in terms of simple letter transitions. In the case of CAR this means that -0, -S, -'S, and -S' are possible transitions, but -RY is not. By associating the CAR-node with the reference address for the network, -RY will not be analysed as an affix and the lexical specification of CAR need not be accessed. Figure 87 illustrates the combination of a discrimination network with simple transition nets (the possibility of orthographical alternations has been ignored).

In any case, multiple-access and affixation is a problem. In section 4.2.4. we discussed the problem of pseudo-affixation, where humans incorrectly analyse poly-morphemic words, such as *defensive*, into three components: DE-FENS-IVE. Even though it is not clear whether such items are stored

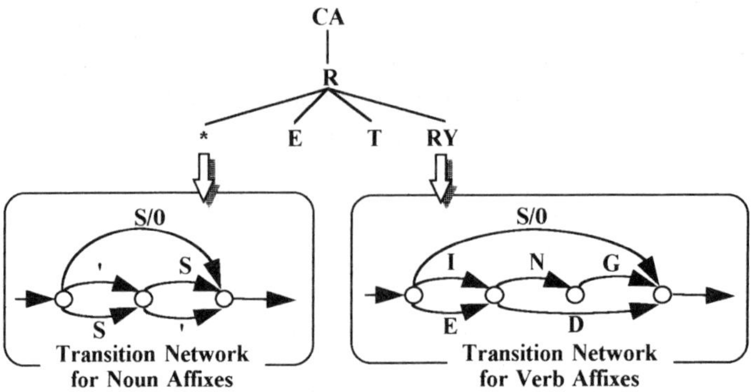

Figure 87. Discrimination networks and transition networks combined[18]

as complex forms or whether humans apply a morphological decomposition strategy, multiple-access phenomena as a result of the structure of a discrimination network, e.g. the CAR-RY-phenomenon, are highly unlikely in the mental lexicon.

Despite the disadvantages discrimination networks have proven a very useful architecture for the lexical access file in machine-readable lexicons: they allow fast data access and they are efficient means of handling orthographical variants. Even though they are unlikely to be correct models of human word recognition (Sproat 1992: 113), they can simulate at least some psychological aspects of word recognition (see section 5.2.5.2.). Let us therefore turn to the details of implementing the access file as a discrimination network.

5.2.5. Implementing the Access File as a Discrimination Network

In implementing the set of lexical access units as a discrimination network, we have the choice between simple character trees, as used in the KIMMO-system (Karttunen 1983), and the more compact "syllable" trees. While in character trees each letter of each access unit represents a branching node, in syllable trees only those parts of the access units (letters or larger units) represent branching nodes that are shared by other access units.[19] Figure 88 illustrates both structures on the basis of a few selected access units.

The differences between the two structures have been discussed at length in Deiß et al. (1990: 99ff). Primarily, they concern the following aspects:

- file compilation (how well can the network be generated from an ASCII-file?)

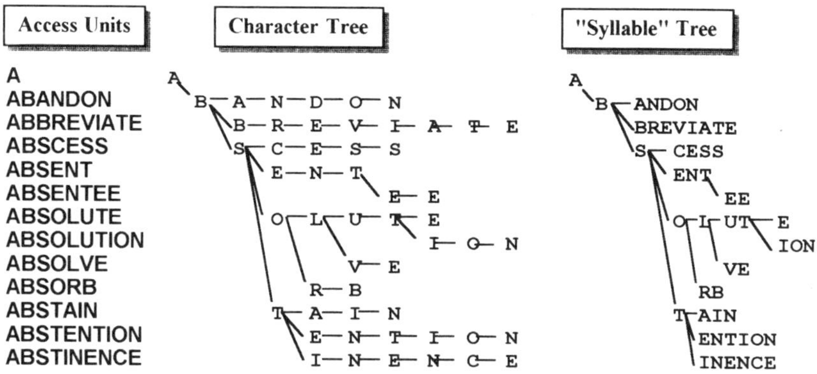

Figure 88. Types of discrimination networks

- file administration (how well can the existing network be administered?)
- search efficiency (how fast is access?)
- memory management (how much storage capacity is required?)

While the first two aspects favour a character tree, the latter two strongly argue for "syllable" trees. Especially if we consider the size of the respective network, we can very quickly see that a "syllable" tree is much more compact than a character tree. Another argument in favour of "syllable" trees is psycholinguistic in character. It is well known that words can be recognised without having been read in their entirety. This effect can be simulated by both network types: as soon as there are no further branching nodes on the search path, a word may be recognised. For example, using the networks in figure 88, ABBREVIATE can be recognised after ABB-, ABSTAIN after ABSTA-. Of course, this requires that the access file contains the entire set of the words in a language. A "syllable" tree is more efficient in simulating this effect. Once a recognition point has been reached, e.g. ABB- in the ABBREVIATE-branch, the remainder of the access unit can simply be retrieved. In a character tree, by contrast, there are further potential branching nodes to be processed after the recognition point.

For these and other reasons "syllable" trees will be preferred to character trees. Interestingly, there are various similarities between "syllable" trees and Marslen-Wilson's Cohort model of spoken word recognition (section 4.2.1.). For example, processing proceeds along the same lines. It starts with the entire network and is narrowed down very quickly to a small set of potential candidates, and, in the case of success, one item is left. Furthermore, as we will see below, "syllable" trees can be used to simulate a number of psycholinguistic effects. Because of these affinities between "syllable" trees and cohorts, and also due to the fact that "syllable" trees do not really employ syllables, we will henceforth refer to this data and file structure as *cohort network.*

5.2.5.1. Partitioned Cohort Networks

As already pointed out, a discrimination network, whether a character tree or a cohort network, is a huge list. The cohort net of figure 88, for example, can be converted into a list as illustrated in figure 89, where each asterisk represents a terminal node in the network, i.e. a potential word candidate.

```
(A *   (B   (ANDON *)
            (BREVIATE *)
            (S      (CESS *)
                    (ENT *   (EE *))
                    (O       (L      (UT       (E *)
                                               (ION *))
                                     (VE *))
                             (RB *))
                    (T       (AIN *)
                             (ENTION *)
                             (INENCE *))))))
```

Figure 89. A cohort network in a list representation

As outlined above each access unit establishes a connection to its lexical specification, represented by a pointer. In an actual implementation of a machine-readable lexicon this is a numerical value denoting the position on an external storage device where the lexical information associated with an access unit can be found. In order to generate these pointers we have to use a specific compilation program that performs numerous highly complicated operations:[20]

- It splits all lexical entries into their access units and their lexical specification.
- It generates the following files:
  - the lexical access file as a cohort network,
  - data file I, containing the formal specifications, as a sequentially ordered linear structure,
  - data file II, containing the lemmas, as a sequentially ordered linear structure.

– It associates pointers with all access units.

Input to such a compilation algorithm is an ordinary ASCII-file where all lexical entries are represented according to a simple format of the kind:

> ACCESS UNIT; Phonology ; Morphology ; Syntax ; Semantics ; Further-Information

From such a simple file, the lexical access file, represented as a cohort network, is generated, where each numerical value represents a readpointer into the data file. Figure 90 represents such an access file on the basis of arbitrarily chosen readpointer values.

```
(A 1  (B  (ANDON 21)
          (BREVIATE 102)
          (S      (CESS 306)
                  (ENT 407    (EE 522))
                  (O     (L    (UT      (E 678)
                                        (ION 864))
                         (VE 1023))
                         (RB 1239))
                  (T     (AIN 1465)
                         (ENTION 1890)
                         (INENCE 1987))))))
```

Figure 90. A simple cohort network with readpointers

Note that processing in such a cohort net is very simple. Each input item is analysed letter by letter, in an attempt to match its structure within the cohort net. Basically, the algorithm has to take three decisions:

(a) branching

Let us imagine the word *abscess* has to be analysed. The first three letters of the input can be processed very quickly, since only A- can be analysed as a potential access unit, while AB- and ABS- cannot. Note that such nodes have embedded lists as their successors, while access units are directly coupled with readpointers.

(b) word recognition

Having processed ABS-, the algorithm has now reached the branch ((CESS 306)(ENT 407 (EE 522))). A simple comparison of -CESS with this branch activates (CESS 306). Since this node is coupled with a readpointer, the lexical specification of ABSCESS can be read at position 306 and further processing, for example, orthographical and morphological analysis, can be invoked.

(c) branching and word recognition

Now consider the processing of *absentee*. In principle, the same steps are performed. However, after the processing of ABS- and the matching of the remainder -ENTEE with the remaining branch, we are confronted with the following list: (ENT 407 (EE 522)). This structure provides the algorithm with two alternatives. On the one hand, it could read the information at position 407 and analyse the remainder of the input, -EE, as an affix. On the other hand, it could continue search in the subnet branch (EE 522) and retrieve the lexical specification of ABSENTEE from position 522. Hence, here we are faced with the problem of multiple-access. This problem can be overcome by using additional transition networks as shown in figure 87, which would exclude -EE as an affix of ABSENT-. Note that the same problem of multiple-access concerns all words beginning with A-, since *a* represents a word in English. Thus, for items, such as ABSENTEE, a first analysis attempt would be to identify A- as a root and -BSENTEE as an affix. This has to be avoided by means of such strategies as introduced in section 5.2.4.

A fundamental disadvantage of a cohort network as introduced in figure 90 is its enormous size. Machine-readable lexicons that are operative in natural language processing systems beyond the experimental phase, for example, in tutorial systems, contain several thousands of lexical entries. A cohort network representing several thousands of access units, however, is too large to be held in a standard machine's working memory. With every new entry inserted into the cohort net, the situation becomes worse. In other words, we are likely to lose control over the size of the cohort net.

One possibility of regaining control is a method of *partitioning*. In a *partitioned cohort network* the access file is split into a main network and a number of 'subnet files'.[21] The main network contains the first three letters of all access units, the subnet files the respective remainders.[22] Due to graphotactic restrictions the main network is limited in size, because the combinatorial possibilities of the first three letters decrease with increasing word length. While word-initially all 26 letters of the English alphabet can occur, clusters of two letters, and even more so triplets, are combinatorially heavily restricted. For example, the Z-branch does not allow a continuation with any consonant; *ZB, *ZC, *ZD, etc., are all impossible word-initially in English. In fact, ZLOTY, the name of the Polish currency, is one of the rare examples of word-initial Z+consonant clusters. These combinatorial possibilities are even more constrained if three characters are concerned. Hence, if a sufficient number of access units is collected, the main network will soon reach its limits. In terms of size this limit is roughly 20 KB. Such a file can easily be loaded into working memory.

The number of subnet files depends on the number of letters in the alphabet of a language, i.e. 26 in English, 29 in German (26 plus Ä, Ö, and Ü). While the main network is now constantly available in working memory, the subnet files can be reached via a subsidiary pointer system. In other words, items that consist of three letters only can be directly found in the main network, whereas longer words lead to an activation of a subnet.

The system of partitioning requires a modified overall structure of the machine-readable lexicon. This new structure is represented in figure 91. (The sizes of the main net and the subnet files are actual values from the LexEcon program to be presented in chapter six).

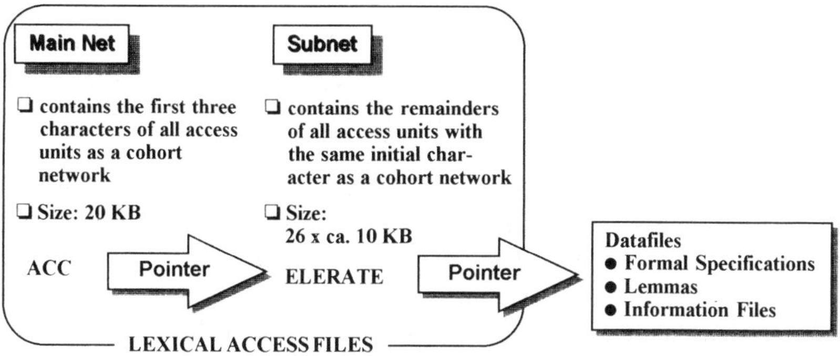

Figure 91. Access files in a partitioned cohort network

The system of using partitioned cohort networks heavily reduces the pressure on working memory. In fact, irrespective of the machine used, the lexicon can now grow in size up to infinity. Its overall size is only constrained by the capacity of the external stores that contain all lexicon files (e.g. by the size of a harddisk). However, in contrast to a simple cohort network, as introduced in figure 90, we have to modify the processing strategy according to which access units are recognised, since we are now confronted with three possibilities in the main network:

(a) three-letter combinations or units smaller than three letters that can be directly identified as access units, examples: A, ACE,
(b) units larger than three letters that are not access units in the main network and require search to be continued in a subnet,
(c) three-letter combinations that can be directly identified as access units and at the same time may constitute the initial part of longer access units to be continued in a subnet, example: ACT, ACT-IVATE.

Figure 92 illustrates these possibilities on the basis of a fragment of the main net of LexEcon.

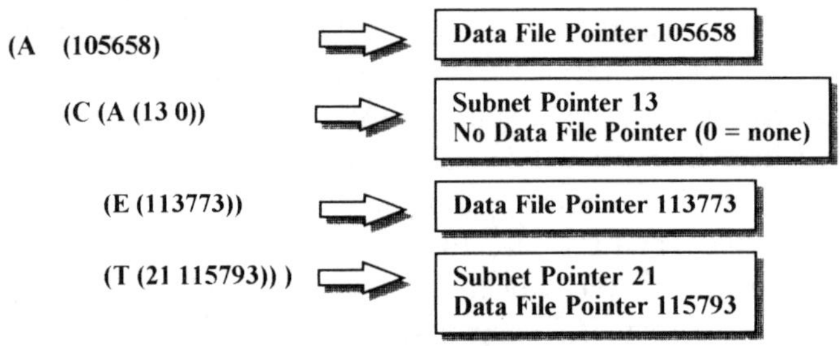

Figure 92. Evaluation strategies in the main network

Now all those branching nodes are coupled with numerical values that either allow a continuation in a subnet or directly represent an access unit. If only one numerical value is associated with a branching node, we are confronted with an access unit whose lexical specification can be directly retrieved from the data file via this pointer value, e.g. A or ACE. Items that can be continued in a subnet are connected with two values. If the second value is zero, they have no representation in the main net, for example, ACA-. Their remainder can be found in the subnet file that contains all cohorts for access units beginning with the word-initial letter at the position expressed by the first numerical value. In the case of ACA-, this is the subnet file for all elements beginning with A-, and the relevant cohort is at position 13. A somewhat special case concerns those items that can be identified as access units in the main network but can also be continued in a subnet, for example ACT-, which can be identified as the access unit ACT or may represent the first part of ACT-IVATE. In such cases the first numerical value is the pointer for the item's continuation in the subnet (e.g. ACT-IVATE) and the second the pointer to the item's lexical specification in the data file (e.g. ACT).

In order to use this system of main network and subnets, an additional administration system has to be employed. Before we turn to the problem of administering the partitioned cohort network, we have to introduce a larger fragment of the main net with its actual pointer values in figure 93.

Network Structure (Main Net)	Possible Word	Pointer into Subnet	Pointer (Data File/Form)
(A (105658)	A*	-	105658
(B (A (1 0))	ABA-	1	-
(B (2 0))	ABB-	2	-
(S (10 0)))	ABS-	10	-
(C (A (13 0))	ACA-	13	-
(E (113773))	ACE*	-	113773
(T (21 115793))	ACT*/-	21	115793
(U (22 0)))	ACU-	22	-
(D (A (23 0))	ADA-	23	-
(D (24 116694))	ADD*/-	24	116694
(E (25 0)))	ADE-	25	-
(ER (33 0))	AER-	33	-
(F (A (34 0))) ....)	AFA-	34	-

Figure 93. A fragment of the main network with its pointer values

Now imagine a new access unit is to be entered into the lexicon. If it consists of only three or fewer than three letters, only the main network has to be modified in its structure, and the readpointer to the new item's lexical specification in the data file has to be generated. However, if the new item is longer than three letters, the subnet file responsible for all access units with the new item's initial letter has to be altered. Changes in the main file may be necessary, too, but are less likely. In large lexicons almost all branching possibilities in the main network exist. Nevertheless, there are cases where the branching structure of the main network has to be changed, especially, if graphotactically illegal but widely used letter combinations have to be entered into the lexicon. Such cases arise with common abbreviations, such as I.C.B.M., H.M.S.O., etc., where even punctuation marks may be integrated into their orthographical structure. While the alteration of the main network is relatively unproblematic, changes to the subnets have far-reaching consequences.

Let us assume the word *abstemious* is to be entered into the lexicon. In such a case, the subnet cohort responsible for the remainders of all ABS-elements has to be altered. In the main network the ABS-branch (A-B-S (10 0)) already exists (see figure 93). To understand the principles of modifying the subnet structure, let us have a look at the ABS-cohort before the insertion of *abstemious* in figure 94. Note that the "syllable" structure is much more obvious in the subnet than in the main network.

Network Structure (ABS-cohort)	Possible Word	Pointer (Data File)
[(CESS (105658)	ABSCESS	108596
(EN (CE (108654))	ABSENCE	108654
(T (108723)	ABSENT	108723
(EE (108922)))	ABSENTEE	108922
(O (L (UT (E (109054))	ABSOLUTE	109054
(ION (109127)))	ABSOLUTION	109127
(VE (109209)))	ABSOLVE	109209
(RB (109298)))	ABSORB	109298
(T (AIN (109383))	ABSTAIN	109383
(ENTION (109459))	ABSTENTION	109459
(INENCE (109525))	ABSTINENCE	109525
(RACT (109582)	ABSTRACT	109582
(ION (109745))))	ABSTRACTION	109745
(URD (109817)]	ABSURD	109817

Figure 94. The ABS-cohort of the A-subnet

To enter ABSTEMIOUS into the subnet, the letter combination TEMIOUS has to be inserted into the T-branch of the ABS-cohort in the subnet, i.e. into the branch responsible for all word remainders with (ABS)T-. The first three letters, ABS-, can be ignored now, since they are represented in the main network. The insertion of TEMIOUS leads to the following new structure of the subnet T-cohort.

```
(T   (AIN (109383))
     (E        (MIOUS ("eof"))
               (NTION (109459)))
     (INENCE (109525))
     (RACT (109582)
               (ION (109745))))
```

The new value "eof" represents the pointer into the data file where the lexical specification of ABSTEMIOUS is stored. This pointer value is actually the end-of-file ("eof") value, since new lexical specifications are simply appended to the end of the data file. After the insertion of TEMIOUS the ABS-cohort has grown in size. This has an unpleasant side-effect. The new ABS-cohort cannot be stored at its original position, since its new, enlarged size would change the positions of all other cohorts below ABS- in the same file, e.g. the position of the ACA-cohort, the ACE-cohort, the ACT-cohort, etc. (see figure 93). This means that all pointer values that locate the positions of any of these subnet cohorts from the main network would have to be changed (see the values in column three of figure 93).

To cope with this problem one can use a kind of index system which takes over the administration of all cohorts in a subnet file. Instead of coupling all branches of the main network that lead to any subnet cohort with true readpointer values, they are connected with values that do not directly point to the relevant subnet cohort but to a highly specialised table in the subnet file. In Deiß et al. (1990: 104) we referred to this table as *handle*. A handle constitutes the first part of each subnet file. It consists of two components:

Part 1: HEAD, NUMBER-of-COHORTS,
MODIFICATION-COUNTER
Part 2: POINTER-VALUES-to-COHORTS

Let us look more closely at the internal make-up of a handle. All parts of the handle are realised in terms of numerical values. The HEAD represents the length of the subnet file in bytes, NUMBER-of-COHORTS is self-explanatory, and MODIFICATION-COUNTER is initially zero and is incremented each time the subnet file is altered. The second part is a list that contains the pointer values to all cohorts. While the first part of the handle is only required for changes in the lexical access files (insertion, deletion, etc., of access units), the second part is loaded whenever a subnet file is activated.

Let us now return to the insertion of ABSTEMIOUS. To store our new (ABS)T-cohort it is simply appended to the end of the subnet file. The old (ABS)T-cohort, however, remains in its original position. This leads to a modification of all values of part one of the handle system: HEAD will now receive a higher value; NUMBER-of-COHORTS and MODIFICATION-COUNTER are incremented by one. In part 2 of the handle the old pointer value leading to the position of the original (ABS)T-cohort is replaced by the new value. The only problem with this system is that subnet files may heavily grow in size each time new access units are entered and appended at the end. In order to shrink the subnet file again, a 'garbage collection system' can be used that rewrites all cohorts and updates all values of the handle, until MODIFICATION-COUNTER is zero. The entire system has been introduced and discussed at length in Deiß et al. (1990).

Now the overall system of administering lexical access units should be clear: lexical processing involves the loading of the main network into the machine's working memory. If an input item can be identified within the main network, its lexical specification is directly retrieved from the data file via its readpointer. Words that are longer than the main network structure, that is longer than three letters, activate a cohort from the subnet file via a handle. This subnet cohort, whose maximum normally does not exceed 3 KB, is read from an external store via the value associated with the handle and loaded into working memory. Depending on the speed of the external store (e.g. harddisk access time) processing will continue after a few milliseconds.

The partitioned cohort network has proven to be a highly efficient lexical access system. Even though the administration of this system is very complicated, this is compensated for by two extremely important aspects. First, the set of access units can grow up to infinity, because the partitioned structure supersedes any working memory limitations, and, secondly, this data and file structure allows enormously fast access. The average processing time per access unit is less than 200 msec. Hence, it satisfies two important demands on databases: memory management and search efficiency.

In the following section we will show that this structure of lexical access files is not only very efficient as a realisation of the first component of a machine-readable lexicon but it also serves as the basis for the realisation of some fundamental aspects of human lexical processing.

5.2.5.2. The Simulation of Psycholinguistic Effects

In section 4.2. we defined three fundamental effects that a model of lexical processing should be able to explain:

- the lexicality effect
- the frequency/recency effect
- contextual effects
  - the lexical context
  - the sentence context

In addition to this, any lexical processing model should provide an explanation of the length effect via a word's recognition point (see section 4.1.). Moreover, it should be able to account for the processing of distorted input. As we saw in chapter four, none of the leading models can sufficiently explain the entirety of these effects. In many cases they introduce fairly abstract concepts to account for these facts. For example, they all have problems with the integration of contextual effects, especially with the sentence context, and attribute this to higher levels and to the possibility of top-down effects. Furthermore, word frequency effects are explained in terms of rather abstract internal groupings of the access units (Marslen-Wilson's Cohort model), or they are not represented at all (McClelland's TRACE model). In other words, no model is conclusive with regard to explaining speech processing effects.

Let us now turn to our computational model of lexical processing, the *partitioned cohort network model.* Can we simulate the word processing effects using this model, and do we gain anything from modelling these effects?

(a) the lexicality effect

The lexicality effect is no problem for the model. It automatically emerges from the system's network structure. However, a distinction between types of non-words (regular vs. illegal) in terms of processing latencies cannot be drawn. Let us exemplify this on the basis of the cohort network as presented in figure 93 and 94 and the following two non-words and a real word as examples:[23]

(60)	illegal non-word:	**abceadle	rejection time:	30 msec
(61)	regular non-word:	*abseadle	rejection time:	120 msec
(62)	real word:	absolve	recognition time:	150 msec

Superficially, the latency values seem to confirm the psycholinguistic finding that illegal non-words are processed faster than regular non-words. However, the fact that real words are processed most slowly contradicts the experimental observations about word processing. Using a cohort network, all latencies can be attributed to the overall structure of the network and the fact that search efficiency is a function of the number of branching nodes on the search path. If many nodes have to be bypassed, processing is slow; if few or no branching nodes have to be analysed, processing is fast. Illegal non-words, such as (60), are rejected very quickly since the branch ABC- does not exist in English. In (61) search goes on until the algorithm finds out that the branch ABSEA- does not exist. Real words take relatively long to analyse, since search has to be continued until no more branching nodes can be found on the search path and the remainder of the input can be matched with the remaining cohort. In other words, processing time depends on a word's recognition/rejection point.

However, there is a second variable that affects word processing. It has to do with the idea of partitioning the access networks. Let us illustrate the differences between the examples above on the basis of the number of branching nodes on the respective search path, assuming all cohorts are in alphabetical order:

(60') two nodes: A-(B-*C)
rejection point: -CEADLE

(61') six nodes: A-B-S-(CESS EN *EA)
rejection point: -EADLE

(62') nine nodes:A-B-S-(CESS EN O (L (UT ✓VE)))
recognition point: -VE

The main difference between (60) and the other cases is related to the system architecture, i.e. to the partitioning of the access file into main network and subnets. While illegal non-words, such as (60), can be rejected solely on the basis of the main network, most regular non-words and real words require that the relevant subnet has to be loaded before they can be identified. Hence, the latency difference between (60) and the other examples can primarily be explained in terms of subnet loading time (roughly 100 msec), while the other differences depend on the number of nodes on the search path.

Another factor that affects processing time has to do with the complexity of the subnet cohorts. Let us compare two real words to illustrate this effect:

(63) absolve recognition time: 150 msec

(64) abandon recognition time: 146 msec

The analysis of both words involves the same main network search path for the first two letters. While ABSOLVE invokes the loading of the relatively large ABS-cohort via handle 10 (see figure 94), ABANDON requires the ABA-cohort via handle 1. This latter cohort is much smaller:

```
((CUS (213955))
 (NDON (214031) (MENT (214125)))
 (SE (214205))
 (TE (214305) (MENT (214424))]
```

Depending on its size, the loading of a subnet cohort from a harddisk occupies more or less processing time (the cohort has to be read via a pointer). Thus, it is not surprising that smaller cohorts, such as the ABA-cohort, are loaded faster and the access units are retrieved at a higher speed. This explains the latency differences between (63) and (64).

In summary, non-words are rejected very fast in the partitioned cohort model; however, no distinction is drawn between illegal non-words and regular non-words. Basically, word processing is affected by two variables:

by the number of branching nodes on the search path, and by the inherent architecture of the system, i.e. by the size of subnet cohorts and their loading time. Nevertheless, the partitioned cohort framework comes pretty close to its mental counterpart since it processes words and non-words differently due to its general architecture.

(b) the frequency/recency effect

Like the psycholinguistic models of lexical processing, whether for spoken or written language, the partitioned cohort network has enormous problems simulating the most unequivocal fact about human word processing, the frequency effect. It suggests that no matter how the mental lexicon is organised, it must at least have the property that frequent words are easier to get at than infrequent words.

In order to incorporate this important variable of word recognition, each access unit would have to be marked to indicate its frequency status. This could be done in terms of a numerical value or in terms of an internal system of ranking or ordering. To couple the frequency effect with the recency effect would furthermore imply that the lexicon allows constant internal regrouping. In a linear list (section 5.2.3.2. (a)) we could simulate the frequency/recency effect relatively easily: whenever an access unit is found, it is retrieved from the list and reinserted in the first position. This system guarantees that frequent words are among the initial elements of the list, and recently processed words at the top. However, for reasons of data management and processing efficiency we rejected a linear file structure and suggested a discrimination network instead, at the expense of a much lower degree of internal dynamics in such a structure. One consequence is that the frequency effect cannot be simulated using a discrimination net. Nevertheless, there are possibilities of handling word frequency.

For example, one could group the main network top nodes according to a statistical frequency distribution instead of an alphabetical order. It is commonly known that in English words the letter E is more common than the letter A. In other words, it is possible to establish a statistical ranking in terms of the letters. This ranking, in descending order, is ETAOINSHRDLU (Hoftstadter 1979: 671), i.e. branching nodes with E- are processed first, nodes with T- second, and so on. Due to this internal grouping we gain an average processing time of ca. 2 msec, admittedly a very small value.

Other ways of accounting for word frequency effects in machine-readable lexicons involve a split of the lexical access file. In a machine translation system, where the lexicon is interfaced with other natural language processing modules, this is a very common method. For example, in SYSTRAN, one of the most well-known machine translation systems, the lexicon is subdivided into two basic components: a stem 'dictionary' and a high-frequency 'dictionary' (Wheeler 1987: 194).[24] While the stem 'dictionary' contains all standard words, the high-frequency 'dictionary' contains unambiguous entries such as AND, BUT, OR, as well as numbers or punctuation marks and idioms. Such a lexical split leads to a speeding up of the overall system since the access algorithm can now be programmed in such a way that high-frequency words are examined first.

Smith (1991: 109ff) suggests an even more advanced strategy of organising the access units to incorporate the frequency effect. Instead of one general access file he proposes a stratified organisation of the lexicon. At the first level, the most common high-frequency words are represented in terms of weighted, i.e. prearranged, binary trees. This initial part of the lexicon contains only a few dozen items, which are organised according to frequency of occurrence.[25] If the target word does not occur in the high-frequency lexicon, search continues in a 'circular queue' that contains several dozen words used most recently. This second level is not realised by a binary tree but as a mere list which is restricted in length and constantly updated. If no item is found in either the high-frequency tree or the recency queue, the general lexicon, which contains all other access units, is approached.

The third method of simulating the frequency effect makes use of activation levels, where high-frequency words will be associated with a lower activation threshold than low-frequency words. In a machine-readable lexicon activation levels could be realised in terms of numerical values. However, for the partitioned cohort network this would imply a waste of search potential. If we were to couple all branching nodes that represent word candidates with an activation value and tried first to access those with a low value, then those with a higher value, and so on, we might have to look up the same access unit more than once. This is certainly an undesirable option that would drastically slow down word recognition. Hence, the introduction of activation values to simulate the word frequency effect does not lead to an acceleration but to a delay of word recognition.

Finally, we have to think about the recency effect, according to which infrequent words when heard often enough are promoted to high-frequency words. In other words, all lexical access units may constantly change their frequency status depending on their recency of occurrence. If this effect is to be simulated in a machine-readable lexicon, one would constantly have to regroup the lexicon structure, perhaps after the processing of each word.

Such a procedure would not only be an enormously complicated enterprise, but it would also lead to very little gain in processing efficiency. Smith's (1991) proposal of a circular queue is probably the best way of simulating this effect of word processing in a machine-readable lexicon. However, his technique makes use of a simple linear list which has proved to be a rather inefficient way of accessing data.

In summary, then, apart from the option of breaking up a machine-readable lexicon into several access lexicons, there is no further possibility of simulating the frequency effect that leads to a higher system performance.

(c) contextual effects

Like the frequency effect, contextual effects are enormously hard to simulate. In section 4.1. (g) we discussed two types of context: the lexical context and the sentence context. Both contextual effects may excite word recognition. Using the lexical context simply means that the content of the lexicon itself influences word recognition. We discussed this possibility at length in section 4.2.2. (d), when we considered the handling of distorted input in the TRACE model. The facilitation of word recognition by means of the sentence context is achieved by integrating the meaning of all items into a general conceptual representation. Words that match this representation are recognised faster than words which semantically deviate from it.

Our partitioned cohort network simulates neither of the two contextual effects. If we integrate it into a natural language processing system that analyses sentences, however, we can utilise the sentence context by some sort of top-down processing strategy. Whenever a word is analysed, its lexical specification is temporarily saved. The analysis of subsequent words in the same sentence will then not only be based on general recognition procedures but it will also make use of the lexical specification of the previous item. Such a strategy makes sense if the input to the system has to be "understood". Let us illustrate this on the basis of an example from machine translation where an ambiguous word in English has to be translated into German:

(65) a. He put the book on the *table*. (table = Tisch)
b. He read the figures in the *table*. (table = Tabelle)

There are various ways of arriving at the correct meaning of the word *table*. The most complex strategy is to integrate the semantic specification of all words into a general conceptual representation and interpret the meaning of *table* in terms of the overall meaning. Such a strategy is used in *interlingua systems*, where machine translation is defined as a process that converts the input from the source language into a semantic representation, or *interlingua*, from which the translation is generated (Lehrberger/Bourbeau 1988: 34). A much simpler possibility involves the inspection of local context which is searched for specific cues. For example, a comparison between "on the table" and "in the table" might indicate that "on + table" is likely to be interpreted as "on + furniture", whereas "in + table" has to do with mathematics. Further strategies can be used if the lexical specification of TABLE is coupled with examples of use or with statistical values. In *transfer* systems, where the input is not converted into an internal conceptual structure, semantic ambiguities can be resolved by reference to previous analyses or statistical probabilities based on the text-domain. For example, in mathematical texts *table* is more likely to be translated as "Tabelle" than in journals for craftsmen.[26]

In summary, the realisation of contextual effects in machine-readable lexicons is very problematic. If the context is only employed to facilitate word recognition, the simulation of contextual effects is too costly. However, if the context is not primarily used for word recognition but for ambiguity resolution, it makes sense to couple the lexical processing algorithm with a strategy that not only inspects words in isolation but also refers to the context.

(d) the length effect

The length effect has been exhaustively discussed above. It has been pointed out that the partitioned cohort network makes exactly the same predictions as Marslen-Wilson's psychological counterpart. Word recognition is independent of word length; rather it is a function of the position of a word's recognition or rejection point.

(66) absolve recognition time: 150 msec

(67) trespass recognition time: 90 msec

In both cases, word recognition occurs within the respective subnet. While TRESPASS can be recognised after TRE-, ABSOLVE cannot be identified before the last two letters. This difference can be explained in terms of the complexity of the subnet cohorts. While for TRESPASS there is only one cohort (-SPASS) with no further branching nodes, ABSOLVE has two more branching nodes in the subnet (figure 94). Thus, even though TRESPASS is longer, it can be identified earlier.

(e) the handling of distorted input

The incapability of Marslen-Wilson's early version of the Cohort model to handle distorted input was a main argument for McClelland to develop a connectionist alternative, the TRACE-model. Marslen-Wilson reacted and presented the idea of parallel cohorts which take care of alternatives (see figure 56).

The partitioned cohort network faces the same difficulties. In principle, it is incapable of handling distorted input. There is no chance to analyse *p?ug* as *plug*. In section 4.2.2. we showed that the analysis of such distorted input requires massive parallelism and top-down processing. Using the partitioned cohort net, this is impossible. However, there is a possible way to present alternatives on the basis of the respective cohort structure. Whenever a potential word rejection point is reached in the network, all possible alternatives can be recursively generated on the basis of all those letters that have already been processed. For example, if the initial three letters ABS- have successfully been analysed, all words from the ABS-cohort will be generated as alternatives (see figure 94, column two).

There are two reasons why this technique only works if at least the first three letters have been analysed correctly. First, we are faced with the standard problem of memory management. While the number of alternatives based on the first three letters does not normally exceed several dozens of items, we would be confronted with several hundreds of alternatives on the basis of just two initial letters. In other words, we might lose control over the system's working memory. The second reason is once more related to the partitioned network architecture. Alternatives can only be generated if a subnet cohort has been loaded. This is the case after the processing of at least three letters. The generation of alternatives from the main network, i.e. after one or two letters, would imply that several cohorts have to be loaded and analysed. This has proven to be far too costly in processing efficiency.

An alternative way of solving the problem of processing distorted input in a partitioned cohort network connects the main network with a list of graphotactically legitimate letter combinations. Before processing starts, a comparison between the items in this list and the first three letters of the input is made. If the comparison is successful, word recognition can proceed, if not, alternatives will be suggested.

In principle, all psycholinguistic effects of word recognition can be simulated using the partitioned cohort model, with one exception: the handling of distorted input via top-down effects. While some effects can be represented relatively easy (the lexicality effect and the length effect), the integration of others (the frequency/recency effect) is possible, but would not lead to an increase of processing performance. Rather, they would require enormously complex administration and lexicon updating techniques. Last but not least, the integration of the context is not solely confined to the lexicon structure itself but it is a matter of interfacing the machine-readable lexicon with other processing modules.

5.3. Lexical Specification

Building the lexical specifications of the entries in a machine-readable lexicon we are confronted with a number of variables. They concern the necessity, the character, and the complexity of the various aspects of the lexical specification and depend on the nature of information to be recorded and on the type of the lexicon (full-forms, morpho-graphemes, roots). Furthermore, it is important to think about the realisation of all these aspects in terms of software engineering.

(a) the necessity for information

The necessity for phonological information, for example, only arises in a root lexicon. Flanking orthographical alternations, such as *refer*+(r)*ing* or *cater*+*ing*, can only be correctly analysed if the lexicon provides the system with information about the segmental and non-segmental phonological structure of the entry, in this case, about the syllable structure and the word-accent pattern (*refer*, rɪ|'fɜ: vs. *cater*, 'keɪ|tə).

(b) the character of information

The character of the morphological information is different in full-form lexicons and root lexicons. While in a full-form lexicon it is primarily a simple statement of the morphological properties, the morphological specification in a root lexicon is often procedural in character. A feature such as N (= noun) not only marks an item's word-class but it may also be a specific symbol that determines a root's continuation, e.g. -S is a possible affix but -ED is not.

(c) the complexity of information

Many aspects of the lexical specification of an entry are contingent on the overall purpose of the system, for example, on the domain within which the system is meant to operate. In a limited domain, such as geography, chemistry, etc., with a restricted number of entries, the representation of the meaning of each item in the lexicon can be much more exhaustive than in a general-purpose system with several thousands of entries. Or take the difference between interlingua and transfer systems in machine translation. While interlingua systems make every effort to represent their entries in terms of detailed conceptual aspects, transfer systems dispense with a semantically-based meaning representation in favour of relationships across the lexicon.

A number of decisions about the complexity of the lexical specification are subject to theoretical linguistic considerations. The representation of the morphological specification, for example, depends on the syntactic theory used. Traditionally, word-classes have been represented in terms of simple items, such as N, V. In more recent frameworks, they have been defined as an unordered set of feature specifications where each feature consists of an ordered attribute-value pair (Ritchie et al. 1992: 42). According to such a format verbs are characterised as (V +)(N -), while nouns have the feature specification (V -)(N +). We will return to this issue in section 5.3.2.

Over and above the decisions about the necessity, the character, and the complexity of the lexical specification, we are confronted with general aspects of software engineering (Lehrberger/Bourbeau 1988: 60).

For most current commercial systems the user is responsible for building lexical entries. The designer of a machine-readable lexicon provides a base lexicon with the system and the user supplements the lexicon with new entries of his choice. This may be a highly complicated enterprise depending on the complexity of the lexical specification required for the entries and can often only be performed by computer experts or linguists. Since most users are neither computer scientists nor theoretical linguists, one should make sure that they have at their disposal computer tools for the management of the lexicon.

Let us now turn to the various components of the lexical specification and the possibilities of representing them in machine-readable format. By analogy with the specification of an entry in the mental lexicon (section 2.3.) at least the following aspects, or *fields*, constitute an entry's lexical specification:

- the phonological field
- the morpho-syntactic field[27]
- the syntactic field
- the semantic field

In addition to these central fields we might want to include further fields such as graphotactic information for the generation of words, fields entirely dependent on the system's application, e.g. a statistical field for machine translation systems, or fields that provide the user with important information, such as examples of use or etymology.

5.3.1. The Phonological Field

The incorporation of phonological information depends on the processing mode. Obviously, ASR-systems with the possibility of generating spoken output require highly sophisticated phonetic aspects which specify an entry's pronunciation in terms of detailed acoustic properties. Machine-readable lexicons that are not interfaced with a speech-processing component do not require such complex information. In fact, in most machine-readable lexicons this field does not exist at all. Many researchers have almost nothing to say about it and only include it for completeness (Ritchie 1992: 4). However, there are good reasons to specify lexical entries phonologically, especially if orthographical variants which arise by affixation have to be analysed and generated. In English five orthographical rules are responsible for this type of orthographical variation (Karttunen/Wittenburg 1983: 218ff). In (68) they are exemplified from the perspective of language analysis, where processing words, such as *watches*, requires the deletion of -E- before the affix -S:

(68)	a.	E-deletion:	watch+(e)s, rush+(e)s,
	b.	consonantal doubling:	swim+(m)ing, refer+(r)ing,
			but: cater+()ing
	c.	E-insertion:	mak(e)+ing, hat(e)+ed
	d.	I-to-Y change:	carry+ed
	e.	Y-to-IE change:	dy+ing $\rightarrow$ die+ing

Note that word generation requires a reversal of these processes. Now *watches*, whose internal structure is WATCH+S, requires the insertion of -E- before -S.

Interestingly, in word recognition, one can subdivide the rules and the resulting changes into two groups: word-internal changes (68c-e) and flanking changes (68a-b). While word-internal changes have to be made before the recognition of the root boundary, flanking changes occur after the identification of the root. Thus, word-internal changes, as in *making*, must be performed without the availability of an item's lexical specification. Since an item such as MAK does not exist in the lexicon, one has to test the possibility of altering its orthographical structure solely on the basis of its letter structure. Flanking changes, by contrast, occur after word recognition, or, more precisely, after the identification of a potential root. In cases such as *watches*, the lexical specification can thus be used to judge the legitimacy of E-deletion and S-affixation. While the analysis of the affix is performed on the basis of the morphological specification of WATCH, the orthographical analysis is normally based on the configuration of the individual letters, i.e. on purely orthographical grounds. Karttunen/Wittenburg (1983: 218), for example, defined a rule which deletes an -E after the root-final segments -CH, -SH, -S, -X, -Z, or -Y/I before the affix -S. This rule can be simplified if the phonological information is made available. It is well-known that the application of E-deletion in cases such as *watches*, *rushes*, *bosses*, and *foxes* does not depend on the root's orthographical but on its phonological structure, i.e. E-deletion is possible after /ʃ/ and /s/.

In some cases the processing of the orthographical structure of words is not only more efficient on the basis of phonological aspects, but is impossible without it. Reconsider our examples of consonantal doubling, *referring* and *catering*, and two further examples, *developing* and *stopping*. Looking at the first two examples one might assume that doubling occurs in all those cases where the last vowel of the root is not /ə/. This would explain why *cater* /ˈkeɪtə/ does not involve consonantal doubling. However, then *develop* /dɪˈvelɒp/ should reduplicate its final consonant. Hence, the segmental phonological information alone, i.e. the information about the phoneme structure, is not sufficient. What we need in order to decide whether consonantal doubling may occur is a precise statement about the root's syllable structure and the placement of the word accent. While in *refer* and *stop* the primary stress is placed on the last syllable, *cater* and *develop* have unstressed final syllables. The latter ones do not allow consonantal doubling. Thus, in order to account for such aspects of orthographical alternation, the phonological field should represent each lexical entry in terms of its phonemic and syllabic structure. This can be achieved by using standard phonemic transcription or, if the extended symbols of this notation are not available, one can use a simple ASCII-format where each symbol represents a specific phoneme. Here are some examples:

(69) a. 'wOtS (watch), 'rUS (rush)
b. 'swIm (swim), rI|'fÖ: (refer), 'ke|ItE (cater)

Internally, each of these symbols stands for a phoneme, for example, O stands for /ɒ/, S stands for /ʃ/, and so on. Syllable boundaries are represented by a separator (|) and stress marks by '. With such a format the phonological structure of lexical entries can not only be translated into real phonemic transcription by means of a reference table but it can also be incorporated into the analysis and generation process.

5.3.2. The Morpho-Syntactic Field

If full forms are to be stored as access units, then there is no point in performing morphological analysis as part of the lexical look-up process. All that is required is the specification of each item in terms of its own morphological properties. This can be done by means of a direct representation or by associating each entry with a reference symbol that points to a large table where the morphological information is stored. For example, one could couple all plural count nouns with the symbol NPL. This symbol would then function as a pointer to a table from which the information (Noun Plural Count) can be inferred. This technique reduces the degree of redundancy in the lexicon and guarantees that the information can be utilised by a multitude of lexical entries.

In a root lexicon we have to couple each entry with its morphological continuation possibilities. The noun *fly*, for example, could be associated with the continuation class N1. Furthermore, we need an additional store that contains all those affixes that take part in regular morphological processes such as inflection. Such an affix lexicon would have to contain the morphological specification of all N1-nouns. Figure 95 illustrates this relationship between the morphological classes of two lexical entries and a fragment of the morphological information in the affix lexicon.

According to this system the N1-access units can be realised as singular and plural forms, N2-items are restricted to singular forms (the item MEN could then be classified as N3, allowing only plural forms). Note that a technique of establishing internal relationships between the items in the affix lexicon is used to reduce redundancy. The first part of the N1-entry is N2, where N2 serves as pointer to all N2-entries, i.e. to the singular forms.

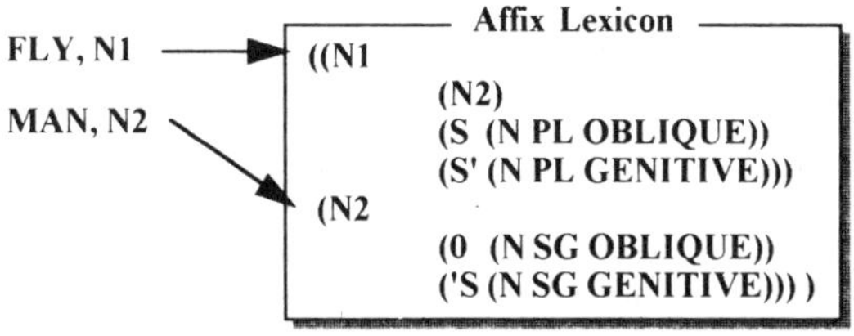

Figure 95. Morphological class and affix information

Further reductions can be achieved by the use of morphological default rules. For example, in figure 95 case information is explicitly listed. This could be avoided by a rule which associates the oblique case with all those items whose case is not specified elsewhere. Other default values could be (+ sg) (+ count), in the case of nouns, (+ positive) in the case of adjectives, or (+ present) in the case of verbs. These values would then be inferred unless they are explicitly overwritten. Alternatively, one could present some of these aspects as a part of the morphological specification of the entry itself. Noun features such as (± count) or (± common), for example, are not required for the morphological analysis process. Rather, they are needed for the integration of a noun into syntactic structures, i.e. 'can the noun be preceded by a determiner or not?'. Hence, we can directly encode this information in the lexical entry.

The link between roots and affixes is established by a computational mechanism that relates surface structures (the actual word forms, such as *carries*) to lexical representations (the root-affix structures, such as CARRY+S). In an excellent summary Sproat (1992: 124) discusses the variety of approaches available. The most well-known formalisation of computational morphology that relates the surface level and the lexical level makes use of *finite-state machines* or *finite-state transition networks*. Such transition networks handle a fair amount of concatenative morphology, i.e. the possibility of generating and analysing sequences of affixes. Figure 96 illustrates such a network on the basis of some selected noun and adjective roots and the derivational affixes -ISE, -ATION, and -AL, which theoretically may be concatenated infinitely often.

It is commonly known that such transition networks can only come into operation at morpheme boundaries. An adequate lexical structure to represent morpheme boundaries is the discrimination network as discussed above, where each terminal node is associated with a morphological class that denotes the affixational possibilities of a root and triggers the relevant transition network.

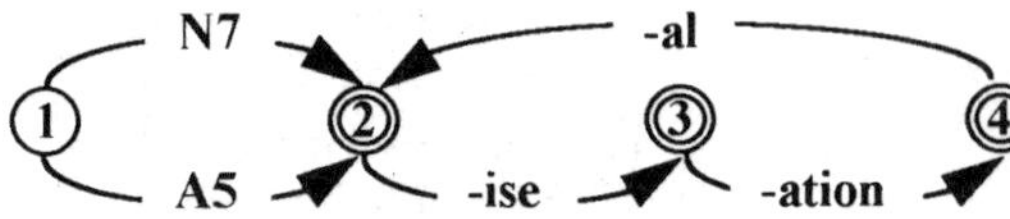

Figure 96. A finite-state transition network for a fragment of English morphology Annotations: N7/A5 = Nouns and Adjectives that take the suffix *-ise* (e.g. *motor*, *moral*); single circles = non-finite states, double circles = finite states, i.e. possible word-forms

A somewhat enhanced method of using finite-state machines not only inspects the affixational possibilities but can also transduce surface structures into lexical structures, taking into account phonological or graphological alternation. The most prominent implementation of finite-state transducers has become known as *two-level morphology* and was first used in the KIMMO-system (Koskenniemi 1983; Karttunen 1983). Basically, KIMMO makes use of two finite-state machines, or *tapes*, that constantly compare surface representations and lexical representations, such as C-A-R-R-I-E-S (the surface form) and C-A-R-R-Y-S (the lexical form).[28]

In many cases the representation of morphological information crosses the boundary between morphology and syntax. Features such as (± count), for example, suggest that morphology and syntax are closely connected. The subsumption of this information under morphology or syntax not only depends on the lexicon format but also on the type of syntactic theory used.

In unification grammars, for example, items of lexical, morphological, and syntactic information are matched against each other to generate well-formed tree structures. These grammars represent the morphological information as a set of attribute-value pairs. Some of the attributes directly relate to the syntactic structure into which these elements can be inserted. For example, a plural noun could be associated with the feature specification

{(N +) (V -) (PLU +) (BAR 0)}

where (BAR 0) expresses the fact that the item is a potential terminal node in a syntactic tree. Note that such an attribute-value pair is no longer entirely morphological in character since it is not required to define a word's morphological properties. Rather, it relates to the syntactic aspects of a lexical entry. Further features of this type specify syntactic agreement (AGR) and subcategorisation (SUBCAT) (see Ritchie et al. 1992: 42ff). Other techniques of combining morphological and syntactic information are *directed acyclic graphs* (DAG), where morphological features are directly integrated in displaying the internal structure of constituents (Gazdar/Mellish 1989:

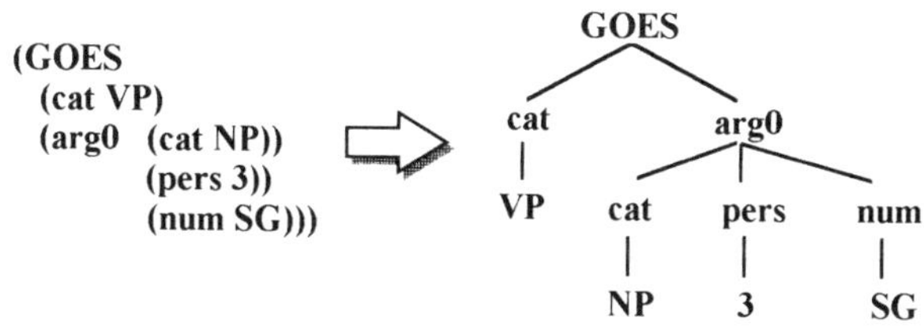

Figure 97. The morpho-syntactic feature representation of *goes* as a DAG

219ff). Figure 97 represents the morpho-syntactic structure of GOES as a full-form entry in a list notation and its conversion into a DAG.

Such a morpho-syntactic representation can directly be mapped on to a tree where syntactic properties, such as subject-verb-agreement, can be examined. However, these structures clearly cross the morphological boundary since they are not required in order to identify the affixational possibilities of a given root. Rather, they are the result of the morphological analysis and are part of the syntactic specification of a lexical entry.

For the morphological specification of a lexical entry, we suggest a representation in terms of a single symbol, such as N1, V13, etc. This serves as a pointer to the morphological component, where the affixational properties are evaluated and a set of feature specifications is generated. Over and above the information about the affixes, the morphological component has at its disposal a number of principles, such as feature inheritance or default values, and a computational mechanism that relates surface structures to lexical representations.

5.3.3. The Syntactic Field

All linguistic theories have in common that they accept a general division of labour between grammatical rules and the lexicon. However, there is disagreement about the amount of information contained in each. At one extreme, we have context-free grammars that hardly make use of lexical features and the lexicon basically associates lexical items with categorial information. In such frameworks, the grammatical rules encode almost all information. At the other extreme, we find feature-based grammars, where the lexicon contains the majority of linguistic information, and the contribution of the rules is only marginal. The encoding of the syntactic specification of an entry in a machine-readable lexicon depends on the theory selected. All theories agree that two central aspects have to be represented as part of the syntactic specification of an entry (section 2.3.3.1.):

– the general syntactic context in terms of the argument structure of the entry
– syntactic idiosyncrasies

Furthermore, it is generally accepted that the syntactic specification must be defined in such a way that a semantic interpretation of an input sentence can be built. By semantic interpretation we mean a logical form with intra-linguistic relevance, rather than a conceptual representation which relates to external domains (see section 1.3.4.). However, there is disagreement about the encoding of the rules and principles that lead to a logical form, i.e. is it directly represented in the syntactic specification of a lexical entry or not?

Today, there seems to be a strong tendency to favour the lexical extreme, where as much syntactic information as possible is encoded in the syntactic specification of a lexical entry. In such feature-based or unification-based theories, processing is essentially a process of pattern matching or *unification*, where the syntactic specifications of the words of an input sentence are unified to form larger structures. The most prominent variants of unification grammar are:

– lexical-functional grammar (LFG)
– generalised phrase structure grammar (GPSG)
– head-driven phrase structure grammar (HPSG)[29]

In HPSG, for example, lexical entries are defined as presented in figure 98.[30]

```
[ (sem: (be)+easy ( ① , ② ))
  (syn.loc.subcat:
          (subj:      (syn: NP-nom)
                      (sem:  ③ ))
          (pp-for:    (sem:  ① ))
          (xcomp:     (syn:  VP-inf)
                      (sem:  ② )
                           (slash: (sem: ③)))) ]
```

Figure 98. The syntactic specification of (be)+EASY in the HPSG-format

The syntactic specification of (be)+EASY accounts for the following sentence structures (Flickinger/Nerbonne 1991: 14):

(70) a. Bill is easy to talk to.
b. It is easy to talk to Bill.
c. Bill is easy for Mary to talk to.
d. It is easy for Mary to talk to Bill.

Note that this "syntactic" specification also exhibits some sort of semantic information in terms of the essential arguments of (be)+EASY. This is achieved by means of the encircled numbers, which identify elements as the same across the entire lexical specification. For the semantic interpretation of (be)+EASY (sem: (be)+easy ..) this means that the semantic arguments 1 and 2 are obligatory. With reference to the example sentences in (70), argument 1 is "Mary" and argument 2 the embedded infinitival clause, which in turn contains "Bill" as argument 3.

The HPSG-representation format unites functional and categorial information. For example, it indicates that element 3 may surface as the grammatical subject of the sentence, e.g. in (70a) and (70c), and that it occurs in the nominative case. Even though the nominative case normally does not exist in English, this overspecified representation guarantees that pronouns as surface subjects and standard nouns receive the correct case (syn: NP-nom). Since HPSG is closely related to the framework of Generalised Phrase Structure Grammar (GPSG), which goes back to Gazdar et al. (1985), it encodes syntactic information along similar lines. For example, the feature "slash" in the infinitival complement (xcomp) of (be)+EASY indicates that element 3 may be missing, as in (70a) and (70c). In such cases it is realised as the grammatical subject of the main clause.

The slash feature is more directly encoded in GPSG, where the lexical entry of (be)+EASY would be associated with an immediate dominance rule of the following type (Gazdar et al. 1985: 247):

$$AP \rightarrow H[42], VP[INF]/NP[\text{-}NOM]$$

Essentially, this rule expands the AP-node into A-bar and a slash-category following, in this case a VP with a NP missing from it.[31] H[42] is a simple, arbitrarily-chosen reference number. It says that (be)+EASY is "Head-type" number 42 within a list of all English heads (Gazdar et al. 1985: 150). The syntactic specification of (be)+EASY in GPSG can be directly converted into a syntactic tree of the type presented in figure 99.

The representation of the syntactic specification of a lexical entry in terms of a GPSG-format or HPSG-frames such as presented in figure 98 is very popular. It integrates categorial aspects, subcategorisation information,

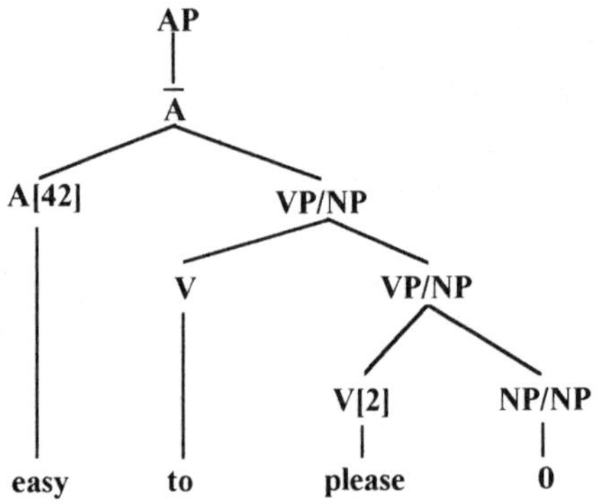

Figure 99. Syntactic specifications as tree structures, the GPSG-entry (be)+EASY

and the possibility of realising the individual arguments of an entry in terms of different syntactic functions.

The presentation of functional aspects, i.e. the exact specification of syntactic functions, such as subject or object, is central to the definition of lexical entries in LFG. Figure 100 shows the fundamental properties of the lexical entry (be)+EASY in the LFG-format after Sells (1985: 154ff).

$$\begin{bmatrix} \textbf{(PRED} \quad = \textbf{'be+easy<(}\Uparrow\textbf{ XCOMP)> (}\Uparrow\textbf{SUBJ)'} \\ \textbf{(}\Uparrow\textbf{ SUBJ) = (}\Uparrow\textbf{ XCOMP OBJ)} \end{bmatrix}$$

Figure 100. The syntactic specification of (be)+EASY in the LFG-format (simplified)

Lexical entries in LFG consist of attribute-value pairs. The attributes are names of grammatical functions, such as subject or object. The associated values can occur as simple symbols, complex semantic forms, or so-called 'functional structures' (see Kaplan/Bresnan 1982: 177). For example, the attribute PRED is associated with the semantic information represented in quotes.[32] The "up-arrows" can be interpreted as functions that assign the information to the respective mother nodes in the syntactic tree. For example, the verbal node in the tree is associated with the information about the functional environment of the PRED. In the case of (be)+EASY, this functional environment is a semantically restricted infinitival complement (XCOMP), such as "to please someone". Furthermore, (be)+EASY subcategorises a non-thematic subject. This is expressed by the fact that (↑ SUBJ) is external to the angle brackets. The complement of (be)+EASY has to contain an object (↑ XCOMP OBJ). This guarantees that constructions where the complement of (be)+EASY contains an intransitive verb are ungrammatical unless the grammatical subject of (be)+EASY is realised by the empty *it* in the sentence. Here is a minimal pair that illustrates this contrast:

(71) a. *Bill is easy to go.
b. It is easy for Bill to go.

However, if the embedded complement has an object, like *talk* in the examples (70a) to (70d), this object may surface as the grammatical subject of (be)+EASY. This relationship is expressed by the equation (↑ SUBJ) = (↑ XCOMP OBJ).

The inclusion of semantic information in terms of argument structures or functional information to generate a logical form is also quite common in machine-readable lexicons. However, the degree of semantic information often depends on the purpose of the system. In the following section we will see that machine translation systems always generate some sort of semantic structure; however, there are enormous differences. In the TAUM-Meteo system, for example, both syntax and semantics are fully integrated. In fact, the analysis process is syntax-driven but it receives semantic guidance (Isabelle 1987: 254). In other words, while the syntactic information is converted into a tree, a semantic evaluation takes place. This evaluation process projects all semantic features of terminal nodes to non-terminal nodes, e.g. from nouns to NPs, and performs a semantic calculus that assesses the compatibility of the constituents of the sentence. For example, if a verb and its object are semantically incompatible, no syntactic structure will be built.

In section 2.3.3.2. we discussed numerous theoretical approaches to semantics, ranging from static representations, such as feature theories, to more procedural representations, such as networks, conceptual dependencies, or prototypical information realised as frames. In the following section we will see how and to what extent these approaches can be made use of in actual implementations and why the definition of semantic aspects is almost insurmountably difficult.

5.3.4. The Semantic Field

The inclusion of a semantic specification depends on a number of basic considerations. First, the contents of the semantic field are a matter of system architecture, i.e. whether the system should be enabled to 'understand' what the words and sentences really mean. A second important decision concerns the representation format. In section 2.3.3.2. we introduced a number of representation formalisms, from simple feature matrices to complex frames which are dynamically filled with information during sentence processing. Thirdly, the programmer has to think carefully about the computational formalism used to represent meaning. There are a number of different conventions for doing this, but for any one program there should be a uniform organisation (Winograd/Flores 1986: 89).

5.3.4.1. System Design: Meaning Representation or not?

In the mid-1960s, researchers into processing natural language with computers were disillusioned by the failure of the highly funded and enthusiastic machine translation projects. There was a feeling that the computer would always be incapable of dealing with the complexities of natural language. However, it became clear by this time that for an adequate analysis of natural language inputs the mere identification of the lexical items, or the shuffling of words to analyse and generate syntactic structures alone, was insufficient. Any program had to deal with what the words and sentences *mean*. In other words, realistic natural language processing on computers involves *understanding*.

In the wake of this disillusionment, but with many innovative ideas in mind, researchers developed a number of new programs that achieved some sort of understanding. Each of these programs worked in a limited domain (baseball, algebraic problems, family relationships, etc.) within which it was possible to represent meaning in terms of a systematic manipulation of a formal representation. Winograd/Flores (1986: 108) listed the following claims about the relationship between such formal representations and meaning:

- Sentences in a natural language correspond to the facts about the world,
- It is possible to create a formal representation system such that:
    - for every fact about the world there is a corresponding representation,
    - there is a systematic way of correlating real sentences with formal representations,
    - there are formal operations on representations to allow reasoning.

Of course Winograd/Flores knew that this view was far too simple. Words may acquire specific meanings when put to use in actual contexts, referential relations may cross sentence boundaries, sentences may be interpreted differently by different speakers, etc. For these and other reasons it soon became clear that despite the early successes of limited-domain programs, such as Winograd's (1972) SHRDLU, the representation of meaning involves formalisms and interpretative techniques that are much more complicated than previously thought. In fact, it has turned out that the representation and analysis of meaning in natural language processing systems is so complex that there is still no computer system capable of achieving real *understanding*. However, because of the needs of commercial systems, alternatives have been developed. Let us look more closely at the situation of today's machine translation systems to illustrate the present situation.

Machine translation systems can be classified into three types (Hutchins 1986: 54ff): direct systems, interlingua systems, and transfer systems. Figure 101 illustrates this typology.

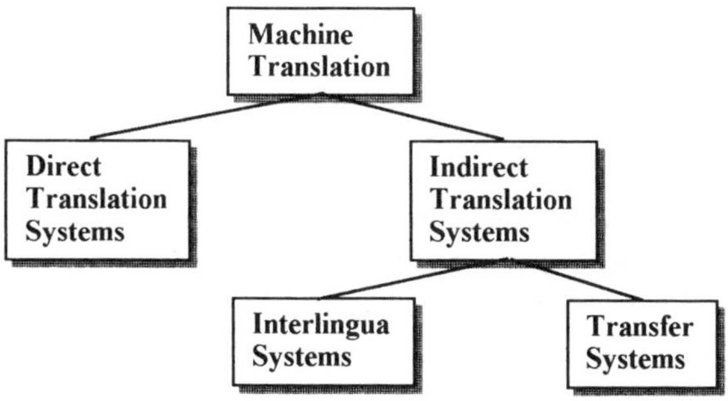

Figure 101. A typology of machine translation

In the *direct approach*, which was used in the early days of machine translation, systems are designed for a particular pair of languages. The basic assumption of this approach is that only little parsing is necessary to convert the source language into the target language. Rather, translation can be generally viewed as a process of matching one language with another. Direct translation systems rely heavily on well-defined lexicons, morphological processing, and a number of language-specific principles responsible for word order patterns. The conversion of the input into a semantic structure, however, was not performed. The classic example of a direct translation system is the Georgetown system, a Russian-to-English machine translation system developed in the 1950s by IBM®at Georgetown University, U.S.A.

Today, the majority of machine translation systems do not translate directly from one language into another but on the basis of an intermediate internal representation. In such *indirect systems*, a major strategic decision is the design of the internal representation. In *interlingua systems*, the internal representation is some sort of semantic structure from which it is theoretically possible to translate into any one language. While in artificial intelligence this conceptual structure is referred to as *knowledge representation*, in machine translation it is called *interlingua* (Nirenburg 1987: 6). Well-known attempts to incorporate semantic analysis into machine translation were made by Schank (1975 1977), whose conceptual dependency representation was used in a number of systems in the 1970s and 1980s.[33] Schematically, the process of translation in such systems can be characterised as a "slot-filling-mechanism", where for each source language element a semantic frame is retrieved from the lexicon. These frames contain a number of slots in which variables have to be matched against the input. Let us use an actual example to illustrate this technique.

(72)
a. The student *enters* the classroom.
German: *betreten* (come into)
b. The robber *enters* the house.
German: *eindringen in* (intrude)
c. The man *enters* the horse in the race.
German: *anmelden* (register)
d. The thought never *enters* my head.
German: *ankommen in* (arrive at)
e. The young man *enters* the services.
German: *einrücken in* (join)
f. The young man *enters* service.
German: *werden* (become a butler)
g. The defendant *enters* a plea of not guilty.
German: *plädieren* (plead)

In order to translate these sentences into another language, an internal representation for each sentence has to be generated that accounts for the different senses of *enter*. This representation has to reflect the fact that the interpretation of *enter* depends on the semantic status of its grammatical subject and object. Using the CD-format, *enter* would, among others, be connected with the following basic frame:

(73)
```
(event ENTER01
       (action PTRANS)
       (actor ?SUBJECT)
       (object ?SUBJECT)
       (from ?VAR)
       (to ?OBJECT))
```

Essentially, this frame says that one interpretation of *enter* (ENTER01) is "an action of physical transfer" (PTRANS), in which the actor (realised by the grammatical subject) transfers the object (also realised by the grammatical subject) from a variable location to a location denoted by the grammatical object. Mapped on to example (72a) it means that "the student transferred himself from an unknown place to the classroom". In terms of slot-filling, ?SUBJECT is "the student", ?VAR "an unknown location", i.e. NIL, and ?OBJECT "the classroom". Unfortunately, this representation would also be apt for (72b). In this case, ?SUBJECT is realised by "the robber" and ?OBJECT by "the house". In order to distinguish the two senses of ENTER01, we have to incorporate the precise semantic details of the elements that realise the grammatical subject (?SUBJECT) and object (?OBJECT) of *enter*. Using semantic features and the CD-format of (12), (72a) and (72b) could be converted into a more detailed CD-representation:

```
(74)    (event ENTER01
               (action PTRANS)
               (actor (SUBJECT: physical-object (animate (human))))
               (object (SUBJECT: physical-object (animate (human))))
               (from nil)
               (to (OBJECT: physical-object (building, part-of-building))))
```

This representation clearly distinguishes (72a/b) from the remaining examples. In (72d), for example, the subject is not a physical object; in (72g) the object is semantically abstract rather than physical. Also, (72d) and (72g) involve actions of mental rather than physical transfer. Hence, the activation of the ENTER01-frame and thus the translation of *enter* as *betreten* (*come into*) or *eindringen* (*intrude*) relies on the identification of the subject as "animate" and the object as "building or part of it". The difference between (72a) and (72b) depends on the attitude towards the subject. If the subject has the connotation of "being not friendly", the translation will be *eindringen*, if the subject is semantically neutral, the standard interpretation *betreten* will be chosen. This distinction can be drawn on the basis of a discrimination network (see Charniak et al. 1987: 149ff).

To summarise, interlingua systems generate a semantic representation on the basis of a semantic lexicon from which predefined frames are retrieved. These frames are filled by a slot-filling-mechanism. Additional techniques in such systems are semantic hierarchies and discrimination networks. In any case, the semantic representation serves as the basis for the translation into any target language.

Transfer systems generate internal structures that are less semantic in character and are tailored for the language pair involved. Ambiguities, such as the meaning of *enter* in (72), are not resolved on the basis of semantic features in the lexicon or stored semantic frames. Instead of generating a precise semantic or conceptual representation, a transfer system makes use of a special 'transfer' lexicon from which the translation into the target language is generated. In such a lexicon, ambiguity resolution can be carried out on the basis of cross-references, statistics or probabilities, or passages of text that have already been translated. The level of transfer differs from system to system. It varies from purely syntactic deep structures to annotated syntactico-semantic structures which contain information about thematic roles (Tucker 1987: 23).

To sum up, in modern machine translation systems we are confronted with two central strategies: a multilingual semantically-based interlingua strategy and a bilingual transfer strategy. The integration of semantic analysis into a machine translation system has both advantages and drawbacks. The most important advantage of interlingual systems is the possibility of true multilingual translation by the abandonment of language-specific transfer grammars. While transfer grammars are large, amorphous systems, which contain a set of ad-hoc rules that map phrases from one language into their corresponding counterparts, the interlingua or knowledge-based approach only requires a parser and a system that generates a semantic representation (Carbonell/Tomita 1987: 75).[34] This sounds very simple and immediately evokes the question why machine translation designers bother about transfer systems at all. The problem with knowledge-based systems is the enormous size of human knowledge that has to be represented. At present, it is not possible to develop knowledge-based systems that encompass the entirety of human knowledge. For this reason, the difference between transfer systems and knowledge-based systems boils down to the complexity of the domain to which a machine translation is to be applied. If the domain is limited, such as weather forecasts, technical reports, etc., knowledge-based systems are to be preferred; if it is unconstrained and the purpose of the system is not restricted, transfer strategies are advantageous.

The question of representing semantic information does not only apply to machine translation. Whenever engineers design a natural language processing system, one of the most important questions concerns the integration of a knowledge base. In systems with limited semantic domains, the knowledge base remains relatively small and easy to survey. In semantically less restricted systems, the knowledge base may become so complex that it can hardly be administered any more.

5.3.4.2. The Representation Format

In section 2.3.3.2. we discussed the most influential approaches to the representation of meaning in the mental lexicon. In a machine-readable lexicon we have the same choices. Depending on the semantic domain we can formalise the knowledge by means of feature lists, semantic networks, frames, etc. However, in implementing these structures we have the choice between *procedural* or *declarative* representations. This distinction has a long tradition in artificial intelligence. While declarative representations stress static aspects of knowledge, such as facts about objects, events, etc., procedural representations emphasise strategies of how to use the knowledge, i.e. inferencing strategies, fact-finding strategies, etc. (Barr/Feigenbaum 1981: 172ff).

Before we discuss the implications of both approaches, let us use an actual example to illustrate the difference between them.

(75) a. John is going.
b. John is going to London.
c. John is going from London to New York.

In all three examples GO has an obligatory subject (John) which is the main actor of the action. The action itself can be characterised as an action of "physical transfer". This action has an optional source (from) and an optional target (to). In a declarative representation this could be expressed by the following frame.

(76)
```
[go: V;
        (subj-np (ACTOR))
        ((ptrans (ACTOR)
                  (to NP)(from NP))
        (<PP (from NP)>
        <PP (to NP)>)]
```

This frame would be triggered via the semantic specification of the lexical entry GO. In a matching process, the variables ACTOR and NP would then be filled. The information provided by the declarative frame, however, is static. It does not contain any clues as to how the variables have to be filled and where the relevant information can be found.

This situation is different in a procedural representation format. Now the information is coupled with a number of procedures that tell the system what to do with it. In CD-theory, for example, semantic specifications are procedural. Represented in LISP, a simplified procedural format of GO can be expressed like this (Schank/Riesbeck 1981):

```
(77) [go ((assign
          (*cat* 'v)
          (*cd-form*'((ptrans(actor ?var1)(object ?var1)
                      (to ?var2)(from ?var3)))) )
         ((test (eq *cat* 'pp))
          (assign (var2 *np*)))) ]
```

This procedural frame not only contains static aspects of knowledge, such as the CD-frame (ptrans..) itself, but also explicit procedures that decide what to do with the information. The procedure ASSIGN, for example, sets variable values, while the procedure TEST examines the formal properties of words and categories. In some cases the application of ASSIGN is dependent on the result of TEST. For example, *var2* is assigned the value **np**, if **cat** has the value *pp*. This guarantees the optionality of the "to-phrase", as in (75b) and (75c).

The main advantage of procedural representations is their possibility of representing what theorem should be used and what goals should be tried first. In a representation such as (77), for example, the assignment of the actual value to *var2* can only be carried out if the test that a "to-PP" has been found is successful.

Even though procedural representations allow a high degree of control, there are drawbacks. They concern the complexity and consistency of information in such representations, and the lack of modularity. In a procedural representation, the interaction between various facts is essential. All levels of representation are connected by explicit mappings that produce structures depending on conditions at the present and the preceding level (Emele et al. 1992: 62). This makes it difficult to express conditions on non-adjacent levels. Therefore, modifications at one level, for example at the level of knowledge representation, might have more far-reaching consequences than in declarative representations. Even though the superiority of the declarative representation format in natural language processing systems is now widely accepted, no recent commercial system makes use of purely declarative rule systems (Henschel/Höser 1991: 98). Rather, today's systems integrate procedural rules into declarative-oriented representations.

Whether declaratively or procedurally, the semantic specification of a lexical entry must capture as many generalisations as possible. This means that associated information is represented in terms of bundled packets. This guarantees the reusability of data and allows a considerable reduction of redundancy. For example, a frame such as (76) is not only confined to the verb GO, but also applies to all sorts of motion concepts, such as DRIVE, RIDE, SWIM, FLY, WALK, RUN, etc. In other words, this information can be reused in various places in the lexicon. A common technique for making shared knowledge available is the use of *default inheritance networks*. In such structures lexical entries are coupled with information that directly represents specific aspects and with aspects that are inherited from larger structures contained in specific databases. Examples of this technique can be found in numerous representation formats, such as PATR-II (Boguraev/Briscoe 1989b), or in semantic representations of the CD-type, where one discrimination network is shared by a number of related verbal concepts.

5.3.4.3. Examples of Semantic Fields

On the basis of the discussion above, we have to distinguish between true semantic fields and fields that are referred to as semantic but are not. In most transfer systems, for example, we find "semantic" specifications that are syntactic structures enriched by some semantic information rather than true semantic representations. For example, the EUROTRA-project dispenses with true semantic aspects and confines itself to the association of 'semantic' cases, such as agent, patient, time, etc., with verbal entries, and the definition of some selected semantic features, such as animate, human, abstract. On the basis of this information, a case frame structure or 'interface structure' is built (Arnold/des Tombe 1987: 132). Hence at one extreme, the semantic specification of an entry is merely an enriched syntactic structure of the type:

(concept (role$_1$ X)(role$_2$ Y) (role$_N$ Z))

At the other extreme, we have semantic specifications that integrate syntax into semantics and are clearly semantic-conceptual in character. Cullingford/Onyshkevych (1987: 295) make use of such lexical entries. Basically, these entries consist of a header C_N, where $_N$ stands for an arbitrary numerical value and C for concept. For example, the representations for JOHN (C48) and MARY (C27) have the following format:

C27: (person (gender (fem)) (persname (MARY)))
C48: (person (gender (masc)) (persname (JOHN)))

Verbal concepts are associated with complex frames based on the CD-format outlined above. Cullingford/Onyshkevych use PUNCH (C55) as an example.

```
C55: (propel  (actor (person ?C1))
              (object (bpart (bytype (HAND))(part-of (person ?C1))))
              (to (physcont val (bpart (bytype (HAND))
                 (part-of (person ?C2)))
              (time ?Time)
              (mode ?Mode))
```

Essentially, this representation defines an action where a person (?C1) propels a hand which is part of ?C1 into physical contact with a part of a different person ?C2. This action may take place at any time (present/past) and with different degrees of intensity. By matching C55 with C27 and C48, this representation can be used to generate or analyse "Mary punched John on the nose".

Between these two extremes there are numerous possible ways of representing semantic information. The machine translation system SUSY, for example, uses a feature representation format in terms of classic values such as 'human', 'abstract', 'concrete', etc., but confines this information to nouns and pronouns (Maas 1987: 236). More sophisticated semantic representation systems, such as Nirenburg et al.'s (1987) TRANSLATOR, define specific interlingua entries in terms of concepts. The representation format used here is a mixture of semantic hierarchies in terms of semantic networks and frames. The combination of these two techniques allows the application of feature inheritance and default values. For example, the semantic specification of COMPUTER-USER in the interlingua lexicon of TRANSLATOR is represented as

```
(COMPUTER-USER (computer-user
                     (IS-A person)
                     (AGENT-OF (+ operate))
                     (SUBWORLD computer-world)))
```

This frame contains pointers to other frames. For example, the IS-A slot will eventually inherit the entire information from the person-frame, i.e. that a person is a creature, that it has a body, etc.; and the AGENT-OF slot will be associated with a list of verbal concepts, such as TAKE, PUT, FIND, etc., which themselves are non-terminal nodes of semantic networks. In other words, frames of this type are shortened versions representing bundles of information that can be retrieved via inheritance and other types of associations.

Whatever type of semantic representation is selected it seems clear that the complexity depends on the system's purpose and application. In domain-specific systems we can employ fairly elaborate semantic information, while in general-purpose systems the lexical entries are associated with only limited semantic information. Nevertheless, the previous discussion should have pointed out the enormous effort and difficulty in representing semantic aspects at all.

In order to represent the semantic specification of lexical entries and account for aspects such as reusability of information, feature inheritance and cross-references, a high degree of externalisation must be employed. Especially if we are confronted with a limitation of a machine's working memory, the semantic specification of a lexical entry should be kept as small as possible. Hence, in terms of implementing the semantic specification, the entire information might be defined by a short list of symbols which are internally interpreted as readpointers to a semantic database that contains the relevant information.

5.3.5. Lexical Specification; a Summary

While there is agreement that serious natural language processing systems have to associate their access units with lexical information, there is disagreement about the complexity, the format, and the implementation of this information in a machine-readable lexicon. Probably the only similarity between the lexical entries across natural language processing systems is the presence of morphological and syntactic information. The formalisms to represent and the algorithms to implement this information, however, are different. The availability of further aspects is dependent on the theory used and on the application of the system. In section 5.3.1. we discussed the necessity of phonological information not only as a means of information about an item's pronunciation but as an important basis for the generation of orthographical variants. That the incorporation of semantic information into the lexical specification, and thus the possibility for a natural language processing system to achieve some sort of understanding, increases the complexity of a lexical entry has been illustrated in section 5.3.4. Because of the difficulty of representing semantic information, one of the most crucial decisions in designing the lexicon of a natural language processing system is whether 'understanding' is required or not.

Over and above the basic 'linguistic' fields associated with each lexical access unit, there are further kinds of lexical information. Again, these additional aspects depend on the system's overall purpose. For example, in text retrieval systems, i.e. in systems that are capable of applying search and sorting operations to texts, aspects that deal with actual examples of an item in context, or with etymological information, may be of valuable support. Furthermore, one might couple a number of lexical entries with visual information. Especially in tutorial systems for children the presentation of lexical entries as pictures has proved beneficial. Last but not least, we might also encode each access unit acoustically. Even though the acoustic presentation of an access unit is dependent on the availability of particular hardware extensions, the possibility of listening to the actual pronunciation of an item might be very helpful in natural language processing systems with a tutorial background.

5.4. Mental and Machine-Readable Lexicons; a Summary

The previous sections have shown that some but not all aspects of human lexical processing can be handled by machines. The main similarities between the mental and a machine-readable lexicon concern the general organisation of lexical entries and their subdivision into several fields. Also, the separation of a lexical access unit from its lexical specification makes sense both for humans and for machines. Psycholinguistic evidence, as pointed out in chapter four, as well as processing efficiency and memory management, supports the partitioning of lexical entry into access unit and lexical specification.

By contrast, the realisation of the well-established effects of word recognition in machine-readable lexicons is problematic in many ways. First, not all effects can be simulated by machines. We saw that the frequency effect is a good case in point. Furthermore, it has been shown that the realisation of these effects in terms of specific data or file structures does not necessarily lead to an increase in computational performance. For example, the internal dynamics of the mental lexicon, that is, its possibility of constantly regrouping its access units according to their recency of occurrence, does not make sense in constructing a machine-readable lexicon. At the expense of highly complicated operations responsible for database reorganisation, we might gain a few milliseconds in word recognition. The price we have to pay is too high. Enormously complex administration mechanisms would complicate database management. Especially in lexical file systems that make use of indices or pointers this would be far too costly.

The most important difference between humans and machines concerns their ability to pre-process the input. In order to segregate the words from the input stream, enormously complicated strategies have to be applied. Irrespective of the input mode, humans are far superior to machines at present. The human speech recognition system, for example, draws on vast amounts of knowledge, ranging from features to high-level information. Even though ASR-systems will be capable of handling spoken input as flexibly as humans one day, the variation in the human speech signal in normal conversation is incomparably greater than anything that has been tackled by modern ASR-systems (Lobacz 1984: 85). The recognition of written language by machines, however, has made enormous progress and in the foreseeable future fully automatic OCR-systems that can identify even hand-written information with great precision will be available.

Table 11 summarises the basic insights into the mental lexicon with regard to their realisation in their machine-readable counterparts.

Table 11. Mental lexicon and machine-readable lexicon

Mental Lexicon	Machine-Readable Lexicon
Speech perception	ASR: rudimentary
Perception of written language	OCR: possible
Roots as access units	possible
Partitioning of lexical specification (Form/Lemma)	possible
Administration of	
– frequency effect	via file systems
– contextual effect	via contextual statistics
– length effect	– possible in discrimination networks
– lexicality effect	– possible in discrimination networks

In the following chapter, we will look at an actual implementation of a machine-readable lexicon that realises a number of the principles introduced in this chapter. It operates within a natural language processing system, it uses the partitioned cohort structure, and recognises words on the basis of roots. This system, developed by the author and his colleagues, is called *LexEcon*.[35]

6. LexEcon; an On-Line Machine Readable Lexicon

> *"Success in programming depends on designing a representation and set of operations that are both 'veridical' and 'effective'. They are veridical to the extent that they produce results that are correct relative to the domain: they are effective to varying degrees, depending on how efficiently the computational operations can be carried out."*
> *(Winograd/Flores 1986:85).*

The basic idea behind LexEcon is to provide a variety of information about words in written documents. This information may be the translation into another language, at present English to German and German to English are available, information about synonyms, etymological and contextual aspects, and last but not least, information about the pronunciation of an item. Furthermore, the system informs the user about the linguistic properties of an item, and, in some selected cases, it may also present lexical entries visually.

The user of LexEcon can freely switch from one source language to another, at present from English to German and vice versa. While the English to German lexicon contains approximately 25.000 entries, the German to English lexicon is still in the build-up phase and features only 4.000 entries. All basic entries have been handcrafted. The economy vocabulary has been scanned in from various economy dictionaries, automatically converted into a machine-readable format, and postedited by hand.

The possibility of presenting a wide range of information about the words in a language alone does not differentiate LexEcon from ordinary databases used as spell-checker or thesaurus in word processing software. In contrast to such 'unintelligent' programs, LexEcon applies numerous linguistic analysis procedures before the information about an item is presented.

(a) pre-lexical processing

LexEcon neither accepts spoken input nor does it handle written information. It analyses textual data solely in terms of ASCII-code. There are two ways to initiate analysis. In the direct mode, words are simply typed using the keyboard. In the indirect mode, words are forwarded to LexEcon from standard software applications, such as word processors or graphics applications. In this mode a word is marked first and then – together with its environment – transferred to LexEcon for further analysis. While in the direct mode no preparation of the incoming data is necessary, each word being directly analysed in terms of its ASCII-code, the indirect mode requires some sort of pre-lexical processing. Whenever a word is forwarded to LexEcon in the indirect mode, it is not just one word that is analysed but also its context. The maximum context that is prepared for one analysis is a sentence. Sentences are defined as units between two punctuation marks, such as full-stops, colons, exclamation marks, question marks, and semicolons. Alternatively, sentences can start or end with two or more blanks, with one or several empty line feeds, for example, at the beginning or the end of a paragraph or the entire document. In other words, in the indirect mode LexEcon analyses the information to the left and to the right of the item marked, until a sentence can be isolated. By the application of a filtering mechanism, this sentence is converted into the ASCII-format and passed on to the central analysis component of LexEcon. Figure 102 outlines the sentence identification strategy used in LexEcon's indirect mode.

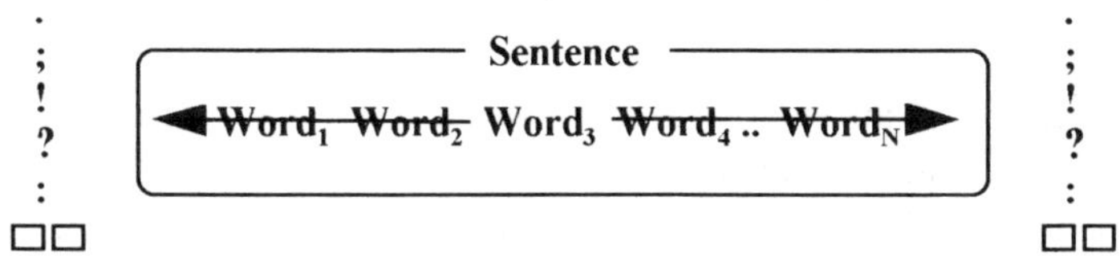

Figure 102. Sentence identification in LexEcon; indirect mode (target item: $Word_3$)

(b) lexical processing

LexEcon has two lexicons, one for English and one for German. Both lexicons contain roots as access units and are coupled with an additional affix lexicon for each language. Hence, the lexical look-up process involves morphological and orthographical rules that handle affixation and orthographical alternation at root boundaries.

(c) post-lexical processing

In order to disambiguate words in context LexEcon uses a strategy of context analysis that inspects the local context of the item marked. This strategy is based on the syntactic information about the neighbouring words drawn from the lexicon. Like the machine translation system, SYSTRAN, LexEcon looks both to the left and to the right (Wheeler 1987: 198).

To cope with all these aspects lexical entries in LexEcon are defined according to the following format:

Access Unit: FLY

Phonology: ˈflaɪ
Morphology: N1
Syntax: NC1
Semantics: NET4
Further:

– Translation:	"Fliege"	
– Synonyms:	SYN2478	optional
– Etymology:	E3	optional
– Example:	FLY.EXM	optional
– Visualisation:	FLY.BMP	optional
– Acoustics:	FLY.VOC	optional

Since various aspects of an entry's lexical specification are entirely optional and are not required during the analysis process, each lexical entry exhibits a high degree of externalisation. Whenever the lexical specification of an entry is accessed, only the phonological and the morphological information are directly accessible. However, the straightforward availability of these aspects is confined to Type 3 words, i.e. to only those words which permit morphological and orthographical changes (see table 10, section 5.2.1.). Type 2 words, that is words that allow affixation processes but no orthographical changes, have direct access only to their morphological specification, while the remaining words are analysed without their lexical specification.

All parts of an entry's lexical specification, except the translation, essentially function as pointers to other components of the system or to external files that contain the relevant information. For example, N1 is the morphological continuation class of the nominal specification of FLY, allowing singular and plural forms to be analysed. NC1 (Noun Class 1) defines

FLY as a count noun and thus defines the possibility of unrestricted syntactic premodification, such as the occurrence of a preceding determiner. NET4 defines the semantic network from which the semantic features can be retrieved.[1] Further aspects, such as the entry's acoustic representation or information about examples of the item in context are contained in specific files, such as FLY.BMP (a bit map file) or FLY.VOC (a sound file), or they are represented by specific symbols that serve as pointers to external databases (SYN2478, for example, is a pointer to the synonym file).

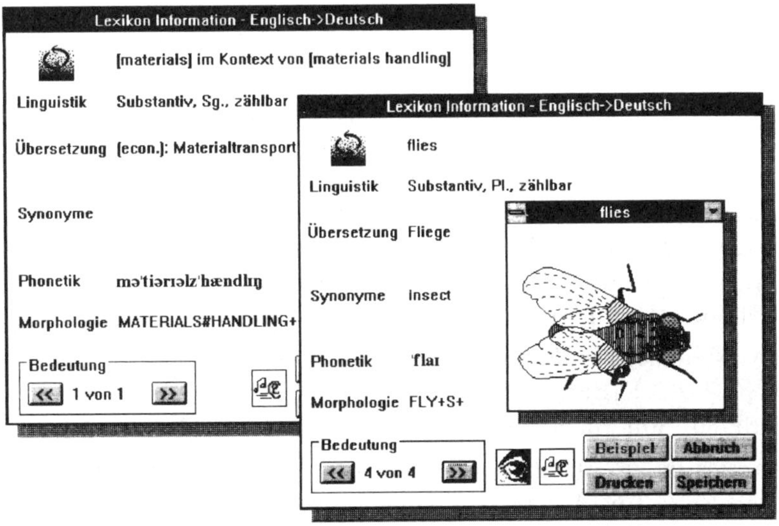

Figure 103. Analysis results in LexEcon

In summary, lexical entries in LexEcon exhibit a high degree of externalisation. This guarantees the reduction of redundancies in the lexicon and the reusability of information. Figure 103 illustrates the analysis result of the items *materials* (as a compound modifier) and *flies* (as an individual item) by LexEcon.

In figure 103, the analysis of *flies* illustrates the direct mode where one word is forwarded to LexEcon as an individual context-independent item.[2] The analysis of *materials*, by contrast, shows the indirect mode, i.e. the analysis of a word in its context, here in the context of "materials handling". Note that *materials* has only one meaning (Bedeutung/meaning 1 von/of 1), whereas LexEcon provides four (4 von/of 4) interpretations of *fly*. Note that FLY is also coupled with a picture, which has been optionally retrieved via the eye-button.

Including pre-lexical processing, morphological and contextual analysis, and the preparation of the information as a user-friendly output, the entire process lasts roughly a second. The linguistic analysis alone, i.e. word recognition and the retrieval of an item's lexical specification, takes less than 150 msec.

In the following section we will outline the basic components of LexEcon and the underlying implementation strategies.

6.1. The Implementation

LexEcon runs under Windows 3.1 and is programmed in LISP and C.[3] The principles of linking two programming languages have been explained in detail in Deiß (1991) and Otto (1991). Basically, LISP is responsible for all natural language tasks, while C interfaces the basic modules of LexEcon with Windows and various Windows-applications. The link between LISP and C is administered by a number of Assembler-routines. The following interpreters/compilers are used in LexEcon:

- Turbo Assembler 3.1 (Borland)
- Turbo C ++ 3.1 (Borland)
- muLISP-86 (Soft Warehouse, Hawaii)[4]

LexEcon runs on any standard microcomputer that has a harddisk and at least 4 MB RAM (for Windows). It requires about 10 MB free disk space and not more than 300 KB free RAM-capacity.

6.2. The Main Modules

LexEcon consists of the following basic components, one for each language.

- the main lexicons
- the affix lexicons
- the morphological and orthographical components
- the disambiguation components
- the information components

All components have been implemented as partitioned cohort networks, i.e. they make use of a cohort tree that contains the access units, a data file that provides the relevant information, and a number of subnet files where the access units that exceed the length of three letters are continued (see figure 90).

The heart of the system is the main lexicon, which contains ca. 25.000 English root entries and ca. 4.000 German root entries. As outlined in section 5.2.2. an economic way of representing the access units in languages with little morphological and orthographical variation is the use of morphographemes. Since LexEcon is not confined to English but is also applied to more inflected languages, such as German, the system uses a uniform representation format of the access units in terms of roots.

The morphological information associated with a lexical entry is represented in terms of continuation classes. These serve as a pointers to the relevant entries in the affix lexicon. On the basis of the affix lexicons, one for each language, all inflectional processes and a number of semantically stable derivational processes, such as deverbal nominalisation in English, WALK → WALKER, are handled. Less productive derivational aspects, such as -ION affixation, are directly represented in the lexicon. The analysis of compounds, such as the economics term "materials handling", is dealt with on the basis of the main lexicon, where the lexical specification of MATERIAL is coupled with the information that it may occur as a compound modifier. In turn, the lexical specification of HANDLING is marked for the possibility of being the head of a compound and is therefore associated with the relevant lexical specification. Let us look more closely at the representation format of these special senses of MATERIAL and HANDLING:

```
(HANDLING
        (PHONOLOGY      mE'tIErIElz'hÄndLIN)
        (MORPHOLOGY     N2)
        (SYNTAX         NC2)
        (SEMANTICS      NIL)
        (TRANSLATION    (econ.): Materialtransport)
        (SYNONYMS       NIL)
        (ETYMOLOGY      NIL)
        (EXAMPLES       NIL)
        (COMPOUND       @MATERIALS))
```

In order to analyse "materials handling" the lexical representation of HANDLING contains one sense in which it is combined with the modifier MATERIALS (@is an arbitrary symbol which is internally interpreted as the modifier marker). In such a case, the analysis routines of LexEcon inspect the context to the left, seeking the word *materials*. Note that the modifier must be *materials* and not *material*. If the lexical specification of MATERIAL is coupled with the possibility of occurring as a compound modifier, the compound interpretation will be retrieved; if not, HANDLING will be interpreted in its general sense as the participle of HANDLE.

In order to permit MATERIALS to be a compound modifier we have to include this information in the lexical specification of MATERIAL:

```
(MATERIAL
        (PHONOLOGY      mE'tIErIEl)
        (MORPHOLOGY     N1)
        (SYNTAX         NC1)
        (SEMANTICS      NIL)
        (TRANSLATION    Material Stoff Substanz
                        Werkstoffe Unterlagen)
        (SYNONYMS       7633)
        (ETYMOLOGY      1)
        (EXAMPLES       NIL)
        (COMPOUNDS      (MATERIALS)))
```

Note that MATERIAL is only associated with MATERIALS but not with the actual senses of "materials handling". This implies that MATERIALS is neutral with regard to its own meaning and can occur as a modifier in a variety of compounds, such as "materials flow", "materials management", etc. The root MATERIAL itself can also constitute the modifier of a compound, such as in "material supplies", "material budget", etc. The processing of such compounds is guaranteed by a similar strategy. The lexical specifications of the heads SUPPLY and BUDGET, for example, are associated with possible compound modifiers, in our case with @MATERIAL. That MATERIAL is a potential compound modifier is not explicitly stated in the lexical specification of MATERIAL. This information is generated by a default rule, which appends to the compound field of every open-class word (in English to nouns, verbs, and adjectives, see Selkirk 1982: 10ff) the information that they are potential compound modifiers. Thus, compound modifier information only needs to be explicitly stated in those cases where not the root itself but an alternate form, such as MATERIALS in "materials handling" or BALANCED" in "balanced economy", constitutes the compound modifier.

This system of compound analysis, however, is entirely lexically-driven. It depends on the information in the lexicon but does not freely interpret and generate the meaning of compounds on the basis of their component parts.

Like the main lexicons the affix lexicons make use of the partitioned cohort network structure and can thus use the same processing algorithm. However, the morphological information associated with the affixes is extremely compact and is primarily represented in terms of arbitrary one or two-letter symbols. For this reason a division of the affix lexicon into access file and data file is not necessary. For example, the entry for -ED, the regular past tense suffix in English looks like this:

Access Unit: ED
Morphology: V ED

where V simply stands for "verb" and "ED" for "past tense".

Orthographical variants are handled via transition networks applying the principles of two-level morphology (see section 5.4.2.). In order to handle orthographical variation as efficiently as possible, a distinction has been drawn between word-internal and flanking changes as outlined in section 5.4.1. While flanking changes, such as WATCH-(E)S, are processed on the basis of phonological changes, word-internal alternations, such as MAK(E)-ING, try to match the letter structure with the access units in the cohort network.

One essential property of LexEcon is its ability to handle categorial disambiguation on the basis of local context. Let us consider the following two examples:

(78) a. He is a little boy.
b. He has little money.

While in (78a) *little* is an adjective, it has to be analysed as a quantifier in (78b). Ideally, disambiguation makes use of a knowledge base on the basis of which a semantic representation is generated. However, in a lexical retrieval system, such as LexEcon, this would considerably prolong processing time and thus delay the presentation of the analysis results. For this reason, LexEcon employs a disambiguation strategy which fully relies on the analysis of local context. Whenever a word is to be analysed that allows more than one syntactic category, the system analyses the context to the left and right and works out the syntactic categories to the left and to the right. In the case of (78a) and (78b) we are faced with the following contextual patterns:

(78) a′. DET little NOUN *a* = determiner, *boy* = noun
b′. AUX/VERB little NOUN *has* = auxiliary or main verb, *money* = noun

The lexical specification of LITTLE itself is connected with the information that it can be an adjective or a quantifier. With this categorial information we can replace *little* in (78a') and (78b') and arrive at the following triplets:

(78) a″. DET ADJ/QUANT NOUN
b″. AUX/VERB ADJ/QUANT NOUN

With these patterns we can consult a specific disambiguation lexicon that combines possible categorial patterns, such as ADJ/QUANT, with probable contextual patterns. In such a "lexicon" items such as ADJ/QUANT function as access units, and patterns of the type DET ? NOUN constitute the lexical specification. We can implement such a disambiguation lexicon as a cohort network along the lines of the other lexicons and use the same access algorithm. Furthermore, we can use a strategy of partitioning where access units such as ADJ/QUANT are evaluated in the main network on the basis of their initial letters and continued in a subnet. To avoid unnecessary loading times we have used a shorthand notation that reduces the access unit ADJ/QUANT to AQ. Now no subnet has to be activated and the processing time required for the disambiguation pattern hardly delays the overall analysis. The lexical specification associated with AQ can be represented as a list of patterns of the following type:

```
(AQ   (DET * ADJ)
      (VERB * QUANT)
      (AUXVERB * QUANT)
      (ADJ * QUANT)
      (ADJVERB * QUANT))
```

This format associates simple patterns with its access units. The pattern (DET * ADJ), for example, says that an access unit, such as LITTLE, is an adjective if the item to the left is a determiner and any item exists to the right (any item = *). Thus we have a general interpretation format of the type ("item-to-the-left" "item-to-the-right" "result"). It is not claimed here that this method is capable of resolving all categorial ambiguities. However, in a text-retrieval system with fast access, such as LexEcon, a disambiguation capability of roughly 90% of all categorially ambiguous cases is a very good result. Over and above the categorial disambiguation we can now use this technique to analyse compound interpretations as presented above.

The main lexicons, the affix lexicons, and the disambiguation lexicons fully exploit the partitioned cohort network structure. Thus, it is not surprising that those components that prepare the lexical information for the user also rely on the cohort structure. In order to present the morphological and syntactic information on the screen, internal linguistic symbols, such as V ED, or N SG CT, have to be translated into a user-friendly language, where V means "verb", ED "past tense", N "noun", SG "singular", and CT "count". This translation is performed on the basis of yet another cohort network, where the access units, such as N or ED, are coupled with the relevant information. Since most of the internal symbols are shorter than three letters, the main network of this "information lexicon" has been confined to two letters. This reduces search time on the one hand and it also relieves working memory since the main network, which has to be loaded into RAM, becomes smaller.

In summary, four "lexicons", all implemented as partitioned cohort networks, constitute the heart of LexEcon. Table 13 lists these lexicons, in terms of their number of entries, their main network size, and the memory space they require.

Table 13. Lexicons in LexEcon; language: English

Lexicon	Entries	Length of Main Net	Size (KBytes)
Main Lexicon	24.987	3 letters	20.3
Affix Lexicon	31	2 letters	0.2
Disambiguation Lexicon	43	2 letters	0.2
Information Lexicon	248	2 letters	1.5

6.3. Additional Components

Over and above the analysis components, LexEcon has a number of components that establish a connection between the kernel system and the user. These are

- error detection components for the presentation of orthographical alternatives
- speech synthesisers

– a graphics interface for the visualisation of lexical entries
– a menu-driven lexicon extension component

(a) the handling of errors

The language-specific error detection component has two tasks: the presentation of alternatives and the identification and correction of spelling errors on the basis of the orthographical rules. As already mentioned in section 5.3.4.2. (e), alternatives in the partitioned cohort network can only be presented if at least the letters of the main network, in our case, the first three letters, are correct. The presentation of alternatives involves two steps. First, a list containing all alternatives is generated by a recursive mechanism that scans the active cohort. In a second step this list is presented in a user-friendly format from which alternatives can be chosen. Figure 104 exhibits this menu on the basis of the input *ABSESS.

Figure 104. The presentation of alternatives in LexEcon[5]

Basically, the possibility of presenting alternatives can be considered as some sort of error detection and correction mechanism. However, there is a more "intelligent" way of handling input errors. Due to its orthographical knowledge, i.e. its knowledge about the rules of orthographical alternation as presented in section 5.4.1., LexEcon is capable of identifying and correcting illegal input automatically. For example, if the present participle form of SWIM is accidentally spelt with one M only (**swiming*), LexEcon will still analyse it, since SWIM is a lexical access unit and -ING one of its legitimate affixes. Furthermore, the availability of the rule of consonantal doubling will inform the user that *SWIMING can be recognised but that the correct orthographical form is *swimming*. Over and above this simple information, the system is also capable of telling the user why this is so. In the case of **swiming*, a suitable comment could be: "swim requires the doubling of M before ING".[6]

(b) auditory and visual representation

Two further utilities can be exploited in LexEcon, sound and vision. Many of today's microcomputers are equipped with sound cards for the integration of music and speech into multi-media applications. LexEcon is configured in such a way that it first examines whether a sound card is installed or not. If a sound card can be detected, lexical access units can be acoustically synthesised, giving the user a more or less good idea of their pronunciation.

Especially for younger users of LexEcon a large number of lexical entries have been associated with bit-map-files that represent lexical entries in terms of 200 x 200 dot matrices. These pictures are not only helpful and informative resources but they can also be forwarded to other programs by means of special hot keys.

(c) lexicon editing[7]

One central disadvantage of root lexicons is the difficulty of adding new information. If new words have to be entered, it is not sufficient to enter their root and their word-class, but each entry also has to be assigned a morphological continuation class, syntactic specifications, and all the other lexical aspects. In other words, the organisation of new entries heavily relies on the user's linguistic background and common sense knowledge. However, only few users have this knowledge at their disposal.

There are two possible ways of handling this problem. Either the system is programmed as a closed system, which does not allow any data manipulation, or it is fully open. In the latter case, it must be interfaced with a highly specialised menu-driven component that interacts with the user in such a way that he only has to confirm the suggestions made by the system. In LexEcon this component operates according to the following principles:

Step 1:
Only nouns, verbs, and adjectives can be entered (closed class words are contained in LexEcon anyway).

Step 2:
Whenever the new item's word-class has been selected from a menu, the system generates sets of possible word forms, where each set is associated with a specific morphological continuation class. All the user has to do is to select the right set and, thus, the right continuation class.

Step 3:
Syntactic information such as (± count), (transitive/head-type 23), etc., are also pregenerated and presented in terms of various menus.

Step 4:
Now the various lexical aspects (translation, synonyms, etymology, etc.) can be entered. Aspects such as the translation into German or synonymic information, can be typed in directly; other fields, such as the etymological information, examples in context, etc., are generated via a system of menus. Pictures can be associated with lexical entries via their filenames. They can be drawn in any graphics program. The only convention is that they are saved as .BMP-files.

These steps are repeated until all senses of a new entry have been defined. The addition of the phonological information is problematic. No user can be expected to be familiar with phonological transcription, let alone with the internal presentation format. For this reason, phonological defaults are generated on the basis of the spelling of the root.

Nevertheless, there are problems. These concern the semantic representation of lexical entries. Since LexEcon does not analyse entire sentences but only local contexts, no suggestions about the semantic properties of a new item can be generated.[8]For this reason, new entries cannot be specified semantically.

6.4. Summary

LexEcon is an efficient tool for word retrieval from texts. Even though it contains a considerable lexicon and also realises a number of linguistic processes, such as morphological analysis and categorial disambiguation, it retrieves and presents information at an enormously high speed. This is due to the use of the partitioned cohort network structure of all access files (main lexicon, affix lexicon, disambiguation network, and information component) throughout the system. The cohort network is very economical as far as the use of working memory is concerned, it is relatively close to its mental counterpart (see section 5.3.4.2.), and it allows high-speed word recognition. Figure 105 summarises the structure of the access files used across the system.

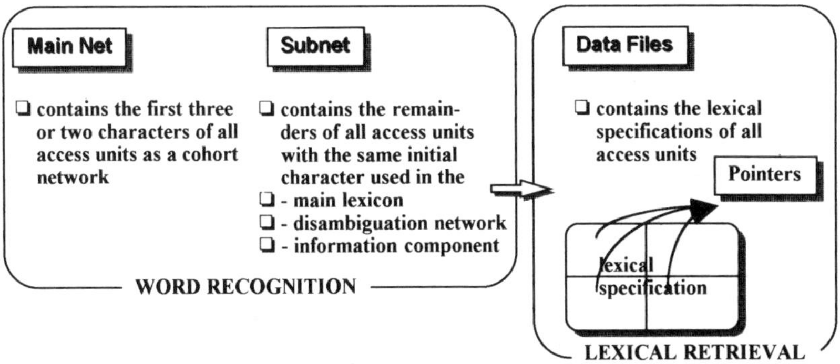

Figure 105. The access file system used in LexEcon

All lexicons exhibit the same internal structure; however, due to their small size and the restricted nature of their access units, at least two lexicons can be simplified. The affix lexicon and the information lexicon can clearly dispense with subnet files, since their access units are defined in such a way that the length of two letters is never exceeded. Thus, the main networks of these "lexicons" can be built in terms of two letters only.

Another difference concerns the inclusion of morphological and orthographical alternation routines. In order to use the same processing algorithm throughout, we have to make sure that the morphological and the orthographical routines only apply as a link between the main lexicon and the affix lexicon but not to the other lexicons of the system. For example, we do not want items such as AQ (ADJ/QUANT or SG = "singular") to be analysed morphologically. Furthermore, such access units are not subject to graphotactic conventions and the presentation of alternatives has to be suppressed. In order to avoid all this, the processing algorithm is steered by a number of Boolean variables (Handke 1991b: 78).

Figure 106 illustrates the function of and the interaction between the modules of LexEcon on the basis of the English input *flies* in the indirect mode, i.e. embedded within a sentence. Since most modules exist twice, one for English, one for German, they have been drawn as double boxes.

After having isolated the sentence in which the target word *flies* occurs, an attempt is made to match the input with the units in the access file of the

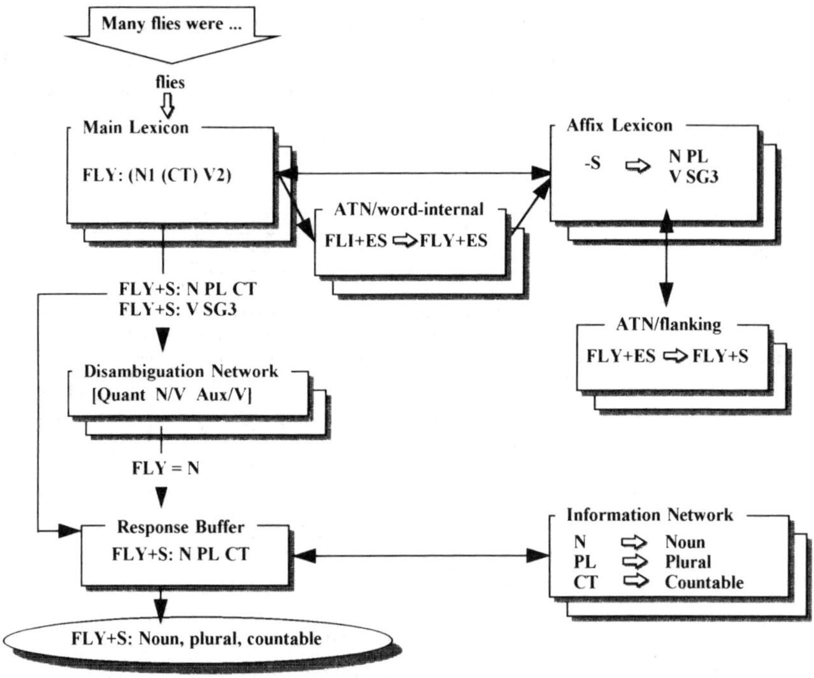

Figure 106. LexEcon: system architecture and processing

main lexicon. By means of a word-internal orthographical I-to-Y change and a second flanking orthographical change that deletes the E before -S, FLY can be recognised as a root and -S as its legitimate affix. As a result of this operation, *flies* will be analysed as a count noun (continuation class N1) and as a verb (continuation class V2).

In the indirect mode, categorially ambiguous items, such as FLY, are automatically forwarded to the disambiguation component. Items that are not ambiguous or are analysed without context may circumvent this optional component. For *flies* in the context of "Many flies were...", the disambiguation component generates a pattern of the kind ("Quantifier" "Noun/Verb" "Auxiliary/Verb"). This pattern helps to disambiguate *flies* to its nominal sense. The result of this analysis is temporarily saved in a response buffer, from where the relevant information, for example the word's translation, or its synonyms, can be retrieved. Before the presentation of the result, all linguistic symbols, such as N, V, CT, etc., are translated into an informative user-friendly code.

7. Summary

"It is a striking fact that computers are virtually incapable of handling the routine mental feats of perception, language comprehension and memory retrieval that we humans take so much for granted."
(Elman/McClelland 1984: 337).

In this book an attempt has been made to integrate human and computational strategies of word processing. Irrespective of the enormous differences between the human mind and presently available computers, the central steps of word processing are the same. First, the incoming signal is analysed and converted into a structure that can be forwarded to higher levels. At a second stage, a decision is taken as to whether the input is a word of the language or not, and, thirdly, the relevant parts of the item's lexical specification are retrieved. In other words, word processing can be separated into three levels:

- pre-lexical processing
- word recognition } lexical processing
- lexical retrieval

All three levels have access to the central word store, the lexicon. The subdivision of word processing into three distinct levels, however, does not necessarily imply a strict sequential order. It has been shown that interaction between these levels is likely. For example, the contents of the lexicon, i.e. the access units which are inspected at the level of word recognition, influence low-level processes and help to identify the nature of the input signal. Other sources of knowledge, such as phonotactic or graphotactic knowledge, or knowledge about the contextual probabilities of lexical items, are also interactively made use of.

Central to these levels of word processing is a store that contains the information about the words, the lexicon. It has been pointed out that this is a highly complex database that encompasses thousands of entries associated with enormously complicated packets of information. The lexicon is not isolated. It has access to a general knowledge base that integrates the meaning of the lexical entries into larger knowledge structures.

In looking at the macrostructure of word processing, i.e. the central levels and components, a distinction between humans and machines cannot be drawn. However, as pointed out in chapter five, presently available machines are not capable of utilising parallel processing. That natural language processing requires massive parallelism is a well-established assumption (see Tyler, 1981, for a discussion). Knowledge from various sources is integrated parallelly to handle the complexity of language processing. There have been attempts to turn conventional computer architectures into parallel machines. At present, several parallel machines with a large number of processors working in parallel are being constructed. These range from modest parallelism, where a few dozen processors operate parallelly, to massive parallelism, where up to a million processors are connected (Watson 1991: 12).[1]

The theoretical computational background of such parallel computers is the relatively young discipline of connectionism. It has been shown that the connectionist approach not only uses parallel processing techniques but also provides a suitable tool for the many requirements of pre-lexical and lexical processing. Even though connectionism has proven to be a promising alternative to conventional computing, it is fairly restricted at present due to the number of processing units and connections to be established. While the human brain, the natural counterpart of connectionist models, is capable of establishing up to 10.000 connections between each of its several billions of processing units, presently available implementations of neural networks at best realise a few hundred fully-connected processing units. Nevertheless, it seems that connectionism is the most promising computational as well as psychological approach, especially at the level of low-level processing.

The microstructure, i.e. the internal organisation of the levels and the modules of word processing, exhibits enormous differences between humans and machines. The most striking fact about the mental lexicon concerns its computational properties. It is amazing how efficiently the information in the lexicon is administered and made available. The ease and the speed with which items are retrieved from the lexicon is astonishing. Furthermore, the internal dynamics, i.e. the possibility with which the entries in the lexicon can be rearranged and manipulated, is unrivalled by any machine.[2] In order to implement a reasonably efficient machine-readable lexicon that serves as a basis of natural language processing systems, we have to employ techniques that make use of some but not all aspects of their natural counterpart. The most radical differences between the mental and a machine-readable lexicon concern the nature of the lexical processing units. While the mental lexicon is likely to use a structure which is based on the syllable, such structures have not been defined for machine-readable lexicons. However, if we assume some sort of cohort structure for a machine-readable lexicon, as introduced in chapter five, we come closer to the concept of the syllable and can at least simulate some effects of human word processing, such as the lexicality effect and the length effect. Yet, the simulation of these effects alone would not be of any help; rather, the cohort structure itself is highly efficient as regards the speed of access.

In looking at the contents of the lexicon, i.e. the information associated with each lexical entry, we were confronted with another problem. While aspects such as phonology, morphology, and syntax can, at least to some extent, be handled relatively satisfactorily by machines, the representation of meaning is an almost insurmountable enterprise. At present, machine-readable lexicons are not capable of integrating their entries into larger knowledge structures such as semantic networks or frames. Even though modern machines have an almost unlimited memory and allow fast data access (sometimes even faster than humans), the handling of meaning is still in its infancy. For this reason, many computational systems have to be restricted to specific domains or they have to dispense with meaning-based interpretation strategies and confine themselves to a semantic interpretation in the sense of a logical form.

Probably the most fundamental difference between man and machine concerns the building and manipulation of the entries in the lexicon. While the mental lexicon constantly changes its contents (items are newly learnt, forgotten, or altered), machine-readable lexicons find it hard to manipulate their entries: lexical editing has to be performed by a handful of experts or on the basis of complicated software; and lexicon production has to be carried out by complex conversion procedures that require a good deal of human interference and post-editing (see Appendix B and C). Lexical acquisition in the sense of human strategies is not possible at present. Even though there are suggestions of automatically incorporating unknown items into machine-readable lexicons (see, for example, Schank et al. 1980), these techniques are by no means safe and are only rudimentary attempts to simulate acquisition strategies.

In summary then, machine-readable lexicons are inferior to their human counterparts. In their internal organisation they are highly restricted and do not permit the same flexibility of data manipulation and data acquisition. Moreover, they are not capable of accounting for a number of psycholinguistic effects such as word frequency and recency. The most important difference between human and machine, however, concerns the integration of knowledge of all kinds. While machines are confined to a few sources, humans utilise knowledge of all kinds to process natural language. For example, in order to interpret the words of an interlocutor we also integrate *paralinguistic knowledge*, such as gestures and bodily movements, and general aspects of vision. Sometimes this might even lead to misunderstandings. A well-known effect of this kind is the "BL/L-effect". An auditory pattern such as [ˈlaɪnd] is interpreted as "blind" if the lips of the interlocutor are shaped to form an initial [b]. However, even in such cases, misunderstandings are unlikely to occur. The integration of higher-level knowledge, such as the sentence context, will help out and lead to a correct interpretation as "lined". It is this flexibility that makes man superior to machines and it will probably be a few more decades before machines reach a level comparable with human intelligence.

Appendix A. Writing Systems

Not all natural languages have writing systems. According to Haarmann (1990: 18ff), more than 5.000 natural languages have been attested and, of these, only a minority of 13% have a writing system. However, the speakers of these languages constitute the majority of 60% of the world's population. Languages such as Chinese, English, Spanish, French, Russian and German alone comprise more than 50% of all speakers. In other words, written language in terms of reading and writing is an important factor in human communication.

Not all writing systems encode information in the same way. Early systems emerged from symbols that represented animals and other images. This symbolic period can be dated back thousands of years. Modern writing systems still make use of symbols, however, in a different sense.

Any writing system is defined as a system of symbols that represent the elements of spoken language (words, syllables, phonemes). Such writing systems can be subdivided into two central branches: logographic systems and phonographic systems. Figure 107 illustrates this subdivision and the respective variants.

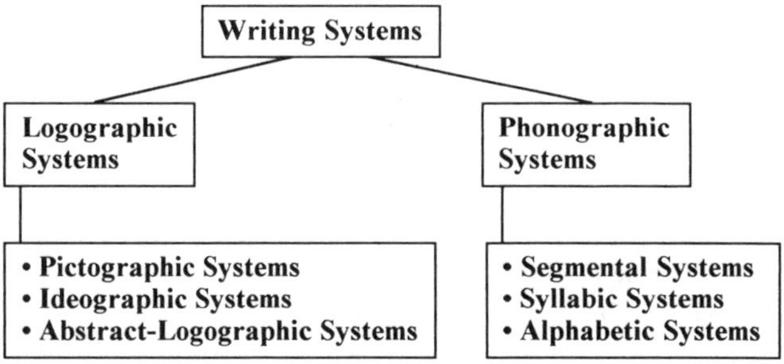

Figure 107. Writing systems[1]

Logographic writing systems make use of symbols that represent words or concepts (Greek: *logos* = *word*, *idea*). The shape of the symbols employed is often closely related to the meaning of the respective concept. In phonographic systems, by contrast, the meaning of the objects denoted by the symbols does not play a role. *Phonographic* or *'sound based' writing systems* establish a relationship between the symbols employed and the pronunciation of the elements denoted. That there are alternative ways of representing the letter-sound relationship will be illustrated below. While logographic systems have been in use for a long time, phonographic systems are relatively young and represent a more advanced level of written language.

A1. Logographic Writing Systems

In the earliest logographic writing systems the relationship between symbol and object is clearly visible. Such variants of logographic writing systems are referred to as *pictographic*. Pictographs are pictorial symbols that directly represent the object to which they refer. Documents with pictographs can thus be interpreted without reference to other linguistic levels. One of the earliest examples of a pictographic system was used in the Sumerian period at around 3000 BC (figure 108).

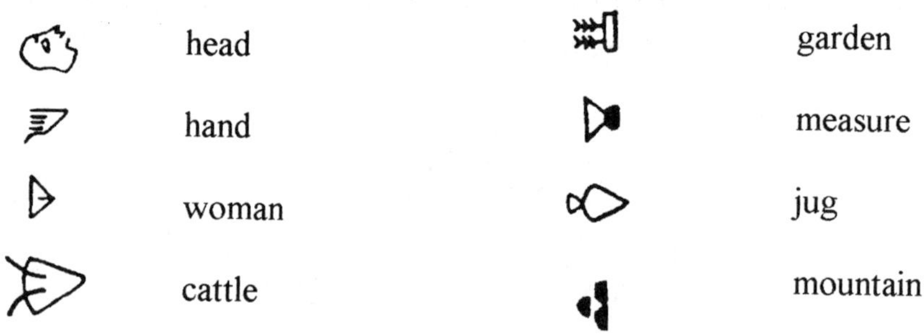

Figure 108. Simple Old-Sumerian pictographs and their meanings (3000 BC, after Haarmann 1990: 152)

Simple pictographs constituted the bulk of the symbolic repertoire of the system. In addition to simple pictographs a large number of concepts were expressed by a combination of two or more simple symbols. Figure 109 exhibits such a complex symbol.

The interpretation of the complex pictorial symbol in figure 109 as "slave" is beyond our judgement. The component parts, "woman" and "mountain" rotated by 90 degrees, hardly suggest the compound meaning. However, if we incorporate the cultural environment of that time, where

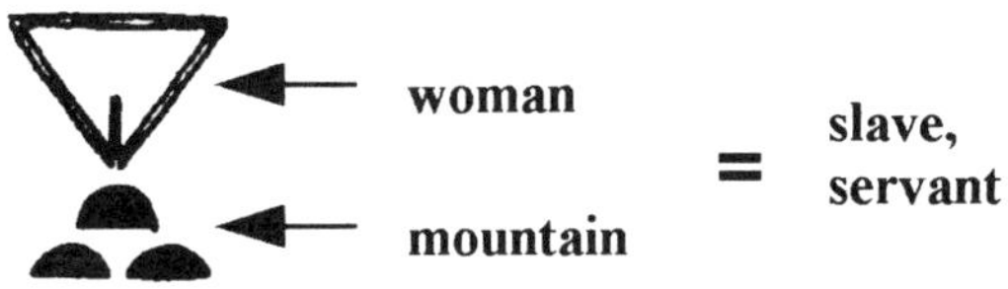

Figure 109. A complex Old-Sumerian pictograph and its meaning (3000 BC, after Haarmann 1990: 154)

slaves, especially young men and women, were held in captivity in the mountains, the interpretation becomes more transparent. The symbol exhibited in figure 109 illustrates an obvious problem of the pictographic system. First, writing demands a considerable skill, and secondly, in view of the fact that the possibilities of combining simple pictographs into complex ones are theoretically unlimited, there are a great many signs to remember (Henderson, 1982:14).

A second way of relating logographic symbols to concepts is the use of *ideograms*. Unlike pictographs, the shape of *ideographic symbols* is not a direct representation but an associative representation of a concept. The use of the modern symbol ✂, used to evoke a cutting process, denotes such an associative relationship. Ideographic symbols are often mixed with pictographs. Figure 110 illustrates this mixture on the basis of Egyptian hieroglyphs:

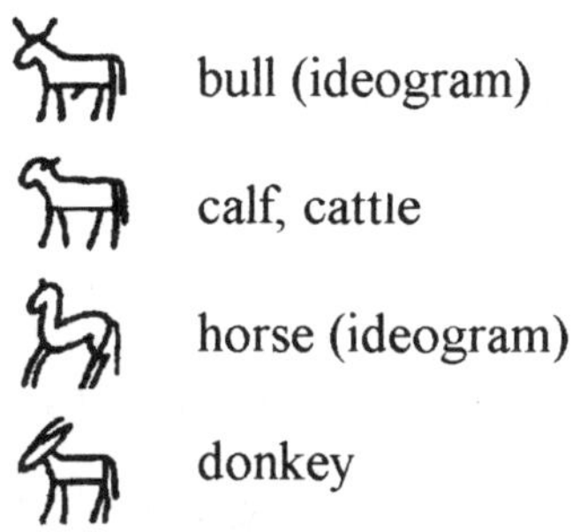

Figure 110. Ideograms in the Egyptian hieroglyphic system

The third group of logographic writing systems makes use of *abstract-logographic* symbols whose meaning is no longer identifiable from their shape. Even in phonographic writing systems, numerous abstract-logographic symbols are employed, for example, §, %, or &. The relationship between the different types of logographic writing systems can be

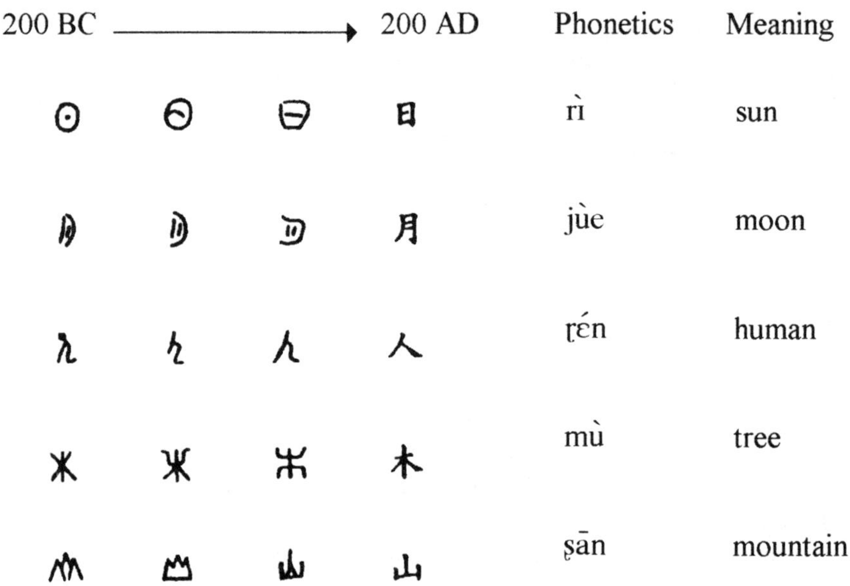

Figure 111. The development of Chinese logographic characters during the Han-Dynasty

illustrated very nicely by comparing the early phases of the development of the Chinese logographic writing system (figure 111).

While the original symbols (left-hand column in figure 111) can almost be interpreted without any further explanation, more modern versions of Chinese characters hardly bear any relationship to the objects they denote.

The main reasons for moving away from a pictorial to a more abstract logographic system were the increasing abstractness of representation and the tendency to adopt one symbol for one word. This in turn led to a more direct relationship between symbol and sound, hence between written language and speech.

Today, modern Chinese as the most representative member of logographic writing systems combines pictography with phonography by using characters of the following kind (Henderson 1982: 17):

- pictographs
- ideographs
- compound ideographs
- phonetic loans
- phonetic compounds

However, the references to phonetics in the Chinese writing system are rudimentary. In phonetic loans, for example, characters which represent the same sound are used across words, and phonetic compounds combine semantic information with phonetic clues based on similar words, e.g. rhyming patterns.

A2. Phonographic Writing Systems

Phonographic writing systems establish some sort of relationship between the written symbol and its pronunciation. There are three possible ways of realising the symbol-sound relationship.

The most advanced and historically the most recent technique makes use of a limited inventory of symbols, where ideally one symbol stands for one sound. Such systems, which are common to the Indo-European and many Asian and African languages, have become known as *alphabetic writing systems*. The one-to-one relationship between sound and symbol, however, has been obscured in many languages. Take the English alphabetic writing system, where one character or one character cluster can have various realisations in pronunciation, and the same phoneme can be realised in writing in different ways. The cluster "ou", for example, may occur in *rough* /ˈrʌf/, *dough* /ˈdəʊ/, *cough* /ˈkɒf/, *plough* /ˈplɑʊ/, *you* /ˈju:/, *thorough* /ˈθʌrə/, the phoneme /u/ can be written as "o" as in *do*, "oo" as in *zoo*, "oe" as in *shoe*, "u" as in *rule*, "ue" as in *Sue*, "ew" as in *few*, or "ou" as in *you*. Hence, there is no longer an ideal relationship between sound and symbol in English. It has been already mentioned that, in addition to the standard set of vowels and consonants, alphabetic systems make frequent use of non-alphabetic symbols such as $ or &. In addition to these, symbols can also be a combination of both alphabetic and non-alphabetic, for example *4th* or *1990s*.

Another variant of a phonographic writing system, the *syllabic writing system*, represents the pronunciation of entire syllables by specific symbols. Syllabic writing systems are relatively old. They have their origin in logographic systems. The progress from logographic symbols towards a syllable structure was usually accompanied by a reduction in the number of signs and simplification of their shape (Gaur 1992: 131). One of the earliest versions of a syllabic writing system, the Crete Linear B system, is illustrated in figure 112. Note that one character may not only represent complex consonant/vowel combinations but also just a vowel, which may constitute a syllable.

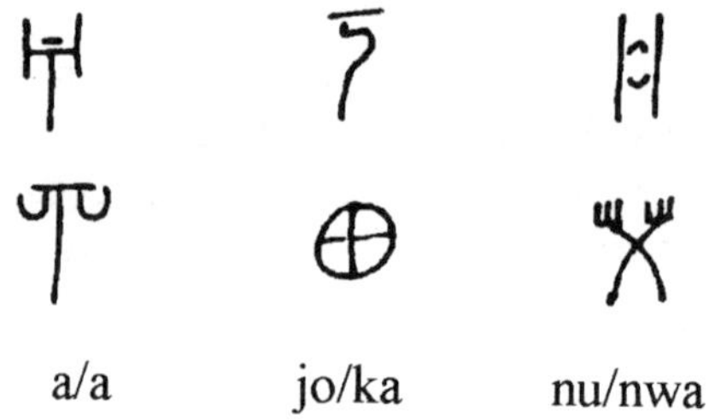

Figure 112. The Crete syllabic writing system Linear B, 1450 to 1250 BC (after Haarmann 1990: 248)

Syllabic writing systems are still in use. One of the most well-known representatives of a syllabic phonographic writing system is Japanese. It supplements a set of logographic characters, the *Kanji*, with two types of syllabic systems. One is known as *Katakana* and is generally reserved for loan words. The second system, the *Hiragana*, is employed for grammatical formatives. Both systems make use of a limited number of symbols which can be combined or may be supplemented with diacritics in order to represent the relatively small repertoire of Japanese syllables.[2]

The third and oldest way of showing the pronunciation of words by means of a phonographic writing system is the segmental method. In a *segmental writing system*, only selected phonetic aspects, primarily the consonants, are realised by orthographic symbols. The most common system of this kind is the Egyptian system of hieroglyphs, where a symbol may stand for a consonantal skeleton. Vowels were not represented in writing; they had to be added during the reading process by reference to syntax and semantics. Figure 113 exhibits a selection of single and double consonants of the hieroglyphic system.

Segmental writing systems such as the Egyptian system are somewhat of an exception. First, they share a number of properties with logographic systems, since the symbols used are in many cases pictures with a certain meaning. How these pictures acquired phonetic values is not clear (Haarmann 1990: 214). Secondly, all that is known about these systems is the consonantal values of the skeletons. Vowels, and thus syllable structures, have not been worked out yet.

Phonographic systems have proven to be very successful. While the syllabic and the segmental variants are of minor importance, alphabetic writing systems are used all over the world. Despite the differences among the alphabets used (Roman, Cyrillic, Arabic, Korean, etc.), the speakers of the languages with an alphabetic writing system have at their disposal a system with a limited set of characters whose combination allows them to infer the pronunciation of words from spelling. That alphabetic systems

Symbol	Meaning	Consonantal Value
𓅓	owl	m
𓈖	water	n
𓂋	mouth	r
𓉔	yard	h

Symbol	Meaning	Consonantal Value
𓁹	eye	ir
𓅨	bird	wr
𓉐	house	pr

Figure 113. A segmental writing system, single and double consonants, ca. 3000 BC (after Haarmann 1990: 215ff)

are extremely economical and efficient can be seen in the development of written Vietnamese. Originally a logographic system, Vietnamese adopted an alphabetic phonographic system in the 20th century. This writing system has been retained until today, despite the politically-influenced replacement of many European loan-words by newly coined Vietnamese terms to wipe out the European influence on Vietnamese.

Appendix B. Lexicon Production

In embedding a machine-readable lexicon into a large natural language processing system the question arises how to produce such a lexicon. The construction of the lexicon for LexEcon (chapter VI), for example, involves a small group of experts who write most of the entries in an unformatted ASCII-format using an ordinary text editor. On the basis of various charts and tables they associate lexical entries with morphological continuation classes, subcategorisation information, phonemic transcription, etc. Admittedly, these are highly specialised tasks which require a lot of expert knowledge. To produce the actual machine-readable format we apply a complicated lexicon compiler that separates the access units from their lexical specifications and generates the partitioned cohort network structure (see Deiß et al. 1990). Furthermore, the compiler replaces the various lexical fields with pointers, thus externalising various aspects of an entry's lexical specification and considerably reducing the size of each lexical entry. Nevertheless, there is a lot of user-engineering involved.

The confinement of lexicon construction to a handful of experts, however, is undesirable for the following reasons. First, it is an extremely time-consuming task. Since only few people are actually capable of lexicon construction, the development of a large lexicon takes a long time.[1] Secondly, humans make mistakes. Each lexical entry has to be defined with great precision. The use of the wrong morphological continuation class, the absence of a syllable boundary, or the assignment of a stress mark to the wrong position, may have disastrous consequences for the analysis process. However, since humans in general and lexicon- engineers in particular are not infallible, error-free machine-readable lexicons constructed by hand are the exception rather than the rule.

For these reasons it is plausible to apply computational methods to the construction and maintenance of a machine-readable lexicon. These methods can be interactive tools that allow the user to construct new or to manipulate existing entries. Furthermore, we might employ automatic procedures that convert lexical information extracted from dictionaries first into the ASCII-format and then into the internal format required for the machine-readable lexicon.

In the following two sections we will discuss the theoretical background of interactive lexicon editors (Appendix B1) and lexicon conversion (Appendix B2). The actual algorithms, and further tools, will be introduced in Appendix C.

B1. Interactive Editing

One method of supporting the human lexicon engineer in constructing and editing lexical entries is the application of an interactive lexicon editor. Such a tool can be used autonomously for the construction of new entries or as an add-on component to the program within which the lexicon operates.

Basically, an interactive lexicon editor is a tool that makes suggestions where feasible but at the same time heavily restricts the freedom of the human user. In LexEcon's root lexicon, for example, we have 4 nominal, 16 verbal, and 7 adjectival morphological continuation classes. If a new word is to be entered into the lexicon, it has to be coupled with the correct class. The new adjective ABSTEMIOUS, for example (we discussed its insertion to the cohort network in section 5.3.4.1.), has to be assigned the continuation class A3. This class is associated with all those adjectives that can form a LY-adverb (*abstemiously*) but do not allow other forms. The selection of this continuation class can be done in a user-friendly lexicon editor that first asks for the word-class (figure 114) and then generates theoretically possible word forms.

Note that the introductory menu in figure 114 only allows the addition of the main open-class words, i.e. nouns, verbs, and adjectives. The option "Further" permits the insertion of complex or idiomatic expressions on the basis of subordinate menus. Even though the user still has to make up his mind about the word-class of a new item, his choice is restricted to these four possibilities.

Having chosen the word-class, a new menu presents further options (figure 115). Depending on the user's choice in the first menu (figure 114) a number of additional questions are asked to define the morphological continuation class. For this purpose, the lexicon editor has been coupled with orthographical analysis and generation routines as introduced in section 5.4.1. and 6.2. These routines allow the orthographically correct generation of most morphological variants: since the phonological information of the new entry has not been made available at this point, flanking orthographical changes may be overgenerated in some rare cases. Nevertheless, we

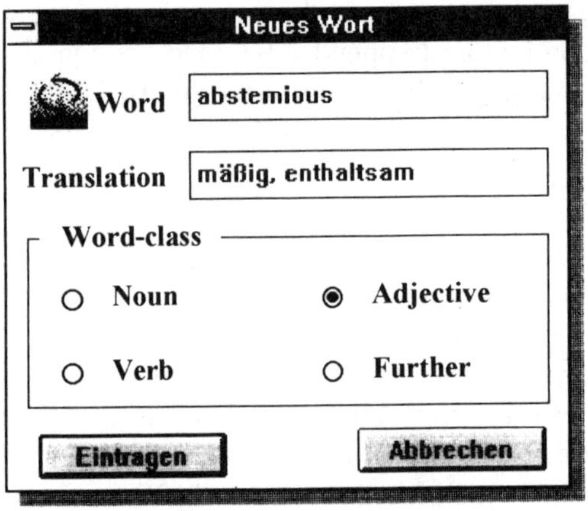

Figure 114. Interactive lexicon editing: word-class selection
Annotations: Eintragen = enter, Abbrechen = Quit

can now ask the user whether certain additional forms are possible. In the case of adjectival roots, such as ABSTEMIOUS, one question concerns the generation of adverbs, another the possibility of grading the adjective, a third the possibility of turning an adjective into an EN-verb, such as *hard* → *harden*. All these questions are asked interactively and are accompanied by the respective word patterns. Figure 115 shows this technique on the basis of the formation of adverbs.

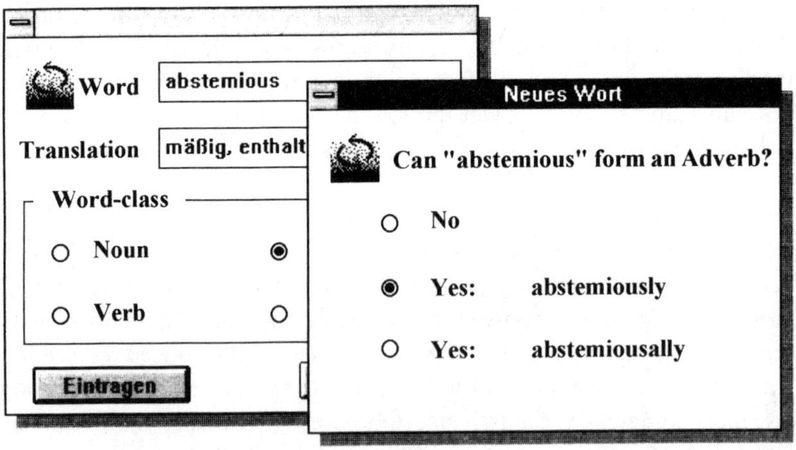

Figure 115. Interactive lexicon editing: adverbs

In this case, the user has to select option 2 via mouse button press, allowing ABSTEMIOUS to form a standard adverb. Depending on the initial word-class chosen, further subordinate menus of this type are presented to the user. At the end of the morphological selection phase the user has to confirm his previous selection in a menu of the type presented in figure 116.

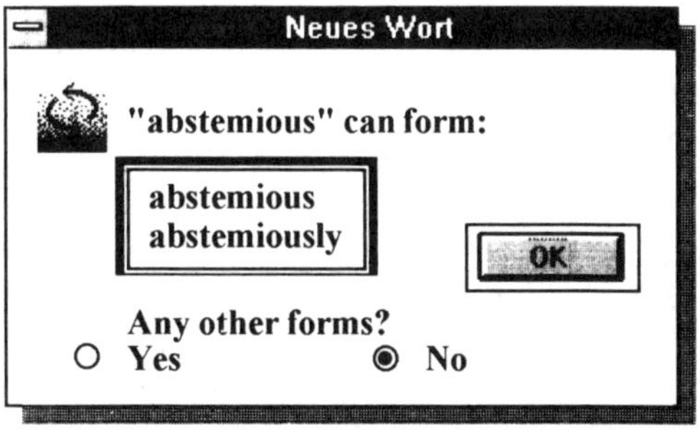

Figure 116. Interactive lexical editing: final confirmation

After the selection phase the system will internally generate the morphological continuation class A3, which will constitute the morphological field of the lexical specification of ABSTEMIOUS. By analogy with the generation of the morphological class, syntactic aspects, etymological information, etc., will be added on the basis of a similar system of menus.

Lexical tools of this type are very helpful for generating the type of information which is internally required to make up the machine-readable format of lexical entries. However, as user-friendly as such a component may be, the actual use of such a component is a tedious enterprise. Experienced users prefer the use of a style sheet which allows them to insert new lexical entries using a simple editing program.

Thus, the use of interactive tools has advantages and disadvantages. For the layman it is possibly the only method of editing lexical entries. It heavily restricts the editorial freedom but reduces mistakes to a minimum. Of course, if the user selects the wrong forms, e.g. he does not accept the adjective *abstemiously*, then there is no chance for the lexicon to process such a form on the basis of the root. Nevertheless, interactive lexicon tools of this type are certainly useful. The experienced user with linguistic background, however, will generally prefer a printed manual which defines the format of an entry and the conventions for the definition of morphological, syntactic, classes, etc.

B2. Automatic Conversion

In constructing a machine-readable lexicon we have to define a source from where we get the raw data. Such a source is normally a book dictionary. As we saw in chapter two an essential problem with dictionaries is their inconsistency of presenting lexical information and their failure to present a number of aspects which are required in machine-readable lexicons.

For example, the syntactic specification of a lexical entry is often very crude and totally insufficient for a machine-readable format. If the syntactic specification is defined in terms of a unification grammar format as presented in section 5.4.3., then even the most sophisticated syntactic aspects used in dictionaries, such as LDOCE, are insufficient. Verbs, for example, are associated with information such as [I] or [T1] indicating their transitivity status (I = intransitive, T1 = monotransitive + NP-object). However, the subcategorisation of a verb in terms of thematic relations, such as agent, theme, etc., cannot be inferred from this information. Furthermore, the assignment of functional information to items, such as (be)+EASY (see section 5.4.3.), is not possible using the syntactic information of a dictionary.

Especially difficult is the derivation of semantic information from a dictionary. As stated in chapter two the definition of an entry in a dictionary is basically a paraphrase that restates the meaning in other words. However, there are possible ways of restricting the freedom of doing this. The LDOCE is most rigorous in this respect. It uses a controlled vocabulary for its main entries. All definitions are composed of words belonging to a list of approximately 2.000 words selected on the basis of frequency (Lipka 1992: 31). This list is given at the end of the dictionary. Words that do not belong to this list but are used in the specification of an entry's meaning are capitalised. The careful use of this technique allows the establishment of cross- references in the lexicon and thus the association of lexical items with specific semantic fields. Nevertheless, the semantic definition of a lexical entry is still not sophisticated enough to generate semantic frames of the CD-type (section 5.4.4.2.) nor to integrate a lexical item into a semantic network.

Hence, whenever we think of implementing conversion procedures, we have to restrict the program to those aspects of the lexical entries in a dictionary that can safely be converted into a machine-readable format.

That the LDOCE is among the most consistent dictionaries as far as the definition of syntactic and semantic information is concerned is undisputed (see Boguraev/Briscoe 1989, Appendix F). For this reason, it used as the basis in many machine-readable lexicons. The LDOCE presents its lexical entries according to the following general principles (Boguraev/Briscoe 1989b: 85):

- Each lexical entry is a paragraph.
- Each lexical entry is preceded by the access unit.
- If an entry has several syntactic categories (word-classes), it is ubdivided into several access units with different numerical indices.
- Hyphenation possibilities are indicated by dots within the access units.
- Each access unit is followed by its phonemic transcription, which is presented in slant brackets, e.g. /flaɪ/.
- The syntactic information is presented in angular brackets, e.g. [T1] = transitive + object, as in *kick* or *blow up*.
- The semantic information follows the syntactic specification. It ends either before one or several examples in context or before the next sense or entry.
- If examples in context are included in the lexical specification of an entry, they follow a colon after the semantic specification.
- Several examples in context are separated by vertical strokes.

In addition to these general principles, each aspect of an entry's lexical specification, for example, the phonological information, follows specific conventions (see Appendix C).

Here are some simplified examples:

(79) fly1 /flaɪ/ v **flew** /flu:/, **flown** /fləʊn/ 1 [I] to move or be moved through the air by means of wings: *Most birds and some insects fly | A bee flew in through ...*

(80) flu•ent /ˈflu:ənt/ adj **1** [(in)] (of a person) speaking, writing . . . : *He is fluent in five languages*

(81) fly half /ˌ•ˈ•/ n (in RUGBY) a fast-running player

If an access unit has irregular inflectional variants, such as FLY, they are presented in bold face print at the beginning of its lexical specification, i.e. after the statement of its word- class and before the syntactic and semantic specification of the first sense. A further convention concerns the presentation of several senses: entries that have only one sense have no numerical information in their specification.

With these conventions we can develop an automatic procedure that converts a large number of lexical entries into a machine-readable format.

An adequate algorithm will first split the access unit from the entry and transform it to a standard form. For example, we do not want hyphenation information or numerical indices in the access unit itself. Secondly, the conversion program will strip off all those aspects of the lexical entry that are not confined to specific senses, i.e. hyphenation information, phonemic transcription, word-class, and information about irregular inflections. As a third step, the algorithm will translate the syntactic specification into the desired format. Boguraev/Briscoe (1989b: 98) illustrated the conversion of the syntactic specification of LDOCE-entries into a machine-readable format on the basis of the entry HATE:

(82) hate v . . . 1 [T1, 3, 4; V3, 4]

The syntactic notation "T1, 3, 4" accounts for the fact that HATE is transitive and takes a direct object. This direct object can be realised by a NP or by a non-finite sentence. Here are the actual syntactic possibilities:

(83) a. Someone hates someone. [T1]
b. Someone hates to do something. [T3]
c. Someone hates doing something. [T4]

"V3, 4", by contrast, denotes the possibility of having one object and a non-finite sentential complement:

(83) d. Someone hates someone to do something. [V3]
e. Someone hates someone doing something. [V4]

As a result, the conversion procedure could translate the syntactic information into a syntactic frame of the following type (simplified):

```
((Sense1
        (NP NP)                ;83a
        (NP Infinitive)        ;83b
        (NP ING-form)          ;83c
        (NP NP Infinitive)     ;83d
        (NP NP ING-form)))     ;83e
(Sense2 ...))
```

Depending on the representation within which the machine-readable lexicon operates, this information may be coupled with thematic roles, categorial information about the tree structure, or with functional aspects, such as in LFG. However, most of this work has to be done by hand.

In summary, the use of conversion procedures that translate standard dictionaries into a machine-readable lexicon is an important means to ease the construction of machine- readable lexicons. Moreover, the use of standard dictionaries is a much safer method to generate lexical information than the reliance on the intuitions about the words by the human lexicon-engineer. However, even the most sophisticated conversion procedures require post-editing by their human users, because one can never be sure whether the dictionary information is totally consistent and correct, and, furthermore, it is by no means guaranteed that the conversion program operates absolutely perfectly. We must never forget that both dictionary and conversion procedures have been written by humans, or at least with human assistance.

In Appendix C we will outline the basic steps of conversion algorithm of the sort that can be applied to dictionary entries of the LDOCE-format.

B3. Testing

Even the most efficient tools and the most intelligent fully-automatic conversion procedures may produce errors. As pointed out above, incorrect morphological continuation classes may have fatal consequences for the analysis and generation of words. Furthermore, the generation of syntactic frames from dictionary information, and, even more so, the generation of semantic aspects, cannot be taken for granted. The conversion of lexical entries from dictionaries into machine-readable format ultimately rests on the accuracy of the lexical entries in the dictionary (Boguraev/Briscoe 1989b: 101). Likewise, the information generated by the interaction between a lexicon editing program and its human user may involve omissions and mistakes. For these reasons, any machine-readable lexicon must be carefully tested before it is actually put to use.

In Appendix C an example of a simple testing algorithm is presented.

Appendix C.
Tools

In the following sections we will introduce a selection of programs written in LISP. The first program converts an ASCII-file into machine-readable format (Appendix C1), the second illustrates how lexical entries in machine-readable lexicons can be automatically tested for correctness (Appendix C2), and, finally, we will discuss a program that can be used as a tool for performance evaluation (Appendix C3). All programs have been written in muLISP-86.[1]

C1. Conversion Procedures

In the following we will outline the central procedures for converting a lexical entry from LDOCE into machine-readable format. The conventions of representing lexical entries in the LDOCE have been outlined in Appendix B2.

Input to the conversion program is an ASCII-file that contains the lexical information. This ASCII-file can be generated using a scanner and an OCR-program, or it can be made available using the electronic version of LDOCE. The format of the output depends on the purpose of the machine-readable lexicon and the requirements of the various aspects of an entry's lexical specification. On the basis of our discussion in chapter five we will convert each lexical entry according to the following principles:

- Access unit and lexical specification will be separated.
- Each lexical specification will be split up into the following precisely defined fields:
  - phonology specified in terms of simple ASCII-symbols,
  - morphology in terms of continuation classes,
  - syntax in terms of syntactic frames,
  - definition field (semantics) in terms of keywords,
  - example in context as specified in LDOCE.

Hence, the conversion algorithm must perform the following basic operations: it must isolate each access unit and convert each lexical field into the desired internal format. In addition to this, various subordinate tasks have to be performed. These concern the insertion of boundaries between the lexical fields, the generation of filenames which contain less important aspects, such as synonyms, and the translation of specific symbols, such as phonemes, into an internal, machine-readable format.

With the exception of the morphological field, which is presented as a mere statement of an item's word-class in LDOCE, all these operations can be done without human interference. For the generation of the continuation classes one can apply an interactive lexicon editor as presented in Appendix B1.

(a) isolating the access unit

Let us repeat the basic conventions of presenting the initial part of lexical entries in LDOCE (also see Appendix B2).

- Each lexical entry is a paragraph.
- Each lexical entry is preceded by the access unit.
- If an entry has several categories each access unit has an index.[2]
- Hyphenation possibilities are indicated by internal dots in the access unit.
- Each access unit is followed by its phonemic transcription, i.e. by a slant bracket.

Here are some examples:

(84) fly1 /flaɪ/

(85) flu•ent /ˈflu:ənt/

(86) fly half /ˌ•ˈ•/

The first step which the conversion algorithm has to perform is to separate the access unit from its lexical specification. To do this the algorithm examines all input information which occurs before the first slant bracket, i.e. before the beginning of the phonemic information. Four LISP-functions are responsible for these tasks: C-GO initialises the program and reads the entries from the input file, C-SPLIT-HEAD cuts off the access unit, C-HEAD prepares it for further processing, and C-HEAD-AUX transforms it into the desired format.[3] C-GO initiates the program. It reads an ASCII-file paragraph by paragraph until the end of file is reached. Each paragraph is internally analysed as a string of theoretically unlimited length (*linelength*

= NIL). Input to C-GO is the name of the file to be analysed. From this file C-GO reads a string, passes it on to further analysis and writes the results into an output file. These operations are repeated until the end of the input file is reached. Prior to these operations, a number of basic variables have to be introduced. These concern a word-counter for statistics (**ctr**), the access-unit-separator (**sep**), the hyphenation-symbol (**hyph**), an association list that converts the LDOCE word- classes into an internal shorthand form (**mor**), the digits of the decimal system represented as strings (**num**), word-separators, such as **blank**, and word- delimiters (**wdl**). The syntactic frames are loaded via the function C-READ-SYN (see below).

```
(defun c-go (inputfile *phon* *hyphen* linelength)
   (setq *ctr* 0
         *sep* "/"
         *hyph* (ascii 249)
         *blank* (ascii 32)
         *mor* '((ADJ A)(N N)(V V))
         *num* (list "1" "2" "3" "4" "5" "6" "7" "8" "9")
         *wdl* '(\. \! \, \; \? \[ \]))
   (c-read-syn)
   (clear-input)                                              ;a
   (rds inputfile)                                            ;b
   (wrs 'lex.out)                                             ;c
   (loop
         ((= (readptr) (readptr 'eof)))                       ;d
         ((null rds))                                         ;e
         ((c-split-head (read-line))                          ;f
         (write-line "Break!")) )                             ;g
         (rds)                                                ;h
         (list *ctr* 'entries 'counted))                      ;i
```

Having instantiated the global variables, C-GO clears the keyboard-buffer (line a) and prepares the input file LEX.ASC for reading (b) and the output file LEX.OUT for writing (c). Note that two global variables are used dynamically in the entire program: **phon** (the phonological code) and **hyphen** (the syllable structure of the access unit). These variables are introduced in the parameter list of C-GO.

The LOOP is terminated if the end of the input file is reached (d) or if the file to be analysed cannot be found (e). The line-by-line reading process is carried out in (f), where each line is forwarded to C-SPLIT-HEAD as a string. If the conversion process is interrupted by a key press, the S-expression (f) evaluates to T and a comment will be displayed (g). The remaining operations close the input file (h) and provide us with a simple statistical information (i).

C-SPLIT-HEAD is responsible for the separation of the access unit and its lexical specification.

```
(defun c-split-head (strg pos rds read-char)
   ((listen))                                                  ;a
   ((null (setq pos (findstring *sep* strg)))                  ;b
    (c-head&tail                                               ;c
     (c-head (substring strg 0
       (setq pos (sub1 (findstring *blank* strg)))))           ;d
       (substring strg (+ pos 2))))                            ;e
   (c-head&tail (c-head (substring strg 0 (sub1 pos)))         ;f
                (substring strg (add1 pos)) t))                ;g
```

Input to this function is one lexical entry as a string. C-SPLIT-HEAD generates a list headed by the access unit as an atom and an ordered set of lexical specifications associated with the access unit. For the entry FLUENT the list in (87) will be the result of the conversion process:

(87)	FLUENT	;access unit
	$ ‘flu:Ent	;phonology
	$ flu•ent	;syllable structure
	$ A3	;morphology (word-class)
	# %IN	;syntax
	$ person speaking writing	;semantics (keywords)
	$ EX279	;example
	$ fließend geläufig	;translation
	$ SYN279	;synonyms
	$	;etymology
	#	;end-of-sense 1
	$ ...	;specifications of sense 2
	#	;end-of-sense 2

The converted entry is written into an output file from where it can be subjected to further conversion procedures, such as the generation of the continuation class in terms of an alpha-numerical symbol, or the externalisation of the various aspects of lexical specification.

Such a machine-readable format uses a number of precisely defined conventions:

- The lexical fields are internally separated by $.
- The phonological information contains normalised symbols, such as E for /ə/.
- The morphological information is a mere statement of the entry's word-class.
- The syntactic information is represented by a simple item, in this case an optional one. The internal symbol for optionality is %.
- The semantic keywords are simply listed.
- Different senses are separated by #.

Note that the LDOCE information has been supplemented by information from bilingual dictionaries to obtain the translation into German, and by synonym dictionaries to generate the synonymic information. Moreover, synonyms and examples in context are represented by filenames that contain the relevant information.

Let us return to the conversion program. Once an entry has been read and passed on to C-SPLIT-HEAD, the following operations are carried out. First, the possibility of program termination is allowed (a). In this case the S-expression in (a) returns the value T and the LOOP in C-GO is aborted.

The second S-expression of C-SPLIT-HEAD, line (b), finds the initial position of the element following the access unit on the basis of the predefined separator (**sep** = /). In the LDOCE-format **sep** introduces the phonemic transcription. If no **sep**, i.e. no phonemic information, can be found we are confronted with entries which are subordinate to other entries and have a second word-class. For example, the nominal meaning FLY occurs subsequent to the verbal meaning. In these cases, the phonemic transcription is stated only once and omitted in subordinate entries to avoid the replication of information. Lines (c) to (e) in C-SPLIT-HEAD account for these facts.[4]

The remaining S-expression transfers *head* (the access unit) and *tail* (the lexical specification) to C-HEAD&TAIL, where they will be subjected to further analysis (f/g). To indicate that the phonemic information has been found, the special form T is explicitly forwarded to C-HEAD&TAIL. Prior to that the access unit has to be inspected to distinguish between different types of access unit (examples (84) to (87)).

C-HEAD transfers the head, which is still a string, to C-HEAD-AUX where it is converted into an atom. For C-HEAD-AUX to operate successfully, the string (*strg*) has to be bound to **hyphen**, which stores the syllable structure of the access unit (d), has to be converted into a list of individual symbols (c), and reversed for further inspection (b). To make sure that no superfluous blanks occur at the right flank, these are removed beforehand (e). In other words, the following operations are performed in C-HEAD (*strg* = "fly1 "):

(e) "fly1 " → "fly1"
(d) "fly1" → = syllable structure
(c) "fly1" → (/f /l /y /1)
(b) (/f /l /y /1) → (/1 /y /l /f)

```
(defun c-head (strg)
   (c-head-aux                                                    ;a
     (reverse                                                     ;b
       (unpack                                                    ;c
         (setq *hyphen*                                           ;d
           (string-right-trim *blank* strg))))))                  ;e
```

In C-HEAD-AUX, the access unit, represented as a reversed list of individual characters, is cleared of superfluous information and converted into a list of one or more atoms. In the case of the access unit "fly1", this list will be (FLY). Note that, in program lines (f) and (g), information about hyphenation can now be ignored and numerical indices relating to different senses can be removed.

```
(defun c-head-aux (lst remain out)
   (loop ((null lst)(cons (pack remain) out))              ;a
         ( ((eq (car lst) *blank*)                         ;b
          (push (pack remain) out)                         ;c
          (setq remain)                                    ;d
          (pop lst))                                       ;e
          ((or (eq (car lst) *hyph*)                       ;f
                 (member (car lst) *num*))                 ;g
          (pop lst))                                       ;h
          ((member (car lst) *wdl*)                        ;i
          (pop lst))                                       ;k
          (push (char-upcase (pop lst)) remain)))) ;l
```

After these basic steps the access unit is ready for storing and we can turn our attention to the various aspects of the entry's lexical specification.

C-HEAD&TAIL is the top-level function for the conversion of an entry's lexical specification.

(b) the conversion of the lexical specification

Now the entry's lexical specification (*tail*) has to be inspected more closely. The following LISP-functions take over this task: C-MAKE-PHON isolates the phonological specification, C-MAKE-MOR picks up the entry's word-class and converts it into a simple format, and C-MAKE-REST-SPEC takes care of the information that is specific to each sense of an entry, i.e. syntax, semantics, and example of use.

In addition to these basic functions, we need a procedure that trims the lexical fields and removes superfluous material, such as blanks and numerical indices, and a procedure that writes the converted lexical entry into the output file.

C-HEAD&TAIL prepares the various aspects for writing:

```
(defun c-head&tail (head *tail* phon *cat* *spec*)
   (if phon (c-make-phon *tail*))                            ;a
   (setq *spec* (c-make-rest-spec (c-make-mor *tail*) 1)) ;b
   (c-write
   head                                                      ;c
   (list *phon*                                              ;d
         (string-right-trim *num* *hyphen*)                  ;e
         *cat*)                                              ;f
   *spec*))                                                  ;g
```

C-HEAD&TAIL first examines whether the entry has a phonemic specification (a). If this is the case, *phon* is not NIL, and the phonemic information will be generated (C-MAKE-PHON). If not, it has already been bound to the global variable **phon**. These cases occur if an entry has no phonemic information, such as the nominal interpretation of FLY. In line (b) the remaining lexical fields are inspected. Lines (c) to (g) forward the result of conversion to C-WRITE. This procedure writes the information into the output file. Note that **hyphen**, the information about the syllable structure, is trimmed, i.e. if present, numerical indices are removed.

The phonemic information is built in C-MAKE-PHON.

```
(defun c-make-phon (strg pos)
   (setqpos (findstring *sep* strg)                        ;a
        *phon* (substring strg 0 (sub1 pos))                ;b
        *tail* (c-trim (list *sep*) (substring strg pos)))) ;c
```

Basically, this function locates the position of the right-hand phonemic bracket (a), binds the phonemic information without the brackets to **phon** (b), and redefines the remainder, i.e. the variable **tail** (c). Note that **tail** has an indefinite extent. It has been preset to NIL in C-HEAD&TAIL and is manipulated in the functions belonging to the same lexical block, that is in all functions subordinate to C-HEAD&TAIL.

C-MAKE-MOR and C-MAKE-REST in C-HEAD&TAIL are responsible for the remainder of an item's lexical specification.

C-MAKE-MOR cuts off the word-class information (a/b), associates it with the list **mor** (c), and redefines the lexical specification (d):

```
(defun c-make-mor (strg pos cat)
  (setq pos (findstring *blank* strg)                      ;a
        cat (substring strg 0 (sub1 pos))                  ;b
       *cat* (cadr (assoc (string-upcase cat) *mor*)))     ;c
  (c-trim (list cat) strg))                                ;d
```

Having worked out those aspects which are shared by all senses of an entry, we can now take care of sense-specific information.

Since we do not know in advance how many senses an entry has, C-MAKE-REST is programmed as a LOOP which iterates until all senses of an entry have been processed. The beginning of each new sense is marked by a number starting with 1. To isolate different senses all the algorithm has to do is to find the positions of two adjacent numbers and define the material between them as belonging to one sense of the entry. For this reason, C-MAKE- REST receives two variables: *strg* = the string of all senses, and *ctr* = the sense-counter, whose initial value is 1.

For example, *strg* could be:

(88) "1 [V1] to do something 2 [V1] . . . 3 . . . ."

```
(defun c-make-rest-spec (strg ctr pos res)
  (loop
   (setq strg (c-trim *num* strg))                          ;a
   ((null (setq pos (findstring (incq ctr) strg)))          ;b
   (reverse (cons (c-get-spec strg) res)))                  ;c
   (push (c-get-spec (substring strg 0 (sub1 pos))) res)   ;d
   (setq strg (substring strg pos))))                       ;e
```

Since the first sense-counter always occurs at position one of the input string, it can be cut off (a). Now *strg* has the following value:

(88') "[V1] to do something 2 [V1] . . . 3 . . . ."

In order to find the right-hand side of the first sense, *ctr*, whose initial value is 1, has to be incremented.

If no further numerical value can be found in the string, all interpretations have been processed (b); if not, the input string is shortened to its remainder, i.e. to:

(88") "2 [V1] . . . 3 . . . ."

The processing itself, i.e. the conversion into the desirable format, is carried out in C-GET-SPEC (lines c/d in C-MAKE-REST-SPEC).

Since machine-readable lexicons differ enormously in terms of syntactic and semantic information, C-GET-SPEC is not elaborated any further here:

```
(defun c-get-spec (strg)
   strg)
```

However, for the experienced programmer it is relatively easy to adapt C-GET- SPEC to the specific requirements of his machine-readable lexicon. All that has to be done is to parse the central variable *strg* into its individual fields and convert each field into the respective format.

C-GET-SPEC receives one sense of a lexical entry as a string. Thus, when forwarded to C- GET-SPEC, *strg* may have the following possible forms:

(89) a. [I] to move . . . by means of wings: Most birds . . . fly | A bee flew
b. [(in)] (of a person). . . : He is fluent in five languages
c. (in RUGBY) a fast-running player

This information can now be forwarded to further analysis. The syntactic information can be identified on the basis of the presence of square brackets []. The separation between the entry's explanation and possible examples of use is indicated by a colon, and so on.

The conversion program makes use of a central utility function which trims the left end of strings. It removes superfluous blanks and other symbols contained in *lst:*

```
(defun c-trim (lst strg)
   (string-left-trim (cons *blank* lst) strg))
```

The conversion of LDOCE's syntactic information into syntactic frames such as presented in Appendix B is carried out on the basis of an association list of the type:

```
((I (H1 NP))
 (V1 (H2 NP NP))
 ...)
```

This list is loaded from a file and bound to the global variable **syntax**. The function C-READ-SYN is called from C-GO, the top-level function of the conversion program:

```
(defun c-read-syn ()
   (rds syntax.doc)
   (setq *syntax* (read))
   (rds))
```

Having converted a lexical entry into the new format, it is enriched with new separator symbols ($ and #), see (87), and written into the output file. C-WRITE and C- WRITE-AUX are responsible for this operation:

```
(defun c-write (head form lemma wrs)
   (incq *ctr*)
   (setq wrs t)
   (loop (prin1 (pop head))
         ((null head))
         (prin1 #))
   (c-write-aux form " $ ")
   (c-write-aux lemma " #")
   (write-line " #")
   nil)
```

```
(defun c-write-aux (strg-lst symb)
   (loop ((null strg-lst))
         (write-string symb)
         (write-string (pop strg-lst))))
```

This simple algorithm is by no means complete. It does not take into account any inconsistencies or additional aspects, such as information about dialectal variants or further symbols associated with specialised information. However, it should illustrate the basic steps of lexical conversion, i.e. of using dictionary information in order to generate a machine- readable lexicon.

C2. Lexicon Testing

Any machine-readable lexicon, whether generated by hand or by the application of automatic conversion procedures, has to undergo careful and rigorous testing at many levels.

At one level we have to examine whether the internal structure is organised as required. In particular, we have to check the correct number and location of field separators, the legitimacy of the contents, and the representation format of each field.

At another level, the linguistic specifications associated with a lexical entry have to be inspected. For example, we have to ascertain that neither the morphological continuation class nor the syntactic specification of an entry leads to an overgeneration or to an underspecification of an entry's grammatical behaviour.

Let us illustrate the importance of testing on the basis of the phonological field. In the LDOCE all those lexical entries that consist of only one syllable are not assigned a stress mark, since monosyllabic words presented in isolation are stressed anyway. Polysyllabic words, by contrast, exhibit at least one stress mark and one or several unstressed syllables. Syllables are indicated in the access unit itself by means of the separator "•", in terms of the ASCII-code by ASCII-value 249. Hence, we have two possible presentational variants:

- monosyllabic words with no non-segmental phonological information
- polysyllabic words with a stress mark in the phonological code and one or several syllable separators in the access unit

That the presence and the correct format of the phonological information is indispensable for natural language processing has been stated in section 5.4.1. If the information about the syllable structure or the stress mark of polysyllabic words is incorrect or missing, a word recognition program may run into trouble with forms such as *developing/*developping*. Thus, the precise statement of the phonological information is highly important. Clearly, one can test this by hand. An automatic test procedure, however, is much more economical in this respect.

Such a testing program is fairly simple: it successively reads all entries from the machine- readable ASCII-file, into which the dictionary has already been converted, it inspects the lexical fields in question, and examines the respective information. The input file to this program is no longer the original LDOCE-file but the file generated by the conversion program introduced in Appendix C1. In this file each entry has the following format:

FLY $ flaI $ fly $ V $ # specification1 # specificationN#
FLUENT $ 'flUEnt $ flu•ent $ A # specification1 # specificationN#

Field_1 contains the access unit, field_2 the phonological code, field_3 the syllable structure, and field_4 the morphological information. The remaining fields constitute the specification of the senses of an entry.

The top-level function is similar to the general conversion program presented in Appendix C1. It successively reads each entry until the end of the input file is reached. Each entry is forwarded to C-SPLIT-ENTRY, where the access unit and the phonological information are separated from the rest.

```
(defun c-phon (*inputfile* linelength wrs)
   (setq *ctr* 0
       *sep* ''$"
       *blank* (ascii 32))
   (clear-input)
   (rds *inputfile*)
   (wrs 'phon.err)
   (loop
       ((= (readptr) (readptr 'eof)))
       ((null rds))
       ((c-split-entry (read-line))
       (write-line ''Break!")) )
   (rds)
   (list *ctr* 'entries 'counted))
```

In C-SPLIT-ENTRY the relevant fields are isolated:

```
(defun c-split-entry (strg fields rds read-char)
  ((listen))                                          ;a
  (incq *ctr*)                                        ;b
  (setq fields (c-find-fields strg 3))                ;c
  ((c-check-phon                                      ;d
    (unpack (cadr fields))(unpack (caddr fields)))   ;e
  nil)
  (c-error fields)                                    ;f
   nil)
```

Since all lexical fields are now neatly separated by $, the isolation of the individual lexical fields can be performed by a central function C-FIND-FIELDS. This function is activated in line (c) of C-SPLIT-ENTRY.

```
(defun c-find-fields (strg ctr res)
  ((> ctr 4))
  (loop ((zerop ctr) (reverse res))                      ;a
        ( ((setq pos (findstring *sep* strg))            ;b
          (push (c-trim 'string-right-trim (list *sep*);c
                   (substring strg 0 pos)) res)          ;d
          (setq strg                                     ;e
           (c-trim 'string-left-trim
                   (list *sep*) (substring strg pos)))
          (decq ctr)))))                                 ;f
```

C-FIND-FIELDS receives one lexical entry (*strg*) and a counter indicating how many fields are to be isolated (maximum 4). The counter (*ctr*) is decremented (f) until its value is zero (a). The COND-clause (b) finds out the position of the first separator, pushes the first field into *res* (d) and redefines the input-string (*strg*) (line (e)). Prior to that, the field is cleared of superfluous material (c). As a result, C-FIND-FIELDS generates a list of the form (“access unit” “phonology” “syllable-structure” “morphology”), where “access unit” is the CAR, “phonology” the CADR, and so on.

The COND-clause in C-SPLIT-ENTRY (lines (d) and (e)) constitutes the heart of the program. It passes the phonological information (*cadr fields*) and the syllable structure (*caddr fields*) to C-CHECK-PHON. C-CHECK-PHON consists of a combination of tests concerning the legitimacy of phonological information. These tests evaluate to T, if the phonological code contains an apostrophe, i.e. a stress mark (a/d), and the head the ASCII-value 249, i.e. a syllable separator (b/c); or none of them (e). In all other cases C-CHECK- PHON returns NIL. If the result of C-CHECK-PHON is NIL, the function C-ERROR is evoked in C-SPLIT-ENTRY:

```
(defun c-check-phon (head-lst phon-lst)
  ((member '\' phon-lst)                  ;a
   ((member (ascii 249) head-lst)))       ;b
  ((member (ascii 249) head-lst)          ;c
   ((member '\' phon-lst)))               ;d
  t)                                      ;e
```

Depending on the result of C-CHECK-PHON, C-ERROR is activated to write the error into the output file PHON.ERR. This output file has been prepared for writing in C-PHON:

```
(defun c-error (lst wrs)
   (setq wrs t)
   (print lst))
```

The error file will eventually contain all access units which have an illegal phonological form. The actual error correction, however, has still to be done by hand. However, a simple comparison between the entries in main file and in the error file considerably reduces this task.

Programs of this type are enormously useful tools for the examination of the correct structure of lexical entries. Using the same top-level function we can easily develop programs that test the morphological field or check the consistency of translation fields, e.g. the correct placement of internal commas, spaces, etc. In other words, we can isolate each lexical field and inspect its contents.

C3. Performance Tests

The following two LISP-procedures illustrate the performance efficiency of a simple operation using lists of different length. Lexical entries can be internally represented as lists consisting of several pieces of information:

- formal specification (morpho-syntax and phonology)
- lemma specification (syntax, semantics, example, etymology, further)

Here is an abstract example of the lexical specification of a lexical entry in terms of the global variable *entry*. It consists of two aspects of a formal information and several lemma aspects represented as simple lists with arbitrary symbols.

```
(setq entry
   '((a b c)              ;form1:  morphology
     (d e f)              ;form2:  phonology
     (g h i)              ;lemma1: syntax
     (j k l)              ;lemma2: semantics
     (m n o)              ;lemma3: example
     (p q r)              ;lemma4: etymology
     (s t u)              ;lemma5: acoustics
     (v w x)              ;lemma6: visual representation
     (y z 1)))            ;lemma7: statistics
```

The function TEST illustrates the behaviour of a program that receives lists of different length as input. TEST receives a list and an arbitrary numerical value as its input. The function performs two operations: it reverses the list and decrements the numerical value *ct* until it is zero. The numerical value is needed to prolong the reverse-operation and illustrate the time factor.

```
(defun test (lst ct)
   (loop ((zerop ct))
         (reverse lst)
         (decq ct)))
```

TEST can be activated as follows:

```
$ (test entry 1000)
T
```

With a simple benchmark macro we can illustrate that loading the entire list considerably slows down performance.

```
(defmacro u-bench (form)
  (list 'progn '(time t) form '(* 10 (time))) )
```

Here are the results in msec:

```
$ (u-bench (test (firstn 2 entry) 2000))  ;loads only the form
110
$ (u-bench (test entry 2000))             ;loads the entire entry
170
```

If we realise that a lexical access algorithm performs far more complex operations than a simple list reversion, it becomes clear that the loading of parts of the lexical specification of an entry on request, and not in its entirety, is an efficient means of increasing the performance of the overall program.

Notes

Chapter 1

1 In computer science the term 'natural language' is used for ordinary human languages, to distinguish them from constructed formal or artificial languages, such as the predicate calculus or computer programming languages (Winograd/Flores 1986: 107).
2 *Phonology* is the British English term; in American English the slightly obsolete term *phonemics* may be used instead.
3 The term *syntactic category* will be used henceforth to replace the traditional term *word-class*.
4 Most theoretical linguists define semantics and pragmatics as two independent branches of linguistics. While semantics is confined to the study of meaning, reference, and truth, pragmatics deals with language use and its relation to language structure and social context (Akmajian et al. 1984: 527ff).
5 If we replace "the eagles" by "the mountains", the interpretation of (1e) becomes clear, since mountains do not fly.
6 Prior to 1995 when Finland, Sweden and Austria became new members of the EU.
7 This is not the place to introduce the reader to the ingredients and the problems of machine translation. For an overview the following monographs are recommended: Hutchins 1986; Niremburg 1987; Lehrberger/Bourbeau 1988. However, we will return to the central issues of using lexical information in machine translation systems in chapter five.
8 For a description of a natural language based operating and help system see Wahlster et al. (1988).
9 A good overview of early CAI/ITS can be found in Barr/Feigenbaum (Volume II 1982: 225ff).
10 Even though English does not provide as many examples of this kind as German, there are some similar cases where the position of the hyphen may lead to a difference of meaning: *menswear* (*men-swear vs. mens-wear) or *bookshop* (*book-shop vs. books-hop) are good cases in point. However, the results, e.g. hyphenated **men-swear* may well not be recognisable English words.
11 According to Kurzweil (1990: 266) we typically speak about three words per second. Assuming an average of six phonemes per word, the average speech rate is about 18 phonemes per second. In rapid speech, by contrast, as many as thirty phonemes per second may occur (Moore 1977: 218).
12 Some characters, such as A and a, constitute the same orthographical value but have to be defined as distinct graphemes due to their different geometrical

structure. In the case of characters such as W and w one grapheme suffices to capture all possible orthographic realisations.

13 For a typology of writing systems, see section Appendix A.

14 In section 4.5. we will reconsider the term 'lexical access' in relation to general models of word processing that comprise word recognition and lexical retrieval.

15 By convention lexemes are spelt with capital letters.

16 The branch referred to as *lexical morphology* here is often referred to as *word-formation* (e.g. in Bauer 1983). There are good arguments to avoid this term. On the one hand, the term *word-formation* is unfortunate for various reasons (Matthews 1974: 38) and secondly, the use of the alternative term *lexical morphology* correctly implies that the forms involved are primarily stored in the lexicon rather than being generated by morphological rules.

17 The combination of the stem *nationalise* with the nominal affix *-ion* is accompanied by a phonological process which changes the stress pattern of the stem from /ˈnæʃnəlaɪz/ to /næʃnəlaɪˈzeɪʃn/ and inserts the diphthong /eɪ/ between stem and affix.

18 The basic syntactic functions of a sentence are subject, verb, object, adverbial and complement (Quirk et al. 1985: 49ff).

19 The term 'aspect' is used in Quirk et al.'s (1985: 188ff) sense here, i.e. as a grammatical category describing the relationship between verb action and time.

20 This generalisation is only an approximation for the sake of illustration. Obviously, there are cases where a much more flexible interpretation strategy has to be applied, for example, "The president put democracy under fire."

21 This is not the place for a more elaborate treatment of the maxims of conversation. Good overviews of the Gricean maxims can be found in Kempson (1976) and Levinson (1983).

22 The term *grammar* is used in the sense of theory of language here (see section 1.1.1.).

23 In this context, the term 'bottom-up' means that low-level information is processed before higher-level information. This sense is not to be mixed up with 'bottom-up parsing', where the analysis of words precedes the unfolding of phrase structure rules (Winograd 1983: 90).

24 See Tyler (1981) for a summary of the Marslen-Wilson experiments.

25 Like the term 'bottom-up', 'top-down' is also used differently. A 'top-down parsing' strategy begins by looking at the rules, normally starting with the sentence, and proceeds until it reaches words (Winograd 1983: 90).

26 The Connection Machine is a product of Thinking Machines Inc. and it comprises several thousand processors operating in parallel.

27 John von Neumann was a physicist and a pioneer of computer science. Apart from putting forward many theoretical ideas, he acted as a consultant in the creation of ENIAC, the world's first digital computer, between 1943 and 1946. The 'von-Neumann computer' or 'von-Neumann machine' is a system architec-

ture that relies on a single processing unit accessing its program from the same memory that holds the data (Kurzweil 1990: 185).

28 For reasons of illustration not all excitatory and inhibitory connections are represented in figure 17.

Chapter 2

1 Alternatively, machine-readable dictionaries are often referred to as *electronic dictionaries* or *electronic lexical databases.*

2 *Homonyms* are words which have identical orthographical and phonological structures but different meanings. Words with identical pronunciations but distinct spellings, such as *rain* and *reign,* are referred to as *homophones,* words with distinct pronunciations but identical spellings, such as *lead* /'led/ and *lead* /'li:d/, are referred to as *homographs.*

3 The term *morpho-grapheme* has been chosen by analogy with *morpho-phoneme.* Morpho-phonemes are abstract phonemic symbols. They are normally represented as capital letters and serve as placeholders for the members of a set of related variants; for example, the morpho-phoneme /S/ may stand for all plural realisations in English, or the morpho-phoneme /D/ for all past tense forms.

4 For a subdivision of the processes of morphological alternation see figure 8.

5 *Agglutinative* languages belong to the synthetic type. The words in such languages are formed by a concatenation of morphemes, where each morpheme can be associated with a specific meaning or grammatical function. Example (Turkish): *adam* = man-singular, *adam-lar* = man-plural, *adam-lar-in* = man-plural-genitive.

6 There is a difference between British English and American English, though. While BrE. gives more weight to morphological and etymological considerations, AmE. practice is to respect phonologically natural points (Quirk, et al 1985: 1613).

7 The fact that *round* can also be realised as a preposition is not totally surprising. Prepositions are somewhat of a hybrid case. Traditionally, they have always been subsumed under closed-class items. In generative syntax, however, they are defined as major categories along with nouns, verbs, and adjectives, since they can be classified in terms of syntactic features such as [$\pm$ N] and [$\pm$ V] (see Gazdar, et al. 1985: 20ff).

8 The LDOCE is more detailed in this respect. It includes subcategorisation information by means of a symbol system (see Appendix B1 for more details).

9 The OED uses normal brackets () instead of phonemic ones //.

10 We will not discuss the exact format of the graphological representation of an entry in the following. First, it is an entirely optional part of the formal specification of an entry, since not all languages have a writing system, and, secondly, it is not clear whether the representation format is a mere declaration of the graphological structure, or a procedural presentation of grapheme-phoneme relationships. Furthermore, there are languages whose writing system is not based

on the phonology but on the meaning of the respective words (see section 3.2.1. for further details).

11 The terminology used here is British. In American English the following alternative terms are used: AmE. *supra-segmental* = BrE. *non-segmental.*

12 Examples such as *strengths* /ˈstreŋkθs/ or *sixths* /ˈsɪksθs/, apparently pose a problem since they contain four consonants within the coda. However, inflectional and derivational affixes, such as -s and -th do not belong to the basic syllable template (Durand 1990: 212).

13 See figure 9 (section 1.3.3) and the examples (16) to (18) in this chapter for an illustration of these processes.

14 According to the generative framework, verbs assign semantic roles, or Θ-roles (Θ = Greek: Theta), to their arguments. The subject of the verb *believe* in the sense of "John believes ...", for example, receives the Θ-role of "believer". A verb like *rain,* by contrast, has a semantically empty subject, which is not assigned a Θ-role (see section 2.3.3.1. for more examples).

15 For a precise definition of these and related constructions see Hawkins 1986.

16 The original version of Ogden/Richards' *semiotic triangle* can be found in most introductory books to semantics, for example, in Palmer 1981: 24, or in Kempson 1976: 15.

17 Terminology is very fluid in this area. Some semanticists (e.g. Kempson 1976: 84) refer to 'antonymy' as 'incompatibility', since there are several different types of 'oppositeness of meaning' and the term 'antonymy' should be reserved for one specific type of incompatibility.

18 The formula to calculate the number of semantic features to distinguish a given number of lexemes from each other is $ABS(\sqrt{n}) + 1$, where n stands for the number of lexemes.

19 A good overview of the design and development of semantic networks can be found in Collins/Loftus 1977, and in Brachman 1979.

20 The representation format employed in semantic networks varies considerably. Nodes can be drawn as dots, circles, boxes, or simply as words, arcs as arrows or as lines. If arcs are presented as lines, they implicitly express top-to-bottom relationships, or else the direction of the relation is indicated by the direction of the arrow.

21 According to Lakoff 1982, the term *prototype theory* is misleading, since the notion of prototypes manifests just one aspect of a more general theory of categorising objects. For this reason, Lakoff 1982: 19 suggests the term *theory of natural categorization.*

22 Frames as a means of knowledge representation are related to a number of similar concepts. Rumelhart/Ortony 1977: 100 use the term *schema* to account for a variety of related representation techniques such as Minsky's 1975 *frames,* or Schank/Abelson's 1977 *scripts.*

23 To keep the representation format as simple as possible, aspects such as tense and specific states that describe each concept more specifically have been omitted here.

Chapter 3

1 There is still a third type of input channel, the tactile one. Its use, however, is restricted to a relatively small group of people, the blind. They use this highly specialised channel for the interpretation of the Braille writing system.
2 For a detailed typology of writing systems see Appendix A.
3 An alternative term for *typeface* is *fount,* often reduced to *font* in the case of word-processors.
4 There are languages with voiceless or devoiced vowels (e.g. Japanese), where the phonetic environment influences the neighbouring vowel. A good example is the Japanese word for the English pronoun *I* [wʌ'tʌçi̥ʌ], where the voiceless fricative [ç] devoices the subsequent vowel [i]. The *diacritic* for devoicing is a circle below the vowel.
5 Spectrograms are printouts displaying the frequency and energy patterns of sounds, using a spectrograph. For a detailed description of spectrograms, and the use of spectrographs, the reader is referred to the experimental phonetics literature, for example Fry (1979), Pickett (1980), or Borden/Harris (1980).
6 A burst is a short puff of air that characterises the acoustics of plosive consonants.
7 While Miller (1981) supposes 0.03 seconds as the VOT boundary, Garman (1990) mentions a value of 0.04 seconds.
8 We will not speculate about the status of such patterns here. In section 4.3. we will see that various possibilities, ranging from subphonemic patterns to syllables, can be taken into account.
9 Readers unfamiliar with the typology of writing systems should consult Appendix A before the subsequent sections.
10 The term *envelope* is normally used with reference to the wave form in acoustic analysis. In this transferred sense it relates to the visual shape of a word.
11 See section figure 54 (section 4.1.) for an overview of experimental stimuli.
12 Actually, humans often fail to decipher unfamiliar handwriting, too
13 The following remarks are based on Kurzweil, one of the leading researchers in OCR (Kurzweil 1990: 238ff)
14 Due to the influential role of the motor theory, active theories are sometimes alternatively referred to as *motor theories.*
15 The Oxford English Dictionary defines a template, among other senses, as "an instrument used as a gauge or guide in bringing any piece of work to the desired shape". In association with other senses, the terms "frame" or "pattern" are also used.

16 A common technique for showing the waveform envelope makes use of the oscilloscope, where the envelope is a curve presenting pressure variations as different voltage values.
17 An expert manager is some sort of supervisory program that organises the co-operation of the feature detectors.
18 For reasons of illustration, only a limited number of low-level feature detectors have been represented. On the basis of an 8-dot matrix, the total number of low-level detectors would be 64, one for each pixel.
19 That there are opposite views about the processing of Chinese characters, such as Sproat (1992: 122), was shown in section 2.1.4.
20 XTC is the name of a British rock band of the 1980s and 1990s.
21 Segmentation problems in written language are fairly exceptional. They can primarily be found at the level of complex words, where, depending on grapho-logical junctures, different interpretations can be manifested. A good case in point is the German word *Staubecken* (see section 1.1.3. (d)) which can be identified as *Stau-becken* or *Staub-ecken*. Also, there are marginal cases, such as *preposition,* where the initial syllable can either be analysed as an integral part of *preposition*, or as a prefix in *pre-position.*
22 See section 4.1. for a discussion of the experimental techniques used in studying lexical processing.
23 After all, the lexicon itself is a source of high-level information.
24 Recent research has shown that this differentiation is based on various phonetic aspects that constitute the particular speech rhythm of a language, rather than on the phenomenon of isochrony alone. Hence, the classification of languages into stress-timed and syllable-timed should be represented as a continuum and not by a strict dichotomy (see Dauer 1987 for more details).

Chapter 4

1 Note that some stimuli types relate only to the process of written word recognition. Exceptional words, whether they exist or not, arise only by an exceptional relationship between sound and symbol. Without reference to written English, *demon* and *sew* would not be exceptional. Likewise, pseudo-homophones exist only in a written representation, since the phonological form of an item such as /'breɪn/ has only one written counterpart, *brain* but not **brane.*
2 Originally, a *cohort* was a special unit of the Roman army (Lat. *cohors praetoriae* = 1000 soldiers).
3 It is difficult to present different activation levels graphically. For this reason figure 56 differentiates between high-frequency and low-frequency words only in terms of specific boxes around the access units.
4 There are two different versions of the TRACE model. TRACE I, the first version, essentially focused on speech perception and especially on the identification of phonemes from real speech. TRACE II, the 1986 version, integrates

word recognition into phoneme identification. It is this model that is described in the subsequent sections.

5 Originally, the framework according to which the TRACE model was set up was referred to as *interactive* or *spreading activation framework* (McClelland/Elman 1986: 2).

6 See McClelland/Elman 1986: 35ff for a discussion of the simulation of categorical perception in the TRACE model.

7 The initial phonemes of the targets, i.e. /p/ and /b/, were changed along a continuum, such as that presented in section 3.1.1., figure 40.

8 Further arguments in favour of the TRACE model concern its pedagogical usefulness. Goodfellow (1991:32) argues that language teaching involves the representation of lexical knowledge, and in particular, the integration of frequency and collocability. By establishing links of appropriate strength between two words the network model can represent these relationships most adequately.

9 In fact, Taft (1986:304) allows for the possibility of access codes other than the BOSS by putting in brackets 'primarily via their BOSS'.

10 The basic architecture of the model has been taken from Harris/Coltheart (1986:150). In addition to this model, a level of pattern detectors has been introduced which incorporates the idea of case distinctions and transgraphemic patterns (see below).

11 Essentially, the OCR-process involves a translation of a geometrical figure into a code that can be interpreted as one letter or several individual letters. More specifically and in terms of real computer applications, this means the translation of the contents of a graphics file (e.g. a .TIF-file, or a .GIF-file) into an ASCII-file. (TIF = Tagged Information File, GIF = Graphics Interchange Format, ASCII = American Standard Code of Information Interchange). In an ASCII-file each symbol can be unambiguously associated with an ASCII-value: A = 65, a = 97, B = 66, b = 98, etc. Hence, the ASCII-file corresponds to the level of grapheme detectors with the only exception that a distinction between upper and lower case is drawn. This distinction is made in a principled way: upper case letters = lower case letters minus 32.

12 See section 1.6. for a discussion of the differences between connectionism and conventional symbolic computation.

13 Because of the similarities between the search principles in Forster's model and the search for books in libraries, the Search model is often referred to as the *Library* model (see section 4.5.1.).

14 In 1987, Marslen-Wilsen showed, however, that the sentential context can excite but not inhibit word recognition (Marslen-Wilsen, 1987:92; also, see our discussion of the examples (48a) to (48c) in section 4.2.1.).

15 Note that Klatt (1981:23) uses the term 'lexical access', even though his model is meant to describe the process of speech perception.

Chapter 5

1 The performance of modern computer systems is measured in FLOPs (Floating Point Operations/Instructions per Second). Further common abbreviations are MFLOPs (Mega FLOPs = a million FLOPs), and GFLOPs (Giga FLOPs = a billion FLOPs).

2 Notational conventions:
(a) C# → CE# if #I/E: an E is appended to the final root consonant (C# → CE#) if an I or an E follows (if #I/E).
(b) ing: V[V _]: ing has the syntactic category V and attaches to verbal roots ([V _]).

3 Note that we always refer to machine-readable lexicons in the plural. This is due to the numerous ways of implementing such a store. While psycholinguists agree that there must be one uniform structure of the mental lexicon but disagree which one, computational linguists have yet not provided a general conception of a machine-readable lexicon. At present, there are many ways of implementing and accessing machine-readable lexicons, depending on the domain in which they operate and the purpose for which they have been designed (Boguraev/Briscoe 1989: 10ff).

4 In real-time a machine processes information without delay. This mode must be contrasted with the 'batch-mode', where the information is first forwarded to the machine, then processed, and the result is presented later.

5 The most commonly used input devices to OCR-systems are full-page scanners, while ASR-systems establish their connection to the outside world via microphones.

6 There are OCR-systems that can be taught to recognise certain patterns. However, these teaching sessions are extremely tedious for the human teacher, and they have to be done for every new hand-writing.

7 OCR-software used: WordScan, Version 1.08, Calera Recognition Systems, Inc.®

8 A real-time natural language processing system can be coupled with routines that interact with the user (asking questions, seeking confirmation, presenting ambiguities).

9 In 1988 computer memory cost only 10^{-8} of what it did in 1950 (Kurzweil 1990: 481).

10 RAM = *r*andom *a*ccess *m*emory, commonly referred to as 'working memory'.

11 In terms of computer programs 'pointers' are digits that determine the location of an item on an external storage device, such as a harddisk. They are generated and retrieved using the relevant commands of the programming language employed. For example, most LISP-dialects include the primitives WRITEPTR, for the generation, and READPTR, for the retrieval of pointers.

12 In Appendix C a small test-program written in LISP is introduced that illustrates the reduction of the system's performance on the basis of one operation applied to two differently complex lexical entries.

13 In fact, in English, type 3 words do not constitute more than 18% of all words. On the basis of a sample of 50.000 actual word forms and a root lexicon with morphological and orthographical alternation procedures, it has been established that 10% of all words undergo word-internal changes (e.g. *mak*-e+*ing*) and 8% undergo flanking changes (e.g. *watch*+(e)*s*). Roughly 2% of all words undergo both processes (e.g. *carries*; word-internal: carries → *carry*+*es*, flanking: *carry*+*s*).

14 The TAUM-Meteo system (TAUM = *T*raduction *A*utomatique de l'*U*niversite *M*ontreal) has a full-form lexicon that contains approximately 1.500 entries of primarily meteorological character, including idioms and place names used in this domain (Isabelle, 1987:263).

15 The access unit DIE exhibits the maximum degree of orthographical variation in English. In terms of morpho-graphemes it has to be presented in three different ways: DIE-s, DI-ed, and DY-ing.

16 dBASE is a registered trademark of Borland.

17 The term *discrimination network* is primarily used in computational linguistics and artificial intelligence. Computer scientists alternatively refer to this data structure as *trie*, a term that represents the affinity with trees but is derived from re-**trie**-val. However, in order to distinguish it from *tree*, it is pronounced as /ˈtraɪ/ (Smith, 1991:111).

18 For a discussion of the mechanism of transition networks and their augmentation by conditions which have to be coupled with the arcs (e.g. S-S or E-N-G are impossible continuations) see Winograd (1983:195ff).

19 The term "syllable" is misleading in this respect. The access units are not integrated into the network on the basis of their syllable structure; rather, they are represented in terms of units larger than single letters.

20 We will not introduce the compilation program in this book because it is described exhaustively in Deiß et al. (1990, Chapter five and Appendix C).

21 The term 'subnet' stands for 'subordinate network'.

22 The number three has proved to be very efficient for English: many words are fairly short and can thus be reached without accessing any subnet file, and, moreover, the main network remains relatively small in size. A further argument for confining the depth of the main net to three letters has to do with the generation of alternatives (see section 5.2.5.2. (e)). Nevertheless, this figure is arbitrary and has been chosen purely for practical reasons. Psychologically, there is nothing special about this value.

23 The following latency values are based on the partitioned cohort network used in LexEcon, which is introduced in chapter six. This cohort net contains ca. 25.000 access units as roots and a morphological component. All latencies include the time required for morphological analysis.

24 According to our classification in section 2 (figure 18), SYSTRAN's word store should not be referred to as 'dictionary' but as 'lexicon'.

25 In fact, Smith only lists thirty-one items for the binary tree, with OF being the top node, THE and FOR the next level, and so on.

26 We will come back to the typology of machine translation systems and their strategies of semantic interpretation in section 5.3.4.

27 In section 5.3.2. we will see that the information subsumed under the heading of 'morphology' is often also syntactic in character. For this reason we renamed the 'morphological' field the 'morpho-syntactic' field. Similar arguments, for example the influence of a verb's transitivity status on affixation, can be found in section 2.3.2.2.

28 Since the KIMMO-system and the augments to the original version are discussed in Ritchie et al. (1992:21ff), and, at length in Sproat (1992), we can dispense with a detailed introduction to two-level morphology in this book and refer the reader to these publications.

29 A special version of a unification grammar is McCord's *Slot Grammar*, which gives an enormous amount of control to the lexicon and thus reduces the complexity of syntactic rules (McCord, 1989:2). However, Slot Grammar is not meant as a general model of syntax processing but is intended as a grammar system to be used for source analysis in machine translation.

30 This example is based on Flickinger/Nerbonne's (1991:6) definition of lexical entries in HPSG.

31 The GPSG-notation A/B simply means constituent A with B missing from it. Hence VP/NP, to be read as "VP slash NP", is a VP without a NP.

32 Note that the term 'semantic' information again relates to the logical form, i.e. the argument structure of the predicate, but not to the detailed specification of the meaning.

33 The basic ingredients of the conceptual dependency theory are discussed in section 2.3.3.3. (e).

34 The term 'knowledge-based approach' is often used as a synonym for interlingua. However, some researchers refer to systems as 'knowledge-based' as soon as they incorporate explicit linguistic rules of any kind (Boguraev/Briscoe, 1989:4). We will use the term in Carbonell/Tomita's (1987) sense, which means that a system is capable of mapping a source text into a language-free meaning representation.

35 *LexEcon* stands for *Machine-Readable lexicon for Economy vocabulary.* It is a commercial product, and was developed by Klaus Deiß, Jürgen Handke, and Lothar Otto.

Chapter 6

1 At present only a fraction of the entries in the lexicon have been associated with semantic information, for demonstration purposes.

2 The comments in LexEcon depend on the target language. Thus, the translation into German uses German comments. Here is an explanation of the German lexical terms used: 'Linguistik' = 'linguistic information', 'Übersetzung' =

'translation', 'Synonyme' = 'synonyms', 'Phonetik' = 'phonetic information', 'Morphologie' = 'morphological structure', 'Bedeutung' = 'Meaning'. Furthermore, the menu-buttons exhibit the terms 'Abbruch' = 'quit', 'Beispiel' = 'example', 'Drucken' = 'print', and 'Speichern' = 'save'.

3 Windows is a registered trademark by Microsoft.

4 Borland and Soft Warehouse products are registered trademarks

5 Annotations: "Wort nicht gefunden" = "Word not found" "Wählen Sie eine Alternative" = "Choose an alternative"

6 Comments of this type have been dispensed with in LexEcon, since LexEcon is not a tutorial system but a commercial text-retrieval system. The usefulness of such comments has been shown in an intelligent language tutoring system by the authors of LexEcon. This program, called WIZARD, uses the same lexicon architecture and similar linguistic analysis algorithms.

7 See Appendix B 1 for more details.

8 Schank et al. (1980) propose a number of techniques for generating the semantic structure of unknown words. However, these techniques involve the use of a highly sophisticated knowledge base.

Chapter 7

1 The best known example of such a massively parallel computer is the Connection Machine Thinking Machines Inc.

2 All those readers familiar with computer programming and database organisation are stunned by the efficiency of the mental lexicon, especially since they know about the difficulties of implementing databases which allow fast access, manipulation of their entries, and which are theoretically unlimited in size.

Appendix

1 Henderson (1982: 8) adapted a slightly different classification from Gelb (1963) which distinguishes between *non-writing systems* (pictures), semasiographic *forerunners of true writing systems* that use symbols without direct reference to speech, and *full writing systems* of the phonographic type.

2 English, with a set of 16 vocalic and 24 consonantal phonemes, has over 4.000 different phonetic syllables as defined by phonemes alone, and more than 31.000 different phonetic syllables if prosodic variations are included (Pickett 1980: 194). Japanese, by contrast, allows only around 120 different syllables (Kurzweil 1990: 268). This is due to the smaller phoneme inventory (only 5 vocalic and 15 consonantal phonemes) and a limited set of phonotactic rules. Hence, Japanese is a much better candidate for a syllabic writing system than English.

3 The construction of LexEcon's first 5.000 entries, which were all handcrafted, took over a year.

4 MuLISP is a registered trademark of Soft Warehouse, Honululu, Hawaii, U.S.A. It is based on Common-LISP and is one of the most economic and efficient LISP-interpreters for the microcomputer. The exact relationship between muLISP and Common-LISP, and and the differences between them, are discussed in Deiß et al. (1990).

5 In the original LDOCE-format the index is presented as a superscript. However, the OCR-procedures can be influenced in such a way that they ignore superscripts and subscripts.

6 To refer to the LISP-code or parts of it the following notational conventions have been used: LISP-functions are written in capital letters, variables in small letters and italics. Global variables and variables with indefinite extent are represented between asterisks. Furthermore, all functions that belong to the same algorithm begin with a common initial letter (C = conversion, U = Utility, etc.).

7 Likewise the morphological information, i.e. an entry's word-class, is only stated once.

References

Abelson, Robert P.
1981 "Psychological Status of the Script Concept". *American Psychologist* 7: 715-729.

Aho, Alfred V. – John E. Hopcroft – Jeffrey D. Ullman
1987 *Data Structures and Algorithms*. New York: Addison-Wesley.

Aitchison, Jean
1987 *Words in the Mind. An Introduction to the Mental Lexicon*. Oxford: Basil Blackwell.

Aitchison, Jean
1992 *Introducing Language and Mind*. Harmondsworth: Penguin Books.

Akmajian, Adrian – Richard A. Demers – Robert M. Harnish
1984 *Linguistics. An Introduction to Language and Communication*. Cambridge, Mass.: MIT Press.
[1985] [2nd edition.]

Allen, James
1983 "ARGOT: A System Overview", in: Nicholas J. Cercone (ed.), 97-109.

Allen, James
1987 *Natural Language Understanding*. Menlo Park, California: Benjamin/ Cummings.

Allen, James
1989 "Natural Language Understanding", in: Avron Barr – Paul R. Cohen – Edward A. Feigenbaum (eds.), 195-239.

Allerhand, Michael
1987 *Knowledge-Based Speech Pattern Recognition*. London: Kogan Page Ltd.

Allport, Alan – Donald G. MacKay – Wolfgang Prinz – Eckart Scheerer (eds.).
1987 *Language Perception and Production*. London: Academic Press.

Allwood, Jens – Lars-Gunnar Anderson – Östen Dahl
1977 *Logic in Linguistics*. Cambridge University Press.

Altmann, Gerry T.M.
1990 "Cognitive Models of Speech Processing: An Introduction", in: Gerry T.M. Altmann (ed.), 1-23.

Anderson, John R.
1983 *The Architecture of Cognition*. Cambridge, Mass.: Harvard University Press.

Anderson, Richard C. – Rand J. Spiro – W.E. Montague (eds.)

1977 Schooling and the Acquisition of Knowledge. Hillsdale, New Jersey: Lawrence Erlbaum Ass.

Archangeli, Diana
1988 "Aspects of Underspecification Theory", *Phonology* 5: 183-207.

Arnold, Doug – Louis des Tombe
1987 "Basic Theory and Methodology in EUROTRA", in: Sergei Nirenburg (ed.), 114-135.

Austin, John L.
1962 *How to Do Things with Words*. Oxford: Clarendon Press.

Barkey, Reinhild – Lothar Lemnitzer – Wolf Paprotté
1989 Zur Entwicklung eines lexikgraphischen Werkzeuges. *Sprache und Datenverarbeitung* 13/1: 3-24.

Barr, Avron – Edward A. Feigenbaum (eds.)
1981 *The Handbook of Artificial Intelligence*, Volume I. London: Pitman.

Barr, Avron – Edward A. Feigenbaum (eds.)
1982 *The Handbook of Artificial Intelligence*, Volume II. London: Pitman.

Barr, Avron – Paul R. Cohen – Edward A. Feigenbaum (eds.)
1989 The Handbook of Artificial Intelligence, Volume IV. New York: Addison-Wesley.

Bauer, Laurie
1983 *English Word-formation*. Cambridge University Press.

Bischof, W.F.
1976 "Psychology of Language and Memory." in: Eugene Charniak – Yorick Wilks (eds.), 185-203.

Blank, Michelle A. – Donald J. Foss
1978 "Semantic Facilitation and Lexical Access during Sentence Processing", *Memory & Cognition* 6: 644-652.

Blatt, Achim – Karl-Heinz Freigang – Klaus Dirk Schmitz – Giesela Thome
1985 *Computer und Übersetzen, eine Einführung*. Hildesheim: Georg Olms.

Bock, J. Kathryn
1982 "Towards a Cognitive Psychology of Syntax", *Psychological Review* 89: 1-47.

Boguraev, Bran – Ted Briscoe
1989a "Natural Language Processing", in: Bran Boguraev – Ted Briscoe (eds.), 1-40.

Boguraev, Bran – Ted Briscoe
1989b "Utilising the LDOCE Grammar Codes", In: Bran Boguraev – Ted Briscoe (eds.), 85-116.

Boguraev, Bran – Ted Briscoe (eds.)
1989 Computational Lexicography for Natural Language Processing. London: Longman.

Borden, Gloria – Katherine Harris
1980 *A Speech Science Primer*. Baltimore Press.

Bosshardt, Hans-Georg (ed.)
1986 Perspektiven auf Sprache. Berlin, New York: de Gruyter.

Brachman, Ronald J.
1970 "On the Epistemological Status of Semantic Networks", in: Nicholas V. Findler (ed.), 3-46.

Bresnan, Joan (ed.)
1982 The Mental Representation of Grammatical Relations. Cambridge, Mass.: MIT Press.

Bumbaca, Frederico
1988 "Intelligent Computer-Assisted Instruction: A Theoretical Framework", *International Journal of Man-Machine Studies* (UK), 29: 227-255.

Butterworth, Brian
1983 "Lexical Representation", in: Brian Butterworth (ed.), 257-294.

Butterworth, Brian (ed.)
1983 Language Production Volume 2: Development, Writing and Other Language Processes. London: Academic Press.

Caramazza, Alfonso – G. Miceli – C. Silveri – A. Laudanna
1985 "Reading Mechanisms and the Organization of the Lexicon: Eevidence from Acquired Dyslexia", *Cognitive Neuropsychology* 2.1: 81-114.

Carbonell, Jaime G.
1970 "AI in CAI: An Artificial Intelligence Approach to Computer-Aided Instruction", *IEEE Transactions on Man-Machine Systems*, Vol. MMS- 11, No. 4: 190-202.

Carbonell, Jaime G. – M. Tomita
1987 "Knowledge-Based Machine Translation, the CMU Approach", in: Sergei Nirenburg (ed.), 68-89.

Carroll, John – Claire Grover
1989 "The Derivation of a Large Computational Lexicon for English from LDOCE", in: Bran Boguraev – Ted Briscoe (eds.), 117-133.

Cercone, Nicholas (ed.)
1983 Computational Linguistics. Oxford: Pergamon Press.

Chambers, Susan M. – Kenneth I. Forster
1975 "Evidence for Lexical Access in a Simultaneous Modelling Task", *Memory and Cognition* 3: 549-559.

Charniak, Eugene – Drew McDermott
1985 *Introduction to Artificial Intelligence*. New York: Addison-Wesley.

Charniak, Eugene – Christopher K. Riesbeck – Drew McDermott – James R. Meehan
1987 *Artificial Intelligence Programming*. Hillsdale, New Jersey: Lawrence Erlbaum Ass.

Charniak, Eugene – Yorick Wilks (eds.)
1976 Computational Semantics. Amsterdam: North-Holland.

Chomsky, Noam
1988 *Language and Problems of Knowledge*. Cambridge, Mass.: MIT Press.

Chomsky, Noam – Morris Halle
1968 *The Sound Pattern of English*. New York: Harper & Row.

Church, Kenneth W.
1987a "Phonological Parsing and Lexical Retrieval", in: Uli H. Frauenfelder – Lorraine K. Tyler (eds.), 53-70.

Church, Kenneth W.
1987b *Phonological Parsing in Speech Recognition*. Boston: Kluwer Academic Publishers.

Cohen, A. – Noteboom, S.G. (eds.)
1975 Structure and Process in Speech Perception. Heidelberg: Springer Verlag.

Cole, Peter – Jerry L. Morgan (eds.)
1975 Syntax and Semantics 3: Speech Acts. New York: Academic Press.

Cole, Ronald E. – Brian Scott
1974 "Towards a Theory of Speech Perception",. *Psychological Review* 81: 348- 374.

Collins, Allan M. – Elizabeth F. Loftus
1975 "A Spreading-Activation Theory of Semantic Processing", *Psychological Review* 82: 407-428.

Coltheart, Max
1978 "Lexical Access in Simple Reading Tasks", in: G. Underwood (ed.).: 151- 216.

Coltheart, Max – Karalyn Patterson – John C. Marshall (eds.)
1980 Deep Dyslexia. London: Routledge & Kegan Paul.

Comrie, Bernard
1981 *Language Universals and Linguistic Typology*. Oxford: Basil Blackwell.

Connine, Cynthia
1990 "Effects of Sentence Context and Lexical Knowledge in Speech Processing", in: Gerry T.M. Altmann (ed.), 281-294.

Cooper, William E. – R. Walker (eds.)
1979 Sentence Processing. Hillsdale, New Jersey: Lawrence Erlbaum Ass.

Crystal, David
1971 *Linguistics*. Harmondsworth: Penguin Books.

Crystal, David
1980 *Introduction to Language Pathology*. London: Edward Arnold.

Cullingford, Richard E. – Boyan A. Onyshkevych
1987 "An Experiment in Lexicon-Driven Machine Translation", in: Sergei Nirenburg (ed.), 278-301.

Cutler, Anne (ed.)
1982 *Slips of the Tongue and Language Production*. Amsterdam: De Gruyter.

Cutler, Anne – Jacques Mehler – Dennis Norris – Juan Segui
1987 "Phoneme Identification and the Lexicon", *Cognitive Psychology* 19: 141- 177.

Dauer, Rebecca
1987 "Phonetic and Phonological Components of Language Rhythm", *Proceedings of the 11th Congress of Phonetic Sciences*: 447-450.

Dede, Christopher
1986 "A Review and Synthesis of Recent Research in Intelligent Computer-Assisted Instruction", *International Journal of Man-Machine Studies*, 24 (4): 329-353.

Deiß, Klaus
1991 "Die Generierung komplexer KI-Programme", *Sprache und Datenverarbeitung* Nr. 14, 1-2/1990. Bonn: 23-48.

Deiß, Klaus – Jürgen Handke – Bodo Meyer
1990 *Professionelles Programmieren mit LISP*. Hamburg: McGraw-Hill.

Dell, Gary S.
1984 "A Spreading Activation Theory of Retrieval in Sentence Production", *Cognitive Science Technical Report*: University of Rochester.

Denes, Peter B. – Elliot Pinson
1963 *The Speech Chain*. New York: Anchor Press.

Dirven, Rene – Johan Vanparys (eds.)
1993 Current Approaches to the Lexicon. Frankfurt/Main: Peter Lang. (to appear).

Dunbar, George L.
1988 *The Cognitive Lexicon*. PhD Thesis. University of Edinburgh, Department of Psychology and Centre for Cognitive Science.

Durand, Jacques
1990 *Generative and Non-linear Phonology*. London: Longman.

Eco, Umberto (ed.)
1988 Meaning and Mental Representations. Bloomington.

Ellis, Andrew W.
1984 *Reading, Writing and Dyslexia: A Cognitive Analysis*. London: Lawrence Erlbaum.

Ellis, Andrew (ed.)
1985 Progress in the Psychology of Language. London: Lawrence Erlbaum Ass.

Elman, Jeffrey L. – James L. McClelland
1984 "The Interactive Activation Model of Speech Perception", in: Norman J. Lass (ed.), 337-374.

Emele, Martin – Ulrich Heid – Stefan Momma – Remi Zajac
1992 "Interactions between Linguistic Constraints: Procedural vs. Declarative Approaches", *Machine Translation* 7, No. 1-2: 61-98.

Emmorey, Karen D. – Victoria A. Fromkin
1988 "The Mental Lexicon", in: Frederic Newmeyer (ed.), 124-149.

Engdahl, Elisabeth
1978 "Word Stress as an Organizing Principle for the Lexicon", *Papers from the Parasession on the Lexicon (CLS)*. Chicago: Chicago Linguistic Society: 138-147.

Fant, Gunnar M. (ed.)
1963 A Motor Theory of Speech Perception. Proceedings of Speech Communication Science, Vol. 3. Stockholm: Royal Institute of Technology.

Feldman, J.A. – D.H. Ballard
1982 "Connectionist Models and Their Properties", *Cognitive Science* 6: 205-254.

Findler, Nicholas V. (ed.)
1979 Associative Networks. New York: Academic Press.

Flickinger, Dan – John Nerbonne
1991 "Inheritance and Complementation: A Case Study of *easy* Adjectives and Related Nouns". (lecture manuscript from the 3rd European Summer School in Language, Logic and Information. University of Saarbrücken, Germany, 1991).

Flores D'Arcais, Giovanni B.
1986 "Konzeptuelle Strukturen und das mentale Lexikon", in: Hans-Georg Bosshardt (ed.), 130-148.

Flores d'Arcais, Giovanni – Willem J. M. Levelt (eds.)
1970 Advances in Psycholinguistics. Amsterdam: North-Holland.

Fodor, Jerry A. – Thomas Bever – Merrill F. Garrett
1974 *The Psychology of Language*. New York: McGraw-Hill.

Fodor, Jerry A.

1983 *The Modularity of Mind. An Essay on Faculty Psychology.* Cambridge, Mass.: MIT Press.

Forster, Kenneth I.
1976 "Accessing the Mental Lexicon", in: R. Walker – Roger J. Wales (eds.), 257- 287.

Forster, Kenneth I.
1979 "Levels of Processing in Sentence Comprehension", in: William E. Cooper – E. Walker (eds.), 27-85.

Forster, Kenneth I. – Susan M. Chambers
1973 "Lexical Access and Naming Time", *Journal of Verbal Learning & Verbal Behaviour* 12: 627-635.

Forster, Kenneth I.
1981 "Priming and the Effects of Sentence and Lexical Context on Naming Time: Evidence for Autonomous Lexical Processing", *Quarterly Journal of Experimental Psychology* 33A: 465-496.

Foss, Donald J. – David T. Hakes
1978 *Psycholinguistics.* New York: Prentice-Hall.

Frauenfelder, Uli – Lorraine K. Tyler (eds.)
1987 Spoken Word Recognition. Cambridge, Mass.: MIT Press.

Fromkin, Victoria – Robert Rodman
1981 *An Introduction to Language.* New York: Holt, Rinehart and Winston.

Fry, Dennis B.
1979 *The Physics of Speech.* Cambridge University Press.

Garman, Michael
1990 *Psycholinguistics.* Cambridge University Press.

Garnham, Alan
1985 *Psycholinguistics.* London: Methuen & Co.

Gaur, Albertine
1984 *A History of Writing.* New York: Cross River Press.
[1992] [Revised Edition.]

Gazdar, Gerald – Ewan Klein – Geoffrey Pullum – Ivan Sag
1985 *Generalised Phrase Structure Grammar.* Oxford: Basil Blackwell.

Gazdar, Gerald – Chris Mellish
1989 *Natural Language Processing in LISP.* New York: Addison-Wesley.

Gimson, Alfred C.
1962 *Introduction to the Pronunciation of English.* London: Edward Arnold.

Goodfellow, Robin
1991 "Lexical CALL: An Approach to Vocabulary Processing and Retrieval", *Proceedings of the ICALL Workshop, UMIST*, September 1991: 28-41.

Grice, H. Paul
1975 "Logic in Conversation", in: Peter Cole – Jerry L. Morgan (eds.).

Griffith, P. L.
1987 *The Role of Phonological and Lexical Information in Word Recognition and Spelling*. Ann Arbour: University Microfilms International.

Grishman, Ralph
1986 *Computational Linguistics*. Cambridge University Press.

Gust, Helmar – Petra Ludewig – Mechthild Rickheit
1988 *Die Struktur des Lexikons für LILOG*. Stuttgart: IBM Deutschland GmbH, LILOG-REPORT 29.

Haarmann, Harald
1990 *Universalgeschichte der Schrift*. Frankfurt: Campus Verlag.

Handke, Jürgen
1989 *Natürliche Sprache: Theorie und Implementierung in LISP*. Hamburg: McGraw-Hill.

Handke, Jürgen
1991a "Lexikalische Datenbanken in natürlichsprachlichen Systemen", *Sprache und Datenverarbeitung* Nr. 14, 1-2/1990. Bonn: 49-64.

Handke, Jürgen
1991b "Partitionierte Kohortennetze in natürlichsprachlichen Systemen", *Sprache und Datenverarbeitung* Nr. 14, 1-2/1990. Bonn: 65-82

Hankamer, Jorge
1989 "Morphological Parsing and the Lexicon", in: William Marslen-Wilson (ed.), 392-408.

Hardyck, Curtis D. – Lewis F. Petrinovich
1970 "Subvocal Speech and Comprehension Level as a Function of the Difficulty Level of Reading Material", *Journal of Verbal Learning & Verbal Behaviour* 9: 647-652.

Harris, Catherine L.
1992 "Connectionism and Cognitive Linguistics", in: Noel E. Sharkey (ed.), 1- 27.

Harris, James Wesley
1983 *Syllable Structure and Stress in Spanish: A Non-linear Analysis*. Cambridge, Mass.: MIT Press.

Harris, Margaret – Max Coltheart
1986 *Language Processing in Children and Adults*. London: Routledge & Kegan Paul.

Hawkins, John A.
1986 *A Contrastive Typology of English and German*. Oxford: Blackwell.

Henderson, Leslie
1982 *Orthography and Word Recognition in Reading*. London: Academic Press.

Henderson, Leslie
1985 "Toward a Psychology of Morphemes", in: Andrew Ellis (ed.), 15-72.

Henschel, Renate – Iris Höser
1991 "Lexical and Structural Transfer with the Graph Transformation System GRACOLI", *Sprache und Datenverarbeitung Nr. 15, 1-2/1991*: 83-100.

Hindle, Donald
1983 "Deterministic Parsing of Syntactic Non-fluencies", *Proc. of the 21st Meeting of the Association of Computational Linguistics*: 123-128.

Hofstadter, Douglas
1979 *Gödel, Escher und Bach: Ein endloses geflochtenes Band*. Stuttgart: Klett Verlag.

Horrocks, Geoffrey
1987 *Generative Grammar*. London: Longman.

Huddleston, Rodney
1984 *Introduction to the Grammar of English*. Cambridge University Press.

Hulst, Harry van der – Norval Smith
1982 "An Overview of Autosegmental Phonology", in: Harry van der Hulst – Norval Smith (eds.), 1-46.

Hulst, Harry van der – Norval Smith (eds.)
1982 The Structure of Phonological Representations (Part I). Dordrecht: Foris.

Hurford, James R.
1983 *Semantics: A Coursebook*. Cambridge University Press.

Hutchins, William J.
1986 *Machine Translation: Past, Present, Future*. Chichester: Ellis Horwood.

Hyman, Larry M.
1975 *Phonology. Theory and Analysis*. New York: Holt, Rinehart and Winston.

Isabelle, Pierre
1987 "Machine Translation at the TAUM Group", in: Margaret King (ed.), 247-318.

Jackendoff, Ray
1983 *Semantics and Cognition*. Cambridge, Mass.: MIT Press.

Jackendoff, Ray
1990 *Semantic Structures*. Cambridge, Mass.: MIT Press.

Johnson-Laird, Philip N.
1987 "The Mental Representation of the Meaning of Words", in: Uli H. Frauenfelder – Lorraine K. Tyler (eds.), 189-212.

Johnston, J.C. – James L. McClelland
1973 "Visual Factors in Word Perception", *Perception and Psychophysics* 14: 365-370.

Johnston, J.C. – James L. McClelland
1980 "Experimental Tests of a Hierarchical Model of Word Identification", *Journal of Verbal Learning & Verbal Behaviour* 19: 503-524.

Kaplan, Ronald M. – Joan Bresnan
1982 "Lexical-Functional Grammar: A Formal System for Grammatical Representation", in: Joan Bresnan (ed.)

Karttunen, Lauri
1983 "KIMMO: A General Morphological Analyzer", *Texas Linguistics Forum* 22: 165-186.

Karttunen, Lauri – Ken Wittenburg
1983 "A Two-Level Morphological Analysis of English", *Texas Linguistics Forum* 22: 217-228..

Katz, Gerold G. – Jerry A. Fodor
1963 "The Structure of a Semantic Theory", *Language* 39: 170-210.

Katz, Gerold G. – Paul M. Postal
1964 *An Integrated Theory of Linguistic Descriptions*. Cambridge, Mass.: MIT Press.

Kavanagh, James – J. G. Mattingly (eds.)
1972 The Relationship between Speech and Reading. Cambridge, Mass.: MIT Press.

Kay, Martin
1977 "Morphological and Syntactic Analysis", in: Antonio Zampolli (ed.), 131- 234.

Kempke, Christian
1988 "Der neuere Konnektionismus", *Informatik-Spektrum* 11: 143-162.

Kempson, Ruth
1976 *Semantics*. Cambridge University Press.

King, Margaret (ed.)
1987 Machine Translation: The State of the Art. Edinburgh: Edinburgh University Press.

Kiparsky, Paul
1982 "From Cyclic Phonology to Lexical Phonology", in: Harry van der Hulst – Norval Smith (eds.), 131-175.

Klatt, Dennis H.
1979 "Speech Perception: a Model of Acoustic-Phonetic Analysis and Lexical Access", *Journal of Phonetics* 7/3: 279-312.

Klatt, Dennis H.
1981 "Lexical Representation for Speech Production and Perception", in: Terry Myers – John Laver – John Anderson (eds.), 11-31.

Klatt, Dennis H.
1989 "Review of Selected Models in Speech Perception", in: Wiliam Marslen-Wilson (ed.), 169-226.

Kleiman, Glenn M.
1975 "Speech Recoding in Reading". *Journal of Verbal Learning & Verbal Behaviour* 14: 323-339.

Koskenniemi, Kimmo
1983 *Two-Level Morphology: A General Computational Model for Word-Form Recognition and Production*. Ph.D. thesis, University of Helsinki.

Kunz, Gunnar C. – Franz Schott
1987 *Intelligente Tutorielle Systeme: Neue Ansätze der computerunterstützten Steuerung von Lehr-Lernprozessen*. Göttingen: Hogrefe Verlag.

Kurzweil, Raymond
1990 *The Age of Intelligent Machines*. Cambridge, Mass.: MIT Press.

Küstner, Andreas
1991 "Lexikonzugriff und Flektionsendungsanalyse in VIRTEX". *Sprache und Datenverarbeitung* Nr. 15, 1-2/1991. Bonn: 101-116.

Ladd, Scott R.
1986 *The Computer and the Brain*. New York: Bantam Books.

Ladefoged, Peter
1975 *A Course in Phonetics*. New York: Harcourt Brace Jovanovich, Inc.

Lahiri, Aditi – William Marslen-Wilson
1991 "The Mental Representation of Lexical Form: A Phonological Approach to the Recognition Lexicon". *Cognition*: 245-294.

Lakoff, George
1982 "Categories and Cognitive Models". Reproduced by LAUT (Linguistic Agency of Trier), Series A, No. 96.

Lakoff, George
1988 "Cognitive Semantics", in: Umberto Eco (ed.), 119-154.

Langacker, Ronald W.
1983 *Foundations of Cognitive Grammar. Vol. II. Semantic Structure*. Linguistic Agency of the University of Trier, Series A, No. 100.

Langacker, Ronald W.
1987 *Foundations of Cognitive Grammar. Vol. I*. Stanford: Stanford University Press.

Langacker, Ronald W.
1990 *Concept, Image, and Symbol: The Cognitive Basis of Grammar*. Berlin: Mouton de Gruyter.

Lass, Norman J. (ed.)
1976 Contemporary Issues in Experimental Phonetics. New York: Academic Press.

Lass, Norman J. (ed.)
1982 Speech and Language, Vol 7. New York: Academic Press.

Lass, Norman J. (ed.)
1984 Language and Speech. New York: Academic Press.

Lawler, Robert W. – Masoud Yazdani (eds.)
1987 Artificial Intelligence and Education, Volume 1: Learning Environments and Tutoring Systems. Norwood: Ablex.

Leech, Geoffrey
1974 *Semantics*. Harmondsworth: Penguin Books.

Lehnert, W. – M. Ringle (eds.)
1982 Strategies for Natural Language Processing. Hillsdale, New Jersey: Lawrence Erlbaum Ass.

Lehrberger, John – Laurent Bourbeau
1988 *Machine Translation*. Amsterdam: John Benjamins.

Lenneberg, Eric H.
1962 "Understanding Language without the Ability to Speak: a Case Report", *Journal of Abnormal and Social Psychology* 65: 419-425.

Lenneberg, Eric H.
1967 *Biological Foundation of Language*. New York: Wiley.

Levelt, Willem J.M.
1983 "Monitoring and Self-Repair in Speech", *Cognition* 14: 41-104.

Levelt, Willem J.M.
1989 *Speaking*. Cambridge, Mass.: MIT Press.

Levelt, Willem J.M. – Giovanni Flores d'Arcais (eds.)
1978 Studies in the Perception of Language. Chichester: Wiley.

Levinson, Stephen C.
1983 *Pragmatics*. Cambridge: Cambridge University Press.

Liberman, Alvin M.
1957 "Some Results of Research on Speech Perception", *Journal of the Acoustic Society of America* 28: 117-123.

Liberman, Alvin M. – E.S. Cooper – D.P. Shankweiler – M. Studdert-Kennedy
1967 "Perception of the Speech Code", *Psychological Review* 74: 431-461.

Liberman, Alvin M. – Katherine Safford Harris – Howard S. Hoffman – Belver C. Griffith
1957 "The Discrimination of Speech Sounds within and across Phoneme Boundaries", *Journal of Experimental Psychology* 54: 358-368.

Liberman, Alvin M. – E.S. Cooper – Katherine Safford Harris – P.F. Macneilage
1963 "A Motor Theory of Speech Perception", in: C. Gunnar M. Fant (ed.),

Lima, Susan D. – Alexander Pollatsek
1983 "Lexical Access via an Orthographic Code? The Basic Orthographic Syllable Structure (BOSS) Reconsidered", *Journal of Verbal Learning &Verbal Behaviour* 22: 310-332.

Lipka, Leonard
1992 *An Outline of English Lexicology*. Tübingen: Niemeyer Verlag.

Lipschutz, Seymour
1987 *Datenstrukturen*. Hamburg: McGraw-Hill.

Lobacz, Piotra
1984 *Processing and Decoding the Signal in Speech Perception*. Hamburg: Helmut Buske Verlag.

Lyons, John
1981. *Language, Meaning and Context*. Bungay: Fontana Paperbacks.

Maas, Heinz-Dieter
1987 "The MT System SUSY", in: Margaret King (ed.), 209-246.

MacKay, Donald G.
1970 "Mental Diplopia" in: Giovanni Flores D'Arcais – Willem J.M. Levelt (eds.), 76-100.

MacKay, Donald G.
1979 "Lexical Insertion, Inflection and Derivation: Creative Processes in Word Production", *Journal of Psycholinguistic Research 8:* 477-498.

Marchand, Hans
1969 *The Categories and Types of Present-Day English Word Formation*. München: Beck'sche Verlagsbuchhandlung.

Marcus, Mitchel P.
1980 *A Theory of Syntactic Recognition for Natural Language*. Cambridge, Mass.: MIT Press.

Marslen-Wilson, William
1987 "Functional Parallelism in Spoken Word Recognition", in: Uli H. Frauenfelder – Lorraine K. Tyler (eds.), 71-102.

Marslen-Wilson, William
1990 "Activation, Competition, and Frequency in Lexical Access", in: Gerry T.M. Altmann (ed.), 148-172.

Marslen-Wilson, William (ed.)
1989 Lexical Representation and Process. Cambridge, Mass.: MIT Press.

Marslen-Wilson, William – Lorraine K. Tyler
1980 "The Temporal Structure of Spoken Language", *Cognition* 8: 1-71.

Marslen-Wilson, William – Lorraine K. Tyler
1981 "Central Processes in Speech Understanding", *Philosophical Transactions of the Royal Society of London, B/295*: 317-332.

Marslen-Wilson, William – Lorraine K. Tyler – M. Seidenberg
1978 "Sentence Processing and the Clause Boundary", in: Willem J.M. Levelt – Giovanni Flores D'Arcais (eds.), 219 - 246.

Marslen-Wilson, William – Alan Welsh
1978 "Processing Interactions and Lexical Access during Word Recognition in Continuous Speech", *Cognitive Psychology* 10: 29-63.

Matthei, Eward – Thomas Roeper
1983 *Understanding and Producing Speech*. Glasgow: Fontana Paperbacks.

Matthews, Peter H.
1974 *Morphology*. Cambridge University Press.

McClelland, James L. – Jeffrey L. Elman
1986 "The TRACE Model of Speech Perception", *Cognitive Psychology* 18: 1-86.

McClelland, James L.
1988 "Connectionist Models and Psychological Evidence", *Journal of Memory and Language* 27: 107-123.

McCord, Michael C.
1980 "Using Slots and Modifiers in Logic Grammars for Natural Language", *Artificial Intelligence* 18: 327-367.

McCord, Michael C.
1989 "A New Version of Slot Grammar" *IBM Research Report RC 14506*. IBM Thomas Watson Research Center. P.O. Box 704. Yorktown Heights, New York 10598.

McNeill, David – Karen Lindig
1973 "The Perceptual Reality of Phonemes, Syllables, Words and Sentences", *Journal of Verbal Learning & Verbal Behaviour* 12: 419-430.

Mehler, Jacques
1981 "The Role of Syllables in Speech Processing: Infant and Adult Data", *Philosophical Transactions of the Royal Society of London 1981 – 295*: 333-352.

Mehler, Jacques – Eric C. Walker – Merrill F. Garrett (eds.)
1982 Perspectives on Mental Representation. Hillsdale, New Jersey: Lawrence Erlbaum Ass.

Mehler, Jacques – Jean Yves Dommergues – Uli H. Frauenfelder – Juan Segui
1981 "The Syllable's Role in Speech Segmentation", *Journal of Verbal Learning & Verbal Behaviour* 20: 298-305.

Mehler, Jacques – Emmanuel Dupoux – Juan Segui
1990 "Constraining Models of Lexical Access", in: Gerry T. Altmann (ed.): 236-262.

Mehlhorn, Kurt
1988 *Datenstrukturen und effiziente Algorithmen*. Stuttgart: Teubner Verlag.

Meyer, David E. – Roger W. Schvaneveldt – Margaret G. Ruddy
1974 "Functions of Graphemic and Phonemic Codes in Visual Word Recognition", *Memory and Cognition* 2: 309-321.

Miller, George A.
1981 *Language and Speech*. San Francisco: Freeman.

Miller, George A. – Philip N. Johnson-Laird
1976 *Language and Perception*. Cambridge, Mass.: MIT Press.

Minsky, Marvin
1975 "A Framework for Representing Knowledge", In.: Patrick Henry Winston (ed.): 211-277.

Moore, Brian C.
1977. *Introduction to the Psychology of Hearing*. London: Macmillan Press.

Morton, John
1969 "Interaction of Information in Word Recognition", *Psychological Review* 76: 165-178.

Morton, John
1970 "A Functional Model of Human Memory", in: Donald A. Norman (ed.), 203-254.

Morton, John – John Long
1976 "Effect of Word Transitional Probability on Phoneme Identification", *Journal of Verbal Learning & Verbal Behaviour* 15: 43-51.

Morton, John – John C. Marshall (eds.)
1979 Psycholinguistics 2: Structures and Processes. Cambridge, Mass.: MIT Press.

Morton, John
1979 "Word Recognition" in: John Morton – John C. Marshall (eds.), 107-156.

Morton, John – Karalyn Patterson
1980 "A New Attempt at an Interpretation, or, an Attempt at a New Interpretation", in: Max Coltheart – Karalyn Patterson – John C. Marshall (eds.), 91-118.

Morton, John
1982 "Disintegrating the Lexicon: An Information Processing Approach.", in: Mehler, Jacques – Eric C. Walker – Merrill F. Garrett (eds.), 89-109.

Myers, Terry – John Laver – John Anderson (eds.)
1981 The Cognitive Representation of Speech (= Advances in Phonology 7). Amsterdam: North- Holland.

Myers, Terry – John Laver – John Anderson (eds.)
1981 *The Cognitive Representation of Speech.* Amsterdam u.a.: North-Holland

Myers-Scotton, Carol
1993a. "Language Processing and the Lexicon in the Bilingual Brain". (unpublished manuscript of a key-note lecture given at the LAUD-symposium at the University of Duisburg, 1993)

Myers-Scotton, Carol
1993b "Language Processing and the Lexicon in Bilinguals", To appear in: René Dirven – Johan Vanparys (eds.)

Newmeyer, Frederick (ed.)
1988 Linguistics: The Cambridge Survey. Cambridge: Cambridge University Press.

Nirenburg, Sergei
1987 "Knowledge and Choices in Machine Translation", in: Sergei Nirenburg (ed.), 1-21.

Nirenburg, Sergei (ed.)
1987 Machine Translation. Cambridge: Cambridge University Press.

Norman, Donald A. (ed.)
1970 Models of Human Memory. New York: Academic Press.

Norman, Donald A. – David E. Rumelhardt
1975 *Explorations in Cognition.* San Francisco, Freeman.

Norris, Dennis
1986 "Word Recognition: Context Effects without Priming", *Cognition* 22: 93-136.

Obermeier, Klaus K.
1989 *Natural Language Processing Technologies in Artificial Intelligence.* New York: Ellis Horwood.

Ohlsson, Stellan
1987 "Some Principles of Intelligent Tutoring", in: Robert W. Lawler – Masoud Yazdani (eds.), 203-237.

Otto, Lothar
1991 "Mehrsprachige KI-Programme: LISP und C verknüpft", *Sprache und Datenverarbeitung* Nr. 14, 1-2 1990, 13-22.

Palmer, Frank R.
1971 *Grammar.* Harmondsworth: Penguin Books.

Palmer, Frank R.
1981 *Semantics.* Cambridge University Press.

Perfetti, Charles Albert – Deborah McCutchen
1982 "Speech Processing in Reading", in: Norman J. Lass (ed.), Vol. 7, 237-269.

Pickett, James M.
1980 *The Sounds of Speech Communication.* Baltimore: University Park Press.

Pinkal, Manfred
1993 *Logic and the Lexicon.* Dordrecht: Kluwer Academic Publishers.

Pisoni, David B. – J.R. Sawusch
1975 "Some Stages of Processing in Speech Perception", in: A. Cohen – S.G. Noteboom (eds.), 16-35

Pustejovsky, James – Bergler, S. (eds.)
1992 Lexical Semantics and Knowledge Representation: Proceedings of the 1st Siglex Workshop, Berkeley, California, June 17th 1991.

Pylyshyn, Zenon W.
1984 *Computation and Cognition. Toward a Foundation for Cognitive Science.* Cambridge, Mass.: MIT Press.

Quirk, Randolph – Sidney Greenbaum – Geoffrey Leech – Jan Svartvik
1985 *A Comprehensive Grammar of the English Language.* London: Longman.

Rembold, Ulrich (ed.)
1987 *Einführung in die Informatik.* München: Hanser Verlag.

Rickheit, Gert – Hans Strohner
1993 *Grundlagen der kognitiven Sprachverarbeitung.* Tübingen: Francke Verlag.

Ritchie, Graeme D.
1987 "The Lexicon", in: Pete Whitelock – Mary McGee Wood. – Harold Somers – Rod Johnson – Paul Bennett (eds.), 225-256.

Ritchie, Graeme D. – Graham J. Russel – Alan W. Black – Stephen G. Pulman
1992 *Computational Morphology*. Cambridge, Mass.: MIT Press.

Rosch, Eleanor
1978 "Principles of Categorization", in: Elanor Rosch – Barbara B. Lloyd (eds.)

Rosch, Eleanor – Lloyd, Barbara B. (eds.)
1978 Categorization and Cognition. Hillsdale, New Jersey: Lawrence Erlbaum Ass.

Rubenstein, Herbert – Lonnie Garfield – Jane A. Millikan
1970 "Homographic Entries in the Internal Lexicon", *Journal of Verbal Learning & Verbal Behaviour* 9: 487-494.

Rubenstein, Herbert – Spafford S. Lewis – Mollie A. Rubenstein
1971 "Evidence for Phonemic Recoding in Visual Word Recognition", *Journal of Verbal Learning & Verbal Behaviour* 10: 645-657.

Rumelhart, David E.
1980 "Schemata: The Building Blocks of Cognition", in: Rand J. Spiro – Bertram Bruce – William F. Brewer (eds.), 33-58.

Rumelhart, David E. – Andrew Ortony
1977 "The Representation of Knowledge in Memory", in: Richard C. Anderson – Rand J. Spiro – W.E. Montague (eds.), 99-135.

Salton, Gerard – Michael J. McGill.
1987 *Information Retrieval - Grundlegendes für Informationswissenschaftler*. Hamburg: McGraw-Hill.

Samuel, A. G.
1986 "The Role of the Lexicon in Speech Perception", in: R.C. Schwab – H.C. Nusbaum (eds.), 89-111.

Scarborough, Don L. – Charles Cortese – Hollis S. Scarborough
1977 "Frequency and Repetition Effects in Lexical Memory", *Journal of Experimental Psychology* 3: 1-17.

Schade, Ulrich
1992 *Konnektionismus*. Opladen: Westdeutscher Verlag.

Schank, Roger C. (ed.)
1975 *Conceptual Information Processing*. Amsterdam: North-Holland.

Schank, Roger C. – Robert P. Abelson
1977 *Scripts, Plans, Goals and Understanding*. Hillsdale, New Jersey: Lawrence Erlbaum Ass.

Schank, Roger C. – Jaime G. Carbonell
1979 "The Gettysburg Address: Representing Social and Political Acts", in: Nicholas A. Findler (ed.)

Schank, Roger C. – Michael Lebowitz – Lawrence Birnbaum
1980 "An Integrated Understander", *American Journal of Computational Linguistics* 6, No. 1: 13-30.

Schank, Roger C. – Christopher K. Riesbeck
1981 *Inside Computer Understanding*. New Jersey: Lawrence Erlbaum Ass.

Schwab, R.C. – H.C. Nusbaum (eds.)
1986 Pattern Recognition by Humans and Machines. San Diego: Academic Press.

Schwarz, Monika
1992 *Einführung in die Kognitive Linguistik*. Tübingen: Francke Verlag.

Schwind, Camilla
1986 "Overview of an Intelligent Language Tutoring System", *CIIAM 86: Proceedings of the Second International Conference on Artificial Intelligence*, Marseilles, 1-5 Dec 1986: 389-407.

Segui, Juan – Emmanuel Dupoux – Jacques Mehler
1990 "The Role of the Syllable in Speech Segmentation, Phoneme Identification and Lexical Access", in: Gerry T. Altmann (ed.), 263-280.

Selkirk, Elisabeth O.
1982 *The Syntax of Words*. Cambridge, Mass.: MIT Press.

Selkirk, Elisabeth O.
1984 *Phonology and Syntax*. Cambridge, Mass.: MIT Press.

Sells, Peter
1985 *Lectures on Contemporary Syntactic Theories*. Stanford: Center for the Study of Language and Information.

Sharkey, Noel (ed.)
1992 *Connectionist Natural Language Processing*. Dordrecht: Kluwer Academic Publishers.

Shillcock, Richard
1990 "Lexical Hypotheses in Continuous Speech", in: Gerry T. Altmann (ed.), 24- 49.

Slobin, Dan I.
1971 *Psycholinguistics*. London: Scott/Foresman.

Small, Steven L. – Garrison W. Cotrell – Michael K. Tanenhaus (eds.)
1988 *Lexical Ambiguity Resolution*. San Mateo, California: Morgan Kaufmann Publishers.

Smith, George W.
1991 *Computers and Human Language*. Oxford: Oxford University Press.

Sowa, John F.
1984 *Conceptual Structures*. New York: Addison-Wesley.

Sowa, John F.
1992 "Logical Structures in the Lexicon", in: James Pustejovsky – S. Bergler (eds.), 39-60.

Spiro, Rand J. – Bertram Bruce – William F. Brewer (eds.)
1980 *Theoretical Issues in Reading Comprehension*. Hillsdale, N.J.: Erlbaum

Sproat, Richard
1992 *Morphology and Computation*. Cambridge, Mass.: MIT Press.

Stachowiak, Franz J.
1979 *Zur semantischen Struktur des subjektiven Lexikons*. München.

Stemberger, Joseph Paul
1982 *The Lexicon in a Model of Language Production*. Ann Arbour: University Microfilms International.

Stevens, Kenneth N.
1968 "On the Relations between Speech Movements and Speech Perception", *Zeitschrift für Phonetik, Sprachwissenschaft und Kommunikationsforschung* 21: 102-106.

Stevens, Kenneth N.
1972 "Segments, Features and Analysis by Synthesis, Language by Ear and Eye", in: James F. Kavanagh – J.G. Mattingly (eds.), 47-52.

Stevens, Kenneth N. – A.S. House
1972 "Speech Perception", in: J. Tobias (ed.), 3-62.

Studdert-Kennedy, Michael
1976 "Speech Perception", in: Norman J. Lass (ed.), 243-293.

Taft, Marcus
1979 "Lexical Access via an Orthographic Code: The Basic Orthographic Syllable Structure", *Journal of Verbal Learning & Verbal Behaviour* 18: 21-39.

Taft, Marcus
1986 "Lexical Access Codes in Visual and Auditory Word Recognition", *Language & Cognitive Processes* 1: 297-308.

Taft, Marcus – Kenneth I. Forster
1976 "Lexical Storage and Retrieval of Polymorphemic and Polysyllabic Words", *Journal of Verbal Learning & Verbal Behaviour* 15: 607-620.

Tobias, J. (ed.)
1972 Foundations of Modern Auditory Theory. Vol. 2. New York: Academic Press.

Tucker, Allen B.
1987 "Current Strategies in Machine Translation Research and Development", in: Sergei Nirenburg (ed.), 22-41.

Tyler, Lorraine K.
1981 "Serial and Interactive Parallel Theories of Sentence Structure Processing", *Theoretical Linguistics* 8: 29-65.

Tyler, Lorraine K. – Uli H. Frauenfelder
1987 "The Process of Spoken Word Recognition: An Introduction", in: Uli H. Frauenfelder – Lorraine K. Tyler (eds.), 1-20.

Underwood, G. (ed.)
1978 Strategies of Information Processing. London: Academic Press.

Wahlster, Wolfgang – Matthias Hecking – Christel Kemke
1988 "SC: Ein intelligentes Hilfssystem für SINIX", in: Bernard Bollan – Wolfgang J. Paul – Alwine Schmitt (eds.), 81-100.

Walker, R. – Roger J. Wales (eds.)
1976 New Approaches to Language Mechanisms. Amsterdam: North-Holland.

Waltz, David
1982 "The State of the Art in Natural Language Understanding", in: W. Lehnert – M. Ringle (eds.), 3-32.

Warren, Richard M.
1970 "Perceptual Restoration of Missing Speech Sounds", *Science* 167: 392-393.

Warren, Richard M. – Rosylin P. Warren
1970 "Auditory Illusions and Confusions", *Scientific American* 223: 30-36.

Watson, Mark
1991 *Common LISP Modules. Artificial Intelligence in the Era of Neural Networks and Chaos Theory*. Heidelberg: Springer Verlag.

Wheeler, Peter J.
1987 "SYSTRAN", in: Margaret King (ed.), 193-208.

Whitelock, Pete – Mary M. Wood – Harold Somers – Rod Johnson – Paul Bennett (eds.)
1987 *Linguistic Theory and Computer Applications*. New York: Academic Press

Winograd, Terry
1972 *Understanding Natural Language*. New York: Academic Press.

Winograd, Terry
1983 *Language as a Cognitive Process. Volume I: Syntax*. New York: Addison-Wesley.

Winograd, Terry – Fernando Flores
1986 *Understanding Computers and Cognition*. New York: Addison-Wesley.

Winston, Patrick Henry (ed.)
1975 The Psychology of Computer Vision. New York: McGraw-Hill.

Winston, Patrick Henry
1984 *Artificial Intelligence*. New York: Addison-Wesley.

Winston, Patrick Henry – Berthold Klaus Paul Horn
1984 *LISP*. New York: Addison-Wesley.

Wolff, S.
1984 *Lexical Entries and Word Formation*. Bloomington: Indiana University Linguistics Club.

Zampolli, Antonio (ed.)
1977 Linguistic Structures Processing. Amsterdam: North-Holland.

Zähner, Christoph
1991 "Foundations of ICALL", *Proceedings of the ICALL Workshop, UMIST*, September 1991: 118-126.

Zwitserlood, Pienie
1989 "The Locus of the Effects of Sentential-Semantic Context in Spoken-Word Processing", *Cognition* 32: 25-64.

Index

abstract-logographic 317
abstract-logographic symbol 317
access file 210; 240; 241; 244; 254; 255; 256; 257; 258; 263; 264; 266; 267
access unit 23; 62; 113; 237; 241; 254; 331
acoustic context 121
acoustic cues 21; 119; 121; 134; 135
Activate and Check model 159; 195; 196; 197; 198; 199; 202; 205
activation levels 176; 179; 193; 198; 204
activation threshold 45; 94
activation value 44; 45
active theories of speech perception 133; 134; 135; 137; 138
addressed morphology model 61
affix 26; 109
affix lexicon 108; 109
affixation 27; 78
agglutinative 60
ambiguity 3; 4; 6; 9; 10; 14
ambiguity resolution 9; 15
ambisyllabicity 74; 75; 156
analysis-by-synthesis theory of speech perception 136; 137
antonymy 88; 89; 90; 93; 106
arcs 94
argument structure 82
ASR 143; 154; 230; 231; 295
association 246; 251
attribute-value pair 278; 282
auditory system 125
automatic speech recognition 143; 154; 230; 231; 295
autonomy model 40; 160
autosegmental phonological representation 73

backtracking 9
basic-level categories 99
basic-level results 99
batch-mode processing 356
binarity 91
binary antonyms 89
binary search 248; 249; 251
bird song 139
blackboard 185
blends 70; 73
BOSS 158; 159; 160; 196; 197; 198; 199; 204; 219
bottom-up 40; 115; 160
bottom-up-priority 178
bound morpheme 25; 52

CAI 13
case-change 116; 128
categorical perception 122; 123; 124; 135; 138; 188
CD-theory 36; 37; 103; 104; 106; 286
character tree 254; 255
checking model 216; 217; 218; 219
Chinese characters 318
circumfix 27
closed-class 25; 57
co-operative principle 33
coarse-grained models 155
coarticulation 135; 139
coda 73; 74
cognitive diagnosis 33
cognitive science 2; 14; 15; 19; 39; 97
cohort 374
cohort model 163; 172; 173; 174; 175; 176; 177; 178; 189; 191; 192; 195; 196; 197; 205; 218
cohort network 256; 257; 258; 259; 265; 300; 305, partitioned 258; 259; 261; 264; 265; 267; 268; 269; 270; 271

common ground 32
communication 17; 39; 49
modes of 17; 18
communicative goal 32
competence 1; 33
compounding 56
comprehension 118
computational adequacy 171; 191; 192
computational approach 2
concavities 130; 145
concept 37; 86; 87
conceptual dependency theory 36; 37; 103; 104; 106; 286
conceptual distance 17
conceptual representation 29; 30; 31; 36; 38
conceptualising 36; 41
connection machine 42
connectionism 42; 43; 44; 312
connectionist framework 43; 44; 46
connectionist models 145
connections 43; 44
consonantal doubling 229; 236; 238; 274; 275
constriction 120
context-free grammar 279
contextual effect 170; 172; 173; 177; 178; 187; 189; 190; 198; 202; 207; 215; 216; 218; 269
continuation class 61; 79; 301; 325; 333
conventional computing 42; 43
conversational implicature 34
Crete Linear B 319; 320
cross-modal effects 206; 207
cross-modal link 160
cross-modal priming 153

data file 240; 244; 256; 257; 260; 261; 263; 300
database 235; 247; 251
declarative representation 289; 290
default inheritance network 291
default value 101
deletion 235
derivation 55
derivative 26; 27
dictionary,
entries 62
general 49; 50; 51
machine-readable 49
meaning specification 65
phonological specification 63
syntactic specification 64
types of 49; 61
diphonic clusters 158
direct access 148; 149; 150; 151; 208; 211
direct approach to MT 285
directed acyclic graph 278
disambiguation 303; 304; 308; 310
disambiguation lexicon 304; 305
discourse model 32
discrimination network 250; 251; 252; 253; 254; 256; 267; 277; 287; 291
discrimination-net phase 148
distinctive features 75
distorted input 170; 175; 176; 185; 192; 202; 204; 271
distortion 117; 131
dual access 151

E-deletion 238; 274; 275
E-insertion 224; 225; 238; 251; 274
editing 235
Egyptian hieroglyphs 317; 320; 321
encodedness 134; 138
error handling 306
EUROTRA 242; 291
exceptional words 150; 374
exchange errors 51; 73
excitatory connections 45; 46
expert manager 143

F2-transition 122; 125; 134; 140
feature buffer 145

feature detector models 144; 146
feature detectors 140; 160
feature theories 91; 93; 94; 96; 98; 106
feature-based grammar 279
file administration 250; 255
file compilation 254
filtering 126
fine-grained models 155
finite-state transition network 277; 278
flanking change 275; 377; 303
font 373
formants 119; 121
frames 30; 100; 101; 102; 103; 106
free morpheme 25; 52
frequency effect 166; 167; 170; 172; 175; 176; 188; 192; 198; 202; 210; 213; 214; 215; 220; 267
frequency of occurrence 166; 217
full listing hypothesis 53; 60
full-form lexicon 53; 57; 58; 236; 242; 243; 251; 272
full-forms 57
functional structure 282
fundamental frequency 119; 121
fuzziness 99

garden-path effect 6
general 36; 39; 47
generalised phrase structure grammar 280; 281
geometrical cues 130; 145
GPSG 280; 281; 282
gradable antonyms 89
grammar 25
grammatical encoding 69
graph 245; 246; 251
directed acyclic 278
grapheme 20; 125; 126
grapheme detectors 200; 201
graphological specification 76
graphotactic knowledge 199
graphotactics 129

handle 263; 264; 266; 271
head-driven phrase structure grammar 280; 281
HEARSAY 185
heavy syllable 72
hieroglyphs 317; 320
high-frequency dictionary 268
high-level segmentation 154
Hiragana 320
holistic approach 15; 16; 126; 127
holistic patterns 147
homonyms 52
homophone effect 168; 198
homophones 149; 168; 198
HPSG 280; 281
hyphenation 14; 331
hyponymy 88; 89; 90; 93; 96; 102; 106

I-to-Y change 238; 274; 310
ICAI 13; 33
ICALL 13
ideogram 317
ideographic symbol 317
IFSP technique 189; 190
illocutionary force 33
ILTS 13
image-schema 98
immediate dominance rule 281
incremental 41; 42
incremental processing 226
index 249; 250; 263
indirect access 148; 149; 150; 151; 208; 209
indirect MT system 285
infant 141
infant speech processing 156
inference 30; 106
infix 26
information retrieval 12; 49
inhibitory connections 45; 46
insertion 232; 235; 248; 250; 261
inter-speaker variation 121

interactive 41; 115
interactive lexicon editing 323; 324
interactive model 160
interface structure 291
interlingua 270; 273; 286; 288; 292; 378
interlingua system 270; 273; 285; 287
internal dynamics 312
ITS 13

juncture 22; 156

Kanji 320
Katakana 320
KIMMO 251; 254; 278

LAFS 222
language acquisition 2; 8; 9
language comprehension 19
language production 19
LDOCE 62; 63; 326; 328; 329; 330; 331; 339; 340
legality effect 168
lemma 28; 69; 70; 71; 80; 343
length effect 166; 172; 175; 192; 207; 215; 270
letter-mediated approach 126
LexEcon 259; 260; 295; 296; 297; 305; 308; 322; 358
lexical processing in LexEcon 297
post-lexical processing in LexEcon 298
pre-lexical processing in LexEcon 296
lexeme 25; 52; 55; 90; 108
lexical access 23; 24
lexical acquisition 313
lexical ambiguity 5; 15
lexical context 216
lexical decision 196
lexical decision task 150; 164; 166; 168; 172
lexical effect 164; 170; 190
lexical entry 23; 50; 51; 69; 70; 113
lexical pointer 80
lexical processing 113
lexical retrieval 24; 69; 162; 163; 191; 205; 212; 214; 219; 220
lexical specification 113
lexical-functional grammar 280; 282
lexicality effect 168; 172; 174; 187; 188; 198; 202; 210; 214; 215; 265
lexicon compiler 322
lexicon construction 227
lexicon conversion 323; 330; 333; 340, automatic 326; 329
lexicon editing 234; 307
lexicon testing 234; 340
lexicon use 227
lexicon,
affix 108; 109
full-form 53; 57; 58; 236; 242; 243; 251; 272
general 49; 50; 51; 80; 90
machine-readable 53; 58; 80; 112; 227; 228; 229; 236; 237; 240; 295
mental 49; 50; 51; 52; 68; 112; 254; 295
morpho-graphemic 53
root 53; 54; 57; 58; 59; 108; 237
LFG 280; 282
library model 374
light syllable 72
linear list 246; 247; 251; 252; 267; 269
linear order 245
linguistic approach 1
linguistic universals 2
links 43; 44; 94
LISP 330
listening 125
local context 298; 303; 308
logical form 29
logogen 211; 212; 213
logogen model 193; 211; 212; 213; 214; 216; 217; 218
logographic 113
lookahead 41; 42

loop 130; 145
low-level cues in OCR 130
low-level processes 18; 20; 21; 22; 36; 41; 47

machine translation 11; 112; 240; 285
machine-readable dictionary 49
machine-readable lexicon 53; 58; 80; 112; 227; 228; 229; 236; 237; 240; 295
major sentence 82
man-machine interface 11; 17
markedness 90
masking technique 164; 169
master file 210
memory management 235; 237; 241; 255; 264; 271; 294
mental 23
mental lexicon 23; 49; 50; 51; 52; 68; 112; 254; 295
meronymy 90
metrical tier 76
MFLOP 224
minimal listing hypothesis 53; 59; 60
model construction 32; 34
modular approach 15; 16; 17
monitoring task 165
monosyllabic 340
morph 26
morpheme 23; 25; 36; 52
morpho-grapheme 53; 58; 59; 241; 243; 301
morpho-graphemic lexicon 53
morpho-phoneme 371
morphological analysis 25
morphological processes 25; 36; 55
morphological specification 77; 78
morphology 5; 36; 71
MOS-Technique 224
motor theory of speech perception 136; 137
multiple-access-phenomenon 253
multitasking 226

naming task 164; 167
natural language 369
neoclassical roots 78
neural network 44
neural pattern 137; 139
neurolinguistics 8
nodes 44; 94; 97
nominal concept 94
non-interactive 40
non-segmental 63; 72
non-thematic subject 282
non-word 168; 169; 173; 174; 187; 190
nucleus 73

OCR 21; 130; 144; 145; 204; 230; 231; 295
OED 29; 62; 63; 66; 68; 81
onset 72; 73; 74
open-class 25; 54; 57; 302
optical character recognition 21; 130; 144; 145; 204; 230; 231; 295
orthographic phase 149
orthographical alternation 58; 59
orthographical features 145
orthographical variants 128
orthographical variation 239; 274; 303

paradigmatic sense relation 88
paralinguistic knowledge 314
parallel 125; 132; 143
parallel distributed processing 44
parallel processing 9; 10; 42; 147; 225; 226; 312
PARSIFAL 42
parsing 25; 27; 36
partition 245
partitioning 38; 70; 258; 259; 266; 294; 304
passive theories of speech perception 133; 138; 141
PDP-model 44
peak 73; 74

perception 118
performance 1; 10; 32; 33
performative verbs 33
phone 4; 74
phoneme 4; 5; 23; 75; 119; 124; 125; 131; 132; 134; 136; 139; 142; 147; 153; 155; 156; 158
phoneme detectors 181; 184; 186; 191; 200; 201
phoneme monitoring 165
phoneme restoration 170
phonemics 369
phonetic error 75
phonetic/phonological segmentation 153
phonetics 4
phonological recoding 149; 150; 151; 208
phonological specification 72; 74; 75; 76
phonology 5; 71
phonotactic knowledge 142; 187
pictograph 316; 317; 318
pointer 61; 69; 71; 80; 81; 109; 237; 244; 249; 256; 257
polysyllabic 340
polysynthetic language 61
pragmatic interpretation 33; 34
pragmatically-based ambiguity 7; 14
pragmatics 7
pre-lexical processing 205
pre-lexical unit 155
predicative concept 103; 106
prefix 26; 60
prime 164
priming task 164
primitive actions 37; 104
procedural representation 283; 289; 290
processing unit 43; 44; 45; 180
properties of a module 15
property inheritance 94; 95; 96; 100
prototype 98; 99; 100; 101
prototype results 98
prototype theory 97; 98; 99; 100; 101
prototypical member 98; 99
pseudo-affixation 253
pseudo-homophone effect 150
pseudo-homophones 150; 168; 169; 198; 374
pseudo-parallelism 42
psycholinguistic approach 2
psychological adequacy 171; 191; 192

quantal theory of speech perception 142

RAM 235; 376
readpointer 80
real-time processing 232; 376
recency effect 166; 267
recognition point 172; 174; 192
referential ambiguity 6
referential relation 86; 88
regularity effect 167; 168; 199
relational antonyms 90
relational database 246
relative pronoun deletion 8
resyllabification 71
rhyme monitoring 165
rime 72
root 14; 25; 54; 57; 77; 301
root lexicon 53; 54; 57; 58; 59; 108; 237

SARAH 157
scenes 101; 102
scripts 100; 101; 102
strong 102
weak 102
search 232; 235; 247; 248; 250; 251; 255; 258
search efficiency 246; 248; 251; 255; 264; 265
search model 163; 189; 193; 207; 209; 210; 211; 214; 216
segmental phonology 72

segmental tier 74; 75
segmentation 22; 152; 154
selectional restrictions 29; 65; 83
selective adaptation 140
semantic ambiguity 14
semantic distance 95
semantic interpretation 29; 30; 32; 36
semantic networks 30; 94; 95; 96; 97; 98; 100; 103
semantic representation 270; 287; 288; 291; 292; 293
semantic specification 80; 86; 90
semiotic triangle 87
sense relation 86; 88; 89; 90; 93; 99
senses 29; 52; 68; 93
sequential search 247; 248; 250
serial 40; 115; 132; 160
serial processing 9
shadowing technique 151; 165; 173
sight-vocabulary phase 148
skeletal tier 74
slash feature 281
slot grammar 378
slot-filling-mechanism 286; 287
sorting 235; 249
speech perception 21; 119; 131; 132; 135
speech production 133; 134; 135
stack-principle 8
stem 25; 26; 27; 52
stem dictionary 268
stress-timed 156
strong linguistic reality 155
structural ambiguity 5; 6; 14
sub-lexicons 109
sub-segmental tiers 75
subcategorisation 82
subcategorisation-frame 64; 83; 234; 238
subnet file 258; 259; 263; 300
subvocalisation 149; 208
suffix 26
SUSY 292
syllabic tier 74
syllabification 74
syllable 23; 63; 70; 71; 72; 73; 121; 134; 154; 156; 158; 159; 160
syllable tree 254; 255; 256
syllable-timed 156
synonymy 88; 89; 90
syntactic analysis 25; 27; 32
syntactic category 54; 63; 81; 369
syntactic frame 65; 328; 329
syntactic function 27; 370
syntactic specification 80; 109
syntagmatic sense relation 88
syntax 5
synthetic 36; 58
SYSTRAN 268; 298

TAUM-Meteo 242; 283; 377
template 139; 144
template system 146
text editing 13
theories of character recognition 143
theory of feature detectors 139; 140; 141
theory of template matching 139
theta-grid 83; 84; 85
theta-roles 83
tiers 73
tip-of-the-tongue phenomena 70
top-down 41; 115
top-down feedback 189
TRACE model 172; 179; 180; 181; 184; 185; 187; 188; 189; 191; 192; 200; 201; 205; 221
transfer 287; 288
transfer system 270; 273; 285; 288; 291
transgraphemic features 128; 131; 132; 147; 201; 202
transition network 253
TRANSLATOR 292
trie 377
triphone 158

tutorial system 13
two-level morphology 278

umlauting 244
unification 235; 280
unification grammar 39; 278; 280

variation 131
allophonic 125
general 116
in written language 116
speaker 116
verbal concept 92
Vietnamese 321
vision 125
visual patterns 147
visual perception 125; 126; 132
voice onset time 123; 134; 140
von-Neumann architecture 42; 224
VOT 123; 124; 125

wave form envelope 141
weak linguistic reality 155
word 22; 23; 25; 49; 51; 52; 54; 70; 74; 78; 88; 89
Word Detector model 195; 200; 201; 202; 205; 221
word envelope 127; 128; 131; 132
word recognition 23; 24; 45; 69; 71; 162; 166; 167; 171; 173; 177; 178; 179; 191; 196; 197; 203; 205; 209; 210; 212; 215; 216; 219; 220; 257
word superiority effect 128; 169; 207
word-class 369
word-initial cohort 173
word-internal change 275; 377; 303
word-stores 49
writing systems
alphabetic 126; 319; 320; 321
logographic 127; 146; 149; 315; 316; 317; 318
phonographic 129; 146; 316; 317; 319; 320
pictographic 316; 317
segmental 320
syllabic 319
written word recognition 127

Y-to-IE change 238; 274